CHALLENGING
—— THE ——
MANDATE
—— OF ——
HEAVEN

—— ASIA AND THE PACIFIC ——

Series Editor: Mark Selden, Binghamton University

Exploring one of the most dynamic and contested regions of the world, this series includes contributions on political, economic, cultural, and social changes in modern and contemporary Asia and the Pacific.

Asia
and
the
Pacific

CHALLENGING
THE
MANDATE
OF
HEAVEN

Social Protest
and State Power
in China

ELIZABETH J. PERRY

AN EAST GATE BOOK

M.E. Sharpe
Armonk, New York
London, England

An East Gate Book

Copyright © 2002 by M. E. Sharpe, Inc.

The following permissions are acknowledged:
   Chapter 1: Originally published in *Rebels and Revolutionaries in North China, 1845–1945,* by Elizabeth J.
Perry. Used here with the permission of the publishers, Stanford University Press. © 1980 by the Board of Trustees
of the Leland Stanford Junior University.
   Chapter 2: Perry, Elizabeth J., and Tom Chang. "Tax Revolt in Late Qing China: The Small Swords of Shanghai
and Liu Depei of Shandong," *Late Imperial China.* The Johns Hopkins University Press, June 1985.
   Chapter 3: Perry, Elizabeth J. "The Mystery of Yellow Cliff." *Modern China* (April 1980): pp. 123-160.
Copyright © 1980 by Sage Publications. Reprinted by Permission of Sage Publications.
   Chapter 4: Perry, Elizabeth J. "Social Banditry Revisited," *Modern China* (July 1983): 355-382. Copyright ©
1983 by Sage Publications. Reprinted by Permission of Sage Publications.
   Chapter 5: Perry, Elizabeth J. "Strikes Among Shanghai Silk Weavers, 1927–1937: The Awakening of a Labor
Aristocracy, in *Shanghai Sojourners,* Frederic Wakeman and Yeh Wen-hsin, eds. University of California Institute
of East Asian Studies, 1992.
   Chapter 6: Perry, Elizabeth J. "Labor Divided: Sources of State Formation in Modern China," in *State Power
and Social Forces: Domination and Transformation in the Third World,* Joel Migdal, Atul Kohli, and Vivienne
Shue, eds. Cambridge University Press, 1994. Reprinted with the permission of Cambridge University Press.
   Chapter 7: Perry, Elizabeth J. "Shanghai's Strike Wave of 1957," in *The China Quarterly* (March 1994).
   Chapter 8: Perry, Elizabeth J., and Li Xun. "Working at Cross-Purposes: Shanghai Labor in the Cultural
Revolution," in *Constructing China: The Interaction of Culture and Economics,* Kenneth Lieberthal, et al., eds.
Ann Arbor: Center for Chinese Studies, University of Michigan, 1997.
   Chapter 9: Perry, Elizabeth J. "Rural Violence in Socialist China," in *The China Quarterly,* September 1985.
   Chapter 10: Perry, Elizabeth J. "Casting a Chinese 'Democracy' Movement: The Roles of Students, Workers,
Peasants, and Entrepreneurs," in *Popular Protest and Political Culture in Modern China,* Jeffrey N. Wasserstrom
and Elizabeth J. Perry, eds. Boulder: Westview Press, 1994.

Library of Congress Cataloging-in-Publication Data

Perry, Elizabeth J.
      Challenging the mandate of Heaven : social protest and state power in China / by
   Elizabeth J. Perry.
         p. cm. — (Asia and the Pacific)
      Includes bibliographical references and index.
      ISBN 0-7656-0444-2 (alk. paper) — ISBN 0-7656-0445-0 (pbk. : alk. paper)
      1. Protest movements—China—History—19th century. 2. Protest movements—
   China—History—20th century. 3. Political culture—China—History—19th century.
   4. Political culture—China—History—20th century. I. Series.

DS761.2 .P47 2001
303.6′095—dc21   2001034214

Printed in the United States of America

BM (c)   10   9   8   7   6   5   4   3   2   1
BM (p)   10   9   8   7   6   5   4   3   2   1

Contents

Acknowledgments

When Mark Selden proposed that I put together a collection of previously published essays for his series with M.E. Sharpe, I was happy to comply. I recognized from the outset that this would call for a bit of work. For one thing, a couple of the papers I planned to include had been written during my pre-computer days and would therefore require retyping. For another, I had over the past twenty years rethought many of my earlier arguments, which would therefore require some rewriting. And then there was the matter of reshaping into a coherent whole pieces that had originally been prepared for quite separate purposes. Still, had I realized just *how much* work would be involved in bringing the project to fruition, I never would have agreed!

The biggest headache, it turned out, was mechanical. In addition to the fact that some of the material had not been computerized, the combination of frequent job moves and computer upgrades had wreaked havoc on my disk collection. Although I initially imagined it would be possible to recreate the missing texts by scanning the published versions, it eventually became painfully clear that scanned files simply did not lend themselves to the sorts of wholesale revisions that were required in this case. In the end, almost all the chapters had to be entirely retyped and reformatted, a tedious task that was expertly overseen by Abigail Ladd. To Abby, I owe a deep debt of gratitude for the care and fortitude that she exhibited throughout this trying process. Thanks go also to Stefanie VanPelt of the Fairbank Center for East Asian Research, for help in recruiting and supervising some much needed secretarial assistance along the way.

Now that the frustrations of scanning technology are fading from memory, it is a pleasure to thank the person responsible for this undertaking in the first place: Mark Selden. Mark not only raised the initial idea for a volume; he also made numerous valuable substantive and stylistic suggestions at every stage. I thank him both for his interest in my work and for his unflagging efforts to improve it.

Acknowledgment is due to the journals and presses that permitted the use of materials previously published under their auspices. And a special acknowledgment is owed to those with whom I coauthored previous versions of two of the chapters: Tom Chang and Li Xun. Special thanks also to Angela Piliouras for expert editorial oversight.

The chapters in this volume touch on many disparate topics and time periods, from sectarian rebellion in the nineteenth century to the student protests of 1989. I hope that this very diversity will underscore the continuing importance (as well as the remarkable range) of popular protest in the politics of modern China. I further hope that this volume will contribute in some small measure to the growing dialogue between students of China and students of contentious politics in general.

Introduction

No country boasts a more enduring or more colorful history of rebellion and revolution than China. The Chinese tradition of popular upheaval stretches back well beyond this century; indeed, records allow us to trace it as far back as 209 B.C. when the Chen She Rebellion helped to topple the mighty Qin empire and give rise to the famous Han dynasty. Over the ensuing millennia, popular protest has formed a constant and consequential theme in Chinese political history.

China's impressive record of rebellion and revolution is due not simply to the country's extraordinary size and longevity, but also to the fact that central elements in Chinese political culture have directly encouraged such protests. The Confucian (or Mencian, to be precise) concept of a "Mandate of Heaven" (*tianming*) bestowed instant legitimacy upon successful rebel leaders. This pragmatic precept differed markedly from European notions of a "divine right of kings" or the Japanese belief in an unbroken line of rulers descending from the Sun Goddess, myths that militated against challenges to the powers that be. In imperial China, one who managed to wrest the throne by force thereby gained Confucian sanction for his rule: as the proverb put it bluntly, "He who succeeds is a king or marquis; he who fails is an outlaw." Of course this did not mean that imperial aspirants were free to ignore normative bounds. Future emperors were expected to demonstrate their claim to the Mandate by means of various divine omens, and needed to come to terms with Confucian elites if they were to harbor any hope of a long-lived reign. Still, the relative openness of the system stood in stark contrast to that of other imperial orders. Political challengers in China—be they peasants or foreign invaders—were permitted to make a bid for kingship through popular rebellion.

Although Confucianism was largely discredited in the twentieth century, the connection between mass protest and political legitimacy remained intact. Sun Yatsen's "Three Principles of the People" helped inspire the 1911 Revolution that toppled two thousand years of imperial rule, while Mao Zedong's doctrine of "People's War" fueled the Communist victory in 1949—just as his subsequent call for "Continuing the Revolution" provided justification for a Cultural Revolution in the mid-1960s. Indeed, one of the principal differences between Chinese and Soviet communism lies in the former's emphasis on mass criticism and mass campaigns. Like Mencius's Mandate of Heaven, Mao's Mass Line insisted on the reciprocal linkage between leader and led in staking a claim to higher political morality. Whereas Stalin looked to the secret police to enforce top-down order, Mao repeatedly called upon the Chinese masses to engage in class struggle from below. This certainly did not mean that the People's Republic under Mao eschewed the use of state surveillance—quite the contrary—but it was unusual among communist countries in also requiring ordinary citizens to participate actively in government-sponsored campaigns.

Many assumed that the death of Chairman Mao would spell an end to the importance of mass movements in the People's Republic of China. Deng Xiaoping announced soon after his accession to power that the era of mass campaigns was indeed over. Actually, however, popular protests—some with at least implicit higher-level encouragement—have continued to punctuate the history of the PRC in the post-Mao period. The Democracy Wall Movement of 1978–79, the anti-Japanese demonstrations of 1985, the anti-American protests of 1999, and even the student uprising of 1989 were all stimulated in part by the expectation of support from elements of the central leadership. Although Mao's successors have been less active in instigating political unrest than was the Great Helmsman himself, protesters remain unusually attentive to signals from the central leadership.

Moreover, alongside these expressly political initiatives have occurred a host of other protests—from tax riots to sectarian resistance—that share a remarkable resemblance to patterns of unrest so familiar to students of imperial and Republican China. Farmers have banded together in assaults on tax bureaus to protest the imposition of exorbitant surcharges. Workers have launched strikes and slowdowns to signal their dissatisfaction with factory closures and attendant layoffs. Religious sectarians have insisted on practicing their spiritual regimens in bold defiance of government proscriptions.

In light of China's rich and variegated traditions of resistance, rebellion, and revolution, we should be duly skeptical of claims (such as those proffered by many observers during the Tiananmen Uprising of 1989) that new outbursts of protest represent a fundamental break with the past. Although initial reactions to the 1989 "democracy movement" stressed its novelty, subsequent reflections on the activities of the protesters— including retrospectives by the principals themselves—questioned the extent to which their behavior constituted a genuine rupture with earlier modes of protest. As Tiananmen activist Liu Xiaobo later conceded,

> Most of the resources and methods we made use of to mobilize the masses were ones that the Communist Party itself had used many times before. . . . As soon as we began our revolution, we became extremely conceited—just as if we had reverted to the time of the Cultural Revolution and felt ourselves to be the most revolutionary. As soon as we joined the 1989 protest movement, we considered ourselves to be the most democratic. After all, had we not fasted for democracy and devoted ourselves to it and made sacrifices for it? . . . Our voice became the only truth. We felt as though we possessed absolute power.[1]

Liu's impassioned reflections are a stinging indictment of the Tiananmen protest as an undemocratic movement that unwittingly recreated many of the worst features of Chinese Communist political culture. He suggests that what masqueraded as the sprouts of civil society (e.g., autonomous student and worker associations) or as novel cultural practices (e.g., weddings on the Square) were in reality little more than variations on the repressive theme of Chinese Communist convention. The searing experience of the Cultural Revolution in particular, according to Liu Xiaobo, has inhibited the development of a genuinely democratic perspective among Chinese intellectuals.

While Liu's critique is a poignant reminder that societal initiatives in China continue to reflect the heavy hand of statist influences, we should not thereby conclude that popular protest is forever fated to serve merely as the handmaiden of Communist control. During the 1989 protests, for example, the autonomous workers' federations that sprang up around the country represented a heightened level of antagonism between organized labor and the state in contemporary China.

Challenging the Mandate of Heaven was never an easy accomplishment, but it did periodically occur—in both ancient and modern times. History suggests that a key to the success of such undertakings lay in bridging the (often state-imposed) categories that set various groups of people against one another. Such divisions, although responsible for much of the unrest that has colored the Chinese past, also posed serious obstacles to concerted popular imagination and action against the state. To overcome these hurdles required the intervention of farsighted individuals, who often issued from the lower rungs of the intelligentsia or local elite. Whether drawn from the ranks of students, teachers, militia captains, religious masters, bandit chieftains, or Communist cadres, such leaders have played a catalytic role in converting ongoing strategies of competition into large-scale political movements. The state, too, was a critical variable in the equation; a poorly executed repression effort could stimulate, rather than stymie, the spirit of political protest.

The advent of a new millennium affords an opportune occasion to take stock of the historical legacy of Chinese protest and its continuing impact on the contemporary scene. The PRC has certainly seen its share of mass movements, many (but by no means all) of which were elite-inspired, if not overtly instigated. According to government pronouncements, however, 1999 was to be different. As the fiftieth anniversary of the founding of the PRC, the final year of the old millennium was supposed to be a protest-free annum—a time for officially orchestrated parades, but not for unofficial demonstrations. Stability, rather than spontaneity, was the watchword of the day.

The year 1999 was seen as potentially problematic not only because it marked a half-century milestone in the history of Communist China, but also because it was a banner anniversary year for other critical events in the record of Chinese protests: the 80th anniversary of the May Fourth Movement of 1919, the 40th anniversary of the Tibetan Revolt of 1959, the 30th anniversary of the conclusion of the mass mobilization phase of the Cultural Revolution in 1969, the 20th anniversary of the Democracy Wall Movement of 1979, the 10th anniversary of the Tiananmen Uprising and its bloody June 4th suppression in 1989. Inasmuch as the commemoration of anniversaries is itself a common pretext for protest in China, the year was approached with trepidation by the leadership.[2] To ensure that potential protesters had no space in which to mark these anniversaries, Tiananmen Square was closed for renovations until shortly before the October 1st National Day celebrations. As things developed, however, before the curtain could be rung down on the old millennium, China was rocked with all manner of protests: tax revolts by farmers in the countryside, petition drives by laid-off workers and displaced residents in the cities, student demonstrations against the NATO bombing of the Chinese embassy in Belgrade, and even a convocation of religious sectarians right outside the central leadership compound of Zhongnanhai.

Despite its avowed intention to oppose all forms of protest, the state actually responded in quite different ways to these various expressions of popular discontent.[3] The government ruthlessly repressed the Falun Gong believers who had amassed peacefully outside Zhongnanhai on April 25, despite the fact that they were arguably the least violent of all the demonstrations that occurred in China that year. Toward the protests by farmers and workers, the authorities showed a considerable degree of tolerance. And officials actively encouraged the student protests of May 8th that erupted after the Belgrade bombing.

These seemingly contradictory government responses make considerably more sense if viewed in historical perspective. The central government's muted response to the protests by farmers and workers has an ancient pedigree. From imperial days to the present, economic protests demanding a secure livelihood were generally seen as a signal of *local* distress that should be dealt with by grassroots officials. As Mencius had emphasized, it was the responsibility of government to provide for the people's welfare. But since economic difficulties tended to be localized, the onus of alleviating them fell to local-level officials—county magistrates or provincial governors. Similarly, today it is the mayor of Chongqing municipality or the magistrate of Renshou county who is expected to cope with petitions by laid-off workers or tax revolts by hard-pressed farmers.

"Moral economy" protests launched in the name of subsistence have occurred with remarkable frequency in recent years in both rural and urban China. In 1993, for instance, according to a top-level government report the countryside witnessed some 1.7 million cases of resistance, primarily tax resistance, of which 6,230 cases were classified as "disturbances" (*naoshi*) that entailed severe damage to persons or property. The confrontations that year exacted a staggering toll of deaths and injuries on some 8,200 township and county officials.[4] Farmers were not alone in expressing economic grievances. In the final decade of the twentieth century, according to official statistics, more than 1.5 million industrial disputes were officially recorded and processed by arbitration or mediation committees.[5] Since many more disputes occur than are officially registered, we can assume an impressive level of labor strife as well.

So long as such confrontations limit their demands to calling for a decent livelihood, the central government has generally stayed out of the picture—except to encourage local officials to deal fairly with the protesters. In the case of a taxicab drivers' strike in the city of Changsha, for example, central authorities intervened to persuade the municipal government to rescind its plan to raise license fees to a level beyond the means of many drivers. When tax revolts by farmers have prompted central intervention, it has usually been to remind township and county governments that their fees and surcharges must not exceed 5 percent of farmers' income, as stipulated by national regulations.[6]

In short, the central government—like its predecessors in imperial and Republican China—has demonstrated a certain degree of tolerance and even sympathy toward economically driven protests, provided that they remain clearly bounded in both scale and aspirations. Claims to a basic subsistence that stay within local confines have seldom been deemed especially threatening by Chinese regimes, and so—in contrast to protests motivated by explicitly religious or political agendas—historically have not attracted a great deal of central anxiety or attention.

Nationalistically inspired student unrest is another story altogether, however. In the case of the 1999 student protests against the bombing of China's Belgrade embassy, we find a considerable degree of overt central government support—sanctioning the demonstrations on national television, providing buses to take students to foreign embassies and consulates, and even supplying the slogans that they should shout once they got there. Here, too, the historical lessons are telling. Patriotic student movements have proved politically incendiary in China ever since the Opium Wars of the mid-nineteenth century opened Chinese governments to charges of being soft on imperialism. The May Fourth Movement of 1919, which railed against Japanese incursions after World War I, resulted in the dismissal of the three discredited officials who had signed the Treaty of Versailles. More importantly, it helped give rise to the Chinese Communist Party itself. The Communist revolution was also at core a movement of nationalistically inspired students, who subsequently reached out to other allies—first workers, then peasants—in an effort to topple a government that they charged was remiss in its responsibility to guard China's national sovereignty.

The current regime is thus deeply afraid of jingoistic student movements, especially if they seem likely to link up with other social groups, and only a few years ago it banned student demonstrations that called for recovering the Diaoyutai (Senkaku) Islands from Japanese control. But with the bombing on May 8, 1999 having created visible martyrs, it was simply too risky for the government to try to disallow student demonstrations altogether. Moreover, the incident occurred only four days after the May Fourth anniversary (and less than a month before June Fourth) when historical parallels were on everyone's mind.[7] Jiang Zemin—like his predecessors in 1919—risked being accused of failing to protect Chinese sovereignty unless he seemed to be responding at least as vigorously as the students to this affront to national pride. And thus, within hours of the news of the bombing, the regime reversed its policy of discouraging all forms of student activism and allowed, even encouraged, educated youths to take to the streets to express their patriotic outrage.

Let us turn now, and at greater length, to the Falun Gong campaign—where the authorities adopted a policy of harsh repression, in contrast to the tacit tolerance that they showed toward small-scale economic protests by workers and farmers or the overt support that they provided to nationalistic students. Even more than in these other instances, the Falun Gong case is replete with historical resonance. The government-directed campaign against Falun Gong (or "Wheel of Law" as it is often rendered into English) is reminiscent both of Maoist campaigns against alleged "counterrevolutionaries" and of earlier, imperial initiatives against allegedly "heterodox" sectarians. Inasmuch as the current regime tries to distinguish itself sharply from such antecedents, the campaign has exposed a host of ironies that raise the question of just how modern and reformist the post-Mao leadership actually is. In striking out against the Wheel of Law, were Jiang Zemin and company simply reinventing the familiar wheel of repression of heterodox sects forged by their predecessors? And does history offer any clues as to the likely consequences of this heavy-handed state response?

Government propaganda against the practice of Falun Gong dominated both the air waves and the print media for weeks after the campaign got under way in July of 1999. Thousands were reportedly sent to labor camps, and hundreds to prison, in conjunction with the crackdown. Dozens may have died at the hands of the police. This was of course hardly the first time that the post-Mao authorities had struck out against allegedly "sectarian" activities. During the past two decades, the government has cracked down on all manner of secret societies and underground religious groups as well as on rebellions inspired by a variety of folk beliefs.[8] The fear of *qigong* practices (or breathing and martial arts exercises) turning into political protests is also not a new concern for the post-Mao leadership. At the time of the 1989 demonstrations, government hotlines were established in the major cities to encourage citizens to report any suspicious behavior by *qigong* masters.[9] Nevertheless, the launching of a full-scale campaign against a single organization of this sort is indeed unprecedented. Not since the Suppression of Counterrevolutionaries Campaign in the early 1950s have we seen such sustained national attention directed to the threat of sectarian resistance, and never before have we witnessed an attack of this kind on but a single target.

Why did the leadership elect to undertake this drastic initiative—an initiative so out of step with its attitude toward labor disputes, tax riots, or even student nationalistic demonstrations? Timing, scale, and composition help to account for the difference. As noted earlier, the year 1999 was approached as a moment of potential trouble by the PRC authorities. Public security officials surely thought they had eliminated the threat of mass demonstrations in the capital when they closed Tiananmen Square for renovations during the first half of the year, conveniently preventing would-be protesters from commemorating May Fourth—or, more dangerous still, June Fourth—at the site of those historic events. Thus they were shocked when 10,000 Falun Gong adherents from all over the country and all walks of life suddenly materialized in front of the leadership compound of Zhongnanhai to demand official recognition of their religious association. While the government had shown increasing flexibility toward localized, interest-based protests in recent years (e.g., demonstrations by laid-off workers at particular factories or in particular cities), it remained deeply fearful of cross-regional and/or cross-class actions. Hence the roundup in 1999 of Democracy Party activists (who had established branches across the country with participation from workers as well as intellectuals), and hence the antipathy toward Falun Gong. That the Internet was evidently serving as a mobilizational weapon for Falun Gong practitioners, as it had for Democracy Party members as well, was also highly disturbing to the leadership. This new means of communication was capable of easily transcending spatial and occupational barriers, and was also stubbornly resistant to state surveillance efforts.

Of further concern was the fact that so many Falun Gong adepts were members of the Communist Party, including high-level officials in the government and army. Although participation (and even leadership) by party cadres and PLA soldiers in sectarian unrest is by no means unprecedented, in the past those involved were generally low-level officials without national influence. In this case, however, the former director of the 301 Army Hospital in Beijing—a doctor with considerable standing among the political elite—had been advising high-level cadres to turn to Falun Gong. At a time when CCP leaders find themselves ideologically adrift and presiding over an increasingly moribund party apparatus, the emergence of a large social movement whose diverse membership exhibits remarkable commitment and enthusiasm, has the capacity to mobilize on a nationwide scale, and maintains secure international communications, is anything but a welcome development. Here, too, historical memories are disturbing. Much of the explanation for the Communists' rapid rise to victory half a century ago lay in the defection of so many elements of the *ancien régime*. When Guomindang members at all levels began to go over to the Communist side, the civil war tilted decisively in favor of the revolutionaries.[10] Thus Jiang Zemin was understandably wary of the fact that many CCP members had joined Falun Gong.

Whether one interprets the regime's reaction as rational suspicion or as irrational paranoia, the contradictions of the campaign have laid bare many of the ironies of Communist rule. When the campaign was first launched, the authorities declared Falun Gong to be a "heterodox religion" (*xiejiao*)—the traditional term employed by the imperial Chinese state to designate those groups, such as the millenarian White Lotus Society, whose practices were deemed antithetical to its own Confucian dictates. In such a discourse, "heterodox religion" is contrasted to "orthodox religion"—whether of the Confucian or Communist persuasion. The initial wave of the campaign counterposed the "heterodox" views of Falun Gong leader Li Hongzhi to the correct tenets of Marxism-Leninism. Whereas Marxism-Leninism championed materialism, Falun Gong espoused idealism. Rather than be misled by the false teachings of the charismatic Li Hongzhi, citizens were enjoined to rally around the central party leadership and its proper doctrines. Framing the problem in this fashion had the unintended effect, however, of putting Falun Gong on a roughly equal footing with the Communist Party. On the one side stood Li Hongzhi and his heterodox teachings, on the other side the central leaders and their orthodox teachings. In the interests of stability and unity, ordinary Chinese were asked to reject Falun Gong in favor of the CCP. The unwitting implication was that two competing sects were locked in mortal combat, each vying for the allegiance of the masses. When the state accused Falun Gong of having caused numerous deaths through suicide, starvation, and mental illness, one could hardly help but compare its record favorably against the devastation wrought by Land Reform, the Great Leap Forward, and the Cultural Revolution—not to mention the June Fourth massacre.

Perhaps it dawned on someone in the Department of Propaganda that this was not a particularly flattering way in which to represent the Communist Party. In any event, after a few days of this approach, the campaign took a new turn. Instead of contrasting Falun Gong "heterodoxy" to Communist "orthodoxy," the principal opposition was now presented as one of "superstition" versus "science." Prominent astronomers and physicists from the major universities and research academies were trotted out to denounce Li Hongzhi's apocalyptic prophecies about the end of an age (*moshilun*). Whereas Li had allegedly predicted the advent of a comet which would generate a global explosion that only he could deflect, scientists responded that the chances of such an occurrence that year were a remote one in fifty billion. Nonetheless, they proceeded soberly to calculate the precise force that Li Hongzhi would have to be able to muster in order to repel such a comet were it in fact on its way, and pronounced his alleged boast "impossible!" Meteorologists for the evening television news also took care to reassure viewers that the partial lunar eclipse on July 28 was no cause for alarm—despite popular beliefs that unusual astrological occurrences are a sign of the loss of the Mandate of Heaven.

Physicians and psychiatrists testified to the deleterious physical and mental health effects of Falun Gong. Television cameras took viewers inside mental institutions to observe cases of "*qigong* deviation" (*qigong piancha*), a Chinese category of mental illness allegedly brought on by the practice of Falun Gong techniques. Victims of Falun Gong, not previously noted for filling mental hospitals, were now said to account for more than 40 percent of the patients in Chinese psychiatric wards. Psychologists explained how continuous exposure to the books, tapes, videos, Internet home page, and other paraphernalia of Falun Gong could induce a "true believer" mentality in which followers would be willing to follow blindly any command issued by the supreme leader.

To be sure, government officials were not without some justification in highlighting the bizarre belief system that underpinned the practice of Falun Gong. Followers of the faith were said to derive therapeutic benefits from the regular rotation of a spiritual wheel implanted in their stomachs by the charismatic authority of Li Hongzhi. Those who mastered the regimens of the religion were promised supernatural powers that ranged from levitation to x-ray vision. And, unlike many other *qigong* groups, Falun Gong believers seemed to devote at least as much energy to honoring their leader—who was invested with divine attributes—as to honing their exercise skills.

Attuned to the international backlash that the repression campaign was bound to generate, government television stations invited experts in law and philosophy to explain that suppression of an unregistered, and thus illegal and illegitimate, organization was not a violation of human rights. Social scientists testified that Falun Gong's capacity to amass large numbers of otherwise unconnected people simultaneously was a clear threat to the general social order—something that could not be tolerated in any modern polity. Officially sanctioned religious specialists decried the "feudal superstition" of Falun Gong, in contrast to the "normal religion" that they themselves espoused.

For weeks after the campaign began, each night pictures were broadcast of huge piles of Falun Gong materials that had been either voluntarily turned over by practitioners or confiscated in police raids on bookstores and publishing houses. (Interestingly, the People's Liberation Army press was responsible for a number of Falun Gong publications.) Some were disposed of in gigantic bonfires, others were recycled. Relatives of Falun Gong victims testified about the terrible tragedies that had befallen their loved ones. Former adherents also began to come forward to explain how they had been hoodwinked by Li Hongzhi and to express regret at their gullibility. Physical education teachers pointed to healthy alternatives to Falun Gong in the form of badminton, ballroom dancing, bowling, and the like. Happy pictures of those who had kicked the Falun Gong habit and were now pursuing more benign varieties of exercise began to flood the evening news.

The basic patterns of the government's offensive were familiar from decades of previous such mobilized suppression efforts, from the anti-rightist campaign of the 1950s to the anti–spiritual pollution campaigns of the 1980s. However, judging from discussions with people in China at the time, this particular campaign was not a resounding success. While most accepted that Falun Gong's organizational capacities were a potential danger and assumed that Li Hongzhi was a hustler with a nefarious agenda, be it political or simply pecuniary, they found the government's treatment of the case something of a public embarrassment. The draconian nature of the campaign was suggestive of a deeply frightened and insecure central leadership. People wondered out loud: Had crimes so serious as to warrant the arrest of thousands really occurred?

The state produced no convincing evidence to demonstrate any actual disruption of public order from Falun Gong—aside from the fact that so many of its own cadres had enlisted in the movement.[11] Although the authorities tried to argue that Falun Gong members were interfering with flood control work by amassing outside public agencies, the television footage revealed that entrances and exits to public buildings had been kept conspicuously open by Falun Gong protesters. The gatherings were nonviolent and remarkably disciplined. While the government insisted that these demonstrations were the most serious political threat since the 1989 student uprising, it was hard to see why.

The weakness of the state's case was plain, its accusations rife with obvious inconsistencies, ironies, and exaggerations. The government claimed to be justified in cracking down on the group because it was not officially registered, but the Falun Gong demonstrations had been prompted precisely by a desire for the official recognition and registration that the state refused to grant. The authorities castigated Falun Gong for being feudal, backward, and unscientific, while at the same time denouncing its use of cutting edge Internet technology to propagate its message both nationally and internationally.

One of the greatest ironies of the campaign lay in the state's reluctance to acknowledge the historical considerations that so clearly lay behind its heavy-handed reaction to Falun Gong. As ordinary people in China were quick to point out, the real fear was that the movement would turn into the sort of sectarian-inspired rebellion for which Chinese history is famous. Indeed, by labeling the group a "heterodox sect" (*xiejiao*) and cracking down relentlessly on its practitioners, the authorities invited just such historical allusions. From the Yellow Turbans to the White Lotus to the Boxers, the folk religion and breathing regimens of "heterodox sects" proved to be a volatile mix in times of dynastic crisis. Although the official media did not draw attention to this historical analogy, it was certainly not lost on the public at large. The fact that a popular central television serial chronicled the story of the first Ming emperor, Zhu Yuanzhang—a mendicant monk whose fourteenth-century rise to power came in the midst of a White Lotus–inspired rebellion—served only to highlight the linkage between past and present. Fear of the loss of the Mandate of Heaven was generally seen as the driving force behind the campaign, but this "feudal superstitious" belief could not, of course, be officially admitted.

As the historical record teaches us, the vast majority of Chinese sectarian groups were inclined toward political quiescence. The trigger for protest, more often than not, lay with the state. Government repression was a common precipitant of overt rebellion.[12] Thus if the current effort to eliminate Falun Gong does not succeed, the authorities are likely to have turned a once tranquil friend into an implacable and formidable foe. Like the anti-sectarian efforts of the Qianlong emperor in the eighteenth century, or for that matter of the Guomindang earlier in the twentieth century, their heavy-handed initiatives against "heterodoxy" and "feudal superstition" may well prove counterproductive in the long run.[13]

Whether or not the government prevails in its effort to eliminate Falun Gong as an organization, the suppression campaign exposed profound vulnerabilities in the state's grip on society. Equally important, the sorts of demonstrations sweeping China at the turn of the millennium— whether launched by *qigong* practitioners or by anti-American students— served notice that popular protest in China is not a carbon copy of the social movements familiar in Western societies. As analysts, we would do well to approach such expressions of public sentiment on their terms, rather than assume (as many outside observers did during the Tiananmen demonstrations a decade ago) that the wellsprings of political change lie only with those marching behind a replica of the Statue of Liberty.

Throughout Chinese history, mass protests have played a special role in bestowing political legitimacy—whether according to Confucian or Communist principles. This contributes to a distinctive dynamic of state–society relations. On the one hand, Chinese political culture (whether framed in terms of the Mencian Mandate of Heaven or in terms of Mao's Mass Line) encourages and empowers protesters to rise up from the ranks of society to challenge state leaders. On the other hand, precisely because of the importance of popular protest to political legitimacy, state authorities—be they emperors or general-secretaries of the Communist Party—move aggressively to condone or to condemn particular outbreaks of protest activity. Popular demonstrations that go beyond the articulation of local economic grievances are either welcomed as supportive of the reigning orthodoxy, or else they are banned as expressions of heterodox superstition. As a result, Chinese protesters themselves are unusually attentive to signals from the state. The request by Falun Gong adherents for official recognition and registration is only the latest in a centuries-old tradition of appeals by social movements for government approval.

The close relationship between state authorization and social movements in China raises some questions concerning the applicability of general theories of contentious politics, developed for the most part on the basis of European and American cases. Although these theories have certainly not ignored the role of the state, they have generally been content to suggest a negative correlation between state strength and politically threatening social movements. Revolutions, according to this line of analysis, are facilitated by weak states incapable of repressing challenges to their own survival.[14] There is, of course, an obvious—possibly even tautological—logic to this insight that applies, at least in hindsight, to any revolutionary outcome. But the Chinese experience argues for acknowledging a larger, more pro-active role for the state.

It is not just that state weakness may encourage protest; rather, popular protests are often inspired by the very strength of state exemplars. Take Falun Gong, whose organizational structure closely resembles that of the Chinese Communist Party. In both cases, individuals belong to local branches whose leaders are strictly subservient to the directives of the next level in a tightly organized, territorially based hierarchy. While ordinary members of one branch may have little direct contact with members of other branches, their leaders are plugged into an extremely effective system of communication and command. Prior to the government crackdown, Falun Gong boasted more than 28,000 local branches (known as *liangongdian* or practice points) whose leaders reported to more than 1,900 supervisory stations (or *fudaozhan*) that in turn reported to 39 general stations (*zongzhan*) at the level of province, autonomous region, and municipality. At the center stood the Wheel of Law Research Society (*falun dafa yanjiuhui*).

The structural isomorphism between Falun Gong and the Communist Party was due not only to Falun Gong's desire to elude state surveillance through a dispersed cellular pattern (perfected by the CCP during its own revolutionary years for a similar purpose). The congruence was due also to the fact that the Communist Party represents an extremely powerful, indeed virtually irresistible, organizational template for any group trying to operate in contemporary China. By the same token, territory designated as politically sacred by the Chinese state exerts a tremendous pull on potential protesters. Thus, despite the enormous dangers inherent in public assemblies at Tiananmen Square, members of the outlawed Falun Gong movement are drawn back again and again to that site precisely because it is the state-sanctioned political center of the country. A Reuters report during the lunar New Year's celebrations in February 2000 makes clear this magnetic, mimetic connection between the Chinese state and its would-be challengers:

Defiant members of the Falun Gong spiritual movement kept up protests in Tiananmen Square on Saturday after the banned group marked the Year of the Dragon with one of its biggest demonstrations on the vast plaza. Plainclothes police swarmed the square, detaining at least half a dozen people, the morning after scores of *Falun Gong protesters tried to unfurl Buddhist banners near China's most prominent flagpole bearing the national standard.* As lunar New Year's revelers looked on, police swooped across the square and detained more than 100 people, kicking and punching some, witnesses said. . . . Despite the beatings, Falun Gong members kept up chants of "Falun Dafa"— "Great Law of the Wheel"—even inside the detention centre. The demonstration is the latest evidence that a nationwide crackdown has failed to crush members' allegiance to the group which China's Communist leaders banned in July last year and labeled an "evil cult" in October. Authorities have done their utmost to keep Falun Gong members from the capital, checking identity cards at railway and bus stations, and setting up roadblocks on routes into the city. They have handed out harsh jail sentences to Falun Gong leaders, and detained thousands of members. Yet Falun Gong has been attempting ever bolder acts of protest.

Last month [January 2000], *members tried to hang a giant portrait of their U.S.-based guru, Li Hongzhi, over the painting of Mao Zedong* which overlooks the square, the Information Centre of Human Rights and Democratic Movement in China has reported.[15]

As this news report indicates, intense state repression may work to radicalize—rather than eliminate—popular protest. This phenomenon has already begun to receive some attention in the literature on social movements,[16] but the ways in which state practices themselves encourage imitation by protesters remains underappreciated. The provocative substitutions of Buddhist banners for the national flag and of Master Li's portrait for that of Chairman Mao suggest the tremendous temptations that the official trappings of state hold even for those who rise up to challenge the powers that be.

The tendency for protesters to take cues from official symbols of authority can be found in any polity, but is particularly pronounced in authoritarian systems where the state exercises a virtual monopoly over political discourse. In such contexts, the clever appropriation and inversion of officially sanctioned rituals and ceremonies for subversive purposes is a prominent feature of protest behavior. In China, where popular protest is culturally sanctioned and where the custom of "waving the red flag to oppose the red flag" has an ancient pedigree that long predates the Communist era, this practice has been honed into a high—and often highly ironic—art form.

Just as various democratic political cultures have given definition to distinctive French, English, and American repertoires of collective action, so authoritarian societies also manifest identifiable styles of protest. In China, the ironic invocation (and, through puns, the inversion) of official rhetoric, the creative use of historical allegory, and the counterhegemonic commemoration of state-sponsored funerals and other ceremonies are exceptionally well-developed means of challenging authority (just as Russian political culture is famed for its sardonic jokes). China offers rich material from which to develop a better understanding of such phenomena, while serving at the same time to exemplify a more general type of political system in which the boundaries between state and society are less starkly drawn than in liberal democracies. Although China (with the exception of contemporary Taiwan) has never enjoyed democratic rule, it has experienced a variety of authoritarian regimes: imperial, Republican, and Communist.

Those who hold the reins of power in Beijing today are of course acutely aware of this historical record. It is precisely in light of the familiar Chinese past—including the history of the Chinese Communist Party itself—that the regime's seemingly inconsistent and illogical responses to contemporary protests become explicable. While popular protest in China bears a definite resemblance to unrest in other authoritarian polities, the differences are also stark and significant. Sidney Tarrow writes of authoritarian states in general:

> That authoritarian states discourage popular politics is implicit in their very definition. In particular, they suppress the sustained interaction of collective actors and authorities that is the hallmark of social movements. . . . Repressive states depress collective action of a conventional and confrontational sort, but leave themselves open to unobtrusive mobilization.[17]

Like other authoritarian societies, the PRC has certainly witnessed the development of what James Scott terms a "hidden transcript" of critical dissent.[18] But Communist China parts company with these other countries in having periodically encouraged—indeed compelled—its citizens to express their private criticisms publicly in the form of big-character posters, struggle sessions, denunciation meetings, demonstrations, and the like. The Cultural Revolution was the most dramatic, albeit certainly not the only, instance of this effort. The Communist state's sponsorship of mass campaigns is related to a fundamental tenet of Chinese political culture that links effective popular protest and political legitimacy. Although Mao's Mass Line departs significantly from Mencius's Mandate of Heaven, they share the belief that "to rebel is justified."

The chapters that follow explore continuities and contrasts in protest patterns, and their implications for state–society relations, under three successive Chinese polities: imperial, Republican, and Communist. A central focus is on the social composition of protest. As the Falun Gong case suggests, the Chinese state recognizes the dangers inherent in cross-class and cross-territorial expressions of popular protest. While geographically confined movements aimed at improving the economic lot of one social group are (and were) countenanced, movements that spill across jurisdictional and/or occupational boundaries are (and were) viewed as cause for serious central concern. Imperial edicts condemned sectarian groups not only for their heterodox beliefs, but also for their tendency to attract itinerants and merchants as well as settled peasants, to encourage intermingling of the sexes, and to uproot people from their assigned places in the social hierarchy. The breaching of "proper" societal divisions was—along with heterodoxy—grounds for severe repression. The efforts of the imperial state to divide and rule (diluting ties between officials and their kinsmen and neighbors through a Law of Avoidance that assigned members of the bureaucracy to distant posts, drawing administrative boundaries so as to divide up natural economic regions, and the like) are well known.

Cross-cutting social coalitions emerged more forcefully during the Republican era (1912–49). This was in part a product of relatively weak state capacity during the interregnum period, but it also reflected the appearance of new social classes (e.g., an industrial proletariat) and new social identities (e.g., youths and women). These developments had momentous implications for the nature of protest, helping give rise to such massive and politically significant events as the May Fourth Movement of 1919, the May Thirtieth Movement of 1925, and the Civil War unrest of the late 1940s. Under the Republic, the notion of urban citizenship (*shiminquan*) took on special meaning, implying a new and powerful claim for urban residents of all social classes to participate in local politics. Fueled by an alliance of intellectuals, workers, and merchants, successive waves of popular contention during the first half of this century constituted a dramatic turning point in Chinese history.

Although these expressions of newfound community and discontent paved the way for the victory of communism, the Maoist state reversed such trends, severely constraining the possibility of cross-class initiatives. In a manner to which his imperial predecessors aspired, but never fully attained, Mao proved amazingly adept at limiting potentially threatening societal interaction. During the Maoist period, a rigid household registration system (*hukou zhidu*) was imposed that severely restricted migration and effectively severed relations between villagers and urbanites. Moreover, within cities separate places of recreation were established for workers and intellectuals, while the bourgeoisie was virtually eliminated. Gone were the teahouses and cafes that had served as meeting places for members of different classes during the Republican era. Workers now spent their leisure time at workers' cultural palaces, while intellectuals congregated at writers' and artists' associations. In the post-Mao period, the breakdown of these social restrictions may once again encourage cross-class alliances with a potential for potent collective action and possible regime change.

Despite the inherent hospitality of Chinese political culture to rebellion and revolution, popular protest—even large-scale protest—did not lead easily or automatically to political transformation. An equally important emphasis in this volume is on the difficulties that protesters have faced in mounting a common challenge to state authorities. As the chapters that follow will demonstrate, popular contention in China has been extremely varied, ranging from predatory bandit armies (e.g., the Nian or Bai Lang) launched by peasants for the purpose of garnering scarce resources, to protective societies (e.g., the Red Spears or Yellow Cliff) led by the elite for the purpose of guarding against just such assaults. In some cases, insurgents were mobilized by village or lineage ties; in other cases, by religious affiliation. Even in the same time and place (e.g., Shanghai factories during the Cultural Revolution), we find vastly different forms of protest: rebellion, conservatism, economism. Deep divisions within Chinese society, which pitted some groups against others (often as a direct consequence of state initiatives), were a driving force behind the impressive history of conflict and resistance. But such splits could also militate against unified opposition to the state. Only under unusual circumstances did protest turn into a serious political threat.

In seeking the origins and outcomes of popular protest, then, we must proceed simultaneously along two fronts. On the one hand, we need to understand the local conditions, contradictions, and cleavages that generate enduring patterns of conflict. On the other hand, we need to appreciate the ways in which state actions serve either to immobilize or to intensify these ongoing modes of contention. The past two decades of scholarly exchange with the PRC have opened a wealth of previously inaccessible primary sources for pursuing this dual inquiry. Field work in China, besides facilitating firsthand interviews with protest participants, has also made available rich archival collections from imperial, Republican, and Communist regimes—at both local and national levels. Most of the chapters to follow draw upon such sources to offer new perspectives on state–society relations in modern China.

Chapter 1, extracted from a book-length study of peasant protest on the North China plain, attempts to show how mundane strategies of rural survival—developed over centuries of adapting to a forbidding environment—set the stage for the massive rebellions of the late imperial and Republican periods. Government intervention was a critical ingredient in the politicization of pre-existing patterns of peasant competition, giving rise to the Nian Rebellion in the mid-nineteenth century and the Red Spears tax revolt of the 1920s.

The conversion of everyday strategies of survival into anti-state rebellion was not inevitable, however. Challenging the Mandate of Heaven required the active engagement of energetic leaders who, often inspired by other rebel undertakings, adapted extant ideas and institutions to new political purposes. In Chapter 2 (previously published in *Late Imperial China*), we see how local notables—influenced in part by the Taiping and Nian rebellions—used the institution of the village militia to launch major tax protests.

Chapter 3 (co-authored with Tom Chang as an article in *Modern China*) offers further evidence of the catalytic role of charismatic leaders. Zhang Jizhong, founder of the Yellow Cliff community in the mid-nineteenth century, bears more than a passing resemblance to Li Hongzhi of Falun Gong fame. Both men drew upon a syncretic tradition of healing techniques and religious beliefs to amass a large and diverse following. While both leaders claimed to be loyal to the powers that be, the Chinese state (imperial in one case, Communist in the other) eventually proscribed their teachings as "heterodox" affronts. Figuring centrally in the state's decision was its anxiety about the heterogeneity of the movements' adherents—in terms of occupation, geography, gender, and political status (i.e., the involvement of a substantial number of gentry in the case of Yellow Cliff, and of Communist Party cadres in the case of Falun Gong). Government hostility in turn encouraged at least some of this diverse band of followers, if not the founding fathers of the faith themselves, to undertake overt resistance to the state.

The famous Chinese bandit Bai Lang, a case study of whom is presented in Chapter 4 (published originally in *Modern China*), was also both empowered and constricted by his eclectic entourage. Encouraged by advisors from Sun Yatsen's revolutionary camp, the bandit chief himself displayed a growing political ambition. Ultimately, however, Bai Lang's hard-core peasant followers cut short his revolutionary dreams by insisting upon returning to their village roots in the mountains of western Henan. As the Bai Lang case illustrates, the social base of a movement sets limits on its subsequent trajectory.

The growth of an industrial proletariat following the opening of China to foreign trade and investment by imperialist powers in the mid-nineteenth century generated a new kind of popular protest with roots among factory workers. In Chapter 5, which appeared originally in the volume *Shanghai Sojourners*, we trace the emergence in Republican Shanghai of two very different types of workers within the single occupation of silk-weaving. With different native-place connections, skill levels, and employment conditions, the two types of weavers also exhibited distinctive strike patterns in the 1930s. Both forms of protest were largely economic in motivation, prompted by the effects of the Great Depression. However, they became highly politicized when outside partisans—in the person of Communist and Guomindang cadres—attempted to redirect these labor conflicts toward wider political agendas. The combination of proletarianization and politicization that took place over the course of the 1930s helped to blur the distinctions between the two types of silk weavers, clearing the way for joint revolutionary action in the 1940s.

Chapter 6 (published previously in the volume *State Power and Social Forces*) explores the importance of such cleavages within the Shanghai industrial labor force for the process of state formation. Problematizing the category "proletariat," the chapter shows that different segments of the work force (distinguished, among other things, by divergent patterns of protest) provided a social base for different Chinese regimes. Whereas the Nationalists (1927–49), via gangster intermediaries, relied heavily upon semiskilled laborers from North China, the Communists found skilled workers from the South to be a more receptive audience for their revolution. The regimes established by both political parties were, moreover, substantially constrained by the nature of their working-class support, dissimilar as it was. The reality, or fear, of labor militancy made it difficult for either government to effect fundamental industrial reforms that might threaten the interests of its primary labor constituency. State–society relations are a two-way street: it is not only that popular protests are influenced by state initiatives; a regime's policies, in turn, are shaped by the perceived protest potential of its social base.

In Chapter 7 (published originally in *The China Quarterly*), we examine the massive strike wave that rocked Chinese factories during the Hundred Flowers campaign of 1956–57. Especially pronounced in Shanghai, the strikes demonstrated once again the importance of divisions within the work force (many of which had been created or exacerbated by new socialist policies) for fueling labor unrest. Yet these cleavages also made it difficult for different segments of the work force to see beyond their own economic interests to engage in a more fundamental critique of the socialist system. And, with workers and intellectuals now confined to very different social circles, their protests remained notably separate. In contrast to the politically powerful general strikes of the Republican period, in which the intelligentsia had taken a major leadership role, the strike wave of 1957 was limited in both social composition and political demands.

Chapter 8, which is extracted from a co-authored monograph with Li Xun entitled *Proletarian Power: Shanghai in the Cultural Revolution*, identifies three strands of labor protest among workers during the Cultural Revolution. "Rebellion" was an effort to unseat local powerholders; "conservatism" was an attempt to protect powerholders; and "economism" raised demands for improved working conditions. Each variety of protest, we suggest, stemmed from factors that are best explained by different interpretive frameworks: a psycho-cultural approach in the case of rebellion, network analysis in the case of conservatism, and interest group theory in the case of economism. This chapter underscores the difficulty of trying to capture diverse forms of contentious politics within a single theoretical framework. The study of collective action has been marked by the attempt to force radically different types of political activity into one analytical straightjacket, be it stucturalist, rational choice, or postmodern in design. Here we propose that different modes of popular protest might more fruitfully be explained by different theoretical approaches.

Chapter 9 (which appeared originally in *The China Quarterly*) further develops the implications of the Chinese experience for theories of contentious politics by moving outside the industrial arena to examine rural unrest under the PRC. The continuities with imperial days are striking, both in the rhetoric and symbolism deployed by would-be rebels and in the state's anxiety about heterodox beliefs and heterogeneous believers. Yet the peasant uprisings of the Communist era also depart markedly from their imperial and Republican forebears in terms of scale, social composition, and (at least to date) political significance. Equally important, rural protests have exhibited major changes over the course of the People's Republic—reflecting fundamental transformations in state–society relations from the Maoist to the post-Mao periods. With state-building in China having occurred in the absence of a capitalist revolution, we find that patterns of Chinese rural revolt are not well anticipated by standard social science theories of peasant rebellion, whether based on Third World or on European examples.

Chapter 10, an earlier version of which appeared in *Popular Protest and Political Culture in Modern China*, reflects upon the 1989 Tiananmen Uprising in historical context. The argument is that many of the failings of this so-called "democracy movement" lay in the inability of students to forge alliances with other social elements: entrepreneurs, workers, or peasants. Thanks in large measure to the tight structural links that continued to bind intellectuals to the Communist state, students were more inclined to look for allies among the bureaucratic elite than among society at large. The result was an exclusionary mode of protest that served to reinforce, rather than to overturn, authority relations in the PRC.

State sponsorship of public criticism in China has had a number of important repercussions. For one thing, ordinary Chinese are simply more familiar with modes of collective protest than we would expect of a population living under such tight political supervision. Ritualized as some aspects of mass criticism became during the Cultural Revolution, these routines nonetheless constituted part of a rich repertoire of protest techniques available to city dwellers and country folk alike. Public experience with protest may well explain why it was China that got the revolutionary ball rolling across the Communist world in 1989. It surely helps explain how the Tiananmen protesters proved so skillful at capturing worldwide attention with their dramatic actions: festive marches complete with colorful banners and stirring music; stinging attacks on political authorities in wall posters, speeches, and televised debates; even somber hunger strikes—all found precedents in earlier, elite-inspired campaigns.

Yet ultimately the voicing of the hidden transcript proved far more unsettling elsewhere in the Communist world than turned out to be the case for China. Precisely because protest was both routine and officially circumscribed, once the top leadership initiated a clear course of repression most of the populace was quick to fall into step—with concerns for personal safety as well as stability rapidly overshadowing the euphoria of public criticism. After all, this too was a familiar drill—harking back to the anti-rightist campaign of 1957, the military suppression of Cultural Revolution mass activism in 1969, the clearing of Tiananmen Square in April 1976, and the clampdown on Democracy Wall in 1979. In China, unlike Eastern Europe or the Soviet Union, both leaders and ordinary citizens knew how to put the genie of mass protest back into the bottle of state socialism.

What this augurs for the future is of course impossible to predict with confidence. Certainly the post-Mao reforms are generating new pretexts for protest, as concerns about excessive taxes and factory closures have joined long-standing resentment toward official privilege and bureaucratic corruption. Equally significant, the opportunities for forming cross-class and cross-regional coalitions are expanding apace with the unraveling of many of the state-imposed controls of the Maoist era. Much will depend upon the way in which the government authorities choose to respond to the growing unrest in both cities and countryside. Regardless of how the evolving tensions play out, however, upcoming scenarios are certain to bear the imprint of past practices—including those of Chinese communism itself.

A study of popular protest over the last century and a half underscores the impossibility of drawing a clear dividing line between Communist and pre-Communist China.[19] Maoist initiatives continue to influence modes of thought and behavior in the contemporary post-Mao period, but in many ways China today resembles the China of the Republican— or even the late imperial—era more than it does the China of Mao's Cultural Revolution. As markets reemerge and state-erected barriers crumble, social relations are reconfigured in a manner that may well rekindle the fires of rebellion and revolution that burned so brightly in an earlier age. Much has changed since then, of course, from cultural values to technological advances. And yet, to the extent to which popular protest and political legitimacy remain inextricably linked in the public mind, we may anticipate that future generations of Chinese will also rise up to challenge the Mandate of Heaven.

Notes

An earlier version of this chapter appeared in *Critical Asian Studies* (Summer 2001).

1. Liu Xiaobo, "That Holy Word, 'Revolution,' " in Jeffrey N. Wasserstrom and Elizabeth J. Perry, eds., *Popular Protest and Political Culture in Modern China* (Boulder, CO: Westview Press, 1994), pp. 315, 318.

2. Elizabeth J. Perry, "Chinese Anniversaries in International Perspective," *Harvard Asia Quarterly* (Summer 1999).

3. See Jeffrey Wasserstrom, "The Year of Living Anxiously: China's 1999," *Dissent* (Spring 2000), for an insightful discussion of historically grounded differences in government reactions to two of the three types of movements discussed here—which Wasserstrom dubs the "Solidarity Scenario" and the "Religious Revolt Scenario."

4. Foreign Broadcast Information Service [FBIS], August 8, 1994, p. 18.

5. Ching Kwan Lee, "Pathways of Labor Insurgency," in Elizabeth J. Perry and Mark Selden, eds., *Chinese Society: Change, Conflict, and Resistance* (London: Routledge, 2000).

6. FBIS, June 11, 1993, p. 13.

7. Jeffrey Wasserstrom makes this point in "The Year of Living Anxiously: China's 1999."

8. Elizabeth J. Perry, "Rural Collective Violence: The Fruits of Recent Reforms," in Elizabeth J. Perry and Christine Wong, eds., *The Political Economy of Reform in Post-Mao China* (Cambridge: Harvard University Press, 1985); and Elizabeth J. Perry, "Crime, Corruption and Contention in Contemporary China," in Merle Goldman and Roderick MacFarquhar, eds., *The Paradox of China's Post-Mao Reforms* (Cambridge: Harvard University Press, 1999).

9. *Dangdai* (The present age), no. 39 (August 25, 1990), pp. 14–15; FBIS, December 26, 1990, p. 29.

10. Suzanne Pepper, *Civil War in China: The Political Struggle, 1945–1949* (Berkeley: University of California Press, 1978).

11. In Shanghai, for example, I was told by the vice-director of the Propaganda Bureau that more than 10 percent of the 5,000-plus Falun Gong practitioners in the city were party members.

12. Daniel L. Overmyer, *Folk Buddhist Religion: Dissenting Sects in Late Traditional China* (Cambridge: Harvard University Press, 1976).

13. Prasenjit Duara, "Knowledge and Power in the Discourse of Modernity: The Campaigns Against Popular Religion in Early Twentieth-Century China," *Journal of Asian Studies* 50, no. 1 (1990): 67–83.

14. Charles Tilly, *From Mobilization to Revolution* (Reading, MA: Addison-Wesley, 1978); and Theda Skocpol, *States and Social Revolutions* (Cambridge: Cambridge University Press, 1979).

15. *Reuters World Report*, February 5, 2000. Emphasis added.

16. Donatella Della Porta, *Social Movements, Political Violence, and the State: A Comparative Analysis of Italy and Germany* (Cambridge: Cambridge University Press, 1995).

17. Sidney Tarrow, *Power in Movement: Social Movements, Collective Action and Politics* (New York: Cambridge University Press, 1994), pp. 92–93.

18. James C. Scott, *Domination and the Arts of Resistance: Hidden Transcripts* (New Haven, CT: Yale University Press, 1990).

19. Further discussion of the continuity between pre-1949 and post-1949 protest can be found in Lucien Bianco, *Peasants Without the Party: Conflict and Resistance in Twentieth-Century China* (Armonk, NY: M.E Sharpe, 2001).

CHALLENGING

THE

MANDATE

OF

HEAVEN

1

Predators and Protectors: Strategies of Peasant Survival

In the late imperial period, peasants in North China lived in a highly unstable natural environment. The resultant insecurity cast a dark shadow upon economic, social, and political life in the area. With productive opportunities severely constrained, peasants turned to alternative means of promoting and safeguarding their survival. Many households pursued the familiar strategies of controlling family size, borrowing from others, or moving elsewhere in an effort to obtain or conserve scarce resources. Such solutions, common to peasants the world over, assumed a particular form in North China that was conducive to the emergence of a diverse array of more aggressive strategies. These violent adaptations to a hostile environment can, for the most part, be subsumed within two broad categories. The first category includes offensive attempts to seize the resources of others: the *predatory* strategy. The second is composed of efforts to guard against such attacks: the *protective* strategy.

Although the motivation for these strategies was personal survival, their effect was to provide peasants with valuable experience in cooperation, mobility, and high-risk behavior. It is often assumed that sideline pursuits work primarily to sap rebellious potential.[1] Missing from this view is the point that adaptive strategies are more than simply income boosters. Far from an inevitable fetter upon revolt, involvement in short-

3

term migration, banditry, militia, and the like can actually organize peasants for more dramatic steps.

It is important to remember that these adaptations to the local environment evolved and persisted over generations. Although conditioned by the physical and social backdrop, these were by no means automatic, "knee-jerk" responses to set stimuli. Peasants learned to cope with their predicament in a cumulative history of trial-and-error experience, passing on these traditions to their progeny through oral history, folklore, and direct instruction.

Like all human beings, peasants are not entirely autonomous individuals. Their range of activity is dependent upon and limited by social circumstances and cultural traditions. Conflict over scarce resources is not comprehensible on an individual basis alone. Both the pattern of resource distribution and the struggle for a readjustment of this pattern necessarily involve wider social units. Much of the following discussion of peasant survival strategies will therefore be concerned with identifying the levels of social organization at which particular strategies were employed. Collective action implies organization, but this may be variously based upon kinship, settlement, class, friendship, occupation, or a number of other ties. Only after having clarified the underlying structures of action can we proceed to the central issue: the relationship of these strategies to peasant rebellion.

Theories of group conflict stress the importance of "mobilization"— the process whereby the discontented muster resources for the pursuit of common goals.[2] Collective survival strategies constitute important means of peasant mobilization, thereby facilitating the possibility of rural rebellion. The Nian and Red Spears provide examples of how, at two specific times in history, ongoing predation and protection were transformed into outright challenges to the Mandate of Heaven. Under the pressures of severe natural disaster and political crisis, regular survival strategies could generate anti-state activity. Such dramatic, rebellious expressions should not, however, blind us to the pragmatic and continuous character of these local patterns of survival.

An ecological perspective on peasant revolt does not deny its political nature. In the first place, national policies played a role in creating many of the problems with which Chinese peasants had to cope. Lack of proper dike maintenance by the central government was largely responsible for the devastating flooding of the region. Administrative irrationalities made possible the practice of smuggling. Lax security contributed to the growth of banditry and the need for private forms of defense. Periodic tax increases and marauding government soldiers furthered the protective response. In the second place, rebellion by definition involves opposition to government authority and is therefore a political act. Nevertheless, such opposition is often peripheral to an explanation of how and why traditions of rural violence evolve and persist. For the peasants themselves, armed revolt is often an extension of familiar strategies for making a living, turning into an anti-state position only reluctantly and under outside pressure.

Standard Household Strategies

Peasant households sought to cope with the problem of scarcity by controlling family size and composition, borrowing from others, diversifying their sources of income, and the like. Periodically family members or entire households would also move outside the local area in search of additional resources. These "sedentary" and "mobile" solutions were standard patterns that may at first appear quite unrelated to more aggressive survival strategies. In fact, they did have an important bearing on the likelihood and style of collective violence. Typically adopted at the level of the household—the primary production–consumption unit of any peasant economy—these mundane responses are common to many peasant societies. The form and consequences of these solutions to resource scarcity differ, however, and it is these differences that help to define the nature of peasant action in specific locales.

Sedentary Solutions

One of the most prevalent and tragic solutions to peasant poverty is the killing of infants. In China, where males were the favored offspring for both cultural and economic reasons, infanticide was primarily directed against girl babies. Whereas boys might be expected eventually to contribute to family income, girls were seen as liabilities who had to be reared and then married off at considerable expense. Widespread female infanticide resulted in a glaring imbalance in the sex ratio, with males outnumbering females by a sizable margin.[3]

For the mid-nineteenth century, figures from Xuzhou Prefecture in Jiangsu suggest an average of 129 men for every 100 women.[4] The disparity continued into the twentieth century. Table 1.1 gives figures from a field investigation conducted in sixteen northern Anhui villages in 1932. These statistics show males outnumbering females among the younger residents, with the ratio reversing itself among the elderly. Although in peasant societies female life expectancy is often lower than

Table 1.1

Percentage of Males and Females in Northern Anhui Villages, 1932

Age Group	% Male	% Female
Under 7 years	55	45
7–14 years	54	46
15–54 years	53	47
55+ years	49	51
Average	53	47

Source: Yang Jihua, 1933.

that of males because of higher mortality during the childbearing years, here we see no indication of that trend. Rather, the proportion of women increases steadily over the life cycle. It thus seems likely that the imbalance in the sex ratio was due to female infanticide. Figures from eighteen northern Anhui counties in 1934 range from a low of 108 to a high of 150 males per 100 females. The mean for the area as a whole was 123 men for every 100 women.[5] This sex ratio imbalance was not extraordinarily high by historic Chinese standards, yet the figures suggest that as many as 20 percent of males in the region may have gone unmarried. Although individual peasant families were pursuing a rational policy in rearing sons who were expected to augment household income, the social impact of this policy was a serious surplus of single young males. The dryland wheat farming practiced in this area was an extensive form of agriculture unresponsive to increased increments of human labor. Few family plots were large enough to absorb the labor of many sons. Some of these unmarried men were able to sell their services to more affluent families as hired workers or servants, but unemployment was a chronic problem. The existence of a huge contingent of single men had major consequences for the pattern of intergroup conflict. "Bare sticks," as unmarried males were popularly termed, provided a principal source of recruits for both predatory and protective movements. Smugglers, bandits, crop watchers, and militiamen alike were drawn in large part from their ranks. Thus the practice of female infanticide, though motivated by a family's need to restrict resource consumption, also helped contribute to particular forms of resource competition.

Despite efforts to control family size, many households continued to suffer economic difficulties. A flood, famine, wedding, or funeral could push peasants below the margin of survival, forcing them to borrow grain or money to weather the crisis. If an investigation conducted in four northern Jiangsu villages in 1943 is representative, nearly one-half of all households were in debt. About 80 percent of the debts had been incurred to provide food for immediate subsistence needs. Most of the other borrowing was a response to weddings, funerals, or illness. Less than 5 percent of the debts were for productive purposes such as irrigation improvement or the purchase of seeds, tools, or draft animals. Borrowing from relatives was common, since such loans might carry a more favorable rate of interest.[6]

Besides borrowing from creditors to tide themselves over in immediate crises, peasants organized loan associations as a means of insurance against hard times in the future. Although often based on kinship, such groups involved a level of cooperation higher than the nuclear family, bringing together friends and relatives in a collective strategy for coping with economic insecurity. "Old people societies" were formed to help with the burden of funeral expenses. Dues were pooled and then used to defray the cost of mourning clothes, coffins, and funeral arrangements as the need arose. "Fur garment societies" were organized to provide participating peasants with warm winter coats, which were beyond their individual means. Members paid annual dues that were used to purchase one or more coats each year. The group disbanded when all participants had been duly provided for. In addition to these specialized societies, groups created to provide more general types of loans were also common. These associations, or *yaohui*, typically met once a year, at which time members drank wine and threw dice to determine the precedence for borrowing.[7] Only a thin line separated the *yaohui* from the *huahui*, or illegal gambling societies, which were also prevalent in the area. Gambling had long been a favorite pastime for peasants during the slack season. As the gazetteer of Bo County commented, "Gambling constitutes the most serious and harmful vice of the local people."[8] Those who engaged in this practice usually did so with very little capital, so that losers often had no means of making good their debts. In the case of the Nian, losses at the gambling table were a potent motivation for the move to open banditry.

Incurring debts was obviously only a temporary palliative, one that could readily lead to greater poverty as interest on the loan accumulated. Many peasants thus sought relief beyond the creditor or loan association, in the outside world.

Mobile Solutions

Throughout human history, one common method of alleviating the problem of too large a population for too little food has been migration. Not
a few North China villagers adopted this "exit" solution to rural poverty.
Mobility was a way of life, a clear consequence of the difficult environment in which they lived. Chronic unemployment drove many to seek
seasonal support elsewhere during periods of agricultural slack. Sudden
natural disasters forced whole communities to evacuate their homes at a
moment's notice. Gazetteers state that in times of calamity poor peasants
"rushed to abandon the land," leading women and children down across
the Yangzi River in search of food.[9] Shouldering a few belongings, they
would trudge off to a temporary refuge where they might wait out the
trouble back home. This meant that the population was in a continuous
state of transiency and flux. Although not every member of every family
was on the move every year, many people did in fact migrate both seasonally and in response to unforeseen ecological crises.

Whether individual or group, seasonal or in response to sudden disaster, mobility was a normal feature of peasant life on the North China
plain. The fact that mobility was both continuous and temporary (in the
sense that peasants returned home whenever possible) gave it a special
importance with respect to the development of collective action. Migration, because of its disruptive and unsettling consequences, frequently
militates against group action. In this case, however, migratory experiences could enhance rather than inhibit the emergence of collective action and group conflict.

In the mid-nineteenth century, southern Jiangsu—particularly the city
of Shanghai—was the destination for many migrants from the North who
sought seasonal work as coolie laborers, porters, rickshaw pullers, and
the like. Few jobs were available, however, and many of the new arrivals
were forced into the ranks of the beggar army of Shanghai. Numbers
swelled with the onset of natural disaster. A description of the phenomenon appeared in the October 4, 1865, *Herald:*

> They have come from the northern part of this province, where the
> country has been devastated by locusts, and are traveling with a pass-
> port, given to them by the chief magistrate of the place from which
> they have come—specifying the reasons for their traveling, and testi-
> fying to their good character, declaring that they are good, but *dis-
> tressed* people.
>
> In times of scarcity of provisions—occasioned by inundation,

drought, locusts, and the like, when the government is unable to supply the means of sustenance—such licensed bands of beggars are by no means uncommon to China. As the food cannot be brought to them—there being neither the money to purchase it, nor the ways and means of transporting it if bought—necessity requires that the distressed people should go to the food.

In this land begging is moreover no very dishonorable profession, and when, as in this case, a passport is given to the beggars, they go in high spirits and are very bold; yet they rob nobody, take no denials, grow stout, and when the calamity is passed they usually return quietly to their native places—having traveled perhaps over half the length of the empire.[10]

As this description makes clear, begging in ecologically more stable areas constituted a recognized route for pursuing one's living in a society with few productive options outside agriculture. Begging was often a seasonal phenomenon—an alternative adopted during periods of agricultural slack as a regular method for supplementing family income.[11]

Seasonally mobile peasants created a fluid population not easily subject to government control. Throughout the Qing dynasty, memorials and edicts proliferated with regard to the problem. In 1815, a report on conditions in Anhui by Manchu official Na Yancheng stressed the importance of conducting an annual census of all mobile peasants—the so-called shed people or *pengmin*—during the periods when they returned to their native villages. In 1822 and again in 1824, imperial edicts were issued to the effect that "shed people" must be investigated one by one, with a responsible supervisor chosen for every ten households and accurate family registers posted on all doors.[12]

Local gentry bemoaned the difficulties of instituting the *baojia* security system in this region. As one gazetteer stated the problem, "The people are not attached to their land and there are many wanderers without regular occupations. They may leave for months at a time without returning home. Thus 30 to 40 percent of the dwellings are occupied by outsiders. These intruders may stay for months and are neither easily expelled nor easily incorporated into a security system."[13] Periodic movements of large numbers of people opened the way for a good deal of dislocation, inhibiting government efforts at tight supervision. The result was not chaos, however, for regularized mobility induced a kind of structure of its own. Although usually conducted as a household strategy, migration often generated higher levels of social cooperation and conflict. A revealing illustration of this process is provided by the *hutuan*, or lake associations, which developed as a result of serious inundations in the area.[14] Massive flooding of the Yellow River in 1851 caused two lakes on the Jiangsu–Shandong border to overflow, submerging all the surrounding land on the western shores of these two lakes. The inhabitants of the area (Pei and Tongshan counties in northwest Jiangsu) fled en masse to escape the calamity.

Four years later the Yellow River again burst its dikes, this time inflicting its greatest damage a few miles north of the previous flood. Inhabitants of the southern Shandong area were hardest hit, and disaster victims rushed down across the border by the hundreds of thousands to seek refuge in neighboring Jiangsu. There they found the abandoned lands that had been inundated in 1851, but which by now had partially dried into fertile silted terrain. The newcomers from Shandong erected shacks and industriously set about cultivating the unoccupied lands. Their hard work paid off and soon the immigrants were enjoying bountiful harvests. This prosperity was reflected in the organization of twelve defense leagues, called lake associations, to protect their newfound wealth. With official approval, the settlers constructed forts and stockpiled weapons to safeguard their livelihood against outside intrusion. The immigrants successfully fought off waves of rebel incursions and remained happily settled in their new homes for nearly a decade.

At this point, however, former inhabitants of the region who had fled the 1851 floods began to reappear on the scene. Seeing that their now fertile lands had been claimed by others, the returned natives filed indignant complaints with the local authorities. When no official help was forthcoming, fighting erupted between the original occupants and the immigrant lake associations. The conflict escalated in late 1865 with an incursion of Nian rebels from Anhui, who found supporters among unruly elements in the *hutuan*. The area was on the verge of revolt, and order was restored only when government troops marched in to arrest and execute more than one thousand lake association members. Two *hutuan* found guilty of having harbored rebels were disbanded and their lands confiscated by the government and redistributed to the original owners.

As the example suggests, life in this part of the North China plain was extremely fluid. An unstable natural environment resulted in massive population movement both out of and into the area. In the late nineteenth and early twentieth centuries, the urbanization of South China also drew large numbers of northern residents out of their villages to seek temporary employment. In 1935 the Ministry of Industry reported that more than 50 percent of rural families in northern Anhui had lost some of their members by migration to cities—the national average being only 13.5 percent. Young unmarried males formed the bulk of the emigrants.[15]

Armies were another outlet for the surplus population. The North China plain had historically served as a major recruiting ground for government soldiers in times of national crisis. Although military service paid poorly in terms of salary or provisions, the life of the soldier promised travel and adventure as well as the opportunity to prey upon distant populations. A military career was usually brief, however. After completing a campaign, the troops would be summarily released and ordered to return to their native villages. Accustomed to a life of violence, and seldom able to find regular employment at home, demobilized soldiers were likely candidates for banditry.[16]

Aggressive Survival Strategies

Peasants, we have seen, employed a variety of conventional methods for dealing with the problem of scarcity. These standard and, for the most part, officially sanctioned activities in turn generated a number of more aggressive approaches. It is important to emphasize that no hard and fast line can be drawn between the conventional methods and the more dramatic strategies of predation and protection. As a foreign observer in bandit-infested Henan noted in 1927:

> Personally, after having talked this over with numbers of foreigners as well as Chinese, I am inclined to believe that there really is no distinction as between "bandits" and "people" further than that by bandits are meant those who are at the time under arms and "on the war path" and by people the women and children and the aged who carry on small businesses in the poorly stocked markets or till the land. But that the people are really the fathers and mothers and sisters and brothers of the bandits, and profit by their activity insofar as those who are active in the profession divide their gains with the folks back home.
>
> On the other hand, there is ample evidence that some of the inhabitants, at least on occasions, rebel against being interfered with by anyone. For one comes upon towns which are "sealed"; and have been so for weeks or months. By this is meant that all the gates are closed and banked up behind with earth, so that the wall is, to all intents and purposes, a continuous structure, and no one who does not belong to the community is allowed in under any circumstances. Communities which adopt this measure may be reinforced by soldiers or Red Spears

or both. I have heard of places that had held out in this manner for months, refusing admittance even to the military on official business.[17]

Ordinarily the relative absence of state interference in this region meant that peasants were fairly free to devise their own methods for ensuring subsistence. When agriculture failed, competition for scarce resources intensified. The hungry staged attacks on those with goods; the latter responded defensively. And thus was set in motion a kind of parochial dialectic between predator and protector. Periodically, however, if violence escalated to an unacceptable level, if the central treasury were seriously depleted, or in times of foreign invasion, outside actors might enter the picture: government soldiers, state officials, or Japanese or warlord troops. Their tactics of harsh repression or heavy taxation could drive predator and protector together into a united front against this common enemy from the outside. Although such a synthesis was always fraught with tension, it furthered the potential for massive rebellion.

Predatory Strategies

It is frequently noted that peasants are normally inhibited from rebellious activity by the tyranny of work and the pressures of custom. The young surplus population of the North China plain—unemployed and often well traveled—was less subject to these restrictions. Having engaged perhaps in periodic excursions out of their native villages as beggars, soldiers, or hired laborers, they had acquired valuable exposure to new ways. Denied regular work at home, these bare sticks were on the face of it classic "marginal men"—impoverished and with no stake or position in conventional society. In reality, however, the very fact that the region regularly reproduced this "marginal" class gave its members a certain recognized social place. These young men, we remember, had been reared as part of a household strategy for survival. Although unmarried, they remained a part of their natal families, to whom they might return periodically with remittances of resources secured in their outside activities. For this reason, the predatory strategy—staffed predominantly by such bare sticks—was organized largely along familial lines. Smuggling activities were frequently conducted by lineage, bandit gangs generally encompassed kinship networks, and feuds were often between competing clans. Thus predation need not be seen as the domain of solitary individuals, forced into asocial behavior by their lack of communal bonds. Precisely because these figures were not only "marginal," but also an integral part of the structure of peasant society, their predatory ventures were a form of collective action with strong rebel potential.

Smuggling

Smuggling was an illegal form of seasonal mobility that took peasants to other areas in an effort to supplement their inadequate agricultural income. It differed from begging, migrating, or soldiering in that it was a seizure of resources officially deemed off-limits to the people involved. Smuggling is by definition illegal, and it is this criminal aspect of the behavior that differentiates it from officially sanctioned mobility. In attempting to seize control over resources to which they had no legal access, smugglers were engaging in a type of predatory activity that blended easily into theft, banditry, and open revolt. As early as Huang Chao's uprising in A.D. 874–85, salt smuggling was a prelude to rebellion on the North China plain.

The peculiarities of the government salt monopoly during the Qing made the illegal transport and sale of salt an extremely lucrative occupation for smugglers. Official regulations divided the country into eleven salt zones. Only certain types of salt could legally be sold and consumed in particular zones at fixed prices. The way the boundaries were drawn, central and eastern Henan and the one county of Su in northern Anhui were "Changlu salt" districts, whereas the rest of northern Anhui was restricted to the inferior "Huai salt." To make matters worse, the foul-tasting Huai salt was the most expensive variety of all.[18] In the early nineteenth century, each *jin* of Huai salt cost 40 to 50 *wen*, whereas the more palatable Changlu variety sold for only half the price.[19] Enterprising peasants in the Huai districts thus used the winter slack period to travel to the Changlu zones, load up on salt, and return home to sell the illicit variety at a sizable profit.

Because of the danger inherent in this illegal enterprise, salt smugglers enlisted the services of armed guards to accompany them on their perilous journeys. In 1815, imperial censor Tao Zhu[20] wrote in a memorial that salt smuggling along the Henan–Anhui border was being conducted behind a shield provided by people popularly known as "Red Beards." These strongmen were said to be remnants of the White Lotus Rebellion who now engaged in armed robbery for a living. Their nickname derived from the fact that, in traditional Chinese opera, red beards were part of the stock make-up for the role of the fierce, lawless character. These people often supplied protection for more than a hundred salt carts a day, receiving a fee of 200 *wen* per cart. If the revenue from smuggling proved insufficient to support the extravagant feasting and gambling parties to which they were accustomed, the Red Beards undertook plundering expeditions to secure additional goods. On these forays they gathered into groups, each of which was known as a *nian*, organizational units that Tao described as ranging in size from a dozen to several hundred people. The Red Beards-cum-*nian* were said to have stolen goods, seized women, and committed a host of sadistic atrocities on innocent victims. They were described as well armed and as posing a major challenge to local peacekeeping efforts.[21]

The Nian Rebellion was in many ways intimately linked to salt smuggling. Subsequent rebellions in the area were also connected to conflict over the prized resource of salt. In 1898, for example, an uprising involving some thirty thousand peasants in Guoyang County began with an attack on the market town's largest salt shop. Centered in the same county that had produced the Nian half a century before, these latter-day rebels also set up a five-colored-banner system and chose an alliance commander in obvious imitation of the Nian pattern.[22] Problems with salt continued into the Republican period. In 1928, Xuyi County in Anhui was plagued with more than a thousand "salt bandits" who took advantage of the poorly maintained Huai River system to plunder stranded salt boats as they ran aground on the accumulated silt.[23]

The salt traffic provided a tempting opportunity for poor peasants to augment a meager income. During the Republican era, opium smuggling was also a lucrative profession in this area.[24] As a regular seasonal activity, smuggling was well organized, often according to lineage.[25] The high-risk nature of the enterprise made it imperative for participating peasants to cooperate closely; such cooperation was most easily effected along kinship lines. The fact that the activity was in direct defiance of government authority meant that it was but a short step from smuggler to full-fledged rebel. Thus smuggling was a form of organized predatory behavior especially conducive to anti-state movements.

Banditry

Even nearer than smuggling to rebellion was organized banditry. The North China plain was for centuries known as a hotbed of Chinese brigandage. Here, where natural disaster and warfare swept the countryside repeatedly, large numbers of peasants took to the "green forests" (*lülin*) with equal regularity. Throughout the late Qing and Republican periods, scarcely a day would pass without newspaper and government reports of organized brigandage in the area. Certain locations were particularly prone to bandit occupation. Frequent flooding turned the marshy shores of Lake Hongze into an especially fertile breeding ground for brigands. Provincial and county borders were another favorite refuge.

Ineffective government control made the choice of banditry viable. Officials dreaded assignment to this unruly area and, if they had the misfortune to receive such a post, usually tried to endure the tenure with as little local involvement as possible. Along county and provincial borders the problem of banditry was especially acute. Since officials in each district preferred to pass the buck to their neighbors rather than cooperate for effective control, bandits moved back and forth across jurisdictional boundaries with impunity. In 1823, Anhui governor Tao Zhu characterized the zones of bandit activity as the "three no-governs" (san buguan), where county, prefecture, and province all denied responsibility for law enforcement.[26] Tao repeatedly memorialized, to no apparent avail, on the need for official cooperation along the provincial borders of Anhui–Jiangsu–Henan–Shandong, where banditry was rampant. This region continued to serve as home for many of China's bandits on into the Republican period.[27]

Government ineptitude was itself partially a product of the natural setting. Take as an example an incident that occurred along the Jiangsu–Henan border in 1872. The magistrates of neighboring counties in the two provinces met to adjudicate a case in which a dry-goods store had been plundered by bandits. The problem was that the village in which the incident took place had no tax registers or property deeds, these having all perished in massive inundations some years back. After the flood waters subsided, people in adjacent counties had bought and sold property in ignorance of the earlier provincial boundary line, and it was now unclear to which jurisdiction the village belonged. Only after a lengthy investigation were gravestones unearthed that identified the village as part of Yongcheng County in Henan.[28]

Natural and political factors worked in concert to make this region an unstable ecosystem especially hospitable to banditry. In addition to contextual causes, an ongoing popular tradition among the peasants themselves played a vital role in perpetuating an awareness of and propensity for banditry. As one indication of this local culture, we have the testimony of the famous Qing general Yuan Jiasan, who was horrified to discover on an inspection tour of northern Anhui the existence of extremely ornate temples dedicated to none other than Tao Zhi, the notorious bandit chief of Chinese legend.[29] The profession of banditry thus apparently did enjoy a certain popular prestige.

Folk songs and folk tales collected by historians working in this area offer further evidence of a living tradition of social banditry.[30] The stories are rich in matters of strategy and tactics, suggesting that oral literature was an important means of transmitting practical knowledge from one generation to the next. That bandits considered themselves a part of such a cultural tradition is suggested by their widespread adoption of similar titles and practices. It was common for bandit chiefs to assume names borrowed from the heroes of popular literature, to organize their forces under a system of five banners, and to distribute turbans and tasseled spears to their followers. In addition, bandits in this area developed a distinctive set of expressions to describe their activities, a vernacular that showed surprising stability over time.[31] Thus there existed background conditions and a conscious tradition conducive to the growth of banditry. Yet the question remains as to what this banditry was like and how individual brigands coalesced into organized groups to pursue their common interests.

Bandits often began their journey into crime at the level of petty thievery—robbing graves or individual households by night, seizing crops from unwatched fields, and so forth. Once the group obtained sufficient arms and personnel to pose a credible threat, however, it would escalate to more audacious activities. Frequently bandits set up operations in local markets, requisitioning lavish food and drink from the surrounding populace and extorting protection money from shopkeepers and merchants. Another favorite activity was to lie in wait along trade routes and swoop down upon unsuspecting travelers, robbing them or demanding some set fee for safe passage. Sometimes bandit groups even managed to take control of government customs passes, assuming the authority to levy taxes at will.

One of the most common ways in which bandits acquired money and goods was by kidnapping hostages for ransom. This practice was directed primarily against the well-to-do, since these families could best afford handsome compensation. Bandits often demanded their ransom in opium, which served as a prime medium of exchange in the late Qing and Republican periods. Those who insisted upon this form of payment were known as *xiangzhu*, or "trunk masters," and government reports are replete with references to their bold runs across the North China plain.[32] Even more colorful terms were used to differentiate kidnapping according to the victim involved. In the case of female victims, the act was termed "seizing a goddess of mercy"; in the case of wealthy males, it was "grabbing a fat pig." The ransom price would vary according to the chief's appraisal of the financial means of the household involved. The time limit imposed on payment was also variable. In the case of virgin girls, a special "quick ticket" (*kuaipiao*) might be required if the young woman were to be reclaimed before nightfall. In addition to opium, payment could be demanded in cash, grain, arms, or horses.[33]

During the Republican period, foreigners also became prized targets for kidnap. Perhaps the boldest such instance was an international incident in May 1923, when thousands of armed bandits converged upon the Tianjin–Pukou Railroad as it approached Lincheng station in southern Shandong. Three hundred passengers, including thirty foreigners, were taken hostage in a bid to end the military siege to which the bandits' mountain lair was being subjected by government forces at the time.[34] A decade earlier, bandit chief Bai Lang ("White Wolf") had adopted similar tactics, seizing thirteen foreign missionaries on a foray into northern Hubei. The practice was repeated by his band on a smaller scale in Anhui, Henan, and Gansu (see Chapter 4).[35] Whether such activities represented an incipient anti-imperialism is uncertain; that they were an effort to garner lucrative ransom seems indisputable.

In addition to relying on robbery, extortion, and kidnap, some large and well-organized groups of bandits were sufficiently bold and powerful actually to occupy cities. The famous Henan bandit Lao Yangren was an example. Popularly known as the "old foreigner" because of his height and curly air, this bandit led a force of over ten thousand to occupy a whole string of cities in Henan and Anhui during the 1920s.[36]

Bandit gangs numbering in the hundreds and thousands were not uncommon in this area. For the Republican period, the picture has been reasonably well documented. In 1925, Shandong was reported to have had forty-seven major bandit chiefs with a total of more than seventeen thousand regular followers. In Henan Province, some fifty-two bandit gangs were said to include fifty-one thousand regulars. Xuzhou District in Jiangsu harbored close to five thousand bandits; in one Anhui county alone there were ten gangs with several hundred followers in the early 1930s.[37]

Who were these bandits and how did they organize themselves? In answering these questions, we must keep in mind that there were at least three types of bandit outfits, differing in size, composition, geographical scope, and durability: the ad hoc gang, the semipermanent gang, and the bandit army.

The simplest bandit group—the ad hoc gang—was a regular institution in the North China countryside. This was the small, seasonal gathering of local *youmin* who drifted into occasional brigandage for economic reasons. The *youmin* were chronically unemployed persons, usually young males, who milled about their local market towns gambling, committing petty theft, and the like. They were the surplus sons of poor peasant families, unable to secure a steady occupation within the confines of their unproductive home economy. For them, the world of banditry constituted an appealing alternative to a life of aimless hunger. In fact, their participation in brigandage was often a regular family strategy whereby younger sons would serve as seasonal bandits to augment household income. Bandit gangs composed entirely of *youmin* were temporary, small-scale operations of a dozen or so people that seldom ventured far from home. At harvest time, the members would disband to lend a hand with the farm work.

In bad years, when flood or drought depressed the harvest, ad hoc gangs could evolve into a second type of bandit outfit: the semipermanent gang. Unable to pursue even a seasonal occupation on the land, the bandits began to operate year-round. They selected some safe base from which to conduct their plundering forays, activities that began to spread farther from home to areas less struck by natural disaster.

As banditry took on a more permanent form, it attracted a new type of member. On the leadership level, the *youmin* were superseded by another group that may, for lack of a better term, be called the "village aspirants." Rural North China generated a certain number of ambitious young men, and less frequently women,[38] of relatively affluent families who found their plans for advancement thwarted by the powers that be. These were usually not the offspring of landed gentry, for whom educational and bureaucratic advancement was within reach, but the children of moderately well-off owner-cultivators to whom such channels of mobility seemed far less promising. Unschooled but enterprising, these individuals faced a bleak future in the villages of the North China plain. Since legitimate entrepreneurial opportunities were extremely scarce, some of the aspirants chose instead to seek their fortune in the world of crime.

Often the aspirants were actively coaxed into brigandage by some unfortunate brush with the law. Like Hobsbawm's "noble robber," they might begin their bandit careers as victims of injustice.[39] Occasionally their subsequent activities also reflected an ethic of social banditry: righting wrongs, robbing the rich to assist the poor, and performing other acts of peasant justice associated with a Robin Hood—or Liangshanbo— image. Zhang Luoxing, commander of the Nian alliance, was apparently an outlaw of this sort. Bai Lang, perhaps the best-known bandit of the Republican period, demonstrated similar tendencies. Both Zhang and Bai came from families with sizable landholdings, Zhang's father owning some 140 to 150 *mu* and Bai's about 200 *mu*. Both were illiterate peasants who engaged in a variety of nonagricultural pursuits before turning to open banditry In each case, their fateful brush with the law stemmed from involvement in gambling and interclan feuds. Both carried out individual acts of chivalry and tried to impress upon their followers the importance of discipline and social justice.[40]

The semipermanent gang was based upon a patron–client relationship between village aspirant leaders and *youmin* followers. The bandit chief used his own influence and resources to offer security and material welfare to the otherwise destitute drifter. The *youmin*, for his part, reciprocated by carrying out plunder and performing symbolic acts of deference to the leader.[41] Chieftains brought to the group crucial assets with which to get the enterprise under way. In the case of the Lincheng railroad brigands, for example, the two brothers who founded the gang did so by using the proceeds from selling their family lands to purchase horses and arms.[42] Once the group was in operation, the plunder by the followers supplied the wherewithal to continue. The chief did not lose importance, however, for it was his responsibility to negotiate the necessary protective alliances to keep the gang afloat. The followers provided the economic basis of survival, and the chieftain contributed political resources to the arrangement. It was his duty to serve as a kind of power broker for the group, effecting advantageous coalitions with prestigious individuals, competing gangs, or other potential allies.

Sometimes the hard-core followers of a bandit gang were related to the chief by blood. The impoverished nephew was an especially common committed client. Members of the gang who were not actually related often underwent sworn brotherhood ceremonies and addressed one another with fictive kinship titles. Bandit chief Wu Ruwen, an important brigand operating along the Anhui–Jiangsu border in the early Republican period, claimed more than one hundred "adopted sons" among his entourage.[43] Newcomers to bandit gangs were often assigned new names, one character of which was uniform for all members of their same age or seniority, the same pattern as was used for siblings and cousins in a regular extended family. Thus the gang provided a kind of surrogate family for the *youmin* who attached themselves to it. The structure of the group was highly authoritarian, however, since the chief had final responsibility for all major decisions and held the power of life or death over his subordinates.[44]

In his role as power broker, the bandit chief made short-term alliances with other gangs. According to these arrangements, each chief retained autonomy with respect to his own subordinates but was expected to coordinate tactical plans with other cooperating chieftains. These alliances were the backbone of the third major type of bandit group, the massive bandit armies that staged periodic raids on market towns and administrative centers. Bandit armies were especially likely to emerge in times of chronic famine, attracting to their ranks large numbers of starving peasants from the surrounding countryside.

If particular coalitions proved especially successful, the chieftains might agree to cooperate on a longer-term basis. In this case, they would make a formal alliance, usually selecting as their commander the chief with the largest following. Often the resulting coalition took on a quasi-military organizational structure, assuming divisions such as brigades, battalions, and the like. Some armies adopted formal disciplinary codes and a kind of martial law.[45] Even in these cases, however, the alliances remained in reality cellular and segmented, with primary loyalties continuing to operate at the level of the gang, rather than the army. Military codes were honored mostly in the breach, and discipline was seldom strictly enforced. Since tactical cooperation really pertained only among chiefs, alliances did not involve a basic restructuring of gang commitments. The coalition was always uneasy, with great potential for disharmony and fissure.

Understanding the composition of bandit gangs and armies is crucial in assessing the adaptability of this survival strategy to peasant rebellion. Without such inspection, banditry might appear a natural candidate for incorporation into wider anti-state movements. It was, after all, an enterprise that organized huge numbers of peasants into an aggressive and mobile mode of action. It was led by individuals with concerns that transcended personal or parochial boundaries. What could have been simpler than to convert this ongoing tradition into outright rebellion?

From the perspective of the state, of course, the very existence of banditry augured rebellion, inasmuch as it was an open defiance of official authority. Particularly in China, where the Mandate of Heaven sanctioned the possibility of a commoner rising to assume the throne, the political potential of brigandage must have seemed especially strong. Looked at from the bandit side, however, another picture emerges. Large-scale banditry, we have seen, was an uneasy composite of three distinct layers of rural society. Each of these elements entered the activity for its own reasons, and each implied a different degree of commitment to brigandage as a way of life. The poor peasant who joined up with a marauding bandit army was the least tied to this survival strategy. His allegiance was short-lived and purely pragmatic. Plunder was for him a means of supplementing, but not supplanting, an inadequate income. By contrast, the *youmin* participants demonstrated a stronger allegiance to banditry as an occupation. These individuals might owe their entire livelihood to the bandit gang and were thus unlikely to abandon it unless offered a secure alternative means of survival. Finally, the bandit chieftain had joined the movement for yet a third set of reasons. His motivation stemmed less from temporary or chronic poverty than from a desire to enhance his own position. The aspirant's commitment to banditry was dependent upon its being able to facilitate honor and impact in a wider world than his own village could offer.

These three layers of participation thus implied quite different sorts of motivation and commitment. For our purposes, the crucial point is that none of the three was inherently rebellious. Temporary gain, permanent livelihood, and individual prestige were all a far cry from an attack upon either the personnel or the structure of state authority. Add to this the intrinsic weaknesses of bandit organization—the patron–client basis of the gang; the loose, cellular quality of intergang cooperation; the fleeting attachment of ordinary peasants—and one appreciates the difficulties involved in any effort to convert banditry to the cause of rebellion.

What complicates the picture somewhat is the pivotal role of the bandit chief. This individual, we must recall, was largely interested in expanding his own power. The scope of the chieftain's control depended upon the kinds of outside coalitions he was able to forge. Such coalitions were seen not only as a necessary source of protection for plundering activities, but as steppingstones to a wider world of power and fame. Although ambitious chiefs effected alliances according to strictly pragmatic criteria, the character of the allies had potentially important implications for the subsequent direction of the bandit movement. If the leader's most promising friends were rebels, then it was quite possible that he would change the rhetoric, and sometimes the substance, of his activity to an anti-state position.

Nian leader Zhang Luoxing offers a prime example of this process. In his search for broader sources of support, Zhang effected a crucial alliance with the Taiping rebels that was intended to transform his bandit army into an anti-Qing movement. Similarly, in the Republican period it was assistance from Sun Yatsen's camp that pushed bandit chief Bai Lang toward open revolt. When much-needed arms and military advisors were forthcoming from the revolutionaries, Bai's pronouncements took on an increasingly political tone.[46]

These examples suggest that it was indeed possible for bandit leaders to assume a rebellious position. If wider political circumstances were such that rebels constituted the most available allies, then banditry could change from pure plunder to anti-government revolt. Historically speaking, however, these situations were relatively rare. Since the state usually constituted the most promising power domain, it was far more common for ambitious bandits to turn in this direction. Government cooptation of bandit chiefs was frequent in imperial China. "Pacification," complete with official position, was such a common government tactic that more than a few bandit leaders probably saw their outlaw career as a quick means of attaining bureaucratic rank.[47] The popular novel *Shuihu zhuan* (Water Margin) provided a well-known model of this very pattern. In fact, the phenomenon of pacification was so frequent that a folk saying arose: "If you want to become an official, 'carry a big stick'; i.e., be a bandit."[48] Speaking softly, however, was evidently not required. Exactly when to surrender was nevertheless a delicate calculation, since the larger one's following, the higher the official title one might expect to be offered. Thus there was always a countercurrent at work drawing bandit chieftains away from government control. Because his behavior was not firmly rooted in either economic need or political commitment, the chieftain often assumed a chameleonic quality, vacillating between the worlds of officialdom and crime in a continuing search for personal gain.

Bandits did display a certain consideration toward the people who lived near their base of operations. As the Chinese proverb puts it, "A rabbit never eats the grass around its own hole." Outlaws were obviously dependent upon the goodwill and protection of local inhabitants and were usually related to them by blood. It was thus common to share booty with poor friends, relatives, and protectors back home.[49] For most peasant participants, however, banditry was a survival strategy born of desperation. Whether or not it also exhibited a sense of social justice depended in large part upon the level of affluence and security a particular group managed to attain. Outlaws who did enjoy some degree of safety tended to be both more selective in their targets and more generous in sharing the booty. When starvation no longer loomed, it is plausible that brigands would consciously try to fashion their behavior on a social bandit model. A popular song recorded in one gazetteer reflects this process:

> Bandits make a stir,
> Impoverishing the wealthy, enriching the poor;
> They kidnap for ransom and eat all they can hold;
> Then the leftover silver they give to the old.[50]

Nagano Akira, a Japanese journalist stationed in China during the 1930s, has left us with some of the most informed firsthand accounts of Chinese banditry for that period. Nagano argues strongly in favor of a social bandit characterization of the groups he investigated. As evidence, he quotes from the proclamation of a large bandit gang in Yancheng, Jiangsu: "We signal the masses of the green forest to assemble for one end—liquidation of the corrupt elements in our society. The common folk are our concern and communal property our goal. First we must beat to death all greedy officials and evil rich, destroying the root of China's trouble and transforming this into a pure new world."[51] As further indication of a rudimentary class consciousness, Nagano cites a song popular among the notorious railway brigands of Lincheng, Shandong:

> Upper classes, you owe us money;
> Middle classes, stay out of our affairs.
> Lower classes, hurry to our mountain lair,
> Here to pass the years with us.[52]

Apparently some bandit groups thus did evidence a redistributive ethos. Nevertheless, the dominant motivation for involvement in banditry remained the promise of immediate gain. Even the Lincheng bandits, for all their radical rhetoric, ended up negotiating a deal with the government whereby their chieftain would be made a brigade commander and be allowed to reorganize his followers into the army in exchange for the release of their foreign captives.[53]

In sum, banditry was a complex variety of predatory behavior that incorporated a number of contradictory strains. For most of its participants, the enterprise represented an effort to secure resources in response to sudden or endemic scarcity. In this sense, banditry was only a more organized form of other aggressive strategies for survival. Precisely because of its higher level of organization, however, banditry was sometimes liable to take a more politicized direction. Depending upon the types of coalitions that their chieftains forged, bandit gangs could move toward either open rebellion or calculated capitulation. The outside context was crucial in presenting opportunities and obstacles for wider involvement.

Feuds

An equally complex type of predatory violence was the feud, an enduring form of contention between families and villages. Local gentry being few and far between in North China, conflict resolution was correspondingly deficient. Competition among inhabitants fostered bitter, deadly disputes conducted along clan and community lines. Like salt smuggling and banditry, feuds were usually organized by kinship, as part of a strategy by a household or lineage to improve its livelihood at the expense of competitors. More than these other forms of predatory activity, however, feuding also involved aspects of the protective response. Because parties to the feud were roughly coequals, with each engaging in aggressive assaults on the other, both sides found it necessary to build up their defenses. As protective measures proceeded, feuds often incorporated whole villages. Settlement was often by lineage, and defense was most effectively conducted at the community level. The fact that certain of the disputes revolved about issues that affected entire villages (for example, water rights or territorial boundaries) also helped to organize the violence on a communal basis.

More clearly than in other forms of predation, we can see in the feud an attempt not only to seize scarce resources, but also to eliminate fellow competitors. In this respect, the feud closely resembled primitive warfare. However, its occurrence in peasant, rather than primitive, society lent the phenomenon rebellious potential. Despite its essentially private character, feuding has wider implications. For one thing, this form of predatory behavior encouraged the possibility of armed action on a larger scale. Furthermore, when rebellions did get under way in the area, they were shaped in important ways by these homely roots. Revenge could escalate to draw in increasing numbers of combatants, but the resulting conflict never entirely outgrew the pattern of underlying feuds.

By the nineteenth century, the making of arms for private use flourished in this region. In 1815 in Ying Prefecture, along the Henan–Anhui border, a village ironsmith was running a lucrative business producing guns for the local populace. The county magistrate reported that repeated efforts to confiscate the weapons had failed miserably, both because of the high economic value of the guns and because peasants feared official investigation if they turned in the weapons as requested.[54] As one gazetteer noted, "The riffraff take along knives and swords whenever they venture outdoors. These persons gather into groups of desperadoes who are quick to pick a fight. As a result, ordinary peasant families must also stockpile weapons."[55]

Ethnic feuds were one motivation for the private arsenals. An 1852 memorial by the governor of Anhui states that Muslims and Han Chinese in this area were making their own spears and swords for use in combat against each other.[56] Often, however, the disputes involved no such ethnic overtones.

During the late Qing, reports on feuds were a frequent theme in memorials to the throne submitted by the provincial governors of Anhui, Henan, and Jiangsu. As described in these documents, the conflicts typically originated as disputes over scarce resources between individuals. The controversies then quickly escalated into armed confrontations fought, for the most part, along kinship lines.

A few examples from northern Anhui illustrate the flavor of these feuds. In June 1845, for instance, the governor of Anhui presented a memorial describing a case in a village in Huaiyuan County. The trouble began when livestock belonging to an escaped criminal trampled and devoured beans growing on his neighbor's land. Seeing the damage to his crops, the neighbor initiated a heated argument. After consulting his paternal uncle for advice, a number of relatives were notified, and the following day thirteen of them—some armed with guns—marched on the home of the victim. The neighbor, assisted by several of his relatives, rushed out to meet the intruders. A fight ensued in which many on both sides were wounded or killed. Bystanders who tried to mediate were also injured in the fray.[57]

In October 1848, an armed feud between two families in Shou County was reported as having developed out of a quarrel over the price of a cow. The owner demanded 13,000 *wen*, whereas a prospective buyer would offer only 12,700 *wen*. In March 1859, a feud in Huaiyuan stemmed from an argument over repayment of a debt. Wang Yuanke owed Shao Kuishen 160 *wen* in cash from a loan for the purchase of firecrackers. One day Shao ran into his debtor on the street and asked for the money. Wang responded with loud curses. The next day Shao called together four of his relatives. Armed with spears, they set out to start a fight. Wang and his neighbor were both killed in the melee.[58]

These examples, brief as they are, give some indication of the origins of wider feuds. The conflicts developed out of controversies between individuals over scarce resources: crops, animals, money. From these modest beginnings, interclan wars were generated to buttress the individual disputants' claims.

Eventually communal feuds took on a life of their own. An illustration is provided by a dispute that had endured for generations between the Wang and Guo family villages in Shangqiu, Henan. In 1844, Guo villagers amassed groups of raiders to plunder and kidnap residents of two neighboring villages inhabited by members of the Wang clan, extracting ransoms from more than a hundred families. In 1847, Guo villagers again went on the offensive, this time stealing wheat from the same Wang community. The theft was reported to the county authorities, whereupon two of the raiders were apprehended. As a result, the Guo clan harbored an even deeper grudge against the Wangs. In 1850 one of the imprisoned Guo raiders escaped from jail and stole some millet from the Wang village. Again the government was notified, at which point the Guo clan amassed more than a hundred members, armed with spears and swords, to stage a retaliatory offensive against the Wangs. One member of the Wang clan was seriously wounded and one Guo killed in the melee. Not content to let the matter rest, several of the Guo masqueraded as officials to launch a surprise attack upon Wang households, forcing open doors, breaking windows, and looting at will.[59]

Disputes over water were a common source of lingering intercommunity feuds. In the summer of 1932, for example, such a conflict flared up along the border between the counties of Xiao in Jiangsu and Su in Anhui. When inhabitants of Xiao County drained two riverbeds, thousands of armed Su villagers responded by filling in the trenches dug by Xiao in order to keep their own land from flooding. A similar struggle occurred in the same area in the fall of 1933, in part because enduring animosities had yet to be settled.[60]

Although feuds were usually conducted on a clan basis, often pitting whole lineage settlements against each other, disputes within the kinship network also occurred on occasion. In 1850, for example, we have an account of such a case in Su County concerning an unemployed peasant, Wang Jiabao, who tried to borrow money from his kinsman Wang Jiaxiu. Jiaxiu, who was in mourning at the time, reprimanded Jiabao for the impropriety, ridiculed his lack of a steady job, and summarily refused the loan. Infuriated by these insults, Jiabao gathered eleven followers to attack his relative's home. They robbed the house of money and carted Jiaxiu off to an empty lot north of the village where they proceeded to gouge out both his eyes. When the eldest son arrived to rescue his unfortunate father, his eyesight was extinguished as well. A year later Jiaxiu's second son ran into Jiabao at the market and cursed him vociferously, whereupon Jiabao seized the youth with the intention of gouging out his eyes also. In response to the impassioned pleading of a crowd that gathered in the marketplace, Jiabao released the son but avenged the insult by another attack on the family home in which he stole horses and donkeys that were later sold for cash. Four months later yet another assault was staged. This time Jiabao made off with dishes, pots, and clothing.[61]

An interesting sidelight on these cases is that all were reports of lawsuits filed by the self-declared victims. The initiators were individuals whose persons or property had been harmed or stolen and who used the lawsuit as a means of regaining, or preferably improving upon, their loss. It is important to point out, however, that such people were not only the wealthy or landed gentry. In 1849, for example, a case was filed by a young tenant farmer in response to a bandit attack. Local officials, bribed by the bandit's relatives, took advantage of the litigant's illiteracy to avoid filing a complete report on the incident. Eventually, however, the full facts of the case were brought to light and the victim was compensated for his losses.[62]

Local gazetteers confirm the fact that lawsuits were filed by all sectors of rural society—although with differing frequency and success, one would certainly suspect.[63] That lawsuits were often a strategy for aggressively gaining at the expense of others, rather than a simple effort to redress loss, is borne out by the gazetteer accounts: "The people are frugal, wear rough clothing, and eat coarse food. However, they often gamble and file court cases. Households may easily be bankrupted in this way. Those who are able to take their complaints to the higher courts are regarded as local heroes. Relatives and friends think it normal to give money to support these ventures, which are pursued in hopes of profit."[64] If the cases reported by the provincial governors are any indication, many lawsuits were filed in connection with armed feuds. After loss on the battlefield, a trip to the county magistrate might be a next step in the conflict. Since legal recourse was, however, a less predictable and a potentially disastrous move, most disputes were settled out of court.

Feuds thus usually remained a private form of competition. Nevertheless, they did organize people, typically along kinship lines, to pursue their interests by violent means. To be sure, the feuds of the North China plain were not so elaborate as the massive armed battles (*xiedou*) of southeastern China. There, a more commercialized economy and powerful lineage structure had made possible the development of a sophisticated and expensive type of vendetta that involved hiring mercenaries, performing religious ceremonies, and so forth.[65] Despite its comparatively modest proportions, however, feuding in North China did provide peasants with experience in collective violence. Emergent rebellions, we will see, took advantage of such rivalries to gain supporters from among the competitors. By the same token, the form the rebellions assumed— their geographical spread, definition of enemies, level of political consciousness—was shaped in many respects by those roots in local feuds.

Like banditry, feuding bore a two-sided relationship to rebellion. On the one hand, it schooled peasants in the practice of group violence, a skill that might under certain historical conditions be channeled into more rebellious directions. On the other hand, feuds were inherently divisive, establishing deep animosities that could surface during the course of a rebellion.[66] In the case of both the Nian and the Red Spears, continuing feuds sapped the vitality of the rebel movements and undermined effective cooperation for wider political goals.

Protective Strategies

Predatory activities, we have seen, were methods for aggressively increasing the assets of some individuals and groups at the expense of others. The origins of these activities may be linked to local problems of resource scarcity, but the subsequent directions of particular predatory movements were highly dependent upon the wider political context. The protective strategy can also be traced back to endemic competition among local inhabitants. Those who found themselves under attack rose to the challenge with a variety of countermeasures. Surplus resources were used to sponsor village guards, crop-watching associations, community defense leagues, and fortification projects.

Compared to the predatory strategy, protection was typically organized by community, rather than by kinship. In single-lineage settlements the distinction was of course irrelevant, but in multisurname villages the community can usually be identified as the dominant unit of organization. Since predation often threatened all members of a victimized community, the residents devised cooperative measures of defense.

As with the predatory strategy, the form, strength, and political coloration of such activities were intimately connected to the larger society. Just as outside forces played a critical role in attracting or alienating bandits, so they also had a decisive impact upon the allegiances of protective groups. Official support was crucial in encouraging the evolution of local defense. However, when governments tried to extract more resources in the form of higher taxes, these same protective units could rapidly turn their energies toward open revolt.

Crop-watching

The threat of crop theft was the cause of a good deal of defensive activity across the North China plain. Since stealing from a wheat field was an almost irresistible temptation to the hungry, cultivators found it necessary to provide protection for their ripening crops. The likelihood of theft was exacerbated by the fact that peasant dwellings were clustered together into compact villages a good distance from many of the fields. Although a central location evened out the travel time to the scattered holdings where peasants worked, this settlement pattern had the side effect of leaving fields unprotected by the security of a nearby dwelling. As a result, when harvest time drew near, peasants would send family members out into the fields at night to take turns guarding the household plots. Some affluent families hired regular crop watchers to do the unpleasant task for them. The practice was known as *kanqing*, or "watching the green." Often several families with contiguous holdings cooperated in hiring a guard to protect all their crops until ready for harvest.

When harvest time finally arrived, unemployed laborers would converge upon the local market town in search of temporary work. Large landholders contracted with these laborers by the day, leading them to the fields to help cut the wheat. Additional crop watchers were often hired to make certain that no stealing occurred in the midst of the harvest activity. This variety of crop-watching was known as *kanbian*, or "watching the borders."[67]

As the harvesting proceeded, in many places it was customary to permit poor peasants from the surrounding countryside to go through the fields gleaning leftovers. The practice, intended as a concession to the impoverished, was the root of many a dispute between gleaners and landowners. In some areas, the difficulties associated with this custom led to the emergence of more formal institutions. In Luyi County, for example, the evolution of crop-watching associations was directly traceable to gleaning:

> At harvest time, women from impoverished families descended upon the fields to seize any leftovers. The more cunning sometimes used gleaning as an opportunity for theft. Time and again quarrels and lawsuits occurred over this problem. As a result, the community determined that gleaning was to be prohibited. Anyone who pilfered grain or let loose animals [to graze on the property of others] would be punished severely. These decisions resulted in the *lanqinghui*, or crop-protection association.[68]

By the early twentieth century, crop-watching had in many places changed from a family to a village responsibility. Sometimes the job was performed on a rotating cooperative basis, but more commonly guards were hired by the crop-watching association to carry out the task. Expenses were borne by the villagers, payable in direct proportion to the amount of their holdings.[69] The individuals hired to serve as watchmen were usually the landless poor who had no regular source of support. By hiring some "idle, worthless fellow in the village (not infrequently a thief he is)"[70] the crop-watching association provided an alternative livelihood, thereby channeling potentially lawless behavior into a socially beneficial mode.

Several village studies conducted in North China during the later Qing and Republican periods point to the formation of crop-watching associations as indicating a heightened degree of solidarity and cooperation in the villages of this area.[71] However, Japanese scholar Hatada Takashi presents a quite different explanation for the phenomenon. In Hatada's opinion, crop-watching associations were evidence not of village growth and development, but rather of village decline. His interpretation is based primarily upon investigations sponsored by the Southern Manchurian Railway, which Hatada helped to conduct in six North China villages from 1940 to 1944. According to informants, the organization of crop-watching activities escalated in direct response to the threat of theft. Thus the switch from family- to village-based systems was primarily a defensive reaction against increased robbery, rather than a positive reflection of village dynamism. In Hatada's analysis, the emergence of crop-watching associations was linked to a deterioration in peasant livelihood during the late Qing and Republican eras: growing concentration of land-holdings, dissolution of the single-lineage settlement, decline in village finance, and so forth. As rural poverty increased, so did the incidence of theft, and hence the need for protection. Although the peasants originally tried to conduct crop-watching on a household basis, family plots were usually scattered in small parcels here and there, so it was extremely difficult for one household to guard them all. Crop-watching associations were formed as a more effective means of carrying out the onerous chore. Furthermore, since the most persistent thieves were not outsiders, but impoverished members of the village itself, the practice of providing gainful employment for these individuals was a boon to the other inhabitants as well. In short, in Hatada's view the evolution of crop-watching was a gradual and multifunctional strategy for dealing with the effects of rural poverty.[72]

Significantly, the process was soon coopted by local governments. By the turn of the century, it was common for counties in North China to instruct their villages to form crop-watching associations. The idea was that, by cutting down on the percentage of the harvest lost to theft, more would be made available for taxation. Furthermore, since villagers were quite willing to pay to protect their fields, the county government saw the crop-watching association as an effective vehicle for general tax collection. In many areas, "crop-watching fees" became the center of village finance, only a fraction of which actually went toward the expense of crop-watching operations.[73]

The government thus found it expedient to systematize and convert to its own purposes a practice by which peasants tried to protect their insecure livelihoods. In this respect, the development of crop-watching associations resembled that of local militia—another process that evidenced the overlay of official policy upon pre-existing ecological strategies.

Militia

Whereas crop-watching was designed to protect the outlying fields, other measures were required to defend property within the village. Since the local government was of little assistance in this matter, responsibility for village defense devolved upon the rural inhabitants themselves. Wealthy households hired personal vigilantes—usually the local riffraff—to provide protection. In addition, whole villages cooperated in organizing for common defense. One traditional village defense institution was the night watch. Watchmen patrolled the streets at night and, at two-hour intervals, sounded a gong, the noise of which was intended to scare off prowlers.

Private vigilantes or night watchmen by themselves were, however, inadequate for the defense needs of most villages. The prevalence of large-scale banditry meant that villagers found it necessary to organize from among themselves groups of armed guards, or militia, to provide the requisite protection. Leadership and funding for these defense forces came from the wealthier inhabitants—gentry, landlords, or rich peasants.

An example of a particularly successful defense league was one directed by Niu Feiran of Caoshiji, Anhui. Niu, a degree holder, in 1853 organized the local militia in opposition to growing Nian activity in his area. For a decade, he, his son, and a cousin actively fought against the Nian. Their work was so esteemed by the government that they were officially dubbed the "Niu Family Army." In 1863, Niu Feiran played a leading role in pacifying a Nian chieftain in the area who then proceeded to betray Nian commander Zhang Luoxing to the authorities. For this deed Niu was rewarded with a high bureaucratic position.[74]

The militia was one of those key institutions in China which to some extent represented a convergence of the interests of state and society.[75] For rural inhabitants, a viable defense structure meant protection of their livelihood against the threat of banditry. To the government, the militia was a means of maintaining its mandate in the face of rebellion.

Official encouragement of local defense was forthcoming when the regime found itself unable to cope with serious peasant unrest. Thus in 1853, with the northward advance of the Taiping rebels, the Qing government ordered the formation of militia throughout the area. It is important to keep in mind, however, that official support during times of crisis was being superimposed upon a pre-existing pattern of rural protection. Although state and society shared certain concerns in the matter, tensions reflecting the two strains were inherent in the institution of the militia. To the villagers, self-defense was a weapon against predatory threats to property. In cases where the threat was posed by plundering bandits, those under attack shared with the state a common interest in combating the problem. Often, however, it was the government itself that played the role of predator by demanding resources from the countryside. At such times the militia constituted an effective vehicle for furthering peasant livelihood at government expense.

An illustration of the rebel potential of the defense corps was found in Xuchang, Henan. In 1854, a militia had been established there in reaction to the intrusion of the Taipings. The following year the militia decided to turn its attention to government intrusion as well. For years, government troops had passed through Xuchang on their way to military engagements elsewhere. In the past, the troops had hired carts from the local peasants at the rate of one *liang* of silver per one hundred *li*. Now, under the auspices of the new defense corps, the community demanded one *liang* per day per cart, regardless of the distance traveled. The government stepped in to thwart the proposal, but not without provoking a major riot in which several officials were killed.[76]

In the mid-nineteenth century, the proliferation of militia was associated with a dramatic rise in the frequency and scale of tax resistance.[77] The relationship was twofold. In the first place, the surcharges levied to support the organization of militia were a cause of considerable resentment. In the second place, these same militia in turn offered an organizational base for opposition to government policy.

Massive tax riots were occasioned in part by a steady fall in the price of grain during the first half of the nineteenth century.[78] It has been estimated that prices dropped by about one-half between the years 1815 and 1850, creating an almost 100 percent appreciation in the value of silver.[79] Since taxes were paid in cash, peasants were now forced to sell nearly double the amount of crops in order to be able to pay the same taxes as previously. When one adds on the new surcharges that were being demanded in this period, the magnitude of the burden is readily apparent.

It was in areas where tenancy was low and freeholding peasants numerous that tax riots tended to be most frequent.[80] Higher taxes were of concern to all landholders—large landlords and small owner-cultivators alike. The newly created self-defense forces, led by local landlords and gentry and staffed by ordinary peasants, thus constituted an effective vehicle for tax resistance. In contrast to the secret society, the militia was free to recruit its numbers openly. Under the pretext of local defense, peasants were encouraged to stockpile weapons and participate in military training. As we will see in Chapter 2, the result was a powerful force that could be mobilized to promote local interests when these conflicted with government demands. In 1859, the Manchu prince Senggelinqin reported that all of Shandong was ablaze with tax revolts instigated by the local militia. Hundreds of cases have been recorded of militia leading assaults on county offices, burning tax registers, and killing magistrates and other officials.[81]

In addition to carrying out what were essentially defensive acts against tax collection, the militia sometimes engaged in outright predatory activities themselves. Ironically, the state's promotion of the militia had brought into being a weapon that could be used for plunder as well as protection. The very existence of this institution in the Chinese countryside opened new organizational opportunities for both types of survival strategy. As if to spite a social scientist's search for order, bandits now began to assume the guise of regular militia, secreting their predatory designs behind the cover of protective legitimacy. Government-sponsored militarization during the late Qing gave birth to powerful institutions that could turn from their officially prescribed functions to tax resistance, banditry, and open revolt.

The importance of defense forces to collective violence did not end with the demise of imperial China. During the Republican era as well, self-defense leagues were a crucial basis for local resistance. In the chaos of the 1920s, locally sponsored village militia mushroomed to combat bandits and warlords, often moving to tax revolt in their effort to maintain control over precarious resources. In the late 1930s, when the Japanese occupied much of the North China plain, the central government once again instructed local communities to organize self-defense groups in response. Newspapers of the time are replete with accounts of these forces turning to predatory activities. In 1939, all of Anhui Province was ordered to establish militia units to resist Japanese intrusion.[82] The vice-commander of the northern Anhui self-defense league, a young man by the name of Zhou Tiaofan, used his position as a front for organized banditry. Zhou forced peasants in his jurisdiction to grow opium, which he then sold at considerable profit to himself. For several years, the vice-commander instructed his subordinates to kill, plunder, and kidnap for ransom.[83]

The militia stood as a kind of bridge between the government and the peasantry. As power brokers in the countryside, village defense leagues were intended to mediate the interests of state and society. When those interests proved irreconcilable, however, militia could serve to channel mass action in opposition to government demands.

Fortification

Intimately connected to the emergence of militia was the establishment of fortified communities. To facilitate local defense, villagers erected walls and constructed stockades around their threatened settlements. Throughout Chinese history, the wall has been an architectural response to conflict. Simple town walls of pounded earth date back to Longshan settlements of 2000 B.C. Subsequently the structures became more massive and enclosed greater expanses of territory. Walls were built to fend off bandits, to define the borders of warring states, and to insulate the so-called civilized world from the barbarous outside.

The particular type of fortification associated with the rise of the militia during the late nineteenth century had precedents in practices developed during the White Lotus Rebellion. Local notables instructed the peasants to construct earth fortresses in which to store grain and take refuge. The idea was that when rebels approached there would be nothing in the fields for them to steal, no place to rest, and no people to threaten. Moats were dug around the fortresses and gun turrets built at the corners to make them virtually impervious to rebel incursion.[84]

Construction of these fortified communities may have begun with the White Lotus insurgency, but it mushroomed in response to the Nian and Taipings in the mid-nineteenth century. The fortresses were known in the north Anhui area as *yuzhai*. The term has an interesting etymology. Although the word *zhai*, or stockade, was common throughout North China, the character *yu* had a more parochial meaning. Originally the word referred to land that was effectively protected by dikes against the Huai River. During the late Qing, the meaning was extended to describe the heavy fortifications constructed against banditry and rebellion under gentry supervision.[85] As maladministration of the river system increased, so grew the need for defense against predatory attack. A term that at one time had been reserved for protection from the physical environment was now applied to protection from human competitors.

A cyclical theory of village fortification has been proposed by G. William Skinner, who suggests that each dynastic decline triggered a process of community closure at the local level. According to the theory, during the height of a dynasty's vigor, rural villages were relatively open. In response to the many opportunities for upward mobility, individuals moved out of and back into their rural communities with considerable frequency. Conversely, the onset of dynastic decay caused villages to close their doors in defense against an increasingly threatening and insecure environment. "Coercive closure," as Skinner terms the process, involved a sequence of steps: formation of crop-watching societies, expulsion of outsiders, militarization of local systems, and fortification of key areas.[86]

In the late nineteenth and early twentieth centuries, the process of community closure was well under way in North China—a direct response to the ecological and political instability of the period. Although construction of fortifications was periodically endorsed by the state, it was fundamentally an expression of parochial interests. Local residents rushed to erect walls and stockades when their property was threatened by attack. Construction of *yuzhai* thus neatly mirrored the level of predatory activity in the area. The general pattern is illustrated by data culled from the gazetteers of six counties that have recorded the dates when fortresses were built in their areas (see Table 1.2). As the table shows, the greatest period of construction occurred during the late Xianfeng and Tongzhi reigns (1856–66), when the Nian and Taipings were most active in the area. The early Republican period then witnessed another rise in construction, as Bai Lang, Lao Yangren, and other bandits marched across the North China plain. Unfortunately, most of the gazetteers that included these data were published too early to present an accurate indication of the trends after the turn of the century. However, we know from other accounts that forts continued to be built in opposition to warlords and marauding troops on into the Republican period. It is probably safe to assume that the construction of new forts and repair of dilapidated ones escalated during this period far faster than the table would suggest.

The building of these massive forts had important implications for the configuration of spatial boundaries. As peasants arranged to store a part of their crop in its granary, the stockade began to assume a host of economic functions. In time, the *yuzhai* effectively displaced local mar-

Table 1.2

Construction of Fortified Communities

			County				
Year	Tongshan	Pei	Suining	Feng	Zhecheng	Xiangcheng	Total
1807	1						1
1846	1						1
1850	5					5	10
1853					1	1	2
1854						5	5
1855					1		1
1856	4				2	2	8
1857	6				1	5	12
1858	9		31	5	3	17	65
1859	17		11		12	5	45
1860	27	1	25	16	9	10	88
1861	9	2	7	20	9	24	71
1862	28	1	12	1	16	36	94
1863	7		3		1	8	19
1864	2	1	1	1		3	8
1865	2	1	3			1	7
1866	4	1	2		3	3	13
1867	1	1	1			1	4
1870						1	1
1871	5						5
1875			1			1	2
1880	2						2
1890	1						1
1891	1						1
1894	1						1
1909	2						2
1910						3	3
1911	8					12	20
1920		46					46
No date	23		6	1		36	66
Total	166	54	103	44	58	179	604

Sources: *Tongshanxian zhi*, 1926, 10/1–30; *Peixian zhi*, 1920, 16/9–10; *Suiningxian zhi*, 1887, 6/35–51; *Fengxian zhi*, 1894, 2/7–11; *Zhechengxian zhi*, 1896, 2/15–19; *Xiangchengxian zhi*, 1911.

kets in some areas. Once-prosperous markets turned into ghost towns as commerce shifted to the safety of the walled fortress.[87]

This accretion of economic importance was soon translated into political status as well. In the 1860s, the *yuzhai* replaced the rural town as a quasi-administrative unit in most parts of northern Anhui. By the Guomindang period, the *yuzhai* was formally recognized as a level of rural administration, with 3,721 of these units in the northern portion of Anhui Province alone.[88] Encompassing an average of 400 to 500 households, the *yuzhai* occupied a slot one step above the village in the hierarchy of rural administration. In Guoyang County, for example, the 221 *yuzhai* in operation in 1925 had jurisdictions ranging from 3 to 79 villages, the average being about 25 villages.[89]

The method of operation of these forts and the extent to which they constituted permanent living quarters as opposed to emergency shelters varied from place to place. The differences seem due in large measure to the magnitude and distribution of resources in particular locales. In areas of poor, freeholding villages—which were most typical of North China—*yuzhai* were usually temporary refuges managed cooperatively by all members of the community. However, in places where there was severe landholding concentration, such that one or two families controlled great tracts of property, the construction of forts was likely to be considerably more lavish. Since these affluent households had much to protect and sufficient means to do so, they would build massive fortifications within which they and their subordinates lived permanently.

To illustrate the freeholding pattern, we have the case of Laowo, a large village in eastern Henan that included some 400 households. In 1938 the village learned of a bandit gang numbering over 1,000 that had plundered ruthlessly in the area. The fort was divided into 35 sections, each of which was guarded by 10 members of the community on a rotating basis. In addition to the 350 peasants on stationary duty, there were 8 mobile units that took turns patrolling around the fort. Within the stockade, peasants slept in dwellings they themselves had constructed. A few of the more affluent used bricks, but most dwellings were made of wheat stalks, and some peasants simply laid out straw mats on which to spend their nights, clutching their rifles as they slept. At one point, Laowo joined with neighboring villages to try to combat the bandits directly. Although they managed to mobilize nearly 1,800 peasants in this engagement, the villagers were unable to suppress the menace. As a result, the peasants of Laowo were forced to continue their nightly routine of taking refuge in the fort.[90]

In cases where the *yuzhai* were essentially owned and operated by wealthy landlords, the system was somewhat different. This second pattern has been vividly described for certain sections of northern Jiangsu where land concentration was especially pronounced. The walls of these forts were often constructed of brick or stone, rather than earth. Cannon towers were erected at the four corners of the stockade. In the center of the encirclement was a tiled mansion with its own cannon tower, the home of the large landowner. All around the fortress chief lived the several hundred tenant households who cultivated his lands. Outside the fort were a number of tiny satellite villages, some of whose inhabitants also tilled the fortress chief's lands.[91]

According to observers who conducted field work in the area in 1930, these were extremely self-contained communities, permeated with a thoroughly medieval atmosphere. The fortress chiefs, who were also the commanders of the local self-defense corps, assumed titles such as "King of the Underworld Guo," "Hegemon Li," and the like. Their militia comprised primarily tenant farmers, sometimes supplemented by disbanded soldiers or other peasants in need of employment.[92]

The *yuzhai* under these circumstances operated as autonomous kingdoms, the fortress chief in command of both economic and judicial matters. Militarily such forts constituted a serious challenge to the local government. In Jiangsu's Pei County, for example, in 1930 the county administration itself controlled only eighteen rifles—eight under the militia and ten under the public security office. By contrast, one single fortress controlled fifty-three rifles, nearly three times the government stock. Often several fortresses joined forces to resist the authority of the county administration. They would then refuse to pay taxes and would assume full independence from government control.[93]

Regardless of whether they were initiated and managed by small owner-cultivators or by rich landlords, the forts were essentially a means of promoting security and survival in a threatening environment. Once these structures were built, however, they themselves constituted an important part of the setting to which peasants had to adjust. The *yuzhai*, we have seen, came to assume both marketing and administrative functions. Furthermore, the very physical presence of these walled communities had an important effect upon collective survival strategies in the area. Although they were products of human activity, the forts became, in a real sense, a feature of the local ecosystem.[94] As such, *yuzhai* were an important weapon for predators as well as protectors. Operating on such flat terrain, bandits found the walled fortress a useful substitute for the swamp marsh or mountain lair that their brethren in other geographical regions chose as home base. Just as the construction of fortified communities was an essential method of protection against bandit attack, so the occupation of these same fortifications became a key tactic for successful banditry across the North China plain.

Conclusion

There was a kind of dialectic at work in the relation between the predatory and protective strategies of survival. On the one hand, the two strategies were polar opposites. Predation was an aggressive attack upon the resources of others; protection was its direct countermeasure. On the other hand, far from being mutually exclusive, the two strategies could complement or alternate with one another. Although predation and protection were fundamentally antagonistic, they provided opportunities for cooperation as well as competition. At times, one mode would pass into the other—militias turned to plunder or bandits settled within walled fortresses. At still other times, the two would even join hands, with bandits and defense leagues making common cause in opposition to yet a third enemy: the state. Widespread and long-lasting rebellion in North China was born of this peculiar synthesis. Such an outcome was always fragile, however, inasmuch as it represented two contrary sets of interests and approaches. Particular rebellions had roots in either the predatory or the protective strategy. Large-scale movements necessarily drew to their ranks adherents of the opposite mode, but they could not entirely overcome their origins in the process. The synthesis was never complete, and was often rife with conflict.

The notion of a dualistic tension is implicit in much of the scholarship on traditional Chinese society. The terms of the dialectic are usually defined from the perspective of the ruling elite, however. Thus the dichotomy is typically posed as one of "order versus chaos," "orthodoxy versus heterodoxy," or "state versus society." In this view, the tension in the system arises out of conflict between the government's demand for conformity and the propensity of peasants and local gentry toward an unruly independence. In adopting this perspective, scholars mirror the outlook of the documents they study. It is the *yin* and *yang* as seen from the top that is being applied to society at large.

Although data on the peasant perspective are obviously less accessible and often altogether nonexistent, we do have information about peasant behavior. Building our theory of rebellion from the bottom up, we begin with the notion of peasants adapting to a particular environment, developing individual and group strategies on the basis of the paucity or surplus of their resources. By looking at rural collective action, we can identify a dialectic operating by its own rules at the lowest levels of society.

Notes

An earlier version of this chapter was published as chapter 3 of Elizabeth J. Perry, *Rebels and Revolutionaries in North China, 1845–1945* (Stanford: Stanford University Press, 1980).

1. For example, James Scott has commented, "To the degree that the marginal opportunities open to the peasant do in fact alleviate short-run subsistence needs, to that degree they tend to reduce the likelihood of more direct and violent solutions" (Scott, 1976, p. 204).

2. Anthony Oberschall, *Social Conflict and Social Movements* (Englewood Cliffs, NJ: Prentice Hall, 1973); Charles Tilly, *From Mobilization to Revolution* (Reading, MA: Addison-Wesley, 1978).

3. Ho Ping-ti, 1959, pp. 58–59.

4. *Xuzhoufu zhi*, 1874, 12/53–54, gives the figures shown in Table 1.3, below. See Aird, 1968, pp. 266–267, for some of the methodological problems with sex ratio statistics for Qing China.

Table 1.3

Sex Ratio Among the Population of Xuzhou Prefecture, 1874

County	Males	Females	Males per 100 females
Tongshan	450,903	337,211	134
Xiao	177,087	148,986	119
Tangshan	170,560	170,277	100
Feng	337,536	246,992	137
Pei	272,198	216,536	126
Peizhou	266,750	266,748	100
Suqian	659,330	439,554	150
Suining	260,682	159,991	163

5. *Anhuisheng tongji nianjian*, 1934, p. 68.

6. Zhang Weicheng, 1943, pp. 47–54; Wu Shoupeng, 1930, p. 61.

7. "Tongshan nongcun," 1931, p. 387.

8. *Bozhou zhi*, 1894, 2/29.

9. *Huaianfu zhi*, 1884, 2/4.

10. *North China Herald*, October 4, 1865, p. 38.

11. In Fengyang, Anhui, the practice of begging evolved in an interesting fashion. This county, birthplace of the first Ming emperor, was devastated by turmoil that preceded the founding of the dynasty. To repopulate his home county, the new sovereign forced more than fourteen thousand affluent people from south of the Yangzi to settle permanently in Fengyang. Any who returned to their homes were to be severely punished. Since the displaced persons had a strong desire to visit their family graves, they masqueraded as seasonal beggars to make the risky journey home. In time, it became a regular custom to depart in winter and return for spring planting. The practice had originated because people in Fengyang had enough money to travel, but over the centuries it became in fact what it once had pretended to be, a winter occupation of the poor for supplementing annual income (Inoue Kobai, 1923, pp. 273–274).

12. Ming-Qing archives, National Palace Museum, Taipei, *Gongzhongdang Daoguang* 0008605–1, Xianfeng 001658.

13. *Fengtaixian zhi*, 1882, 4/6.

14. The following discussion is based on *Nianjun*, vol. 1, pp. 13–30; *Peixian zhi*, 1920, p. 16.

15. "Internal Chinese Migration," in Institute of Pacific Relations, 1938, p. 256.

16. See Nagano Akira, 1931, 1938, for a discussion of this area's role in generating soldiers; Wu Shoupeng, 1930, p. 65.

17. *North China Herald*, March 5, 1927, p. 388.

18. Xu Hong, 1972.

19. NCPC, p. 6.

20. For information on the career and policies of Tao Zhu, see Metzger, 1962.

21. NCPC, p. 6.

22. *Fengyangfu zhi*, 1908, p. 4; *Mengchengxian zhi*, 1915, p. 6; Mu Lianfu, 1959, pp. 77–83.

23. *Zhongyang ribao*, August 30, 1928, p. 1.

24. Billingsley, 1974, pp. 118–120.

25. Ma Changhua, 1959, pp. 22–23.

26. NCPC, p. 7.

27. Nagano Akira, 1931, p. 66; 1938, p. 199.

28. *Xiaoxian zhi*, 1874, 4/5–6.

29. Yuan Jiasan, 1911, 5/31.

30. Examples appear in numerous articles in *Minjian wenxue* (Folk literature) during the late 1950s and early 1960s. A general collection is contained in *Zhongguo nongmin qiyi de gushi* (Stories of Chinese peasant uprisings), 1952, Shanghai. Interviews with former north Anhui residents in Taiwan reinforce the impression of a strong bandit tradition, perpetuated through oral storytelling.

31. He Xiya, 1925, pp. 39–41, 65–76; *Nianjun*, vol. 1, pp. 192–288; vol. 4, pp. 210–249; NCPC, pp. 6, 29.

32. NCPC, p. 29; WCT-TK 5/9/26.

33. He Xiya, 1925, pp. 49–56; Dai Xuanzhi, 1973, pp. 61–62.

34. Nagano Akira, 1931, p. 27.

35. Wang Zongyu, 1964, pp. 23–24.

36. *Shanxian zhi*, 1936, p. 1.

37. He Xiya, 1925, pp. 83–94; Nagano Akira, 1938, pp. 226–227; *Shina no doran*, 1930, pp. 27–56.

38. Women bandit leaders were less common, but certainly did exist, in both the Qing and Republican periods. For examples from the late nineteenth century, see NC, vol. 2, pp. 202–288; vol. 4, pp. 210–249. In the Republican period, the best-known female bandit was "Mama Zhao," who led a force of six or seven hundred bandits, all of them women, in southern Shandong (He Xiya, 1925, p. 19; Nagano Akira, 1931, p. 68). Interviews with former residents of the area suggest that there were in fact many more women outlaws than the written record would have us believe. In Anhui's Shou County, for example, a woman bandit known as "Two-gun Zhang" was famous for wielding a pistol in each hand. She is said to have come from a respectable middle peasant family and to have stolen from the rich in neighboring areas to assist the poor of Shou County.

39. Hobsbawm, 1965, pp. 13–29; 1969, pp. 34–49.

40. Ruo Mu, 1959, p. 52; *Guoyangxian zhi*, 1924, 15/6; *Shixue yuekan*, no. 2 (1960): 20; Wang Fanting, 1975, p. 15.

41. Scott and Kerkvliet (1977, p. 443), based on their studies of Southeast Asia, deny the applicability of a patron–client link to the bandit context, noting that the bandit chief is newly arrived with little claim to higher status, and not culturally sanctioned. The typical North China case would seem at variance with this. There the chief usually did come from a relatively secure family and thus brought to banditry a set of resources quite different from those of his followers. Furthermore, there does seem to have been a strong subculture of legitimacy to sustain the bandit leader. Interviews with former residents confirm the fact that in the North China plain the role of "noble bandit" was considered a quasi-respectable one for frustrated youths.

42. Nagano Akira, 1933, p. 269.

43. *Zhongyang ribao*, March 7, 1928, p. 3.

44. He Xiya, 1925, pp. 34–35; Dai Xuanzhi, 1973, pp. 61–62.

45. He Xiya, 1925, pp. 34–38.

46. Friedman, 1974, pp. 151–156; Wang Zongyu, 1964, pp. 20–21.

47. He Xiya, 1925, p. 9.

48. Dai Xuanzhi, 1973, p. 61.

49. *Dongpingxian zhi*, 1935, p. 5.

50. Nagano Akira, 1933, p. 270.

51. Ibid.

52. Nagano Akira, 1938, pp. 149–154.

53. Edward Friedman (1974, p. 164) has noted that the government was finally able to suppress the bandit army of Bai Lang ("White Wolf") only by terrorizing the brigands' families. Their relatives were killed, farms confiscated, and homes burned to prevent the bandits from blending back into the peasantry.

54. NCPC, p. 28.

55. *Fengtaixian zhi*, 1882, 4/5.

56. KCT-Xianfeng 001949.

57. KCT-Daoguang 009663.

58. KCT-Daoguang 010929, 00838.

59. FL 1/1–3.

60. Bianco, 1976, p. 320.

61. KCT-Xianfeng 002504.

62. WCT-Daoguang 29/8/24.

63. *Xiangchengxian zhi*, 1911, 5/47; *Luyixian zhi*, 1896, 9/1; *Suiningxian zhi*, 1887, 3/6.

64. *Fengtaixian zhi*, 1882, 4/5.

65. Harry J. Lamley, "Hsieh-tou: The Pathology of Violence in Southeastern China," *Ch'ing-shih wen-t'i*, 3, no. 7 (1977): 1–39. Although feuds in Huaibei were less elaborate, there was a certain amount of ritualistic behavior. For a description, see NC, vol. 1, p. 387.

66. *Fengtaixian zhi*, 1882, 4/6.

67. *Luyixian zhi*, 1896, 9/3.

68. Gamble, 1963, pp. 69–70; Smith, 1970, pp. 121–122.

69. Mills, 1873.

70. Lamley, 1977, pp. 31–32. Lamley notes that feuds helped give rise to all four of China's major mid-nineteenth-century rebellions: Taiping, Nian, and Northwest and Southwest Muslim. However, he also finds that in the areas of

Southeast China where *xiedou* were most highly developed, large-scale rebellion was uncommon. Apparently, in those areas the conflicts were too intense to permit cooperative struggle against the state.

71. Gamble, 1963, pp. 156–157; Smith, 1970, pp. 119–124; Yang, 1945, pp. 148–149.

72. Hatada Takashi, 1973, pp. 67, 68, 174–224, 225.

73. Ibid., pp. 64, 74–76; Myers, 1970, pp. 60, 100.

74. *Guoyangxian zhi*, 1924, 12/51. Niu's militia was probably related to the Old Cows, a secret society–defense league that carried out bitter opposition to the Nian. One Nian folk tale (*Nianjun gushiji*, 1962, p. 225) suggests such a connection. The Niu militia was located in approximately the area described by Liu Tang (NC, vol. 1, p. 349) as Old Cow territory.

75. See Kuhn, 1970, pp. 10–36, for a discussion of this point.

76. KCT-Xianfeng 007580.

77. Yokoyama Suguru, 1964, pp. 44–45.

78. NC, vol. 2, p. 177.

79. Wang Yeh-chien, 1973, p. 144.

80. Kanbe Teruo, 1972, p. 91.

81. NC, vol. 2, pp. 174–191; vol. 4, pp. 415–444.

82. For details on the evolution and organization of Anhui local defense during this period, see Qiu Guozhen, 1940. Qiu distinguishes three types of defense forces: the "protect-peace corps" (*baoantuan dui*), the guerrilla forces (*youji budui*), and the county self-defense corps (*xianziweidui*). Each had a distinct origin and purpose. The "protect-peace corps" was apparently the most effective in combating banditry. See Zou Renmeng, 1940, for an account of their success in bandit extermination during the Republican period.

83. *Wan bao*, February 22, 1939, p. 3.

84. Hibino Takeo, 1953, pp. 141–155.

85. Guo Hanming, 1938–39, p. 156.

86. Skinner, 1971. Skinner's point about decreased movement in and out of the community during the period of closure is less applicable to North China, where seasonal migration as beggars, salt smugglers, and bandits seems to have increased in response to ecological insecurity. Although mobility for educational or commercial purposes may have declined, periodic forays to obtain scarce resources intensified.

87. *Zhongmouxian zhi*, 1935, 2/2–4.

88. *Anhuisheng tongji nianjian*, 1934, pp. 153–155; *Tongshanxian zhi*, 1926, 10/1–20.

89. *Guoyangxian zhi*, 1924, 2/19–24.

90. Chen Hongjin, 1939, pp. 86–88. Another description of a freeholding type of *yuzhai* is found in Xia Feirui, 1974, pp. 32–33. This western Henan fort included one thousand households with six hundred guns. Slightly affluent households all possessed their own guns, wealthy families had several guns, and poor families cooperated in buying weapons to share.

91. Wu Shoupeng, 1930, p. 71.

92. Ibid., p. 72.

93. Ibid., p. 73.

94. Clifford Geertz explains this same process with reference to the example of the Eskimo's igloo, which, he explains, "can be seen as a most important cultural weapon in his [the Eskimo's] resourceful struggle against the arctic

climate, or it can be seen as a, to him, highly relevant feature of the physical landscape within which he is set and in terms of which he must adapt" (1963, p. 9). As a Chinese scholar described the northern Anhui landscape in 1930, it was "nothing but windswept, dry, dusty fields on which were planted a veritable forest of earthen forts" (Wu Shoupeng, 1930, p. 70).

References

Note: The locations and call numbers of archival materials are supplied in the bibliography of my dissertation, "From Rebels to Revolutionaries: Peasant Violence in Huai-pei, 1845–1945" (University of Michigan, 1978).

Aird, J.S. 1968. "Population Growth." In *Economic Trends in Communist China*, ed. A. Eckstein, W. Galenson, and T.C. Liu. Chicago: Aldine.

Anhuisheng tongji nianjian (Statistical yearbook of Anhui Province). 1934. Anhui Provincial Government Statistics Committee.

Bianco, L. 1976. "Peasants and Revolution." *Journal of Peasant Studies*, 2(3), pp. 313–36.

Billingsley, P.R. 1974. "Banditry in China, 1911–1928." Doctoral dissertation, University of Leeds.

Bozhou zhi (Gazetteer of Bo County). 1894. Ed. Yu Yunshu.

Chen Hongjin. 1939. "Minzhong liliang zai Yudong" (Mass power in eastern Henan). *Kangzhan zhong de Zhongguo nongcun dongtai*, pp. 85–88.

Dai Xuanzhi. 1973. *Hongqiang hui* (The Red Spears). Taipei.

Dongpingxian zhi (Gazetteer of Dongping County). 1935. Ed. Liu Qingyu.

Fengtaixian zhi (Gazetteer of Fengtai County). 1882. Ed. Li Shihang.

Fengyangfu zhi (Gazetteer of Fengyang District). 1908. Ed. Zhu Kongchang.

FL (*Jiaoping Nianfei fanglüe*) (Records of the suppression of the Nian bandits). Ed. Zhu Xueqin. Taipei.

Friedman, E. 1974. *Backward Toward Revolution*. Berkeley: University of California Press.

Gamble, S.D. 1963. *North China Villages*. Berkeley: University of California Press.

Geertz, C. 1963. *Agricultural Involution*. Berkeley: University of California Press.

Guo Hanming. 1938–39. "Anki tochi chosa nikki" (Diary of land investigations in Anhui). *Mantetsu Chosa Geppo*, 18(12), 19(1).

Guoyangxian zhi (Gazetteer of Guoyang County). 1924. Ed. Wang Peijian.

Hatada Takashi. 1973. *Chugoku sonraku to kyodatai riron* (Chinese villages and theories of cooperative systems). Tokyo.

He Xiya. 1925. *Zhongguo daofei wenti zhi yanjiu* (A study of the question of Chinese banditry). Shanghai.

Hibino Takeo. 1953. "Goson boei to kempeki shoya" (Village defense and the policy of strengthening walls and clearing fields). *Toho Gakuho*, 22, pp. 141–55.

Ho Ping-ti. 1959. *Studies on the Population of China, 1368–1953*. Cambridge: Harvard University Press.

Hobsbawm, E.J. 1963. *Primitive Rebels*. New York: Praeger.

———. 1969. *Bandits*. New York: Delacorte.

Huianfu zhi (Gazetteer of Huaian District). 1884. Ed. Wu Kuntian.

Inoue Kobai. 1923. *Hito* (Bandits). Shanghai.

Institute of Pacific Relations. 1938. *Agrarian China*. Chicago: University of Chicago Press.

Kanbe Teruo. 1972. "Shindai koki santosho ni okeru 'danhi' to noson mondai" ("Militia bandits" in Shandong during the late Qing and the peasant village question). *Shirin*, 55(4), pp. 61–98.

KCT (Gongzhongdang) (Palace memorials) in National Palace Museum, Taipei. Citations are given with reign year and memorial number.

Kuhn, P.A. 1970. *Rebellion and Its Enemies in Late Imperial China: Militarization and Social Structure, 1796–1864*. Cambridge: Harvard University Press.

Lamley, Harry J. 1977. "Hsieh-tou: The Pathology of Violence in Southeastern China." *Ch'ing-shih wen-t'i*, 3(7), pp. 1–39.

Luyixian zhi (Gazetteer of Luyi County). 1896. Ed. Jiang Shiche.

Ma Changhua. 1959. "Nianjun de chansheng ji qi chuqi de huodong" (The birth and early activities of the Nian Army). *Anhui shixue tongxun*, 14, pp. 13–27.

Mengchengxian zhi (Gazetteer of Mengcheng County). 1915. Ed. Huang Yujun.

Metzger, T.A. 1962. "T'ao Chu's Reform of the Huai-pei Salt Monopoly." *Papers on China*, 16, pp. 1–39.

Mills, C.R. 1873. In Presbyterian Mission Archives, China Letters, Microfilm Reel no. 197.

Mu Lianfu. 1959. "Niu Ping za yandian" (Niu Ping smashes the salt shop). *Minjian wenxue*, 9, pp. 77–83.

Myers, R.H. 1970. *The Chinese Peasant Economy*. Cambridge: Harvard University Press.

Nagano Akira. 1931. *Tohi, guntai, kosokai* (Bandits, army, Red Spears). Tokyo.

———. 1933. *Shina nomin undokan* (A view of the peasant movement in China). Tokyo.

———. 1938. *Shinahei, tohi, kosokai* (China's soldiers, bandits, Red Spears). Tokyo.

NC (*Nianjun*) (The Nian Army). 1953. Ed. Fan Wenlan. Shanghai.

NCH (*North China Herald*). Shanghai.

NCPC (*Nianjun bieji*) (Collection of the Nian Army). 1958. Ed. Nie Chongqi. Shanghai.

Nianjun (The Nian Army). 1953. Ed. Fan Wenlan. Shanghai.

Nianjun gushiji (Collected tales from the Nian Army). 1962. Shanghai.

Peixian zhi (Gazetteer of Pei County). 1920. Ed. Yu Yunshu.

Qiu Guozhen. 1940. "Zhanshi Anhui difang wuli zhi fadong yu chengli" (The development and reorganization of local military forces in Anhui during the war). *Kangzhan zhong zhi Anhui*.

Ruo Mu. 1959. "Zhang Luoxing zhuan" (Biography of Zhang Luoxing). *Anhui shixue tongxun*, 14, pp. 51–62.

Scott, J.C. 1976. *The Moral Economy of the Peasant*. New Haven: Yale University Press.

Scott, J.C., and B.J. Kerkvliet. 1977. "How Traditional Rural Patrons Lose Legitimacy." In *Friends, Followers, and Factions*, ed. S.W. Schmidt, J.C. Scott, C. Lande, and L. Gausti. Berkeley: University of California Press.

Shanxian zhi (Gazetteer of Shan County). 1936. Ed. Han Jiahui.

Shina no doran to Santo noson (China's chaos and the villages of Shandong). 1930. Dalian.

Shixue yuekan (Historiography monthly). 1960.

Skinner, G.W. 1971. "Chinese Peasants and the Closed Community: An Open and Shut Case." *Comparative Studies in Society and History*, 13, pp. 270–381.

Smith, A.H. 1970. *Village Life in China*. Boston: Little Brown.

Suiningxian zhi (Gazetteer of Suining County). 1887. Ed. Ding Xian.

"Tongshan nongcun jingji diaocha" (Investigation of the village economy of Tongshan). 1931. In *Zhongguo nongcun jingji ziliao*, ed. Feng Hefa. Shanghai, pp. 385–387.

Tongshanxian zhi (Gazetteer of Tongshan County). 1926. Ed. Wang Jiaxian.

Wan bao (Anhui news). Hefei.

Wang Fanting. 1970. "Guoyang shezhi shimo" (The ins and outs of the construction of Guoyang). *Anhui wenxian*, 1(1), pp. 36–40.

Wang Yeh-chien. 1973. *Land Taxation in Imperial China, 1750–1911*. Cambridge: Harvard University Press.

Wang Zongyu. 1964. "Shilun Bai Lang qiyi de xingzhi" (A preliminary discussion of the character of the Bai Lang uprising). *Shixue yuekan*, 12, pp. 20–24.

WCT (*Wai jidang*) (Extra records). In National Palace Museum, Taipei. Citations are given with reign year followed by month and day of lunar calendar.

Wu Shoupeng. 1930. "Douliu yu nongcun jingji shidai de xuhai geshu" (The lingering of Xuzhou and Haizhou in the era of village economy). *Dongfang zazhi*, 27(6,7), pp. 69–79, 59–70.

Xia Feirui. 1974. "Yizhongyuan Huachengzhai" (Memories of Huacheng Fort). *Zhongyuan wenxian*, 6 (9), pp. 32–33.

Xiangchengxian zhi (Gazetteer of Xiangcheng County). 1911. Ed. Shi Qingwu.

Xiaoxian zhi (Gazetteer of Xiao County). 1874. Ed. Tuan Guangying.

Xu Hong. 1972. *Qingdai lianghuai yanchang de yanjiu* (A study of the salt fields north and south of the Huai during the Qing). Taipei.

Xuzhoufu zhi (Gazetteer of Xuzhou Prefecture) 1874. Ed. Fu Shaocheng.

Yang Jihua. 1933. *Wanbei nongcun shehui jingji shikuang* (Socioeconomic conditions in northern Anhui villages). Nanjing.

Yang, M.C. 1945. *A Chinese Village: Taitou, Shantung Province*. New York: Columbia University Press.

Yokoyama Suguru. 1964. "Kenhoki, Santo no koryo fucho to mindan" (Shandong's wave of tax resistance and the militia during the Xianfeng period). *Rekishi Kyoiku*, 12(9), pp. 42–50.

Yuan Jiasan. 1911. "Duanmin gong ji" (Collected works of Prince Duanmin). *Xiangcheng Yuanshijia ji*. Beijing.

Zhang Weicheng. 1943. "Yanyuxiang de jiedai wenti shi ruhe jiejue de" (How the debt problem was resolved in Yanyu). FH, 5, pp. 47–54.

Zhongmouxian zhi (Gazetteer of Zhongmou County). 1935. Ed. Xiao Dexing.

Zhongyang ribao (Central Daily). Shanghai.

Zou Renmeng. 1940. "Anhui baoan tuanti" (Anhui's peace-protection corps). *Kangzhan zhong zhi Anhui.*

2

Protective Rebellion: Tax Protest in Late Qing China

Late nineteenth-century China saw an outburst of anti-tax riots, several of which developed into significant rebellions against the government. In the case of Western Europe, scholars have suggested that the emergence of the tax revolt as a dominant form of collective activity in nineteenth-century Italy, Germany, and France was largely a reaction to a process of state formation under way at the time.[1] For China, by contrast, this was a period when the imperial state was in a process of decline. Not until a century later, with the establishment of the People's Republic, can we find an unmistakably strengthened state apparatus. And yet, to suggest that the hundred years between the Opium Wars and the founding of the PRC saw only the progressive weakening of the Chinese state would be misleading. For in fact Chinese statesmen were drawn inevitably into desperate efforts at state building by the very process that undermined their traditional polity. As Westerners humbled the Chinese empire with their gunboats, they also introduced new models for political activism. Like their counterparts in Europe, Chinese leaders began to seek ways to enlarge the role of the state vis-à-vis society.

The peculiar combination of deterioration and regeneration that marked the reform efforts of nineteenth-century China gave rise to social responses that were apparently similar, yet actually quite different, from movements under way in Western Europe in the same period. Of particular importance in the case of China was the blurred line separating state from society. While this distinction had always been fuzzy—with the gentry acting as critical intermediaries—it became even more confused under the circumstances of the late nineteenth century. Faced simultaneously with the formidable threats of foreign intervention and domestic rebellion, the government found it necessary to place much of the burden of resistance on the shoulders of local society. On the face of it, the call for higher taxes, militia formation, and the like was a classic example of state building. But in the context of late nineteenth-century China, such measures also played into the hands of local strongmen who proved to be serious rivals of the center for power. The battle for control, based organizationally on the local militia and fought over the issue of taxation, suggests the complexity of state–society relations in this period.

While the struggle between state and society was a national one, it was played out rather differently in different parts of the country. This chapter explores some of the commonalities and variations through case studies of two late Qing tax protests: the Small Swords of Shanghai (1853–55) and Liu Depei of Shandong (1862–63). The comparison highlights the central place of the militia, or *tuanlian*, in facilitating tax rebellion and the influence of local environments in shaping the precise forms that resistance assumed.

As theorists of collective action have pointed out, effective popular protest is not an automatic response to government oppression. Before a movement can be launched, some form of organizational base must exist to draw people together in concerted action.[2] In late nineteenth-century China, ironically, the government itself encouraged the formation of just such organizational bases. Faced with the considerable threat of Taiping and Nian rebels, the Qing state called on local communities to provide for their own defense by forming militia. Unwittingly, the government thereby erected the foundation for opposition to its own demands.[3] For in the closing decades of imperial China, it was rebel *tuanlian* that so frequently offered the impetus for resistance to taxation. And, equally ironically, taxes demanded to maintain the institution of the militia were often the very pretext for this protest.[4]

The two cases on which this chapter is based both demonstrate the importance of the *tuanlian* in fomenting large-scale tax resistance. In each instance, local militia units—led by members of the grassroots elite—constituted a critical vehicle for mobilization during the initial stages of rebellion. Yet despite this fundamental similarity, there were also some important differences in the composition and character of the two movements. The dissimilarities were in large measure a reflection of socioeconomic conditions in the areas where the uprisings occurred. Shanghai, in the 1850s already a bustling treaty port surrounded by a commercialized rural economy, saw the emergence of a more complex social movement than the one that developed in the isolated mountains of central Shandong.

The Small Swords of Shanghai

Thanks to their seventeen-month occupation of the city of Shanghai, the Small Swords have gained a certain amount of attention from Western historians. Yet the Western literature has made little effort to link this urban rebellion with the rural tax protest that accompanied it.[5] Actually, the Small Swords of Shanghai were closely connected to tax resistance in the surrounding countryside.

The trouble had been especially acute in the county of Qingpu, a cotton-growing region some thirty kilometers northwest of Shanghai, where household textile production had been threatened by the opening of the treaty port and the importation of foreign cloth.[6] In the summer of 1852, the county magistrate aroused indignant popular opposition when he ordered the payment of grain tribute taxes that had been exempted two years earlier.[7] The local clerk (*dibao*), Zhou Lichun, led several hundred peasants to the county seat to plead for a continued tax exemption on the grounds of bad harvests. They destroyed the home of the official in charge of the local grain tribute collection as punishment for his part in revoking the remission of taxes. When the magistrate refused to be moved, the protesters attacked the county office and delivered a sound thrashing to the magistrate himself. Government troops were dispatched to apprehend Zhou Lichun, but the protection of a united peasant force, armed with farm tools and representing more than twenty villages, saved him from immediate arrest. As a result of this incident, Zhou emerged as a major strongman in the area, a magnet toward whom martial experts, bandits, and ordinary peasants gravitated in large numbers.[8]

Soon important developments taking place elsewhere in China would open new opportunities to Zhou Lichun and his followers. In March of

1853, the Taiping rebels stormed the city of Nanjing and established their Heavenly Capital. Only a few months later, the city of Xiamen (Amoy) was occupied by a group of Triad secret society members calling themselves the Small Swords—a name that had been popular among Triads in Taiwan, Guangdong, Fujian, and Southeast Asia for many years.[9]

Confronted with these startling events, local authorities throughout the Shanghai region began to organize militia units in self-defense. The circuit intendant for Suzhou-Songjiang, a Cantonese by the name of Wu Jianzhang, hastily assembled a corps of local braves, recruited largely from among the thousands of unemployed Cantonese and Fujianese milling about the port of Shanghai. Unable to provide proper training or wages for these rowdies, however, the intendant soon found it necessary to demobilize them.[10] After this summary dismissal, the former braves proved to be a serious problem for peacekeeping efforts in Shanghai. Many of them enlisted in growing secret society gangs, based on native place ties and flavored with a Triad ethos. As these groups became more and more daring—plundering local merchants and generally creating a disturbance—rumors began to circulate of a Small Sword uprising scheduled to occur in Shanghai in early autumn.[11]

Alarmed by these developments, Wu Jianzhang convened a meeting of the directors of the major guilds of Shanghai. As is well known, Shanghai's guilds were established for the purpose of bringing together people in the same line of work or uniting people from the same native place.[12] While individual guilds have often been seen as serving one or the other of these two distinct functions, in fact many of the Shanghai guilds performed the dual role of uniting members of a particular industry who *also* hailed from the same native place. Merchants from Fujian and Guangdong who transported sugar for sale to Shanghai in exchange for the purchase of cotton founded separate guilds to organize native sons into the bustling trade. Guild directors were often the owners of fleets of large junks that plied the waters between Shanghai and the southeastern provinces. Seamen recruited from Fujian and Guangdong to man the merchant junks must have found some comfort in their Shanghai guild—with its hall for the worship of familiar local deities, its stage for the performance of local operas, and in some cases its burial grounds and charitable associations.[13]

By the mid-nineteenth century, the 3,500 seafaring junks operating out of Shanghai had brought a burgeoning population of some 80,000 Guangdong natives and some 50,000 Fujianese to the entrepôt.[14] However, when competition from foreign steamships after the Opium Wars put many of the Chinese boats out of operation, the now unemployed seamen became ready recruits for protest.[15] As contraction in the native shipping trade also undermined the fortunes of some of the guild directors, the stage had been set for their participation in rebellion as well.

Responding to a request for advice by Intendant Wu, directors of seven major guilds presented him with a joint petition on August 11, 1853. Complaining of the growing threat of banditry, the guild directors communicated their intention to train a militia to provide defense. They called upon the indendant to raise the expenses from local gentry and merchants, a request to which Wu Jianzhang agreed.[16]

Wu's approval of the guild-sponsored militia gave birth, however unwittingly, to the organizational base of the Small Sword rebellion. Only a week later, the newly constituted militia (composed predominantly of unemployed boatmen from Guangdong and Fujian, but supplemented by some members from Shanghai and Ningbo) became the fighting force that engineered the dramatic takeover of Shanghai and undertook forays into the neighboring countryside to establish contact with the nascent tax resistance movement there.[17] Although the sources are ambiguous on this point, it is likely that the seven groups which people later said had comprised the Small Swords[18] were none other than the seven guilds that submitted the joint petition on the need for a militia.[19]

The guild directors, despite their respectable positions in Shanghai society, were in reality local bosses who acted as patrons to their displaced fellow provincials. Li Xianyun, director of the Xingan and Quanzhang guilds, supervised the activities of Fujian immigrants in Shanghai. A bearded man in his sixties, Li traveled about in a sedan chair guarded by a large personal security force. His underlings, armed with daggers, regularly prowled the Shanghai wharf in search of plunder. Local merchants had to pay off Li Xianyun if their goods were to be guaranteed safe transport.[20] Known as a man of fierce temperament, Li in July 1851 had led a protest against the Britishers' building of the Shanghai race course.[21] Two years later, he would become a principal advisor to the Small Sword rebels.

Li Shaoqing, director of the Jiaying guild, was a powerful patron for Cantonese immigrants in Shanghai. He had come to Jiangnan as a peddler, but eventually established a teahouse that proved lucrative enough to enable him to buy an official post as expectant magistrate. Such purchased respectability did not, however, prevent Li from keeping a hand in the seamy side of Shanghai commerce: he served as protector to Cantonese opium smugglers in the Yangzi delta. Although Li would later defect to the government side, he played an important leadership role in the early stages of the Small Sword rebellion.[22]

In addition to the three guilds led by Li Xianyun and Li Shaoqing, four other guilds (representing the counties of Guangan, Chaozhou, Ningbo, and Shanghai) were involved in organizing the militia that became the nucleus of the Small Sword rebellion. The Small Swords were a motley association of rough and ready characters from Guangdong, Fujian, Ningbo, and Shanghai. Many of them had served in the short-lived corps of braves that Intendant Wu had hastily assembled and disbanded some months earlier. As a consequence of that experience, they had formed friendships with government clerks, runners, and soldiers—ties that later proved invaluable in facilitating their rebellion.[23] After the braves were demobilized, these individuals had drifted into various secret society gangs: the Double Dagger Society composed of Cantonese; the Bird Society made up of Fujian natives; the Hundred Dragons for Shanghainese; the Lohan Society based outside of Shanghai in the county of Jiading, and so forth.[24]

In the tense atmosphere of the day, these secret societies—which were normally divided by the bitter feelings that prevailed among people of different places—began to join forces. Within the city of Shanghai, this process of amalgamation centered around the leadership of a Triad from Guangdong by the name of Liu Lichuan. Born in 1820 of a peasant family in Xiangshan, Liu had learned pidgin English after moving to Hong Kong in 1845. There he also apparently joined the Triad society, whose practices he took along to Shanghai when he moved there a few years later to become an interpreter for a Western firm.[25] Subsequently unemployed, Liu eked out a living as a medicine man, gaining a reputation for treating the poor free of charge.[26] This reputation, combined with his Hong Kong experience, helped Liu Lichuan assume leadership of the growing Triad community in Shanghai.

In the surrounding countryside, a parallel amalgamation of secret societies was taking place under the leadership of Qingpu strongman Zhou Lichun. Groups such as the Lohans, the Hundred Dragons, and the Temple Gang enrolled by the hundreds under Zhou's direction. Attracted by his reputation for tax protest, these groups in the summer of 1853 pressed Zhou toward full-scale rebellion.[27]

A link between these developments in city and countryside was soon made possible by the commercial networks of the area, specifically the opium trade. Cantonese smugglers regularly transported opium by boat from Shanghai to Suzhou. It happened that in July 1853 a shipment had been intercepted en route by a local strongman acquainted with Zhou Lichun. The Cantonese smugglers, knowing of Zhou's authority in the area, enlisted his aid in recovering their goods. This favor won Zhou immediate recognition from the smuggler's chief back in Shanghai, Jia-ying Guild Director Li Shaoqing. Li subsequently paid a visit to Zhou and persuaded him to go to Shanghai to meet the secret society chieftain of the city, Liu Lichuan, and enlist under his Triad banner.[28]

Soon thereafter, on September 5, Guild Director Li Shaoqing led sev-eral hundred followers to Jiading County to cooperate with Zhou Lichun and other disgruntled members of the local elite and peasantry who had launched an attack on the county seat.[29] The takeover of Jiading was accomplished swiftly by red-turbaned rebels who posted proclamations declaring a tax holiday.[30]

Two days later, inspired by the success of their country cousins in Jiading, the guild-sponsored "militia" of Shanghai took the walled city of 200,000 inhabitants in a few hours. September 7 being the birthday of Confucius, the magistrate of Shanghai was changing out of ceremonial clothes when at 6 A.M. he was knifed to death in his yamen. The assassin turned out to be a Small Sword leader whom the magistrate had impris-oned some months earlier for instigating a fight while serving in the Shanghai braves organized by Intendant Wu.[31] The circuit intendant him-self, who hailed from the same county as Guild Director Li Shaoqing and was also on close terms with Guild Director Li Xianyun, was kid-napped by the rebels but subsequently turned over to American author-ities. The only opposition the Small Swords encountered in taking the city was a group of forty soldiers in the pay of the circuit intendant as his bodyguard, but of these all but seventeen refused to fight because they were Triads themselves.[32]

Over the next ten days, a combined urban-rural force—proclaiming remission of taxes—proceeded to take the county seats of Baoshan (Sep-tember 9), Nanhui (September 10–12), Chuansha (September 13), and Qingpu (September 17). Taking advantage of the power vacuum that had been created by the redeployment of imperial troops (to counter the Taiping threat in the west), the Small Swords managed swiftly to extend their control throughout the Shanghai region. In these attacks on county seats, the rebels carried banners emblazoned with age-old slogans (e.g., "Oppose the Qing, Restore the Ming," "Down with Corrupt Officials," "Prepare the Way on Behalf of Heaven"), sacked government offices and official residences, and released prisoners from jail.[33]

The rural victories were short-lived, however. Once in power in Shanghai, the Small Swords—in need of revenue—reneged on their in-itial promise of a tax holiday and began to press the villagers for funds.[34] Local officials were able to capitalize on this betrayal to encourage the formation of anti–Small Sword militia. Even more important, their urgent petitions to the governor-general of Jiangnan and the governor of Jiangsu resulted in thousands of imperial troops being recalled from their blockade of the Taipings in Nanjing. This powerful government force quickly recaptured the city of Jiading, executing strongman Zhou Lichun on September 22. Frightened by the demise of their ally, other Small Sword leaders made a hasty retreat to the walled safety of Shanghai, permitting the government to retake all of the rebel counties in the space of less than a week.[35]

The loss of rural support was a major setback for the Small Swords, contributing to the severe food shortage that the rebels would soon face. Many remnants of the rural movement who escaped death at the hands of the vengeful local gentry took refuge in Shanghai,[36] thereby augmenting the rebel force by the hundreds, but also adding to the problem of discipline that was to plague the rebellion during its seventeen-month lifetime.

Securing the means to sustain a city the size of Shanghai was a considerable challenge, especially since Small Sword militiamen were promised daily wages of several hundred cash. Initially the revenue came principally from two sources: the plundered yamen treasury and voluntary contributions of wealthy supporters. On the day after they had secured the city, the rebels discovered 200,000 silver taels in the circuit treasury. Although some of the Fujianese wanted to divide the money among the leaders and abscond with their haul, rebels from Guangdong prevailed in arguing that the funds should be used to carry on the rebellion.[37] Further revenue came from financiers among the Shanghai business community. For example, Yu Songnian, one of the wealthiest shipping magnates in the city, contributed more than 180,000 silver taels to the rebel coffers.[38] Before long, however, the rebels were also pressing funds from reluctant contributors. When word leaked out that some well-to-do inhabitants had buried their riches before fleeing the city, a search was undertaken to unearth the treasure. The vast sum of 300,000 taels was dug up at the home of one wealthy refugee, encouraging the rebels to conduct a house-to-house search for additional loot.[39] Furthermore, the city's pawnshops were all assessed the sum of 300–400 yuan, to be paid to the rebel treasury.[40]

The proceeds from these efforts went toward the purchase of arms (supplied by Western merchants), the payment of rebel soldiers, and the procurement of food supplies.[41] Grain boats anchored in Shanghai harbor at the time of the uprising were also seized to provide food.[42] To maintain a circulation of grain and other commodities, the rebels directed all shops and merchants to carry on business as usual. Injunctions against hoarding and speculation were issued repeatedly.[43]

One source of revenue that the rebels were not able to claim was the customs duty levied on foreign goods. As is well known, the Small Sword Rebellion provided the pretext for the foreign plenipotentiaries to take over control of the customs house. Rather than contest this development, the Small Swords actually sent guards to facilitate the turnover. In a bid for foreign support, the rebels also guaranteed the protection of foreign property and willingly released any seized goods that belonged to foreigners.[44]

Patriotic Chinese historiography notwithstanding, there is every reason to believe that the Small Swords actively sought the friendship of the imperialist powers. Indeed, without the initial willingness of the foreigners to adopt a neutral stand, it is hard to imagine how the rebels could have endured as long as they did. To be sure, from the beginning there were numerous disagreements and misunderstandings between the rebels and the foreign powers.[45] Despite these conflicts, however, the Small Swords could count on a reservoir of goodwill from the foreign inhabitants. As Robert Fortune, an Englishman then residing in Shanghai, noted, "The sympathies of the foreigners are generally all on the rebel side."[46] One reason for this support was the interest in supplying the rebels with weapons and ammunition. At the start of the uprising, it was well known that the American consul was using his business position with Russell and Co. to sell American-made guns and bullets to the Small Swords.[47] Beyond this pecuniary interest was the fact that the Small Swords claimed a close connection with the Taiping Rebellion in Nanjing. Although the contention later proved unfounded, it was useful for gaining the sympathy of the foreign residents, especially the missionaries—many of whom at this time were supportive of what they took to be a Christian revival in Nanjing.

Relations with the foreigners were facilitated by the fact that several of the Small Sword leaders had previously worked in foreign employ. Grand Marshal Liu Lichuan, as we have seen, once served as an interpreter in a Western firm. Left Marshal Chen Alin, a leader of the Fujian faction of the Small Swords, had worked in the stables of an Englishman named Skinner.[48] Among rank-and-file Small Swords were a number of English-speaking overseas Chinese from Singapore and even a handful of British and American deserters from merchant and naval vessels.[49] On the day after the Small Swords occupied Shanghai, Liu Lichuan went with much ceremony to visit the American, British, and French consuls to announce his subservience to the Taiping Heavenly King and his desire for friendship with the foreign powers.[50]

Although the survival of the rebellion was due in large measure to the buffer created by the presence of the Taipings in Nanjing and the foreigners in Shanghai, the Small Swords were in fact never able to forge lasting alliances with either party. Part of the difficulty lay with the reluctance of the Small Sword leaders to shed their Triad precepts for the Taipings' quasi-Christian faith. On September 25, shortly after the Small Swords occupied Shanghai, the Reverend Issachar Roberts (the Protestant missionary from whom Taiping leader Hong Xiuquan had received religious instruction in Canton) called on Liu Lichuan in his headquarters at the Confucian temple. There Roberts found the pale, emaciated young rebel chief in the act of smoking opium. Liu told Roberts that he had already sent two letters—one by land and the other by water—to the Taiping Heavenly King, requesting that an emissary be sent from Nanjing to arrange joint operations. Thereupon Roberts showed Liu a copy of the Ten Commandments and told him that the Taipings had adopted them as their sacred code. Roberts went on to explain that he had been the Heavenly King's religious teacher and that he now wished to instruct the eight or nine thousand Cantonese under Liu's personal command. At this suggestion, the rebel chief demurred, saying that all such arrangements should await the arrival of the deputy from Nanjing.[51]

It is possible that neither of Liu Lichuan's letters reached the Taipings at Nanjing.[52] Nevertheless, deputies from Nanjing were apparently sent to make contact with the Small Swords. The *North China Herald* in December 1853 reported the rumor that Taiping envoys had arrived on a special mission to the Small Swords and had immediately denounced the "immoral habits and vicious propensities" of the local rebels as "an insuperable barrier to amalgamation" with the Taiping movement.[53] British observer Thomas Meadows noted that two Taiping emissaries to Shanghai "found the gods all standing in the temples and opium smoking" and reported back to Nanjing in such a way that the Taipings rejected all Small Sword overtures.[54]

The well-known missionary William Medhurst provided further evidence of Taiping overtures. On December 14, 1853, Medhurst received permission to enter the walled city of Shanghai to preach to a large congregation at the London Missionary Society chapel. In the middle of Medhurst's sermon about the folly of idolatry and the necessity of worshiping one god, a man stood up and shouted, "That is true—that is true—the idols must perish and shall perish. I am a Kwang-si [Guangxi] man, a follower of Tai-ping-wang [the Taiping King]; we all of us worship one God and believe in Jesus. . . ." The man went on to inveigh against opium smoking and told the crowd to be swift in abandoning their evil ways, for the Heavenly King was coming and would permit no infringement of his rules. Medhurst, who was fully familiar with Taiping doctrine, observed that this man was thoroughly trained in Taiping beliefs and must have been a Taiping follower.[55]

There is some evidence that these efforts at transforming Small Sword ideology eventually bore limited results. In April 1854, Liu Lichuan issued a remarkable proclamation in which he explained the origin of the universe as God's creation and called on the people of Shanghai to abandon Buddhist and Daoist idolatry, to accept the true God, to pray regularly, and to observe the Sabbath.[56] There is, however, absolutely no evidence to suggest that these injunctions were enforced in any way. And the next month Liu issued another proclamation in which his caution against idolatry drew more from Confucian than Christian inspiration:

> There is a class of ignorant people who repair to the temples, ignite incense sticks, burn paper-money, and contribute to the gilding of the Buddhist images; why do they not with this money purchase articles with which they may show their filial piety and respect towards their parents? . . . Now it behooves us who are brethren of the Hung family [the Triads] with faithful hearts to manifest our patriotism and he who is a son must show filial piety towards his two parents. . . . I have no object in this [other] than to act according to the ancient national laws and regulations of the Ming dynasty, in promoting the practice of loyalty and filial piety.[57]

Ming restorationism, which lay at the center of Triad beliefs, was clearly evident in the practices of Shanghai's Small Swords. Shortly after they had assumed control of the city, Small Sword deputy marshal Lin Afu proclaimed a dress code in line with Ming tradition. On September 17, when the major Small Sword chieftains paraded to the Confucian temple to offer their respects, they were attired in what appeared to be splendid Ming-style robes. (Since there had not been sufficient time to tailor the necessary clothing, however, the robes were in fact costumes borrowed from a local opera troupe.)[58] By May 1854, the Small Swords had issued a proclamation requiring their subjects to grow out their hair in the old Ming style. By July, they were minting their own coins; one side of these coins was engraved with the words "Taiping coinage," while the other side pictured the shapes of the sun and the moon—which, when combined, formed the character "Ming."[59]

Despite the Small Swords' ostensible acknowledgment of Taiping leadership, the gap between their Triad-inspired practices and the Christian-inspired practices of the Taipings remained substantial. As Taiping leader Hong Xiuquan summarized the differences:

> Though I never entered the Triad Society, I have often heard it said that their object is to subvert the Tsing [Qing] and restore the Ming dynasty. . . . We may still speak of subverting the Tsing, but we cannot properly speak of restoring the Ming. At all events, when our native mountains and rivers are recovered, a new dynasty must be established. How can we at present arouse the energies of men by speaking of restoring the Ming dynasty? There are several evil practices connected with the Triad Society, which I detest; if any new member enter the society, he must worship the devil, and utter thirty-six oaths; a sword is placed upon his neck and he is forced to contribute money for the use of the society.[60]

But even had the Taipings been willing to overlook matters of doctrine, there were obvious military obstacles to an alliance with the Small Swords.[61] East of Zhenjiang (where Triad-turned-Taiping Luo Dagang was in charge), Qing control of the Yangzi was secure enough to deter any Taiping effort at linking up with the rebels in Shanghai.[62]

It was the combination of objective obstacles and divergent interests that militated against Small Sword alliances with outside forces.[63] Even so, the rebellion developed within a milieu, infused with foreign and commercial influences, that fostered a more complex composition and outlook than we might expect of the "typical" tax revolt. It was not merely as a pretense to attract outside support that the Small Swords were prompted to adopt certain creeds and symbols.[64] Of particular interest in this respect was their use of the term *Yixing gongsi*, or "Righteousness Company." Small Sword proclamations were stamped with this seal and waist tags imprinted with these characters were issued as identification to rebel supporters. While *Yixing* was a traditional enough name for a rebel or social bandit group to assume, the term *gongsi* has a more modern ring to it. As a recent study argues, the Small Swords' use of the term was a reflection of the foreign capitalist environment in which their members had been nurtured.[65]

In a variety of ways then, we can trace the impact of the treaty port setting on the genesis and character of the Small Swords: cash crop areas affected by the foreign intrusion launched the initial tax resistance; opium smuggling provided the link between rural and urban protest; merchant guilds spearheaded the formation of rebel militia; and foreign ideas influenced Small Sword ideology and symbolism. Nevertheless, the Small Swords remained in many respects what Eric Hobsbawm would term a "primitive rebel" movement. Ultimately, the demise of the rebellion can be attributed as much to the limitations of its own participants as to the failure of outside parties to come to its aid. The leadership was a motley assortment of marginal figures, tied to their followers by little more than native-place affinities, who found it impossible to cooperate among themselves.

The internal dissension among the Small Swords became apparent immediately after the occupation of Shanghai, when members of the Fujian and Guangdong factions feuded over disposition of the yamen treasury. Elements from Fujian loaded a share of the booty on board their junks and threatened to set sail. This faction advocated putting to death the circuit intendant, Wu Jianzhang (who had been kidnapped when the city was taken), and then escaping with the plundered cash to their native homes in the south. The Cantonese faction was more ambitious. As Liu Lichuan informed U.S. Commissioner Marshall on the first day of the rebellion, the Cantonese were quite willing to reinstate Wu as governor of the city if only he would swear loyalty to the new Small Sword dynasty. Then Liu, as commander-in-chief of the rebellion, would proceed immediately to Suzhou to occupy the provincial capital.[66] Unfortunately for these designs, the Americans managed to release Wu, who subsequently played a central role in the Qing government's suppression of the rebellion.

Liu Lichuan was able to convince many of his Fujianese comrades to remain in Shanghai to persevere in the rebel enterprise. Yet despite the seventeen-month endurance of the revolt, it was continuously wracked by tensions and disagreements among its various components. On September 15, for example, Fujian Guild Director Li Xianyun was discovered to have stolen from the rebel treasury.[67] A few months later, as food supplies in the city were running low, rebel leaders disputed whether—and on what terms—to surrender to government peace initiatives. This time it was Liu Lichuan who advocated surrender; Liu informed Intendant Wu that he would relinquish the city in exchange for the offer of an official title. Fujian rebel chief Lin Afu, however, was unwilling to concur in the proposal.[68] About the same time, dissension broke out within the ranks of the Guangdong faction of the rebellion. Several hundred Hakkas, secretly conspiring to give up the city, had set a fire at the East Gate as a signal to the government troops. Once the plot was discovered, seventy-six of the conspirators were beheaded, while the rest were bound and thrown into the fire they had set themselves.[69] Shortly thereafter, Cantonese Guild Director Li Shaoqing defected to the Qing and served as an advisor to the imperial army.[70]

These sorts of problems persisted until the conclusion of the rebellion.[71] When finally the rebels were forced by desperate food shortages to flee the city, their separate paths reflected divergent strains within the movement. Chen Alin, who could speak some pidgin English, negotiated with the British and Americans for help in smuggling his seventy followers out of the city. Compradors of the British firm Bedford and Co. arranged for barbers to shave the foreheads of the former rebels to make it appear that they wore the required queues under their caps. Then other foreign hongs harbored the men in groups of two or three until they could all be smuggled by ship to Hong Kong over the following weeks.[72] Chen Alin himself became a comprador in Siam.[73] Liu Lichuan sneaked back to his home in Guangdong, disguised as a Buddhist nun.[74] Another group of 250 Small Swords surrendered to the French admiral Laguerre. By this time, however, the French had sided with the Qing government. The rebels were all turned over to the authorities and promptly decapitated.[75]

Many of the Small Swords—including the assassin of the Shanghai magistrate—fled the city in the direction of Zhenjiang and Nanjing, hoping to link up with the Taipings.[76] Some of the remnant rebels retreated to Jiading County. Five years later, when the Taipings finally sent a military expedition to Shanghai, these Jiading remnants lent their support to the unsuccessful Taiping venture.[77] Another contingent went to Jiangxi where they participated in a Triad offensive.[78] Yet others, including Fujian chieftain Lin Afu, took to the sea as pirates.[79]

Liu Depei of Shandong

The influence of the Taiping Rebellion extended far beyond the confines of the Yangzi delta. Soon after their occupation of Nanjing, the Taipings dispatched a northern expedition to link up with rebels of the North China plain, in hopes of a joint attack on the Qing capital of Beijing. Unsuccessful as their ultimate ambition proved to be, the Taipings' northern advance managed nonetheless to encourage an impressive outburst of anti-state protest in North China. As in the South, abuses in the collection of grain tribute tax provided a ready pretext for protest, while newly constituted militia units offered an organizational base.

Shandong Province saw an especially active display of tax rebellions for a number of reasons. First, the province was a pacesetter in the formation of *tuanlian* to resist the Taiping rebels. Starting early in 1853, the governor of Shandong launched a major campaign for the establishment of local militia throughout the countryside.[80] These quickly came to serve as vehicles for popular resistance.

Unrest in the area was further encouraged by a series of devastating natural catastrophes that swept the province in the middle of the nineteenth century. The drastic change in the course of the Yellow River—which moved northward several hundred miles across the Shandong peninsula—wreaked enormous destruction on the local populace. Millions perished in the initial floods of 1853–55, and the long-term damage to the system of water control gave rise to repeated natural calamities in the years that followed.

Among the casualties of the Yellow River floods was the Grand Canal transport system. The blocked waterways spelled unemployment for thousands of Shandong boatmen who had made a living by shipping tribute grain northward along the Grand Canal to Beijing. Many of the jobless sailors organized as "turban bandits," and sometimes lent their support to the burgeoning tax protests under way in the region.[81]

The closing of the Grand Canal had serious implications for the grain tribute system. While some grain could be shipped by sea instead, the remainder was supposed to be commuted to a monetary tax.[82] Malfeasance in the conversion process from kind to cash proved to be a major precipitant of the wave of tax riots that soon broke forth. By 1859, the commander of the government's cavalry responsible for keeping order on the North China plain, Mongol prince Senggelinqin, reported that the whole of Shandong Province was awash in tax revolts instigated by local militia.

One of the largest and most enduring of these revolts was centered in the county of Zichuan, a remote and mountainous place located some miles south of the new bed of the Yellow River. The leader of the rebellion, Liu Depei, had been born into a family of pettifoggers in Zichuan. Educated at a local academy, Liu had passed the lowest rung of the official examinations to earn the degree of licentiate. Like his father, however, Liu Depei also practiced pettifoggery for a living. Perhaps it was his experience with litigation that propelled Liu Depei to the forefront of tax resistance. In any event, during the winter of 1860 Liu handwrote several hundred copies of a notice that he posted about the countryside. The posters called on the inhabitants of Zichuan to protest abuses in the tribute system by paying tax in grain rather than silver.[83]

To add legitimacy to the undertaking, Liu included in his posters a namelist of several prominent members of the local elite who allegedly condemned the Zichuan magistrate for his mismanagement of the tribute tax. The magistrate was in fact notoriously unfair when it came to converting copper cash (which the peasants received for the sale of their produce) to silver taels (which were the required currency for tax payment).[84] Widespread resentment over such malpractices allowed Liu Depei to mobilize a mass demonstration of more than 2,000 protesters. Armed with farm tools, they surrounded the county seat to express indignation at the tax abuses.[85]

The magistrate responded to this affront with a full-scale investigation of events leading to the demonstration. When he ascertained that Liu Depei had single-handedly drawn up the inflammatory posters (without the express consent of those whose names he so brazenly appended to it), the magistrate ordered Liu's arrest and extradition to the provincial capital. However, while en route to Jinan to be executed on grounds of sedition, Liu Depei somehow managed to break free from his two guards.[86]

Thanks to his friendships among the local gentry, Liu easily found refuge in the homes of sympathetic supporters. Chief among these allies were Si Guanping, a well-to-do member of the local elite, and Pu Renzhi, a lower degree holder.[87] Pu introduced Liu Depei to militia captains in the area, and by the spring of 1861 Liu had managed to assume command of a private militia corps in a nearby county.[88] Like many local militias, Liu's proved as prone toward aggression as toward defense. That summer, his militia joined with salt smugglers to stage raids on wealthy families in the area. Soon suppressed by government troops, Liu again retreated to the homes of his friends Si Guanping and Pu Renzhi.

While staying with Si Guanping, Liu had the opportunity to get to know another of Si's houseguests—an elderly scholar by the name of Zhang Jizhong. Zhang was a teacher of the syncretic Taizhou school and had persuaded Si Guanping to join his rapidly growing group of disciples among the Shandong local gentry. Two years later, Zhang would perish on Yellow Cliff in a violent confrontation between his community of followers and the suspicious Qing authorities (see Chapter 3). Although the government's charges of "heterodox rebellion" seem exaggerated in the case of Yellow Cliff, it is clear that Zhang and his followers did exemplify a process of alienation from the Qing state that was becoming more and more common among the local elite. Just as members of the Shanghai establishment were seeking refuge in guilds and secret societies, so the rural elite of Shandong were also searching for alternatives to the ineffective Qing state. Thus when Zhang Jizhong, who was known for his skill in physiognomy, dramatically informed Si that he had the bearing of an emperor and Liu and Pu that theirs were the visages of ministers, we can imagine the powerful impression this exercise in fortune telling must have made upon the three men.[89]

That winter, some peasants in the western part of Zichuan again protested the tribute tax by paying it in grain rather than cash. Angered at this flagrant breach of regulations, the magistrate ordered that the protesters be beaten. When one person died as a result of the flogging, Pu Renzhi and several other degree-holders led an infuriated crowd in a march on the county seat. They killed a tax collector and threatened to loot the home of the county clerk. Frightened by this display of strength, the magistrate agreed to adjust the conversion rate.[90] An even more startling indication of the magistrate's loss of control occurred shortly thereafter, when leaders of the tax protest set up their own tribute collection office to the west of the city. Ostensibly discharging their duties as a public service, the new collectors also profited handsomely from the steady source of income. Their appetites whetted by this sudden accretion of power and wealth, the tax protesters began to cast about for yet other means of advancement.[91]

A convenient target was soon found. The Eternal Peace pawnshop, located west of the county seat in the vicinity of the newly established tax collection office, had been looted by Nian rebels some months earlier. Although the proprietor of the pawnshop claimed that all the goods in his shop were lost in the raid, some of the missing items began to show up at the Eternal Prosperity pawnshop—owned by the same proprietor and located in the city of Zichuan. Armed with this discovery, Pu Renzhi and Si Guanping assembled a crowd to march on the Eternal Prosperity to demand repayment for their pawned possessions. They stole a gun and several thousand pieces of cash from the pawnshop before dispersing.[92]

These increasingly bold forays began to generate a good deal of hostility from the victims toward Liu Depei and his friends. To defend themselves against the danger of revenge, Liu, Si, Pu, and some twenty other allies from among the local elite decided to found their own militia force. Dubbed the Sincere Harmony, this militia would serve as the organizational base for subsequent rebellion. The well-to-do contributed money to purchase arms, hire martial arts teachers, and recruit militiamen. Those who joined included, in addition to ordinary peasants, a number of former bandits, attracted to militia service by the promise of food and clothing.[93]

Having already abrogated the power of taxation, Liu and his friends now began to assume judicial authority as well. They were emboldened by the sudden death of the Zichuan magistrate, whose life was ended in a heart attack (brought about, the sources suggest, by the cumulative shock of protest activities in his county). Stepping right into the shoes of the deceased magistrate, Liu's militia unit was willing to settle cases quickly and forcefully. As the Sincere Harmony became increasingly involved in local feuds, several lawsuits were filed against it with the county government. However, Pu Renzhi's close connections with yamen authorities—sweetened by a well-placed bribe to local officials—served to cover up accusations of wrongdoing.[94]

As the threat of Nian incursions grew more menacing, Si Guanping contacted militia chiefs in the nearby county of Boshan to propose an alliance with the Sincere Harmony corps. The commander of the northern Boshan militia forces, a licentiate by the name of Chen Zhiben, strongly opposed the idea of joining forces with the motley crew from Zichuan. But the commander of Boshan's southern militia, which had recently lost a battle to Nian invaders, decided to accept the offer of help. Thereupon Liu Depei and seventy-three followers moved their militia headquarters to Boshan. Before long, Liu Depei had also managed to forge secret connections with Nian and salt smugglers in the area, alliances that greatly augmented the size of his following.[95]

Fearful that Liu was becoming a greater danger than the Nian rebels, Chen Zhiben secretly informed the Zichuan authorities of his suspicions. Accordingly, the official Zichuan militia corps—some 100 members strong—was ordered to guard the city gates against a possible attack by Liu Depei. After a personal visit from Pu Renzhi, however, the new magistrate of Zichuan was persuaded to call off the guard.[96]

The following month, Chen Zhiben's ominous predictions were borne out. In the summer of 1862, Liu Depei and 200 subordinates marched from Boshan through the unprotected gates of Zichuan straight toward the Eternal Prosperity pawnshop. The ferocity of the crowd (who trampled underfoot the new magistrate's hat when he came forth to try to dispel them) convinced the pawnshop owner to offer compensation. He handed over some 800 silver taels, two-thirds of which went directly to Liu Depei's militia.[97]

Liu immediately reestablished his militia bureau in the western outskirts of Zichuan, using his new funds to buy more weapons and enlist yet more followers. Each recruit was given 3,000–5,000 in cash for enlisting, supplemented by free food and clothing and a daily wage of 200 cash. Overnight, the size of the Sincere Harmony militia grew to number in the thousands.[98]

Another bribe from Pu Renzhi convinced the now thoroughly intimidated magistrate to put Liu Depei officially in charge of the county militia. Arming his men with guns and ammunition from the county armory, Liu promptly stationed his followers at the four city gates and assumed effective control of the Zichuan county seat. His headquarters was established at the same academy where he had once studied for the Confucian examinations. But now no longer an ordinary scholar, Liu announced his new title as "Grand Marshal." Although the magistrate soon realized his error and resigned on grounds of poor health, Liu was not to be displaced.[99]

From his stronghold in Zichuan city, Liu sent subordinates out to establish militia units across an area that stretched some 80 kilometers to the south. The miltiamen in the countryside demanded that land and head taxes be remitted directly to them, pressuring wealthy families to contribute additional provisions.[100] Within the city of Zichuan, Liu also exercised his newly established authority. The property of county clerks who had opposed the tax resistance movement was confiscated, and other rivals (including the erstwhile captain of the official Zichuan militia) fled the city altogether.[101]

Troubled by reports of unrest in the Zichuan area, the Shandong governor dispatched Prefect Wu Zaixun to investigate the situation. A cousin of Yellow Cliff teacher Zhang Jizhong, Wu also enjoyed a special connection to Liu Depei. In a much earlier assignment as magistrate of Zichuan, Wu had been personally responsible for reading and assigning a passing grade to Liu Depei's examination paper. This student–teacher relationship between the two men undoubtedly helped prejudice Wu in favor of Licentiate Liu. Instead of taking steps to halt Liu's accretion of power, Wu tried to pacify him with the presentation of official rank.[102]

Encouraged by his meeting with the prefect, Liu moved even more boldly against his local rivals. In the fall of 1862 several hundred of his followers directed an attack on the forces of Chen Zhiben, the Boshan militia commander who had informed on Liu the year before. Chen himself was killed in this assault. Although Prefect Wu still hesitated to take action, further pressure from the provincial governor eventually persuaded him to dispatch troops against Liu's followers in the Boshan area. After several days of intense fighting, the government side succeeded in killing such rebel notables as Liu Depei's son, Si Guanping's father, and Pu Renzhi himself.[103]

To buttress his strength in the face of this serious government suppression effort, Liu Depei made further overtures toward other rebel groups in the area. The Nian, after being suitably rewarded with riches from the city of Zichuan, provided 300 men to help in the city's defense.

Emboldened by this addition to their forces, on October 31, 1862, Liu's followers killed the newly appointed county magistrate and his garrison commander and displayed their severed heads from the city wall.[104]

While alliances with other rebels served to enhance Liu's insurrectionary spirit, these ties had drawbacks as well. Pre-existing patterns of conflict among such groups injected further dissension and political intrigue into Liu Depei's movement. This was clearly demonstrated in dealings with the "turban bandits," the large contingent of local brigands drawn from the ranks of unemployed boatmen in the now defunct Grand Canal trade. Two of the most formidable turban chieftains, Sun Huaxiang and Song Sangang, responded to Liu Depei's call for help. The chieftains were in fact major rivals, Song relying on his large force and Sun on his military skills to claim hegemony. When Song arrived at Zichuan with more than 10,000 followers, the overjoyed Liu hosted him at a sumptuous banquet in the city. This was in striking contrast to his reception for Sun, who showed up with a mere 1,000 men in tow. When the government forces attacked Zichuan, however, Song's massive contingent hid in cowardly fashion within the safety of the city walls, whereas Sun's much smaller following delivered a sound thrashing to the government soldiers. Although Song was forced to depart in humiliation, the competition did not end there. Sun proceeded to stage raids on Song's home base, prompting the once proud turban chief to surrender to the Qing side.[105] Among Liu's own followers, there were also betrayals. One of the co-founders of the Sincere Harmony militia conspired to open a city gate to allow the Qing forces into Zichuan.[106] Although detected and thwarted, the plot indicated the deep divisions among Liu Depei's closest comrades.

If some of his colleagues were having second thoughts about their defiance of state authority, Liu Depei himself marched ever more boldly down the road of rebellion. He openly assumed the title of "Virtuous Ruler of the Great Han," setting up his "Grand Council" offices in the local academy and his "imperial audience hall" in the local lecture auditorium. Outside these offices, Liu hung a couplet with the words: "With one heart support the sun and moon; with both hands transform the universe." The characters for sun and moon, when combined, formed the familiar rebel reference to the Ming dynasty of old. Liu Depei's followers were instructed to cut their queues and grow out their hair—yet another symbol of defiance to the Manchu rulers.[107]

As Liu's rebel aspirations escalated, so too did the government's determination to subdue him. To carry out the final suppression, the Shandong governor dismissed Prefect Wu and called upon the aid of Mongol prince Senggelinqin and his crack cavalry. Government forces laid siege to the city of Zichuan, thereby cutting communication between the rebels in the city and those of the southern countryside. When it was obvious that the end was drawing nigh, Liu Depei tried to commit suicide. Unsuccessful in the attempt, he was captured and put to death by slow torture on August 7, 1863. With the demise of its leader, the tax protest-turned-rebellion quickly crumbled.[108]

Conclusion

In several important respects, Liu Depei's uprising bore remarkable similarities to that of the Shanghai Small Swords. Both movements originated in the tax riots led by rural strongmen and supported by the hard-pressed peasantry. The tax protest associated with the Small Swords developed in Songjiang Prefecture, an area where landlords appear to have been less exploitative than in some other parts of the Yangzi delta. The alkaline soil of Songjiang had rendered the area more suitable to cotton than to rice cultivation, and landlords in this region tended to be resident rather than absentee as in many other parts of Jiangnan.[109] The closer landlord–tenant relationship that apparently prevailed in Songjiang was probably an important stimulus to tax revolt, inasmuch as this form of resistance was typically fueled by cross-class cooperation. Such alliances were facilitated by the establishment of local militias. For Shandong, it has been suggested that areas with a high proportion of freeholders were especially susceptible to militia-based tax protest.[110] But there, too, we have seen that gentry leadership was an important ingredient in the Liu Depei case. In both the Songjiang and Zichuan tax riots, it was lower-level members of the rural elite who assumed the leadership roles. These were persons who, although charged with control of the peasantry, lived in the villages and tended to identify with the plight of their neighbors.[111]

The move from simple tax protest to outright anti-state rebellion that challenged the Qing's claim to the Mandate of Heaven was prompted by wider historical currents as well. Shanghai's recent treaty port status and attendant changes in trade routes had altered the fortunes of boatmen and merchants—key groups in the transition from rural protest to urban-based rebellion. Proximity to the Taiping movement and links with Triad groups in other areas further encouraged Small Sword ambitions. In the case of Liu Depei, the closing of the Grand Canal and the activities of Nian and turban bandits played a comparable role in fueling the rebelliousness of the leaders.

There were, of course, also some clear differences between the two rebellions. In the Zichuan uprising, the initial tax rioters retained a leadership role throughout the course of the rebellion. Until the final weeks of the insurrection, the base of the movement remained centered in the countryside—with Liu Depei's militia branches performing fiscal and judicial functions abrogated by the state authorities. Thanks to the tolerance of the Jinan prefect, the state was slow in bringing decisive power to bear against the insurgents. When finally the cavalry of Senggelinqin succeeded in isolating the city of Zichuan from its rural lifeline, however, the rebel government was able to survive but a few weeks. The Small Swords, by contrast, persisted in an urban area much longer. The force that occupied Shanghai was a more diverse group than the one that had launched tax resistance in the Songjiang countryside. Led by guild directors and pidgin-speaking secret society chieftains, the urban Small Swords were able to sustain links with outside forces—foreign merchants, missionaries, and governments; Taiping and Triad rebels—which prolonged the life of the movement and encouraged a more complex ideology than that developed by Liu Depei in the remote hills of Shandong.

Despite such differences, the Chinese cases do seem to present an identifiable pattern of protest, especially when viewed in comparison with European tax revolts. Perhaps the most striking feature of the Chinese rebellions is the confusing overlap between state and society. Militia units—established within a framework of state sponsorship—served as the institutional foundation for these revolts. The leadership of such units rested in the hands of the local elite, many of whom had state-conferred degrees and offices and enjoyed close connection with high-ranking state officials. The contrast is suggested by George Rudé's characterization of the protesters in pre-industrial France and England:

> Basically, they were the "lower orders" or *menu people* of the towns and countryside, or those who, in Paris and other cities during the French Revolution, were called *sans-culottes*. . . . [N]ormally, merchants, capitalists or the more prosperous householders did not demonstrate, riot, or shoulder muskets to besiege a Bastille or capture a royal palace by force of arms[;] even where the sympathies of a substantial part of the propertied classes were evidentially enlisted on the side of those taking part, such activities were generally left to the common herd.[112]

In China, members of the local elite—linked by education and personal friendships to state agents and institutions—played a central role in the development of anti-state protest. While their activities were in part a defensive response to state-making efforts of the imperial court, they also reflected a growing sense of local community. China was involved in a complicated, and as yet little understood, process of transformation in which _both_ state and local society were endeavoring to expand their control of resources. The Ming restorationist rhetoric of the rebels should not delude us into seeing these protests merely as futile efforts to turn back the dynastic clock. Instead, the struggle over tax revenues and militia forces was in many ways a new battle over recently claimed resources—a battle that both state and local society were anxious to win.

China's past century and a half of state building has not meant the collapse of local community. On the contrary, modern China has seen— by fits and starts to be sure—a _simultaneous_ strengthening of both state and local society.[113] The mid-nineteenth-century tax rebellion, fought out in different ways in different parts of the Chinese empire, foreshadowed the complicated interplay between state and society—at once conflictual and complementary—that lay ahead in the decades to come.

Notes

An earlier version of this chapter was published as an article in _Late Imperial China_ (June 1985).

I am grateful to the Committee on Scholarly Communication with the People's Republic of China for supporting the research on which this chapter is based. In China, Professors Cai Shaoqing and Mao Jiaqi of Nanjing University, Professor Fang Shiming of the Shanghai Academy of Social Sciences, Wang Tingru of the Boshan District Library, and Kong Xiangjun of the Zichuan Foreign Affairs Bureau were most helpful in offering research direction. For the Liu Depei case, I am also deeply appreciative to Professor Tom Chang for sharing materials and ideas. Abbreviations used in the notes: NCH: _North China Herald_, Shanghai; SDZL: _Shandong jindaishi ziliao_ (Materials on Shandong's modern history), vol. 1, 1957, whose section on the Liu Depei uprising, pp. 33–126, is a compilation of fifteen primary sources; XDH: _Shanghai Xiaodaohui qiyi shiliao huibian_ (Compendium of historical materials on the Shanghai Small Swords uprising) (Shanghai, 1980).

1. Charles Tilly, Louise Tilly, and Richard Tilly, _The Rebellious Century_ (Cambridge: Harvard University Press, 1975).

2. See, for example, Anthony Oberschall, _Social Conflict and Social Movements_ (Englewood Cliffs, NJ: Prentice Hall, 1973).

3. See Philip A. Kuhn, _Rebellion and Its Enemies in Late Imperial China_ (Cambridge: Harvard University Press, 1970), for a discussion of the organi-

zation of the *tuanlian*; pp. 99–100 and 161 deal specifically with the relationship between *tuanlian* and taxation.

4. For the relationship between *tuanlian* and tax resistance in Shandong, see Yokoyama Suguru, "Kenhoki santo no koryo fucho to mindan" (Militias and the wave of tax resistance in Shandong during the Xianfeng reign), *Rekishi Kyoiku*, 2d series, 12(9) (September 1964):42–50; and Kanbe Teruo, "Shindai koki santosho ni okeru 'danhi' to noson mondai" ("Militia bandits" and village issues in Shandong during the late Qing), *Shirin*, 55(4) (July 1972):61–98. For the tax problem in the Yangzi delta at this time, see Xia Ding, "Taiping tianguo qianhou changjiang gesheng de tianfu wenti" (The land tax problem in various Yangzi provinces before and after the Taipings), *Qinghua xuebao*, 10(2) (1935).

5. See, for example, Maureen F. Dillon, "The Triads in Shanghai: The Small Sword Society Uprising, 1853–1855," *Papers on China*, 23 (1970):67–86; and Joseph Fass, "L'insurrection du Xiaodaohui à Shanghai," in Jean Chesneaux, ed., *Mouvements populaires et sociétés secrètes en Chine aux XIXe et XXe siècles* (Paris, 1970): 178–195. Valuable firsthand accounts by Westerners who witnessed the Small Sword occupation of Shanghai include John Scarth's *Twelve Years in China* (Edinburgh: T. Constable, 1860); Thomas Taylor Meadows, *The Chinese and Their Rebellions* (London: Smith, Elder, 1856); Robert Fortune, *A Residence Among the Chinese* (London: J. Murray, 1857); and Captain Fishbourne, *Impressions of China* (London, 1855). For an important account that does consider the rural links, published after this article was first written, see Kathryn Bernhardt, *Rents, Taxes and Peasant Resistance* (Stanford: Stanford University Press, 1992).

6. Peng Zeyi, *Zhongguo jindai shougongye shi ziliao* (Materials on the history of China's modern handicraft industry), I: 495.

7. According to some accounts, the taxes had already been remitted, but had been embezzled by the tax collector. For a discussion of the variant accounts, see T. Kujirai, "1853-nen choko karyuiki no nomin ikki" (Peasant uprisings in the Yangzi delta in 1853), *Ochanomizu shigaku*, 3 (1960):20–34.

8. XDH: 1055, 1086–87, 1157.

9. NCH, September 10, 1853: 22. See also Xu Weinan, "Shanghai Xiaodaohui luanshi de shimo" (The full story of Shanghai's Small Sword disturbance), *Yijing*, 26 (March 20, 1937):29.

10. XDH: 933.

11. XDH: 38.

12. These two functions have given rise to differing interpretations of the role of the guilds in facilitating economic development. The guilds are seen as an impediment to capitalism in Peng Zeyi, "Shijiu shiji houqi Zhongguo chengshi shougongye shangye hanghui de chongjian he zuoyong" (The revival and functions of China's urban handicraft and commercial guilds in the late nineteenth century), *Lishi yanjiu*, 91 (February 1965):71–102. For a fine recent study of guilds and native-place associations in Shanghai, see Bryna Goodman, *Native Place, City, and Nation: Regional Networks and Identities in Shanghai, 1853–1937* (Berkeley: University of California Press, 1995).

13. See *Shanghaixian xuzhi* (Shanghai county gazetteer), Wu Qing, ed., 1918, 3/2–8, on activities of guilds in the late Qing period.

14. XDH: 519.

15. In 1848, some 13,000 unemployed boatmen had launched a demonstration against foreign missionaries in the county of Qingpu. See "Qingpu shijian xigao" (A draft account of the Qingpu incident), *Jindaishi ziliao*, 2 (1957).

16. Lu Yaohua, "Shanghai Xiaodaohui de yuanliu" (The origins of the Shanghai Small Swords), *Shihuo yuekan*, 3(5) (1973):9; XDH: 39.

17. Grand Council memorial collection of the Ming-Qing archives, Beijing; Peasant Movement File, supplementary packet no. 582, memorial no. 3 (Xianfeng 5–11–5); "Shanghai Xiaodaohui jishi benmo" (The full story of the Shanghai Small Sword uprising), Taiping Museum Archives, Nanjing; XDH: 36, 126.

18. XDH: 36, 128, 146, 1024.

19. The connection is suggested in Lu Yaohua, "Shanghai Xiaodaohui": 13–14.

20. XHD:983.

21. NCH, August 9, 1851.

22. XDH: 1024–25.

23. XDH: 38.

24. XDH: 1087, 1112, 1158.

25. XDH: 12, 879; NCH, October 1, 1853: 38; Scarth, *Twelve Years*: 196.

26. XDH: 973.

27. XDH: 1055, 118, 1158.

28. XDH: 1055, 1158.

29. XDH: 1102, 1124–1125.

30. XDH: 28, 1056.

31. XDH: 984, 1018–1023.

32. *China Mail*, September 29, 1853.

33. *Taiping tianguo shiliao congbian jianji* (Compilation of historical materials on the Taiping heavenly kingdom), Taiping Revolution Museum, Nanjing, V: 32ff.; XDH: 6–7, 95, 976, 985–986, 1044, 1102, 1106, 1112, 1118, 1124, 1158, 1163, 1193.

34. For the city of Shanghai itself, the rebels did declare a three-year remission of taxes. See NCH, October 15, 1853: 44.

35. XDH: 968, 987, 1007, 1050.

36. Admittedly, the rebel takeover had resulted in a substantial emigration. One source estimates that the population of the walled city was reduced from 270,000 to about 40,000 in the space of a few days; see C. A. Montalto de Jesus, *Historic Shanghai* (Shanghai: The Shanghai Mercury, 1909): 60. Even so, the remaining inhabitants were still substantial in number.

37. NCH, September 10, 1853: 22. According to another source, the rebels took 440,000 silver taels from the treasury on September 7 and another 200,000 taels on September 9; see *Taiping tianguo shiliao congbian jianji*, V: 49.

38. XDH: 48. Yu was not above hedging his bets, however. When the Qing forces attacked Shanghai, he was quick to present them with contributions as well.

39. XDH: 975, 145.

40. XDH: 142.

41. XDH: 145, 152–153, 800; Scarth, *Twelve Years*: 189; *Taiping tianguo*, V: 438.

42. *Taiping tianguo*, V: 49.

43. XDH: 44, 46, 145. However, when merchants found their supply lines severed by the siege that was soon laid on the city by the imperial army, the rebels took to raiding the surrounding countryside for grain. See "Shanghai Xiaodaohui jishi benmo."

44. Scarth, *Twelve Years*: 188.

45. In October 1853, Small Sword commander Liu Lichuan sent the foreign consuls a note protesting that arms from aboard the ship *Antelope* had been handed over to the Qing authorities by the U.S. consul (NCH, October 22, 1853: 46). On December 21, two Chinese catechists were seized on their way to the Roman Catholic cathedral by Small Swords who mistook them for government spies. The incident resulted in a flare-up of hostility between the rebels and the French consulate until the Small Swords acknowledged responsibility for the error (NCH, December 31, 1853: 87). Rebel seizure of an American shipment of silk was similarly resolved (Montalto de Jesus, *Historic Shanghai*: 64–65).

46. Fortune, *A Residence*: 126.

47. XDH: 800.

48. XDH: 781.

49. XDH; Scarth, *Twelve Years*: 191–92; NCH, September 10, 1853: 22.

50. XDH: 881; NCH, September 10, 1853: 22.

51. NCH, October 1, 1853: 34.

52. The one sent by water was apparently confiscated by government soldiers at Ningbo when they impounded a fishing boat carrying foreigners on their way to sell arms to the Taipings. XDH: 245.

53. NCH, December 3, 1853: 70.

54. Meadows, *The Chinese*: 452. This was not atypical of Taiping attitudes toward Triad groups elsewhere. See Charles A. Curwen, "Taiping Relations with Secret Societies and Other Rebels," in Jean Chesneaux, ed., *Popular Movements and Secret Societies in China* (Stanford: Stanford University Press, 1972): 65–84; and Elizabeth J. Perry, "Taipings and Triads: The Role of Religion in Inter-Rebel Relations," in Janos Bak, ed., *Religion and Rural Revolt* (Dover, NH: Manchester University Press, 1984).

55. NCH, December 17, 1853: 78.

56. NCH, May 20, 1854.

57. NCH, May 20, 1854.

58. XDH: 45.

59. XDH: 976–977.

60. Theodore Hamberg, *The Visions of Hung-Siu-Tshuen and Origin of the Kwang-si Insurrection* (Hong Kong, 1854): 55–56.

61. There has been much debate among Chinese historians over whether the Taipings were in fact anxious to ally with the Small Swords. Those who argue for Taiping willingness include: Luo Ergang, *Taiping tianguo shishi kao* (A study of historical facts of the Taiping Heavenly Kingdom) (Hong Kong, 1962), I: 685; and Li Chun, "Taiping tianguo dui Shanghai Xiaodaohui qiyi yundong de taidu wenti" (The question of the Taipings' attitude toward the rebel movement of the Shanghai Small Swords), *Shixue yuekan*, 2 (1958):7–10. Those who argue that the Taipings were not interested in an alliance include Liang Renbao, "Taiping tianguo he Shanghai Xiaodaohui guanxi de shangque" (A debate over relations between the Taipings and the Shanghai Small Swords),

Lishi yanjiu, 2 (1957):52–54; and Lu Yaohua, "Shanghai Xiaodaohui qiyiqian yu Taiping tianguo wuguan kao" (A study of the lack of relations between the Taipings and the pre-rebellion Shanghai Small Swords), *Dushi zhaji*, 5 (1970–71):9–13.

62. According to the *Jiaoping yuefei fanglüe* (Annals of the suppression of the Guangdong bandits), 67:101–2, attempts by the Taipings to move east in November 1853 and August 1854 were blocked by overwhelming government opposition.

63. The confession of Guangdong Triad chief Chen Kai, reprinted in *Guangming ribao*, March 28, 1962: 4, suggested a strong connection between the Shanghai Small Swords and the Red Turban Rebellion in the Guangzhou area. However, scholars in Guangxi (Zhong Wendian of Guangxi Normal University and Li Feiren of the Guangxi Museum) have recently ascertained that this oft-quoted source is, in fact, a forgery.

64. Of course, the adoption of certain Taiping terms did have the intent of facilitating an alliance. Thus Liu Lichuan's dynastic title was changed from "Great Ming Empire" to "Taiping Heavenly Kingdom" as he sought to establish connections with the rebels in Nanjing. (See XDH: 1–30 for the evolution of dynastic titles used in rebel proclamations.)

65. Fang Shiming and Liu Xiuming, "Shanghai Xiaodaohui qiyi de shehui jichu he lishi tedian" (The social base and historical characteristics of the Shanghai Small Sword Uprising), *Lishi xue*, 3 (1979):3–14. Specifically, the authors suggest that overseas members of the Triads had introduced this term into the society's lexicon. On the use of this term by the Small Swords, see XDH: 28–30, 974.

66. NCH, September 10, 1853: 22.

67. *Taiping tianguo shiliao congbian jianji*, V: 422. Perhaps it was this disgrace that prompted Li to return to Fujian (ostensibly in search of aid from the Amoy Small Swords) a couple of months later. When he discovered that the Amoy rebellion had already been quelled, Li fled home where he was captured by the authorities (Grand Council memorial collection, peasant movement packet no. 2712, memorial no. 1, Xianfeng 3–11–25).

68. *Taiping tianguo shiliao*, V: 486; Grand Council memorial collection, peasant movement packet no. 2710, memorial no. 6, Xianfeng 3–12–4.

69. NCH, January 7, 1854: 90.

70. Li did not totally abandon his rebel sympathies, however. He later joined the Taipings, although he was eventually killed by them because of a subsequent betrayal. See XDH: 1025.

71. The rebels' desertion of the city in February 1855 was accelerated by Fujian chief Chen Alin's shooting of Liu Lichuan's secretary. (See NCH, February 24, 1855: 120.)

72. H.B. Morse, *In the Days of the Taipings* (Salem, MA: Essex Institute, 1927): 157–159.

73. Scarth, *Twelve Years*: 219.

74. XDH: 1025, Scarth, *Twelve Years*: 218.

75. Ibid.

76. Scarth, *Twelve Years*: 218; XDH: 1025. There is evidence that some of them succeeded in joining the Taipings. A memorial of Zuo Zongtang reported

the death of the magistrate's assassin, Pan Qiliang, in a Taiping battle in 1865, ten years after the Shanghai uprising had been defeated. See Fang Shiming, "Shanghai Xiaodaohui cong xiancheng chetui hou de douzheng shishi" (Historical facts concerning the Small Swords after their retreat from the county seat), *Xueshu yuekan*, 2 (1963):41.

77. *Shanghai xianzhi*, ch.11.

78. Luo Ergang, *Taiping tianguo shishi kao*: 64.

79. *Taiping tianguo shiliao congbian jianji*, I: 227; XDH: 1025.

80. "Shandong junxing jilüe" (Annals of military activities in Shandong), ch. 22, in Fan Wenlan, ed., *Nianjun* (Shanghai, 1953): IV.

81. Further information on turban bandits can be found in SDZL: 207–8; *Feixian zhi* (Fei county gazetteer), 1896: 8.7b, 8/14a–21b; Lu Zhi, "Shandong fujun douzheng gaishu" (An overview of the struggles of the turban army of Shandong), *Shandong shengzhi ziliao*, 1 (1962); Jiang Di, "Fujun" (The turban army), *Xinshixue tongxun*, 10 (1956):6–10; Li Senwen and Yi Chengyuan, *Fujun* (The turban army) (Jinan, 1960).

82. Harold C. Hinton, *The Grain Tribute System of China, 1845–1911* (Cambridge: Harvard University Press, 1970): 20–24.

83. SDZL: 94.

84. SDZL: 35,52.

85. SDZL: 122.

86. SDZL: 46, 52–53, 62, 122–123.

87. SDZL: 60.

88. SDZL: 36, 53.

89. SDZL: 53, 63.

90. SDZL: 46, 63.

91. SDZL: 53, 63.

92. SDZL: 46.

93. SDZL: 46.

94. SDZL: 46.

95. SDZL: 46.

96. SDZL: 46.

97. SDZL: 46.

98. SDZL: 46.

99. SDZL: 54, 64, 121.

100. SDZL: 38.

101. SDZL: 47.

102. SDZL: 118.

103. SDZL: 55, 65.

104. SDZL: 50.

105. See the sources listed in note 81, and Luo Changlie, "Taiping tianguo geming shiqi Shandong renmin de geming douzheng" (Revolutionary struggles of the Shandong people during the period of the Taiping Heavenly Kingdom), paper presented to the conference on the history of the Taiping Rebellion, Suzhou, 1981.

106. SDZL: 42.

107. SDZL: 58, 72, 121.

108. SDZL: 60, 94.

109. On this point see Banno Ryokichi, "Shanhai shotokai no hanran" (The disturbance of the Shanghai Small Swords), *Rekishigaku kenkyu*, 353 (1969):1–13.

110. Kanbe Teruo, "Shin Koki santosho":76.

111. Further discussion of this point can be found in Yokoyama Suguru, "Shincho chuki ni okeru koryo undo" (Tax protest movements in the mid-Qing), *Rekishi kyoiku*, 2d series, 8(11) (1960):25–31.

112. George Rudé, *The Crowd in History: A Study of Popular Disturbances in France and England, 1730–1848* (New York: Wiley, 1964): 204–205.

113. For further discussion, see Elizabeth J. Perry, "Collective Violence in China, 1880–1980," *Theory and Society* (May 1984): 427–454.

3

Heterodox Rebellion?
The Mystery of Yellow Cliff

In the fall of 1866, an incident characterized by the Chinese authorities as the act of "religious" rebels (*jiaofei*) took place in central Shandong Province on a remote mountaintop known as Yellow Cliff. The government's suppression of the alleged uprising, according to official reports, resulted in the deaths of more than ten thousand recalcitrant rebels. What inspired and organized these droves of diehards? Was theirs another entry in the long annals of heterodox religious rebellion for which China was well known?

Interpretations of the incident are difficult to draw, having given rise to bitter controversy among government officials, Shandong residents, and concerned scholars for generations after the conclusion of the affair. A consideration of the mystery surrounding the Yellow Cliff incident allows us a revealing entrée to the world of late Qing rural society, inviting an assessment of the nature and effectiveness of government penetration of the countryside, the loyalties of the rural elite, the relations of gentry and masses, and the prevailing belief systems of the day. This study, in attempting to reconstruct the mysterious drama of Yellow Cliff, will also address these larger issues.

The Case: Zhang Jizhong, His Friends, and Forebears

The alleged mastermind behind the rebellion was an elderly man by the name of Zhang Jizhong. Some sixty years before the Yellow Cliff incident, Jizhong had been born the seventh child into a prominent Yangzhou family with a history of gentry and official members that stretched back for generations. In his own lifetime, Jizhong's cousin Zhang Jixin attained the high office of governor of Shaanxi Province. Indeed, Jizhong's own elder brother, Zhang Jigong, held the coveted degree of *juren* and served for nearly twenty years in four magistrate posts before an untimely martyrdom in 1854. Jigong and his immediate family met their violent end when the Taiping rebels stormed the city of Linqing where he was then serving as prefect. Inasmuch as Jigong's only son died with him in the Taiping assault, an official hereditary title that he had held passed on to his nephew, Zhang Jizhong's own son, Zhang Shaoling. Shaoling was also in due course to achieve a certain official status; by the time of the Yellow Cliff debacle, he was already an expectant magistrate in Shandong Province.[1]

The record is less clear about their kinsman Zhang Jizhong, branded a religious rebel and sent to his fiery death amid the flames on Yellow Cliff. By one account, Jizhong himself, although well educated as a youth, had failed in repeated attempts to pass the civil service examinations.[2] Elsewhere, however, he is described as a senior licentiate (*gongsheng*) who rose to become an education official.[3] We do know that Jizhong was a protégé of the former governor-general of Huguang, Zhou Tianjue. Through Zhou's recommendation, Zhang Jizhong was appointed in 1851 or 1852 to serve as a member of the government military staff in the critical Jiangxi-Jiangsu-Anhui area at the height of the campaign against the Taiping rebels.[4] In this capacity, Jizhong was able to forge close friendships with other prominent members of the southern gentry active in the suppression campaign.[5] His efforts in the development of local militia even afforded sufficient respect to win him an invitation to a court audience in Beijing.[6]

If Zhang Jizhong felt somewhat dissatisfied with his own rather modest credentials in comparison to those of the august company he kept, he was nevertheless no Hong Xiuquan [leader of the Taiping Rebellion], blocked by examination failure from any hope of advancement or recognition. Zhang's world was the world of the powerful and influential of his day: degree holders, magistrates, governors. Still, he did share with that frustrated rebel from Guangdong at least one common characteristic: conversion to a rather unusual philosophico-religious persuasion.

Yangzhou, city of Zhang Jizhong's youth, was in the early nineteenth century a flourishing commercial center. And among those who came to ply their wares in the bustling marketplace was a magician by the name of Zhou Xingyuan, a man skilled in the art of breath control, dietary restraint, amulets, and other aspects of the occult tradition. Apparently fascinated by these strange powers, Zhang Jizhong apprenticed himself to the master magician. Here again Jizhong was in good company, for Zhou Xingyuan succeeded in attracting to his fold numerous followers from among the scholar-gentry of Yangzhou.[7]

Actually, this interest of the educated upper strata in the teachings and practices of Zhou Xingyuan was not quite as out of character as might at first appear. For despite certain later official accounts anxious to emphasize the "heterodox" side of Zhang and his teacher,[8] there were also a good many respectable elements in their ideological stockpile.

Indeed, the teachings of Zhou Xingyuan had quite a pedigree, tracing their ancestry back to the writings of Ming philosophers Wang Gen (1484–1541) and Lin Zhaoen (1517–98). The teachings of these two apparently unconnected thinkers formed the basis of an important alternative strain of Confucianism within late Ming and Qing intellectual circles. To appreciate the heritage of Zhou Xingyuan and his disciple Zhang Jizhong, let us digress for a moment to consider these earlier progenitors.

Wang Gen, a native of Yangzhou's Taizhou County, hailed from a family of salt farmers. Trained as a tradesman to handle the family business, Wang terminated his formal studies at an early age in order to accompany his father on salt-selling ventures north to Shandong. By age twenty-one, he had become an independent salt dealer based in the bustling trading center of Yangzhou. In addition to his commercial activities, the young man developed an interest in herbal medicine and classical philosophy. Suddenly, at age twenty-eight, he is said to have had a dream in which he single-handedly prevented the heavens from imminent collapse and restored the sun, moon, and stars to working order.[9] This vision aroused in Wang Gen a new appreciation of the self as an active center. Subsequently, he began to formulate his conception of the self (*shen*) as root, and society as its branch. Individual welfare was seen as the foundation of social order. Proclaiming his teachings to be the way of the ancient sages, kings, and Confucius, Wang Gen donned a long gown and ceremonial hat in accordance with ancient ritual texts and set out to recruit receptive followers. Much impressed by another innovator in the

Confucian tradition, Wang Yangming, in 1521 Wang declared himself a disciple of his famous contemporary. He studied with the master until the latter's death in 1529, at which time Wang Gen returned home to Taizhou to open a school of his own.[10]

At his school, Wang Gen lectured on the concept of innate knowledge (*liangzhi*), which he explained as requiring first a love of self and then a love of others. Proper self-cultivation would lead naturally to a well-ordered society. The self was the center of all things, the highest good, the Way. To popularize these principles, which he took to be the essence of Confucianism, Wang resorted to a heavy dose of Buddhist and Daoist language. Study was seen as a spontaneous and joyous awakening of the mind within oneself—a pursuit open to every man and woman, framed in whatever language proved most compatible. Many of Wang Gen's students were drawn from among the poorer strata of society; peasants, woodcutters, craftsmen, potters, and cooks joined members of the scholar-gentry as his followers.

Although Wang Gen offered no developed sociopolitical theory, his commitment to social justice was evident. He was active in charity: during famines he collected grain from the wealthy and distributed it to the needy; during epidemics he dispensed medicine to the afflicted. In 1538, he demanded and won more equitable land distribution for the hard-pressed local salt farmers.[11]

The legacy of Wang Gen, known to later generations as the Taizhou school, was an individualistic approach to Confucianism that stressed personal understanding, aided as appropriate by Daoist and Buddhist insights. Emphasis on self-awareness was matched by a concern for the welfare of the downtrodden to lend a strong flavor of social morality.

Contemporary with, but apparently quite independent of, Wang Gen was another syncretically inclined philosopher: Lin Zhaoen of Fujian Province. Unlike Wang Gen, Lin came from a prominent family that boasted several degree holders and officials during the Ming. Like Wang Gen, however, Lin also experienced an impressive dream. In his vision, Lin was joined by none other than Confucius, Laozi, and Buddha. Each of the three great worthies was said to have revealed the key to his respective teachings: the Way (*dao*), mystery (*xuan*), and emptiness (*kong*). Armed with his special insights, Lin dressed in peculiar garb and set off across southeastern China to attract converts. His lectures, which were accompanied by instruction in healing techniques, won thousands of followers in Fujian, Jiangxi, and Zhejiang.[12] Lin's method of healing, known as *genbeifa*, consisted in advising the patient to concentrate his or her mind on the back of the body. Advertised as efficacious in curing a wide variety of ailments, the exercise was responsible for capturing the allegiance of a number of high officials suffering from eye trouble, nervous disorders, and the like. Lin came also to be credited with the ability to perform such feats as warding off ghosts and quelling storms. Though rumored to be a heretic by some, Lin's impeccable family credentials, high-placed supporters, and record as a philanthropist prevented severe persecution by the authorities.[13]

After the death of Lin Zhaoen, temples sprang up to commemorate his syncretic doctrine. Known as temples to the "three teachings" (*sanjiao*), the institutions drew a large following from among common folk and officialdom alike.[14] In 1744, nearly two centuries after Lin's death, the continued popularity of these places of worship prompted the Qianlong emperor to issue an edict forbidding the establishment of *sanjiao* temples.[15]

In part because of the Qing court's intolerance for anything smacking of a challenge to neo-Confucian orthodoxy, the precise lines of transmission from Wang Gen and Lin Zhaoen to late Qing adherents are less than clear. To be sure, Wang, Lin, and their many latter-day disciples insisted that theirs was an orthodox Confucian creed. Nevertheless, the openness to Buddhism and Daoism, the interest in healing techniques, and the motley membership of officials and unlettered persons placed the followers of their syncretic doctrines under suspicion of heterodoxy.[16]

It was from such roots as these that the magician of Yangzhou claimed his intellectual heritage. Zhou Xingyuan's own teachings—known variously as the Taizhou, Taigu, or Dacheng school—stressed the importance of innate knowledge (*liangzhi*) and practice (*shixing*) in a manner resembling Wang Yangming. Fatherless at an early age, Zhou had spent his youth wandering about in search of instruction. After apprenticing himself first to a Daoist adept in Fujian and then to a Buddhist master in Anhui, he went alone to the mountains to receive enlightenment. There he reportedly discovered the key to Confucian success, or *dacheng*—namely, that mind and breath must be in step with each other.[17] This revelation inspired Zhou to lecture widely on his findings, attracting throngs of followers, including his own former mentors in Buddhism and Daoism. His philosophical insights were augmented by an impressive repertoire of magical-medical techniques that also proved appealing to many. In his later years, Zhou took his popular message to the busy city of Yangzhou. There the sayings of the illiterate preacher were recorded by his students and compiled into philosophical treatises.[18] Although Zhou Xingyuan's disciples included more than a few highly placed officials, his unusual teachings eventually resulted in his imprisonment on order of the governor-general of Liangjiang. Subsequently released, the time in prison had apparently taken its toll, for Zhou died soon thereafter.[19]

In addition to Zhang Jizhong, Zhou Xingyuan counted among his thousands of followers a number of other faithful disciples. Most notable of these was another man from the Yangzhou area, Li Guanxin.[20] It was Li, at the young age of twenty, whom master Zhou called to his deathbed to bequeath authority for carrying on his teachings.[21] After Zhou's death, Li traveled widely throughout the empire proselytizing for his late mentor's faith. Although centered in the West Lake area, Li managed through his travels to recruit prominent followers in many locations. Under his promptings, a top degree-holder (*jinshi*) in Shandong who had been serving as magistrate for a decade gave up his official career to devote all his time to the cause. The provincial treasurer of Gansu, also a *jinshi* degree-holder, became another of Li's chosen converts.[22] While Li Guanxin acted as a kind of roving evangelist, Zhang Jizhong was to adopt a more sedentary approach.[23] After his master's death, Jizhong absorbed himself in writing. In addition to commentaries on Zhou Xingyuan's teachings, Jizhong wrote criticisms on the Daoist works of Laozi, Zhuangzi, and Liezi and applied Daoist and Buddhist concepts to an explication of the Confucian classics. Although Jizhong did not overtly proselytize, prospective disciples streamed to his doorstep. Apparently, some of this popularity stemmed from Zhang's exciting claim that his master's corpse had vanished like a Daoist immortal, setting an example for others who wished to attain immortal life.[24] Despite the unconventional overtones of this assertion, when challenged Jizhong was also able to prove himself among the gentry as a highly competent scholar of the classics.[25]

Before long, however, a peaceful life of scholarship became an impossibility in troubled Yangzhou. With the city now threatened by the advance of the Taiping rebels who had taken his brother's life two years earlier, in 1856 Jizhong felt compelled to flee the area. Since his son was an expectant magistrate in Shandong and a cousin of his, Wu Zaixun,[26] was serving as an official in the same province, Zhang decided to move his family north to Shandong to escape the rebel danger at home.[27] Upon arrival in Shandong, Zhang took up residence along the border of Feicheng and Changqing counties, a mountainous area apparently safe from rebel attack and fortunate to be the home of yet another of his relatives. Despite the secluded location, it was not long before the Yangzhou scholar came to the attention of the local gentry. One member of the Feicheng gentry, a licentiate by the name of Liu Yaodong, was particularly impressed with Jizhong's erudition. Expressing his intention of becoming Zhang's disciple, Liu divided up his own home to accommodate the Zhang family. Jizhong accepted the hospitality and moved into the Liu residence, located as it had been for generations on the top of Yellow Cliff.[28] Perhaps put off by the primitive conditions and isolation of the mountain, however, Zhang soon accepted another invitation to the much more attractive setting of Boshan County, some fifty miles to the northeast. Known for its spectacular scenery, Boshan apparently provided a congenial home for Jizhong for several years. In the winter of 1861, however, the approach of the Nian rebels to the Boshan area prompted Zhang to return to Yellow Cliff.[29] While the mountain may not have offered much in the way of conveniences, its secluded position seemed to render it impervious to rebel attack.[30]

The Setting: Yellow Cliff on the Eve of Destruction

Located some twenty miles northwest of the Feicheng County seat, Yellow Cliff was composed of three jagged precipices in the midst of which lay a sheltered area of about fifteen acres. The sheltered territory itself being over a mile high and accessible only by tortuous paths, it offered an ideal spot for eluding rebels.[31]

As the Nian threat grew ever more menacing in the southern Shandong area, increasing numbers of refugees found their way to Yellow Cliff, attracted by both the protected location and the teachings of Zhang Jizhong. Thanks to the enthusiastic endorsement of cousin Wu, who had just been promoted to the high post of prefect of Jinan, provincial capital of Shandong, Zhang also began to gain an impressive following among the officialdom.[32]

In 1862–63, as the Nian stepped up their Shandong raids, Zhang Jizhong oversaw the construction of a stone fort at Yellow Cliff to provide increased protection for his growing community. A moat was added at the foot of the mountain and weapons were procured and stored in an arsenal. Six months after Zhang's return to Yellow Cliff, the fort withstood its first test. When bandits attacked the surrounding area, members of Yellow Cliff repaired to their stronghold. Having prepared enough gruel and soup to sustain them, the refugees were able to wait out the assault in safety. The success of Zhang's defense measures served, of course, to augment greatly the appeal of Yellow Cliff among the local populace. Soon some eight thousand households—hundreds of them gentry and officials—had moved to the safety of the mountain and its surrounding villages.[33] Many of the new recruits were, predictably, the wealthier families in the area. Bringing their valuables with them, they gave the once desolate Yellow Cliff a sudden reputation for affluence.[34]

Unfortunately, we have little information on the individual members of Zhang's well-to-do entourage. We do know that Liu Yaodong, the scholar originally responsible for Zhang's move to Yellow Cliff, continued to take an active role in the expanding community as one of Jizhong's most trusted lieutenants.[35] Zhang's favorite disciple was his cousin Wu Zaixun, who moved to Yellow Cliff after dismissal from his official position in 1862 on grounds of incompetence in handling the Liu Depei uprising (described in Chapter 2).[36] Two women also served as high-level disciples. One of the two, widowed at an early age, had been married to the grandson of Zhou Xingyuan, Zhang's old mentor from Yangzhou days. The other was Jizhong's own niece. The women were housed in special quarters and anyone who visited them was required to perform nine kowtows, the same ritual as required for an audience with Zhang himself.[37] For military services, Zhang depended upon two members of a local gentry family, the fifth and sixth Zhu brothers. Inasmuch as their elder brother was a degree holder and leader of the militia in the nearby town of Shuilipu, the two Zhu brothers could draw on the help of regular defense forces to provide protection for the Yellow Cliff inhabitants.[38]

From many accounts, however, it seems that Yellow Cliff also relied upon some less savory elements in its quest for defense. To ensure the safety of the many affluent residents, additional personnel were employed as armed guards. These hired watchmen were drawn largely from the "riffraff" of Shandong society and apparently included within their ranks a number of salt smugglers. Zhang Jizhong welcomed such persons as new recruits to his religion, emphasizing that even the lowly could become prized disciples. In keeping with the Taizhou tradition, he proclaimed his doctrine to be one of equality, making no distinction between the mighty and the meek among his followers.[39] As time would show, however, the Yellow Cliff community was to pay dearly for its ties to the less respectable side of Shandong society.

But we are getting ahead of our story. Several years were to pass before the bloody massacre of 1866. And in the meantime, what was life like for the thousands of refugees gathered under Zhang's leadership on Yellow Cliff?

The educational regimen was apparently quite strict. New members were lodged in a sort of schoolhouse where they were put through an intensive instructional program in the ways of the faith. Though Jizhong himself took little part in this educational process, he charged his trusted disciples with responsibility for inculcating his teachings. By the end of the orientation period, believers were expected to be able to recite from memory many of Zhang's writings. Once initiated, followers bared their right shoulders as a mark of commitment and were enjoined against leaving the mountain without permission. Their new life was supposed to be free of concern for material wealth or sexual desire.[40]

To provide continuing spiritual inspiration, Zhang conducted nightly worship services in a large hall atop the mountain known as Sage Hall (*shengrentang*). The ceremonies featured his two women disciples, costumed in lavish attire and armed with swords. Huge quantities of incense and sandalwood were burned, giving off a brilliant illumination that could be seen for miles. Zhang himself dressed for the occasion in ancient garb and pontificated in flowery language. Although the altar where the ceremonies were held was ostensibly dedicated to Confucius,[41] the extravagant form of worship gave rise to suspicions in the surrounding countryside. Only bona fide members of the faith were permitted to attend the proceedings, which were known among the country folk as "Sage Zhang's night rite."[42] Whereas worship services were restricted to the initiated devotees, public lectures drew a much wider audience. Each month, Zhang presented philosophic lectures attended by scholars from throughout the Feicheng and Jinan area. The talks were intended to explicate the syncretic teachings of the Taizhou tradition, pointing out the convergence of Confucian and Buddhist principles and criticizing too narrow an intellectual approach.[43] Although Zhang was adamant in his claim to be elucidating the fundamentals of Confucianism, there was public suspicion. Whether due to lack of clarity in his presentation, a misunderstanding or misrepresentation on the part of the listeners, or to the truly novel content of the message, the lecture series gave rise to widespread rumors that Zhang was preaching a heterodox religion.[44]

Yet however much outsiders may have suspected the goings-on at Yellow Cliff, Zhang's thousands of followers showed no lack of faith. It was the spiritual and material commitment of these believers that permitted Yellow Cliff to develop into a prospering religious and commercial center. New members were expected to contribute half of their wealth to Zhang Jizhong, who managed it on behalf of the mountain community.[45] The influx of faithful adherents and their largess prompted the establishment of a number of shops in the area—all under Zhang's control—to serve the needs of the burgeoning population. Sales profits were then used to meet the expenses of the Yellow Cliff society. The community also opened salt shops at a number of strategic points along the Yellow River, expanding its commercial network until it extended across an area some 300 miles in length.[46] Since the sale of salt was by law a strictly government-authorized monopoly, we are tempted to speculate that Yellow Cliff's entry into the market may have been facilitated by the salt smugglers among its following. Regardless of their possibly illicit connections, the stores were clearly a profitable undertaking.

Economic support for the community also came from three farming villages located in the foothills of Yellow Cliff. Named South, Central, and North Yellow Cliff, the three villages circled the base of the mountain. Apparently, most of the resident peasants declared allegiance to Zhang Jizhong, although many of them proved incapable of mastering the memorization required for full initiation into the faith. Such persons were free to return home to their native villages. The harvest of their agricultural labors, we may surmise, was important for maintaining the community of faithful atop Yellow Cliff.[47]

Two medical centers were established under Jizhong's direction: one located on Yellow Cliff, the other in the nearby town of Shuilipu. Administering the traditional cures for which Zhang's forebears had gained reknown, the centers proved tremendously popular among the neighboring inhabitants.[48]

It is unclear what political structure emerged to manage the Yellow Cliff population with its sizable numbers and diversified activities. The community apparently operated as some form of theocracy, with high priest and teacher Zhang Jizhong nominally in charge. Although the weakness of the system was to be proved by later events, there was at least some effort at institutionalization. Public offices (*gongju*) were set up at both the foot and top of the mountain for registering the population and handling other internal affairs.[49] Defense, as we have seen, depended upon a combination of militia and hired guards.

Yellow Cliff was thus a fully functioning social community, complete with a distinctive set of educational, religious, economic, medical, political, and military practices.[50] But if Yellow Cliff was a community apart from mainstream Chinese society, was it also a community in arms against it? Soon we will hear the government's indictment of the mountain refuge, but before listening to the case for the prosecution, let us turn to one of our most valuable sources: the travelogue of a visitor to Yellow Cliff just ten days before the alleged insurrection.[51]

The visitor was a *jinshi* and several-time magistrate by the name of Wang Baoshu, a resident of Taian County, located about thirty miles southeast of Yellow Cliff. His trip to the mountain was undertaken at the urging of two friends, gentry from nearby Ningyang County, who informed Wang that there was much talk of strange happenings at Yellow

Cliff. To satisfy their curiosity about the situation and take in some sight-seeing along the way, the three headed off to the west, accompanied by two servants.

After several days of travel, the visitors approached Yellow Cliff. Seeing that the villages at the foot of the mountain seemed calm enough, the travelers registered at the public office there and settled in for the night. That evening they were cordially hosted by several members of the Yellow Cliff community: Yu Sun, from a prominent family in Zhejiang, and the two Zhu brothers. The talk was mainly of poetry and literature, and the Yellow Cliff residents remarked on the inaccuracy of suspicions that magic was being practiced in their community.

The following day, Wang and his companions toured the foothill villages and were impressed that the peasants—housed for the most part in caves—were contently going about their farming. The visitors also paid a brief courtesy call on Zhang Jizhong, duly noting his fine family reputation and the respect that he was accorded by the other residents. That evening they stayed at the home of Liu Yaodong, original inhabitant of the mountain and Zhang's loyal disciple. Their conversation together touched on a wide range of topics: the amount of rainfall, Korea's resistance to the West, the whereabouts of the Nian rebels, and the dependability of the Yellow Cliff defense. Apparently much concerned about the rebel threat, Liu suggested that the men should keep in touch so as to exchange information on rebel activities.

After a most pleasant evening in Liu's company, the visitors were taken the following day by Yu Sun and the Zhu brothers on a guided tour of the fort. Leaving the foothill village, the men climbed up narrow trails through rugged terrain for a distance of about a mile until they reached the main gate of the fort, built of square stones and strengthened by an iron gate. Walking along the mountain rim for another 500 yards or so, they came to a second gate. Scattered across the empty field in front of this inner gate were pieces of broken jars. When Wang inquired as to the purpose of the jars, he was told they had originally been placed there by refugees (to serve as storage bins in time of crisis), but had since been damaged by stones thrown by shepherds on the mountain, apparently oblivious to the need for self-defense.

Within the second gate were several cannon, rusted to the point of being very nearly worthless. Asked Wang, "Why don't you put the cannon under the protection of the gate? If you leave them exposed to wind and rain, your defense will be spoiled when the crisis comes." Yu reprimanded the gatekeepers for their negligence and ordered the cannon moved under the gate. Seeing that much of the stockade walls had collapsed, Wang inquired as to why they were not being repaired. Replied his hosts, "It isn't easy to manage public affairs here. The villagers, being accustomed to peace and busy with their farming, are not willing to do the repair work. Fortunately this is a remote and secluded place, treacherous enough to frighten off bandits. Besides, we do have some reliable means of defense. There's nothing really to worry about." Wang pursued his line of questioning, pressing, "With a fort this large how *do* you defend it?" Smiling, Yu answered, "Security is based on the Zhu brothers' 800 hand-picked fighting men. Without their help we'd have nothing to depend upon."

At the summit of the mountain, the visitors came upon another public office, a three-pillar structure overgrown with grass. Next to it were a dozen small rooms, also designated for handling public affairs. The rooms were connected by a winding corridor constructed in the southern architectural style that reflected the tastes of most of the fort leaders, transplanted as they were from homes hundreds of miles to the south. A house supported by two pillars was the refugee residence of Zhang's cousin Wu Zaixun. Primitive, leaky, and unoccupied, the structures were made of stone with thatched roofing. Shelters for the other inhabitants of Yellow Cliff were also constructed of stone, each unit enjoying a space of only a few square feet. Except for weeds on the earthen floors, the rooms were empty. Pampas grass and mugwort covered the mountainside, which harbored not a person in sight.

East of the fort was a strategic spot protected by a foot-high wall of square stones and surrounded by a sturdy fence. On the wall was an inscription naming it the "Joyous Homecoming Terrace." A side gate leading through the wall into the fort had been prepared for the use of villagers on the east side of the mountain. Going out the side gate and climbing another few hundred yards, the visitors saw a winding red banister that led much of the way up the mountain. By its side was a stone tablet designating the path the "Herb-Picking Trail," presumably used in procuring drugs for the Yellow Cliff medical centers. Along the trail was a hexagonal pavilion, and at the trail's end stood a small room in good repair where a man was studying. One of the Zhu brothers explained that these structures had all been built with the odds and ends of wood and bamboo left over from house construction. The banister was intended to keep the children and elderly from falling and had been painted red to look attractive as well. The wall was defensive, but had also been designed for people to stand on. The pavilion and study were resting areas that could also serve as shelters in the event of a bandit attack. Simple as the structures were in reality, when viewed from the foot of the mountain, they reminded Wang of the elaborate Wuyi Pavilion of Fujian Province.[52]

After this tour of the fort, the group returned to the public office at the base of the mountain, where they spent a final night before heading homeward. Just a few days after arriving home, Wang heard the shocking news of the Yellow Cliff massacre.

While Wang's travelogue is silent on many of the critical issues that we would like to explore—the personality of Zhang Jizhong, the nature of political authority, the social composition of the inhabitants—the account does go far toward dispelling any interpretation of Yellow Cliff as a community poised on the verge of rebellion. From Wang's narrative emerges the picture of a settled group, founded upon the toil of a hard-working peasantry and led by urbane intellectuals anxious about the security of their community, but more immediately occupied with other concerns.

Why then the confrontation? What sent government troops up its treacherous mountainside to destroy Yellow Cliff, in the process slaughtering thousands of seemingly innocent inhabitants?

The Plot Thickens: Government Suspicions of Yellow Cliff

That something extraordinary might be happening at Yellow Cliff first came to the attention of the provincial authorities in the late fall of 1865. At the time a man by the name of Wang Xiaohua was arrested by officials in Wei County. Wang had been packing up his entire household in preparation for a move to Yellow Cliff, some 130 miles away. Finding this to be rather peculiar behavior, the Weixian magistrate arrested Wang. Under questioning, Wang testified that he had been recruited to the Yellow Cliff community, had acknowledged Zhang Jizhong as his teacher, and was planning to join the throngs of other believers congregating on the mountain.

The magistrate reported the incident to the governor's office, calling for a full investigation. In response, the governor of Shandong, Yan Jingming, dispatched two emissaries to visit Yellow Cliff. The two officials met with Zhang Jizhong and were impressed by the lofty words and distinguished appearance of the elderly scholar. They took special note of the fact that Zhang's family had been loyal to the throne for generations and that many of Jizhong's closest relatives boasted civil service degrees and official positions. Zhang's teachings seemed harmless enough and his followers were obviously peacefully engaged in farming and studying. Furthermore, the emissaries established that Zhang had never heard of Wang Xiaohua from distant Wei County. In short, there seemed no grounds for alarm. Governor Yan was happy to dismiss the case.[53]

The following year, however, yet another incident was to bring the name of Yellow Cliff to the governor's attention. In October 1866, at a time when the Nian threat to Shandong was particularly acute, a rebel plot was uncovered in Yidu County, some 100 miles northeast of Yellow Cliff. Under interrogation, the captured leader of the forestalled uprising, Ji Zhonghua, claimed that five members of his group, still at large, were students of Zhang of Yellow Cliff.[54] Zhang, he went on, had ordered them to amass people and horses in preparation for a late autumn uprising aimed at occupying the prefectural cities of Yidu and Jinan so as to gain control of the province. Searching within his own city, the magistrate of Yidu reported capturing eleven rebels who also claimed allegiance to Yellow Cliff and also admitted plans for the seizure of Yidu and Jinan. All but one of the prospective rebels was executed; the lucky one was imprisoned, retained as a witness to testify against Zhang Jizhong.[55]

Several other disturbing reports concerning Yellow Cliff reached Governor Yan at about this same time. One was that of an army general by the name of Qi Shan. While passing through the Yellow Cliff area one day, Qi had happened to stop at an inn for lunch. After finishing the meal, the officer was told by the innkeeper that his bill had already been paid by Mr. Zhang, who was inviting him up the mountain for a rest. Suspicious, the general declined the offer and notified Governor Yan.[56] A second report concerned an expectant Shandong circuit intendant who had just been married in the capital. When the bridegroom announced three days after the wedding that he was about to depart for Yellow Cliff to listen to a lecture by Zhang Jizhong, his wife was understandably upset. Although she remonstrated with her husband, he insisted that Jizhong's rules were so strict that he had no choice but to go. The wife then reported this strange behavior to her parents, who feared that their new son-in-law was involved in heterodox religion. Afraid their family might be ruined as a result, the father—also a circuit intendant—informed Governor Yan.[57]

Having learned the unsettling news of these events, Governor Yan again dispatched an investigation party to Yellow Cliff, this time composed of the magistrates of Feicheng and Changqing counties as well as an army captain from the provincial capital. The envoys were to instruct Zhang Jizhong to come to the provincial capital to testify, and to explain to him that because of his advanced age and prestigious family background the government had no intention of killing him. When the delegation, accompanied by the sizable retinue, reached Yellow Cliff, they came across Zhang's cousin, Wu Zaixun. The former prefect of Jinan was in the process of hurriedly moving his family out of the mountain. Wu informed the visiting officials that his cousin was away on a sightseeing trip to nearby Five-Peak Mountain. Suddenly someone rushed forth from Yellow Cliff with a letter for Wu, who, visibly shaken, urged the officials to be on their way.[58] Seeing that something was amiss, the army captain mounted his horse to dash off, but not before one of his servants was killed by someone from the fort. The magistrate of Feicheng managed to enter the fort, but rushed out when he met cannon fire that killed one of his servants as well.[59]

Perhaps, as one source tells us, the inhabitants of Yellow Cliff mistook the officials and their entourage for bandits and fired in self-defense.[60] Perhaps, as other sources suggest, the army captain returned to Governor Yan with a distorted account as so to cover up his own mishandling of the incident.[61] That we do not know. What we do know is that the governor reacted to the news as evidence of an extremely serious crisis brewing at Yellow Cliff. In an apparent effort to prevent an explosion, Yan contacted the son of Zhang Jizhong, Zhang Shaoling, an expectant magistrate awaiting assignment in Shandong. The governor instructed Shaoling to go to Yellow Cliff to convince his father to come forth with an explanation, setting a five-day time limit after which the mountain would be attacked mercilessly.

Although Shaoling went dutifully to persuade his father, Zhang Jizhong remained unmoved. As the story goes, he explained to his son, "I have committed no crime by my teachings. There is no proof that I am a rebel; to go would serve only to verify their suspicions. People simply wish to incriminate me. Greedy officials hope to make a big case out of this to improve their own positions. If you are afraid, go yourself." Tearful pleading from both son and wife did nothing to shake the elderly Zhang from his resolution to remain within the mountain stockade. Insisted Jizhong, "I will not go to the governor's office. To do so would mean my death. I am a gentleman and, while willing to die at the sword, am not willing to die in prison. I will sacrifice my life for my scholarship." Seeing that his father was not to be moved, Shaoling, obedient son that he was, elected to stay in Yellow Cliff as well.[62]

When Governor Yan received no answer from Shaoling, he turned to another of Jizhong's relatives, cousin Wu, for assistance. Now it was Wu's turn to try his hand at talking the elderly Zhang down from his hideaway. However, when he reached the foot of Yellow Cliff, Wu was denied admission to the fort.[63]

While these behind-the-scenes efforts at convincing Zhang to surrender were stalling, other more visible events moved dramatically forward. The day after Yellow Cliff's confrontation with the governor's special delegation, it was reported that all the mountain inhabitants were being moved into the upper stockade. Soon a red flag was raised at the top of the mountain and banners were placed along the fort walls. The trails were jammed with people transporting firewood, grain, coal, and candles into the fort. It was further learned that salt smugglers were delivering arms to the mountain, moving the goods by boat along the Yellow River to Shuilipu. At night, several hundred Yellow Cliff inhabitants, garbed in red turbans, were said to have looted neighboring towns for mules and horses. Several villagers and two postal couriers were killed in the melee.[64]

Climax: The Battle of Yellow Cliff

When government cavalry approached the vicinity of Shuilipu, the market town within six miles of Yellow Cliff that served as headquarters for the Zhu brothers' militia, they came across robbers looting wildly. Several of the culprits were arrested; the rest retreated to the safety of Yellow Cliff. Why now were persons from the mountain plundering the home of their own defense force? It appears that the Yellow Cliff community's main means of defense had abandoned them in this time of crisis—willing, perhaps, to fight bandits but not the imperial state. Certainly, there is no evidence of the 800 hand-picked men in reports of the ensuing battle. And we are told that the Zhu brothers were the only important residents of Yellow Cliff who escaped harm in the debacle.[65]

Whatever the role of the Shuilipu militia, we do know that other local corps in the area fought actively on the government side. One Feicheng resident, Wang Zonggan, had financed the training of braves (*xiangyong*) for the express purpose of battling Yellow Cliff. Because Wang had refused repeated invitations to join the mountain community, his home was reportedly burned by persons from Yellow Cliff during the chaotic days just before the government attack. Although Governor Yan had been intending to annihilate all the surrounding villages, having been informed that they were loyal to Zhang Jizhong, Wang went to explain to Yan that he had not submitted to Jizhong, and offered a battle plan for taking the Yellow Cliff fort. When the governor seemed skeptical, Wang detained some fifty relatives as proof of his good intentions. Joined by his younger brother, a degree holder, he then led his braves against the fort.[66] Official local corps from Feicheng County and Taian Prefecture also added strength to the government forces. The result was a combined army that numbered more than 12,000 troops, of whom about one-third were local braves and militia.[67]

In the initial few days of fighting, the official forces found the steep mountain a formidable obstacle. They could do no more than painfully inch up the treacherous trails. The defenders of the fort controlled the opening rounds of fights, although government cannon fire claimed the lives of Jizhong's disciple Liu Yaodong and more than ten of his companions. Persisting, the government managed to take a few of the lower barricades, where they reported seizing rebel cannon, flags, bamboo poles, and fowling spears.[68]

After several days of intense fighting, the government called a temporary cease-fire to make known its lenient policy for any who surrendered. Again Wu Zaixun was called upon to make contact with his cousin, this time by writing a letter to Zhang Jizhong asking for his surrender. Two days later, Wu's envoy returned with a reply. Zhang's letter read:

> Your letter criticizes my reluctance to come forth and defend myself against the charges. Although willing, I have reasons for not complying with the request. I have never had much appetite for glory or profit, my sole aim being to study. With the world in such chaos, I have sought a life of seclusion in order to pursue my aim. Hearing of my undeserved reputation as a recluse, people were much impressed and thronged to my doorstep bearing gifts. Although there were many good folk among them, there were some reckless elements as well. I had hoped to reform them by my virtue, but I am to blame for not being more selective in my choice of acquaintances. I have been in Shandong for ten years now. Have I dared commit even a single reckless act? Last year I was implicated in the Wang Xiaohua affair, and this year in the Ji Zhonghua incident. With regard to these matters I would certainly have come forward and made an open testimony had I received a written request to do so from Deng Xin and Chen Enshou [magistrates of Feicheng and Changqing counties]. Instead, these two officials came here with soldiers. Fortunately I was away on a trip. Otherwise I would have been bound in criminal confinement long ago. Again soldiers were sent at night, confusing the villagers and prompting them to fight and inflict injuries on the troops.
>
> Knowing that disaster is at hand and that I cannot elude it, I per-

sonally preferred to exercise restraint, to await defeat with no hope of redress for the great wrong that has been done me. However, some of my followers have usurped my authority and I am powerless to deter them. For several days I have hesitated in a state of depression. When the army came I wanted to go forth and explain, but the situation was in such a disastrous state that little could be said. I considered suicide, but was deterred by the violent effect that my death would have had upon my followers, who would surely avenge the injustice. I want to disband my multitude of followers, but they are numerous and not a few are very belligerent. Please grant me time by temporarily withdrawing your troops from the mountain so that we can calmly disperse. When you profess to pacify us while simultaneously attacking militarily, you do not inspire trust. A cornered beast will fight in desperation. How can I convince my followers?[69]

Upon receipt of the letter, Governor Yan again proclaimed his conditions for pacification, declaring that anyone within the fort who surrendered voluntarily would not be punished. A two-day period was set for people to give themselves up, but not a single person ventured forth from the mountain. Instead, weapons were fired from the stockade wall, injuring some of the government forces.

Afraid that both sides would suffer unbearable casualties, Yan again called a temporary halt to the hostilities. On that day, Jizhong's son Zhang Shaoling came out to speak with the governor. He was given one day in which to produce a name list of all the officials residing on Yellow Cliff. In addition, the governor again instructed Wu to write a letter to his cousin promising that he would be spared if he complied with government orders. Outside the fort, Yan ordered that white banners be raised on which were written in red characters: "No punishment for those who were followers against their will; no death to any who surrenders." That evening another letter was received from Jizhong in answer to Wu. It read simply, "The people are agitated and I cannot make any move. We must postpone compilation of the list [of those who would surrender]."[70]

Rumors spread that Zhang's letter was simply a delaying tactic, that spies had been sent from Yellow Cliff to contact salt bandits and Nian rebels for help. Indeed, a report from the magistrate of Caoxian confirmed that a captured Nian spy had confessed to being on his way north to provide assistance to Yellow Cliff.[71]

Fearful of a united rebel offensive from several directions, Yan ordered a full-scale attack on the mountain.[72] A ferocious battle ensued in which thousands were slaughtered and countless tumbled over the cliff to their deaths. Not a single person among the 10,000 inhabitants surrendered, despite the fact that they included more than 200 official families.[73]

When Zhang Jizhong knew the end was near, he gathered his family and closest disciples—some 200 persons in all—to Sage Hall, their place of worship atop the mountain. As may have been customary for their regular worship services, the group arranged itself according to seniority, with Jizhong seated in the place of honor. Gunpowder was spread across the floor. With the news that the fortress gate had been taken, the powder was ignited. The explosion could be heard for miles.[74]

Although a number of other Yellow Cliff followers were captured by the attacking forces, they all insisted that their sole desire was to follow their teacher to death. No amount of pressure from the authorities could wring a confession from them. As Governor Yan described these true believers to the Tongzhi emperor, "Their eyes were fixed in wide stares, as though they were under some strange spell." Thus the fort was annihilated, with only some 400 women and children spared from government fire. Even the women, remarked the governor, "wore expressions of serenity."[75]

The government soldiers, we can imagine, wore rather different expressions on their faces that day. For the slaughter was followed by wild looting on the part of the troops. The repeated orders issued by Governor Yan that night to restrain them had no effect. The soldiers, delerious with the sight of the wonderful riches left by the slain inhabitants of Yellow Cliff, were not to be deterred from seizing their share.[76]

After the chaos had abated, Governor Yan personally climbed the mountain to inspect. Passing through the iron gates and stone walls into the fort, he headed for the worship hall, site of the immolation of Zhang Jizhong and his 200 closest disciples. As the governor reported the scene to the emperor, the hall was filled with a series of staircases and daises, imperial in appearance. Screens were draped with yellow cloth. Tables and chairs were also made of the forbidden imperial color. From the ashes were retrieved yellow silk curtains as well as 100 round and 100 square tablecloths. Other forbidden items had been lost to the flames and could not be salvaged. The charred head of Zhang Jizhong was recovered and gleefully displayed on a pole. Outside the hall swords and bamboo poles were reportedly heaped in a massive pile. Pieces of lead and sulphur were found, along with an inventory of military weapons. Copies of the inventory and of one of Zhang Jizhong's books were sent to the Grand Council for perusal.[77]

Although it was difficult to ascertain the names of the officials who had been immolated together with Zhang Jizhong, Yan ordered that an effort be made to retrieve their bodies from the ashes.[78] The following day local people were called in to identify the corpses, which were buried in a pond in front of Sage Hall—women on one side, men on the other.[79]

The governor instructed local officials to care for the 400 surviving women and children and to make redress to villagers who had suffered from the disturbance.[80] He then ordered investigations of the shops that had been operated under Yellow Cliff auspices. It was discovered that the stores had all closed down just before the official troops had been dispatched, and that their employees had fled. "Rebel" books and pamphlets in "reckless and exaggerated language" were found on the premises. Concluding that the shops had been part of a wide rebel network, Yan had them sealed up. He also ordered that traditional Shandong bandit lairs (e.g., White Lotus Pond) be secretly investigated to ascertain possible connections to the Yellow Cliff incident. The results of these investigations suggested, however, that there was no cause for concern.[81]

As was to be expected in a military undertaking of this magnitude, high rewards were forthcoming for dozens of the officials who had assisted in the government assault.[82] The only major participants who did not receive awards were Chen Enshou, magistrate of Changqing and Deng Xin, magistrate of Feicheng. Since Yellow Cliff was located along the border of these two counties, the magistrates were held responsible for the incident. Deng Xin was dismissed from his post for having turned "a deaf ear and a blind eye" to the rebellion brewing in his jurisdiction.[83] Another who most notably did not benefit from the incident was Jizhong's hapless cousin, Wu Zaixun. Governor Yan recommended that Wu be permanently barred from official position and that he be assigned to the military to work off his disgrace. The emperor was less generous. For a crime as grave as Wu's, nothing less than hard labor in the distant province of Heilongjiang would do, he decreed.[84]

Governor Yan himself seemed humbled by the catastrophe. His summary memorial to the emperor expressed exasperation and puzzlement. Of Zhang Jizhong he wrote,

> His family was not wealthy, yet he was able in the space of fewer than ten years in Shandong to establish markets across the province and trick people with his magic so as to obtain funds for attracting and organizing desperadoes. His followers, numbering hundreds of households, took to the mountain all their possessions, sacrificing both their wealth and their lives for him. I cannot fathom what religion he practiced and what magic he used that could dupe men so thoroughly.[85]

Yet Yan acknowledged that his initial inquiries had suggested Jizhong to be "a learned and upright man." As he confessed to the emperor, "I am ashamed of my own blindness."[86] Shortly thereafter Governor Yan, pleading illness, offered his resignation.

Attempt at a Denouement

The conflagration at Sage Hall destroyed Zhang Jizhong's Yellow Cliff community. It did not, however, destroy the teachings upon which that community had been founded. After the incident, Li Guangxin, favored disciple of Zhang Jizhong's mentor Zhou, continued to propagate the faith, although now in more clandestine fashion.[87]

The government's indictment of Yellow Cliff did not deter a number of prominent persons from continuing to evidence interest in the Taizhou school. One example was Liu E—scholar, official, and author of the famous novel *Lao Can youji*. Liu's studies with Li Guangxin in Yangzhou led him to a kind of religious conversion that is said to have given rise to his well-known sense of social responsibility. The character of Lao Can, a representation of Liu himself, demonstrates the combination of independence and social concern for which Taizhou adherents were famous. Lao Can's dual interest in philosophy and healing techniques shows another characteristic of the tradition.[88]

After Li Guangxin's death, it was Liu E who convinced a fellow Taizhou follower, Huang Guiqun, to resign his magistracy in Shandong and establish a lecture hall in Suzhou, just west of Shanghai. In 1902, Huang, a Yangzhou native, opened his academy in Suzhou. Thanks to the sponsorship of several wealthy supporters,[89] stipends were offered that permitted more than 100 students to live at the school. The curriculum was unconventional; instruction was largely oral, with scant use of written texts. Students were encouraged to discuss popular novels, local gossip, and even to reveal and analyze their nightly dreams.[90]

All told, Huang Guiqun's followers soon numbered in the thousands, scattered across the land and including many members of the elite. Before his death in 1924, Huang designated his top disciple Li Taijie, grandson of Li Guangxin, to inherit the leadership of the Taizhou tradition. Taijie himself died shortly thereafter, however, leaving the school without a master.[91] Around the Yellow Cliff area itself, many people continued to adhere to the Taizhou faith, although over time much of the philosophical content of the teachings disappeared, until the remnant band was little more than a kind of Daoist sect. According to interviews with residents of the Yellow Cliff area in 1957, in the recent past believers still went annually to the mountain to perform religious rites.[92]

The continued popularity of the tradition indicated that more than a few persons looked back with disfavor on the government's handling of the Yellow Cliff affair. In 1906, an imperial censor from Sichuan—reportedly a Taizhou believer—petitioned the Guangxu emperor to reopen the case. In talks with Shandong gentry and officials, the censor had learned that local notables were of the unanimous opinion that Governor Yan had acted improperly in the incident. Frightened by the chaotic situation in Shandong at the time, they said, the governor had overreacted to unsubstantiated rumor, prematurely using force against a group that was primarily defensive in nature. The censor called for an investigation by the current Shandong governor, Yang Wenjing, to determine the true facts of the case and posthumously to exonerate Zhang Jizhong should he be found innocent. Instructed by the emperor to look into the matter, Governor Yang ascertained that although there were probably some persons in Yellow Cliff who had resisted the authorities, Jizhong himself had been a loyal scholar. Nevertheless, not wishing to tarnish the reputation of his predecessor, Governor Yan Jingming, Yang concealed the findings and allowed the matter to be quietly dropped.[93]

If the issue was too controversial to be settled by the Qing authorities, can we with the distance of a century come to any verdict? To be sure, a number of the critical facts are tantalizingly missing. Many of the reports are blatantly contradictory. Yet in trying to put the pieces of the puzzle together, one is hard-pressed to construct a picture of Zhang Jizhong as rebel. This was a man whose brother had died at the hands of Taiping rebels, whose cousin had gained fame by suppressing the Nian, who had himself fought and fled, first Taiping and then Nian.[94] He had led his community through some five years of peace and had in the process drawn hundreds of officials to his cause, attracted both by his teachings and by the shelter that his mountain fort offered in those troubled times. Zhang's was a classic protective movement, inspired and organized by a group of affluent notables whose underlying motive was the defense of persons and property. Faced with a disintegrating and incompetent government, they devoted their energies to building an alternative system that would provide the physical and spiritual security so absent in the larger society. Visitors to Yellow Cliff—from curious gentry to official delegations—were all impressed by the purely defensive motives behind the mountain refuge.

Certainly the government's indictment of the Yellow Cliff community seems contrived. The fact that suspicious persons may have claimed a connection to Zhang Jizhong was hardly convincing proof of rebel intentions on the part of the leader himself. Furthermore, the most incriminating indication of rebellious designs on the part of Zhang Jizhong—the yellow cloth allegedly strewn around Sage Hall—turns out to be open to question as well. According to several sources, after the massacre Governor Yan was distraught at lacking any hard evidence of imperial pretensions on the part of the Yellow Cliff inhabitants. He called in his generals and threatened them with death if they failed within three days to produce some proof that the slaughter had been justified. The generals are said to have hired seven tailors to make the incriminating materials.[95] All seven were later killed to suppress the true story.[96] Indeed, it does seem rather unlikely that silk would have survived the explosion intact.

But why should Governor Yan have felt it necessary to order the assault in the face of such flimsy evidence? Government ineptitude was doubtless a crucial factor in the decision. The Yellow Cliff case offers a dramatic instance of Qing administration in decline. Intelligence was inadequate, communications unreliable, and decisions ill-advised. That Yellow Cliff persisted so long as a separate community beyond the reaches of the state security system is striking evidence of bureaucratic incompetence. That the governor was able to ascertain so little about this group of 8,000 households, including as they did a generous representation of scholars and officials, is even more incriminating.

Yet the finger of blame may well point beyond mere bureaucratic bungling. For beneath the surface of the story seems to lie the outline of a more sinister explanation for Governor Yan's behavior. In the fall of 1866, the Shandong officialdom was hard-pressed for success stories to report to their superiors in Beijing. Tax resistance and rebellion had assumed epidemic proportions in the province, and official careers had plummeted in step. Governor Yan himself had been demoted in rank during the spring of 1866 and was on the verge of losing his official career because of the rampant unrest in his province.[97] Do we pay the man an unwarranted insult in suggesting that Yellow Cliff might have seemed a profitable and relatively low-risk means of regaining lost prestige?[98] In any event, one outcome of the affair—despite Yan's offer to resign—was the restoration of his former rank. Not long after, the governor was promoted to such prestigious national posts as Grand Council secretary, president of the Board of Revenue, and acting president of the Board of War.[99] The suppression of an allegedly heterodox rebellion, in a campaign personally overseen by the governor himself, was undoubtedly of some assistance in furthering Yan's subsequent career.

Yellow Cliff was surrounded by enough circumstantial suggestion of wrongdoing to render it a tempting candidate for the accusation of heterodoxy. First, the syncretic philosophy and healing practices espoused by the community could be construed as a challenge to orthodox doctrine, narrowly defined. The tribute paid to Ming philosophers Wang Yangming, Wang Gen, and Lin Zhaoen in preference to rigid Cheng-Zhu neo-Confucianism implied impatience with Qing orthodoxy and perhaps hinted at sympathies for a Ming restoration.

Even more potentially incriminating was the social composition of the movement. If the position of Zhang's two female disciples is any indication, women were accorded respect and equality. That fact alone opened the group to the criminal charge of "mingling of the sexes." Further difficulties arose from the inclusion of salt smugglers among the mountain community. Yellow Cliff, like most large social movements, was a coalition of a variety of classes and interests. As in many Chinese protective institutions (see Chapter 1)—the night watch, the household guard, the crop-watching association, the village militia—manpower was drawn largely from the lower ranks of rural society. Although the leadership might be propertied and their rationale defensive, ordinary recruits often exhibited a rather different status and outlook.

In the case of Yellow Cliff, the alliance between elite and outcast was sanctioned by the Taizhou tradition. Founder Wang Gen, let us remember, was himself a salt merchant with commercial ties to Shandong outlets. Wang had struggled for the rights of poor salt farmers and had welcomed the lowly as well as the lettered into his unusual school. We do not know whether those same links between Taizhou philosophy and the Shandong salt market had persisted for more than three centuries, preparing the way for Zhang Jizhong's refugee flight north and his contacts with salt smugglers in Shandong. What we do know is that the Taizhou faith was based on the principle of open recruitment. Zhang Jizhong was thus morally bound to welcome to his entourage the less respectable side of Shandong society.

Although Jizhong did not develop his community as a cover or pretext for rebellion, quite the contrary, it is plausible that others on the fringes of his following were willing to undertake such a move.[100] Threatened by government pressure, some of the Yellow Cliff smugglers apparently decided to throw in their lot with the Nian rebels—persons with whom they almost certainly enjoyed business dealings.

The combination of ideology and practical necessity that had attracted gentry and smugglers alike also laid the basis for later disaster. Although it is impossible to reconstruct the exact nature of the ties between smugglers and gentry that bound them in a joint struggle to the death against overwhelming opposition, the merger of outlaw and rural elite in the face of government intrusion was an explosive partnership.

To be sure, Governor Yan had his reasons for acting precipitously. The Nian were closing in, heterodox rebels had recently been captured elsewhere in the province,[101] Yellow Cliff was less than thirty miles from his capital, and its leader was by all reports capable and intelligent. Viewed with the advantage of hindsight, however, it is clear that Yan's hasty and uninformed decisions resulted in the unnecessary slaughter of 10,000 people. It was a classic example of the kind of governmental heavy-handedness that would, over the succeeding decades, serve increasingly to alienate segments of the Chinese rural elite from government authority and to draw protector and predatory bandit together in armed resistance.

Half a century later, as the fledgling Republican state proved no better able to impose control on the countryside than had its late Qing predecessor, religiously inspired protective groups mushroomed across North China. Although originally initiated by local notables against brigandage, the Red Spears movement of the 1920s—boasting at its height a membership of some 3 million—also attracted outlaws to its side in the competitive struggle for survival. Like their forerunners on Yellow Cliff, the Red Spears adopted a peculiar combination of Confucianism and religion symptomatic of their disillusionment with the ineffective Chinese state and its cultural foundation. Again like the gentry assembled on Yellow Cliff, the Red Spears were not initially rebels. They became so only when pressed by misguided government interference.

In the 1860s, cases of large numbers of the rural elite adhering to a peculiar religious doctrine, incorporating outlaws, and resisting government intrusion were rare. Thus the *mystery* of Yellow Cliff. Some five decades later, though with many a change to be sure, such cases were ordinary. And thus the significance of Yellow Cliff.

Notes

An earlier version of this chapter was co-authored with Tom Chang and appeared in *Modern China* (April 1980). The authors gratefully acknowledge the helpful suggestions of David Buck, David Jordan, Robert Kapp, Susan Naquin, and especially K.C. Liu and Joseph Esherick. Appreciation is also extended to Chen Hua of National Taiwan University for his generous assistance in obtaining source materials.

The major source for this chapter is the *Shandong jindaishi ziliao*, vol. 1, 1957. This invaluable collection includes reprints of more than twenty documents on the Yellow Cliff incident.

1. *Shandong jindaishi*, 1957: 129, 133, 173–174.
2. Ibid., 174.
3. Ibid., 134, 164. The accounts may not be contradictory, inasmuch as the purchase of degrees was widespread at the time.
4. *Shandong jindaishi*, 1957: 129, 164, 170. It may well be significant that Zhou Tianjue was an ardent believer in Wang Yangming's theory of innate knowledge. As we shall see, this theory formed a central tenet in the teachings of the school with which Zhang Jizhong was associated.
5. *Shandong jindaishi*, 1957. After the fall of Nanjing to the rebels, Jizhong became a sworn brother to two of his colleagues in the suppression campaign: Qian Jiang, former governor of Shanxi, and Lei Hegao, holder of the *jinshi* degree and vice-president of the Board of Punishments.
6. *Shandong jindaishi*, 1957: 137.
7. Ibid., 174.
8. The most notable of these is the *Shandong junxing jilüe* (Annals of Shandong military campaigns), *Shandong jindaishi*, 1957: 173–180. The annals were compiled by the secretary of Yan Jingming, the governor of Shandong at the time of the Yellow Cliff incident. The account exaggerates the unorthodox aspects of Jizhong's teachings in an obvious effort to exonerate Governor Yan from the suspicion of having overreacted in the affair.
9. The cosmological overtones have led some authors to connect the Taizhou school with the Yellow Turbans of 184 A.D. See, for example, Hou Wailu, 1959: 46.
10. De Bary, 1970: 157–160; Goodrich and Fang, 1976: 13821; Chen, 1908: 21/5–6.
11. De Bary, 1970: 162–171; Goodrich and Fang, 1976: 13821; Huang, n.d.: III, 32/6–7.
12. Goodrich and Fang, 1976: 912–914.
13. Liu Ts'un-yan, 1967: 263–270; Goodrich and Fang, 1976: 913–914.
14. Liu Ts'un-yan, 1967: 277.
15. *Qing shilu*: Qianlong: 218/7–8. A memorial from the Board of Rites at this time noted that in Henan Province alone, more than 590 *sanjiao* temples had been established. The memorial called for the investigation of all academies where such worship centers might surreptitiously exist (*Qing shilu*: Qianlong: 218/7–8).
16. Even during the Ming, followers of the Taizhou tradition suffered persecution. He Xinyin (1517–79) and Li Zhi (1527–1602), disciples of Wang Gen who came from prominent families, both died in prison after their social activism had evoked official rebuke. For more on these important figures in the Taizhou school, see De Bary, 1970: 178–222; Hou Wailu, 1959: 49–52; Huang, n.d.: III, 32/1–4.
17. *Qing bailei chao*, no. 37: 60.
18. *Shandong jindaishi*, 1957: 191; *Qing bailei chao*, no. 37: 60; Liu Houzi, 1940: 92–93.
19. The Annals of Shandong Military Campaigns (*Shandong jindaishi*, 1957: 174) states that Zhou died in prison, but here again we may have an instance of the Annals attempting to frame a case against Yellow Cliff so as to strengthen the argument in favor of Governor Yan's suppression policy. The

Anhui tongzhi (Gazetteer of Anhui) explains that Zhou was wrongly arrested and subsequently released (6/22).

20. By one account, Li and Zhang were maternal cousins (Liu Houzi, 1940: 83).

21. *Shandong jindaishi*, 1957: 191.

22. *Shandong jindaishi*, 1957: 164–165, 192.

23. In addition to Zhang and Li, whose schools were known as the "moderate faction," Zhou Xingyuan had a third important disciple, Jiang Ziming, whose school, apparently centered in northern Anhui, was known as the "radical faction" (*Shandong jindaishi*, 1957: 165).

24. *Shandong jindaishi*, 1957: 174; *Qing bailei chao*, no. 37: 61.

25. *Shandong jindaishi*, 1957: 164, 174–175.

26. At the time of Zhang's arrival, Wu had already served in a number of magistrate posts and had received imperial recognition for his tax collection efforts (*Shandong jindaishi*, 1957: 146).

27. *Shandong jindaishi*, 1957: 170, 175.

28. Ibid., 170.

29. The northward shift of the Yellow River in 1855 had first made Shandong accessible to the Anhui-based Nian. In 1860, the flooding of the Guo and Fei rivers in northern Anhui forced the Nian to vacate their homes and prompted them to invade Shandong in search of food and horses. The sharp rise in Nian cavalry at this time shows the result of the Shandong raids, which continued through the early 1860s. See Chiang Siang-tseh, 1954: 63–64.

30. *Shandong jindaishi*, 1957: 170, 175.

31. Ibid., 196.

32. Ibid., 146, 175. Significantly, Wu received his appointment to prefect as a result of his success in mobilizing local militia against the Nian.

33. Ibid., 170–171, 175, 180–183.

34. Ibid., 185.

35. Ibid., 175.

36. As prefect of Jinan, Wu was ordered by the governor to send troops to suppress Liu Depei, who was one of Wu's students. Wu's poor performance in the task resulted in his dismissal (*Shandong jindaishi*, 1957: 145, 146, 162).

37. Ibid., 163, 166, 171, 175.

38. Ibid., 134.

39. Ibid., 168, 185, 187.

40. Ibid., 175, 195. A surviving document of one of Zhang's sermons to his disciples reads:

> One must not indulge one's own will for fear of becoming overbearing. Happiness must not be too extreme or chaos will ensue. Pride must not flourish or one will lapse into evil. Desire must not go unrestrained or it will transgress proper bounds. Shandong is in a state of disarray, as you know. You disciples live on this mountain, working together. Be not lazy in learning. "To live as a social group and yet not speak of righteousness; what an error." "To be well fed and yet not to exercise one's mind; what an error." Confucius criticized this. I follow him in prohibiting it. You know as much. Obey my words. (Ibid., 156)

41. One source states that Sage Hall, in addition to its Confucian altar, also housed altars to Fu Xi (the legendary ruler credited with the introduction of farming, fishing, and animal husbandry), King Wen (who paved the way for the founding of the Zhou dynasty by his son King Wu), the Duke of Zhou, and Zhang Jizhong's mentor Zhou Xingyuan (*Qing bailei chao*, no. 37: 63).

42. *Shandong jindaishi*, 1957: 163, 175, 191.

43. The text of one of Zhang's lectures reads in part:

> The Buddhist principle of "enlightening the mind and beholding nature" is exactly equivalent to the Great Learning's doctrine of "extension of knowledge." ... The Cheng-Zhu school is based on "sincerity" and "rectification of the mind," but it overlooks the extension of knowledge." With Wang Yangming the "extension of knowledge" began to flourish. But scholars of the day attacked Wang Yangming just as they had Buddhism. Alas, how confused they were. To educate the ignorant, Buddhism begins with the worship of idols ... After Confucius and Mencius, for a thousand years Buddhism kept alive the principle of "innate knowledge." Yet Confucian scholars who follow the school of mind are satirized as monks. Isn't this confusing ... The "original awareness" of Buddhism is equivalent to "foresight" in Confucianism. Only good scholars understand these similarities. (Ibid., 154)

44. Ibid., 183, 186, 195.

45. Ibid., 171.

46. Ibid., 411; *Yuezhedang*: Tongzhi 5/11/10; Xie Xingyao, 1936: 7.

47. *Shandong jindaishi*, 1957: 134, 175.

48. Ibid., 171, 195.

49. Ibid., 134–135.

50. A precedent for the idea of a utopian Confucian community was introduced to the Taizhou tradition by philosopher He Xinyin. He had operated a similar community, known as "Collective Harmony Hall" (*juhetang*). See De Bary, 1970: 180; Zhou Zhiwen, 1977: 33.

51. *Shandong jindaishi*, 1957: 134–135.

52. The deceptively impressive view of this building complex that could be seen from below was, Wang declared, a major cause of the Yellow Cliff calamity. Precisely what he meant by this statement is not clear. Perhaps it was the mere aura of opulence that incited rumors and tempted the government to rush in. Perhaps the structures looked sufficiently imperious to suggest rebel ambition. We do know that the famous Wuyi Pavilion to which Wang likened the Yellow Cliff complex was magnificent enough to have served as the site for a banquet hosted by none other than Qinshi Huangdi in 245 B.C. See *Fujian tongzhi* (Gazetteer of Fujian), vol. 2: 625, reprinted by Huawen shuju, Taibei, 1970.

53. *Shandong jindaishi*, 1957: 129, 176.

54. Ibid., 129–130, 176. Actually, according to one document, the claim was that they were students of Zhang Qi, apparently a homophone for Zhang the 7th. Zhang Jizhong was known by his followers as "Mr. Zhang the 7th" (*Zhangqi xiansheng*) since he was the seventh born in his family (*Shandong jindaishi*, 1957: 176).

55. Ibid., 129–130, 176.
56. Ibid., 149.
57. Ibid., 183, 187.
58. The sources are contradictory on the details of the mission. By one account, Wu did not claim that Zhang was absent, and instead informed the delegation that the mountain fort was now filled with people (ibid., 130). Another version tells us that the magistrate of Changqing went by himself to Yellow Cliff. Learning that Jizhong was away, he left a message for him to present himself at the provincial capital upon his return. Instead of complying, however, Zhang wrote a letter refusing to make an appearance (ibid., 148). By yet a third account, when the magistrate of Changqing went to Yellow Cliff he met up with the father of the magistrate of Yidu County who was a friend of Jizhong's and had gone to the mountain to persuade him to come forth. The father assured the visiting magistrate that nothing was amiss at Yellow Cliff. As the two men were talking, however, a letter was sent out of the mountain to the father. Its contents read: "The magistrate of Changqing has come to the fort to investigate the situation. Please kill him at once." Shocked, the father shared the letter with the magistrate and apologized for his apparent misreading of the situation at Yellow Cliff (ibid., 186).
59. Ibid., 176, 180–181. According to other versions, it was a servant of the Changqing magistrate who was killed (ibid., 130, 148, 186).
60. Ibid., 149.
61. Ibid., 137, 149.
62. Ibid., 176, 181, 184.
63. Ibid., 176–177, 181.
64. Ibid., 172, 177.
65. Ibid., 135.
66. Ibid., 173.
67. Ibid., 130–131.
68. Ibid., 131. This one memorial by Governor Yan also mentions—incredibly enough—seizing more than forty uniforms marked with the insignia of the Taiping Rebellion. The claim is not repeated in another memorial submitted by the governor the following month, nor was it included in the official report of the incident, the Annals of Shandong Military Campaigns.
69. Ibid., 178.
70. Ibid., 178–179.
71. Ibid., 173, 179; *Yuezhedang*: Tongzhi 5/11/10.
72. According to one report, Yan's fury at the news of Nian connections tempted him to order total annihilation of the mountain, but he was persuaded to adopt a more generous position by the magistrate of Changqing County, Chen Enshou. Chen's own visit to Yellow Cliff some days before had apparently convinced him that the community was essentially defensive. Why, he asked the governor, would members have taken along their families and possessions had they been plotting rebellion? On Chen's insistence, Yan ordered that only adult males be killed (*Shandong jindaishi*, 1957:149).
73. Ibid., 143, 179; *Yuezhedang*: Tongzhi 5/11/10. Yan's own accounts state that there were no surrenders. However, according to some reports, although 10,000 people lost their lives, about 1,000 did surrender by the west gate thanks

to the personal efforts of the Changqing magistrate, Chen Enshou (*Shandong jindaishi*, 1957: 182, 186).

74. *Shandong jindaishi*, 1957: 195; *Yuezhedang*: Tongzhi 5/11/10.

75. *Yuezhedang*: Tongzhi 5/11/10.

76. *Shandong jindaishi*, 1957: 184, 188, 195.

77. Ibid., 179; *Yuezhedang*: Tongzhi 5/11/10. The book was subsequently deemed "unintelligible" by the Grand Council.

78. *Yuezhedang*: Tongzhi 5/11/20. According to one account, Magistrate Chen Enshou actually found a name list of Yellow Cliff inhabitants, but decided to burn it so as to spare their relatives (*Shandong jindaishi*, 1957: 150).

79. *Shandong jindaishi*, 1957:195.

80. *Yuezhedang*: Tongzhi 5/11/10. According to one report, however, a great many children were seized and sold by the officials (*Shandong jindaishi*, 1957: 136).

81. *Yuezhedang*: Tongzhi 5/11/10.

82. Ibid., 5/10/10; *Shangyudang*: Tongzhi 5/10/10, 5/11/3.

83. *Shangyudang*: Tongzhi 5/11/15.

84. *Shandong jindaishi*, 1957: 133–134. After arrival in Heilongjiang, Wu was put to work on a variety of frontier affairs: pacification, reclamation of new territory, negotiation along the Sino-Russian border, establishment of the Mogolian boundary. When he had accumulated great merit in this work, he finally was granted an imperial pardon and was allowed to return to his home (*Shandong jindaishi*, 1957: 145–146).

85. Ibid., 179.

86. Ibid., 198.

87. Ibid., 167–168, 194.

88. Liu Houzi, 1940: 82; Liu E, 1952: introduction. Chapter 9 of *Lao Can youji* commemorates Li Guangxin; chapters 10 and 11 commemorate fellow Taizhou adherent Huang Guiqun. As Liu explains in chapter 8:

> The three schools—Confucian, Buddhist, Taoist—are like signboards hung outside three shops. In reality they are all sellers of mixed provisions; they all sell fuel, rice, oil, salt. But the shop belonging to the Confucian family is bigger; the Buddhist and Taoist shops are smaller. There is nothing they don't stock in all the shops. (Liu E, 1952: 97–98)

89. In addition to Liu E, the sponsors included Cheng Enpei and Cheng Bi—brother and son of Hua army general Cheng Wenbing; Mao Shijun—manager of the Jiangnan Arsenal in Shanghai; and Yang Shisheng—elder brother of Shandong governor Yang Wenjing (Liu Houzi, 1940: 90).

90. Ibid., 89–90, 109; Lu Yiye, 1927:73.

91. Liu Houzi, 1940: 90.

92. *Shandong jindaishi*, 1957: 166, 168, 194.

93. Liu Houzi, 1936: 329–334; Liu Houzi, 1937: 205–206. We also have the word of several contemporary officials with intimate knowledge of the case that they personally felt the government attack to have been uncalled for (*Shandong jindaishi*, 1957: 136–137, 166).

94. Further evidence of Zhang's opposition to the Nian is provided in some

of his writings. One, entitled "Xuzhou tuntian shuo" (Discourse on a military camp for Xuzhou), was clearly written as a policy proposal for government defense against the rebels. In the essay Zhang argues that the state should take over deserted floodlands bordering the former Yellow River bed and establish there a military camp to forestall the northward advance of the Nian (*Shandong jindaishi*, 1957: 160–161). A second piece of evidence is a letter written by Zhang in which he noted in alarm that "the poisonous fog of Zhang and Gong (the two main Nian commanders)" had spread to southern Shandong. Zhang described the villages through which the Nian cavalry had passed as "reduced to bones and weeds" (*Shandong jindaishi*, 1957: 157).

95. This is the explanation given for the Taiping uniforms mentioned in one of Governor Yan's memorials as well. See Note 68.

96. *Shandong jindaishi*, 1957: 182, 184, 185.

97. *Qing shilu*: Tongzhi: 3990.

98. The governor's approach seems to have received strong support from nearly all of his subordinate officials. Interestingly, limited opposition to his aggressive strategy seems to have come largely from natives of South China. The one official who tried most earnestly to spare the Yellow Cliff community from annihilation, Chen Enshou, was from Zhejiang, for example. It does seem that sympathy for the Taizhou adherents came primarily from fellow southerners. Conversely, perhaps it was animosity and jealousy on the part of northern officials toward the well-to-do refugees from the South that helped spark the confrontation. Unfortunately, there is not enough information on the backgrounds of all concerned officials to be certain.

99. *Qing shilu*: Tongzhi: 4344; *Qing liezhuan*: 57/18–20.

100. Such a hypothesis is further supported by the arrest of more than thirty bandits and thirteen salt smugglers in southern Shandong about one year after the calamity at Yellow Cliff. Under questioning, the leaders of the group admitted that they had escaped from Yellow Cliff and had joined up with a local smuggling outfit. When the Nian entered the area, they plotted an uprising under the pretext of recruiting guards to provide protection for a wealthy family. After having gathered 300 people, they notified Nian blue banner chief Chen Huaizhong, suggesting a date for the uprising. Their hope had been that a temporary alliance with the Nian would enhance their reputation so that they might be able to attract several thousand followers and develop their group into a full-fledged bandit organization (*Shandong jindaishi*, 1957: 193).

101. *Yuezhedang*: Tongzhi 5/9/24, 5/10/5.

References

Chen Daotan ed. 1908. *Taizhouzhi* (Gazeteer of Taizhou).

Ch'en J. 1970. "Rebels between rebellions." *Journal of Asian Studies* 29: 807–822.

Chiang Siang-tseh. 1954. *The Nien Rebellion*. Seattle: University of Washington Press.

De Bary, William Theodore. 1970. *Self and Society in Ming Thought*. New York: Columbia University Press.

Goodrich, L.C., and Chaoying Fang, eds. 1976. *Dictionary of Ming Biography*. New York: Columbia University Press.

Hou Wailu. 1959. "Shiliushiju Zhongguo de jinbu de zhexue sichao gaishu" (Overview of progressive philosophical trends in sixteenth-century China). *Lishi yanjiu* 10: 39–59.

Huang Zongxi, ed. n.d. *Mingru xue'an* (Scholarly annals of Ming Confucianists). Reprint. Taibei: Taiwan Zhonghua shuju yinxing.

Liu E. 1952. *The Travels of Lao Ts'an*. Translated by Harold Shadick. Ithaca: Cornell University Press.

Liu Houzi. 1940. "Zhang Shiqi yu taigu xuepai" (Zhang Shiqi and the Taigu school). *Furen xuezhi* 9, 1: 81–124.

———. 1937. "Huangyai jiaoan zhiyibu" (Supplement to "Doubts on the Yellow Cliff religious incident"). *Guoli Beiping yanjiuyuan shixue jikan* 3: 329–334.

———. 1936. "Tongzhi wunian huangya jiaofeian zhiyi" (Doubts concerning the Yellow Cliff religious bandit incident of 1866). *Guoli Beiping yanjiuyuan shixue jikan* 2: 195–206.

Liu Ts'un-yan. 1967. "Lin Chao-en: the master of three teachings." *Tung pao* 53: 253–278.

Lu Yiye. 1927. "Taigu xuepai zhi yange ji qi sixiang" (Evolution and ideology of the Taigu School). *Dongfang zazhi* 24, 14: 71–75.

Okubo Hideko. 1953. "Taishu gakko no shominsei" (The mass character of the Taizhou School). *Toho shukyo* 3.

Qing bailei chao (Unofficial records of the Qing). 1972. Reprint. Taibei: Shangwu yinshuguan.

Qing liezhuan (Eminent biographies of the Qing). 1973. Reprint. Taibei: Zhonghua shuju yinxing.

Qing shilu (Veritable records of the Qing). 1970. Reprint. Taibei: Taiwan huawen shuju.

Shandong jindaishi ziliao (Material on Shandong modern history). 1957. Jinan: Shandong renmin chubanshe.

Shangyudang (Record book of ordinary matters). Taibei: National Palace Museum Qing Archives.

Xie Xingyao. 1936. "Daoxian shidai beifang de huangyajiao" (The northern Yellow Cliff religion during the Daoxian period). *Yijing* 3: 6–11.

Yang Shizou, ed. 1915. *Shandong tongzhi* (Gazetteer of Shandong).

Yuezhedang (Monthly Memorial Record Book). Taibei: National Palace Museum Qing Archives.

Zhou Zhiwen. 1977. "Taizhou xuepai dui wenxue xuefeng de xingxiang" (The Influence of the Taizhou School on Late Ming Intellectual Currents). M.A. thesis. National Taiwan University.

4

Predatory Rebellion:
Bai Lang and Social Banditry

Thanks largely to the pioneering work of Eric Hobsbawm, the study of banditry has become a popular scholarly pursuit. By characterizing rural brigandage as a worldwide phenomenon, Hobsbawm's work is an invitation to students of many diverse societies to join in comparative inquiry. Not surprisingly, the findings of these studies have sparked elaborations and challenges to Hobsbawm's original ideas.

The cornerstone of Hobsbawm's contribution lies in the concept of "social banditry." First spelled out in *Primitive Rebels* (1959) and later elaborated in *Bandits* (1981), the concept contains at least three essential and interrelated elements. First, the term suggests a certain *connection between bandits and social classes*. Fundamentally, social banditry is held to be an expression of the peasantry. As such, it enjoys the support, protection, and admiration of the rural communities where it originates. While this peasant base is credited with giving social banditry its strength and cross-cultural similarity, it also places definite limits on brigandage as a mode of political protest. For Hobsbawm, bandits are "primitive" rebels, handicapped by the rudimentary outlook and structure of the peasant society from whence they emerge. Second, the concept refers to a particular *type of behavior*: brigandage that is socially discriminating. Social bandits are of the Robin Hood variety—outlaws who steal from the rich and give to the poor. While Hobsbawm was quick to admit that real bandits often deviate from the ideal type,[1] he held that social banditry was important both as a standard against which bandits and peasants alike measure brigand behavior, and as a primitive form of rural protest. This brings us to the third facet of social banditry: its *relationship to revolution*. According to Hobsbawm's analysis, banditry is highly unadaptable to social revolution. Reflecting the amorphous character of its peasant base, brigandage is inhibited by an undeveloped outlook and organization. Thus banditry (in contrast to millenarianism) is seen by Hobsbawm as a most unlikely candidate for incorporation into a modern revolutionary movement.

Considerable debate has surrounded each of the elements of social banditry. As with most arguments among social scientists, some of the controversy can be attributed to different usages of terminology. For the purposes of this article, let us try to reduce ambiguity by defining several key concepts at the outset. "Peasants" will refer to members of a rural household whose basic subsistence derives from agricultural production. Since in a peasant society the household is the primary unit of production and consumption, its members will be considered as "peasants" even though some of them may engage periodically in nonfarming activities to supplement their family income. "Revolution" will here be defined as a movement that aims at a fundamental restructuring of politics and/or society. A "political revolution" (which may, for example, endeavor to replace an imperial or autocratic regime with a more democratic polity) can be distinguished from a "social revolution," which attempts to reshape the foundations of power and privilege throughout the society at large.

Even when some conceptual clarity has been brought to bear, however, disagreement remains. While much of the controversy has been generated by scholars working on areas of the Western world, students of China have also joined the discussion. On the issue of bandit behavior, some scholars have emphasized a chivalrous (*xiadao*) characterization of Chinese brigands,[2] whereas others have chosen to highlight the depraved, criminal side.[3] Not surprisingly, most Chinese bandit gangs can in fact be shown to have engaged in both malicious and magnanimous behavior. As a firsthand observer noted, "The Chinese bandit is a paradox. He is the terror of the countryside and the guardian of the people. He is an erratic Robin Hood."[4]

More interesting than the question of whether a particular band of brigands assisted or victimized the poor is the issue of the structural relationship between banditry and the peasantry. One of Hobsbawm's critics, Anton Blok concluded from his studies of Sicily that the most important thing about bandits is not their closeness to the peasantry, but rather their use of terror against the rural populace. The key to a brigand's endurance, Blok argues, lies not in garnering the support of the peasants, but in attracting protection from powerholders.[5] Local notables, rather than peasant families, are seen as the beneficiaries of bandit plunder and the reservoirs of bandit strength.

On the issue of revolutionary potential, Blok—like Hobsbawm—considers bandits as poor grist for revolutionary mills. However, he attributes this not to a failing in outlook or organization, but to the fact that a bandit's first loyalty is not to the peasantry. For Blok, brigands impede rural mobilization in two ways: by repressing peasant action through terror, and by carving out avenues of upward mobility.[6] Because it may provide access to new sources of wealth and prestige, banditry in Blok's view dilutes class solidarity and inhibits revolutionary potential.

Scholars of modern China, by contrast, have tended to argue for considerable overlap between banditry and revolution. Edward Friedman, for example, claims that "traditional or transitional social bandits and modern twentieth century revolutionaries should not be conceived of wholly as separate entities. They are really united in fantasy, dream and story, in living models of action, aspiration and opprobrium."[7] But just as Blok and Hobsbawm part company in their explanations for the discontinuity they find between banditry and revolution, so China scholars have offered competing explanations for their claims of continuity. For Friedman, the answer lies in his view that revolutions are "backward-looking": "people in the countryside who had been acting for centuries on millennial, religious and magical notions did not suddenly undergo a transvaluation of values";[8] "the villagers experience the revolution as a reknitting of family."[9] For Fei-ling Davis, on the other hand, the linkage is attributed not to the "backward-looking" quality of revolutionaries, but rather to the "revolutionary" nature of traditional brigands and secret societies. As she phrases it, "secret societies of the Chinese type were socially revolutionary long before they became politically revolutionary. It is in this sense, then, that Chinese secret societies, and those resembling them elsewhere, were not primitive rebels, like those described by Hobsbawm, but primitive revolutionaries."[10]

Questions of bandit behavior, peasant connections, and revolutionary potential are all extremely complex issues that do not lend themselves to definitive conclusions. One way to cut through some of the complexity, to see more clearly the relationships involved, is to undertake case studies of particular bandit outfits. For this purpose, the case of Bai Lang (or "White Wolf,"[11] as he is sometimes referred to in the Western literature) merits special scrutiny. One of the most famous bandits in modern Chinese history, Bai Lang (1873–1914) has already been the basis for much of the speculation in the secondary literature about the nature of Chinese brigandage.[12] Now that several new sets of primary materials on the career of this colorful bandit are available,[13] we are in a better position to compare the Bai Lang case against competing interpretations of banditry.

To date, scholarly treatments of Bai Lang have generally agreed on the Robin Hood flavor of much of the brigand's behavior. Although his subordinates sometimes strayed from Bai Lang's disciplinary injunction, the bandit chief himself seems to have endeavored to enforce peasant justice. In his assaults on more than fifty cities in five North China provinces, Bai Lang's chief targets were the traditional enemies of the poor: government offices, jails, wealthy households. On many occasions, the bandit army is reported to have redistributed a share of its plunder to the local populace.

Regarding the class character and revolutionary potential of the bandit outfit, however, interpretations have differed. Edward Friedman has described Bai Lang's army as comprised of three groups: (1) the local poor of "ex-tillers and ex-villagers" who constituted the majority of the force at any one time, but who stayed with the movement only briefly; (2) the "local constabulary" (whose participation was also temporary); and (3) the "marginal men" who engaged in banditry on a more or less permanent basis.[14] By Friedman's account, none of these groups was representative of the peasantry. In becoming a regular member of a bandit outfit, an individual severed whatever tenuous links to family and community still existed and assumed an altogether new identity. To quote Friedman,

> These permanent recruits . . . had no family to return to. The rebel army became their home, its cause their purpose. . . . This backbone element could move on, move anywhere, because it had no place to move back to.[15]
>
> . . . Men forced to leave their family who then joined a rural band or a secret society found a new family. . . . A villager joining a band is not like a secular Westerner joining a civic club. The rural Chinese is entering a new life, taking on a new identity.[16]

For Friedman, the process of becoming a bandit was religious in nature:

> In a society where men are not complete unless they marry and have male heirs, these village migrants who could afford neither wife nor home probably experienced themselves as immoral. The opportunity to join as a peer a brotherhood of valued comrades may have led to an experience almost of holiness in the fulfillment of the new affirmation.[17]
>
> ... As people joining a rebel band would come to identify with a more universal familial-religion, the particularism of the family was transformed into a synonym for inexcusably selfish corruption.[18]

Friedman sees the heart of Bai Lang's army as composed of non-peasants, of persons who were so pressed by poverty that they renounced family and village ties in favor of a new life. As such, the movement was bound by neither the territorial nor the ideological limitations of a purely peasant operation.[19] While arguing that much of Bai Lang's popular appeal lay in his invocation of traditional legends ("Revolution meant resurrecting the ideal past"),[20] Friedman portrays the bandit chief as a "modern man"[21] who "had to move on . . . toward his political objective."[22] Bai Lang, contends Friedman, "was not a typical bandit, social or otherwise."[23] Influenced by young intellectuals from the revolutionary camp of Sun Yatsen, the movement's horizons reached beyond the confines of parochial peasant concerns to attempt revolutionary struggle.

Others have advanced rather different perspectives. Philip Billingsley characterizes Bai Lang as an "old-style bandit," out of place and thus unable to withstand the military mobilization brought to bear against him.[24] Banno Ryokichi suggests that the Bai Lang uprising was possessed of a dual nature. On the one hand, it reflected the anti-warlordism, anti–Yuan Shikai sentiments of the revolutionary camp; but on the other hand, it perpetuated a tradition of popular struggle against the well-to-do (government officials, gentry, merchants), Christians, and foreign property in general[25]—a struggle that had characterized Chinese peasant movements since the Boxer uprising.[26] For Banno, this popular tradition distinguished the bandits from their revolutionary allies and prevented a full integration of the two movements.

The primary materials on Bai Lang, which provide important information on the origins and subsequent character of the movement, help us to evaluate these various contentions. Thanks to these sources, we are now better able to decide whether this case matches Hobsbawm's characterization of social banditry; we are better able to answer questions such as: What was the social composition of Bai Lang's army? Did the brigands engage in Robin Hood–type activities? To what extent was the movement a revolutionary struggle?

Bai Lang's Social Base

Bai Lang hailed from the hills of western Henan—an area long known for rampant banditry.[27] Like much of North China, Bai Lang's native region (Baofeng, Lushan, and Linru counties) suffered from chronic natural disasters. Waterworks were in poor repair and thus unable to blunt the harsh effects of geography and climate. In 1900 a severe drought and famine resulted in a great increase in the number of bandits in the area. In 1911, on the eve of Bai Lang's own turn to rebellion, a hailstorm destroyed the wheat and bean crop in the area around his native village. This came on top of an extreme drought the previous year that had also decimated the wheat harvest.[28] Repeated natural catastrophes had rendered the peasants of this area exceptionally mobile. Informants from Bai Lang's native village estimated that anywhere from 20 to 60 percent of the inhabitants left the village for part of each year to beg for food in neighboring Hubei Province and returned home when the wheat was ready to harvest.[29]

A second cause of peasant mobility was corvée labor. In Bai Lang's home village of Daliuzhuang, that usually meant lugging coal approximately ten miles from the mines into Baofeng city. Another type of corvée labor, performed during the four-month agricultural slack period between winter and spring, was the repair of irrigation canals in the mountains. Peasants who performed the terracing and ditchdigging were known locally as *tangjiang*.[30] Groups of such laborers—generally young men from poor peasant families—were often the building blocks for other forms of collective action.[31]

In 1877, for example, a severe famine in Lushan County resulted in a grain riot instigated by a large number of *tangjiang*. In the face of recalcitrant landlords who were unwilling to provide relief, the *tangjiang* opened local granaries and distributed the grain to the poor. This act propelled other peasants to join the movement, and the numbers of participants reached tens of thousands. Only by calling up a large contingent of government troops could the riot be quelled.[32]

In 1902, neighboring Baofeng County also experienced an uprising instigated by *tangjiang*. Two years before, the county magistrate had established a tax bureau in the mining district.[33] The bureau was responsible for levying a fee of twenty cash (*wen*) per cart of coal taken out of the mines. Since inhabitants of this area previously had paid no taxes on their haul of coal (which was needed for daily fuel) the imposition of the tax created considerable resentment. Finally, in 1902 the popular antagonism exploded in an attack by groups of *tangjiang* on the tax bureau. After the suppression of the revolt, small groups of *tangjiang* congregated in the mountains as bandit outfits. Members of these gangs farmed by day and gathered at night to engage in brigandage. Their usual practice was to kidnap from wealthy families for ransom. Sometimes outright extortion was attempted; the gang would amass its members outside a target village and announce loudly that a certain household was being charged a specified amount of money to be delivered by a certain date to a stipulated location. Unless the terms were met, the entire village would be attacked.[34] Kidnap victims were called "meat tickets" (*roupiao*); each ticket was worth anywhere from 1,000 to 10,000 dollars in gold, depending upon the resources of the victimized families. Women were prime targets for ransom since their bound feet made their escape almost impossible.[35]

Thus, on the eve of the formation of Bai Lang's bandit group there were already a number of gangs active in the western Henan area. The best known was led by Du Qibin, who hailed from one of the most prominent lineages in Baofeng. His family, which owned more than fifteen acres of land, had produced generations of scholars and officials. Du Qibin himself had received five or six years of education at a private academy. However, when government soldiers were dispatched to arrest him for a robbery he had not committed, Du Qibin decided to turn outlaw. His gang, which was well armed, became the major bandit outfit in the Baofeng–Lushan area. Du emerged as commander-in-chief of a number of other minor bandit chieftains in the area, including—briefly—Bai Lang.[36]

Most of the other chieftains had grown up in less comfortable circumstances than Du Qibin. Qin Jiaohong ("Peppery-red" Qin) came from a landless family; his father worked on a nearby estate as a hired farm hand and his brothers labored in the pottery pits. When one of his elder brothers was beaten to death by the county authorities for trafficking with local bandits, Qin Jiaohong—then seventeen or eighteen years old—became a brigand himself. Although Qin had led several successful assaults on government forces (netting an impressive cache of weaponry) and developed a reputation for social justice among the peasantry, his career was cut short by serious illness when he was still in his early twenties. Arrest and execution followed.[37]

Bai Lang himself was born in 1873 into a fairly affluent family with about thirty acres of land. The family were not landlords, but hired one long-term and several short-term laborers to help them cultivate their sizable holdings. Bai Lang had no brothers and only one sister. He was sent to a private academy to receive a literary education, but dropped out after a year or so, having mastered very few Chinese characters.

When Bai Lang reached working age, he labored on the family farm and married a woman surnamed Guan, from Guan Village in Baofeng County. They had five children: a son and four daughters. In addition to farming activities, Bai Lang (probably during the agricultural slack period) drove an oxcart with government salt. Because of his commanding personality and martial skills, he began to play a protective role toward the other salt carters when they met up with bandits or other dangers. These forays gradually earned Bai Lang a reputation for leadership among the local populace.

The Bai family was the only household by that surname in their village of Daliuzhuang; most of the other inhabitants were named "Wang." From an early age, Bai Lang had been involved in disputes with the Wangs in his village. When he was twenty-five, Bai Lang suffered a sound thrashing as a result of a quarrel with the landlord Wang Zhen. Urged on by a group of supporters, Bai Lang marched to the landlord's house to protest. When Wang Zhen's aged father came forth to argue his family's case, the angered Bai Lang gave the old man a shove. The patriarch fell and died soon thereafter. Although the death was accidental, the Wang family is said to have bribed the county magistrate to imprison Bai Lang, and he was detained for more than a year. His family was forced to sell half of its land to purchase his eventual release. The jail experience, which filled him with a desire for revenge, was apparently a turning point in Bai Lang's life. According to the recollections of his close associates, Bai Lang was fully prepared to take to banditry when he left jail. However, he first returned home to pay respects to his family. There he was dissuaded from embarking on brigandage by his mother's insistent pleadings.[38] Instead, Bai Lang is reported to have enlisted under Wu Luzhen, commander of the sixth division of the Beiyang Army. Bai Lang rose quickly to become a trusted advisor to Wu, but was set adrift in 1911 when the division commander was assassinated.[39]

At this time, natural catastrophe had given rise to unusual levels of bandit activity in the Baofeng–Lushan area. Bai Lang was friendly with some of the brigands, who persuaded him to join them. At this point, his mother—who had been subjected to harassment from the county authorities during her son's absence—willingly assented to his decision.[40] Thus in the fall of 1911, Bai Lang amassed a group of twenty or thirty followers at Yaodianpu, a village seven miles to the west of Baofeng city. Soon his ranks had grown to fifty or sixty, swelled by the effects of a poor harvest in the area.

Bai Lang cooperated with the major bandit chieftain in the region, Du Qibin, but quickly distinguished himself from his ally in two respects: loyalty to his rank-and-file followers, and distance from the local powerholders. The first difference was demonstrated in December 1911 when rumors of an impending government attack prompted Du Qibin to suggest that all local bandit chiefs flee westward to take cover. Du insisted that only those followers who possessed automatic rifles could join the flight to safety; those with homemade weapons would have to return home to take their chances. Bai Lang protested that this would mean abandoning the bulk of his men since most of them were armed with only crude, homemade guns or spears. Even though "Peppery-red" Qin interceded on Bai Lang's behalf, Du Qibin refused to change his position. Angered by this callous attitude, Bai Lang parted company with the bandit commander and led his followers in an assault on the Baofeng county magistrate's battalion.[41] The second difference between the two bandit chiefs was seen in April 1912, when the retiring Baofeng magistrate was preparing to return to the provincial capital with his family and personal belongings. Du Qibin, who enjoyed close relations with landlords and local strongmen, had agreed not to rob the magistrate's procession. Bai Lang, however, refused to go along with Du's decision. With twenty to thirty followers, he ambushed the magistrate and captured sixteen automatic rifles. He kidnapped the magistrate's young son for the ransom of an additional dozen rifles. The outcome was thus a substantial gain in weapons for Bai Lang's band.[42]

Pressed by the mounting bandit threat, the provincial government— in an age-old tactic of Chinese rulers—offered the brigand chiefs official rank in exchange for a promise to abandon their plundering ways. Eighteen bandit chieftains, including Du Qibin, accepted the offer. Encouraged by large gifts of money, the eighteen hurried to Lushan to accept their new titles. Rather than honor its promise, however, the government turned on the surrendering chieftains and executed all of them on October 18, 1912. As one of the few surviving bandit leaders of any reputation, Bai Lang gained a large influx of followers. His force grew to more than 600 persons and was headquartered at Sow Gorge in the mountains along the Baofeng–Lushan border.[43] With no human habitation for some twenty-five miles around, Sow Gorge was a natural fortress. The single entryway was guarded by four sentries, who admitted only persons armed with the gang's secret symbol of identification: a two-and-one-half-inch green-colored queue.[44] The bandits ventured forth frequently from their mountain redoubt to garner supplies from outlying towns. After the Beiyang army moved south to suppress revolutionary activities in the summer of 1913, Bai's followers attacked the city of Zaoyang in Hubei Province, drawing international attention by their capture of American missionaries. The bandit army proceeded to stage lightning raids on cities in Henan and Anhui before marching westward into Shaanxi and Gansu provinces in the spring of 1914.

The core of Bai Lang's fighting force was drawn from *tangjiang* and other peasants from the Baofeng-Lushan-Linru area. Later, as he traveled about, Bai Lang attracted followers from other places and from other walks of life as well. Informants recall that Bai Lang himself had difficulty keeping track of the size of his army. On occasion he would set a certain amount of paper currency by the side of the road and instruct each soldier to take one bill so that he could calculate their number.[45] In early 1914, the brigand army was said to have included about 10,000 men, 3,000 of whom were hard-core bandits.[46] These western Henan regulars were a composite of several different bandit gangs whose original chiefs retained a leadership role under Bai Lang's allied command. Lesser chieftains often led their men on separate plundering expeditions, cooperating among themselves only when pressed by government suppression efforts. Most important among the subordinate chiefs were Li Hongbin and Song Laonian, each of whom controlled about a thousand followers.[47]

Bai Lang was usually able to impose his will in critical strategic decisions. The march westward into Shaanxi and Gansu, for example, had been opposed by Li Hongbin and Song Laonian. Yet although both men were reluctant to desert the familiar ground of Henan, they eventually acceded to Bai Lang's wishes.[48] Even so, the alliance of bandit chiefs was not free from conflict. One chief who could not persuade his 400–500 followers to accompany Bai Lang to the northwest returned to Sow Gorge to hold the fort.[49] Another close associate led his 100 men home when they ran out of ammunition.[50] After Bai Lang retreated to Henan, the problems continued. He executed one of his subordinate chiefs who had tried to desert with 1,000 followers.[51]

The organizational structure of the bandit army was quite loose. Soldiers belonged to units, known simply as "supports" (*gan* or *jia*) that included anywhere from 100 to several thousand followers. Each unit was marked by a small banner on which was inscribed the name of its leader.[52] Bai Lang himself commanded a white-colored banner; a red banner was led by Li Hongbin, and a blue by Song Laonian. Their followers' uniforms were also marked by buttons of corresponding colors.[53] Bai Lang was addressed simply as Elder Brother (*dage*) by all members of his army; the lesser chieftains had no designated titles.[54]

According to government sources, two of Bai Lang's most trusted subordinates were related by blood: his uncle and son. Nicknamed "Bai the Blind," the uncle fought alongside his nephew until he was injured in the attack on Zaoyang in the fall of 1913. He was arrested at his hiding place in western Henan in May of the following year and died during the interrogation.[55] That same month, Bai Lang's son was reported killed in battle.[56]

Functionally, the bandit army was divided into three units: a "plunder" group, a "spy" group, and a "merchant" group.[57] The first group was concerned solely with stealing goods. Opium, silver, guns, and horses were the most prized items of plunder. The second group investigated military conditions and ascertained the whereabouts of the wealthiest local families—information that was then passed along to the plunder group. Bai Lang's spies were often disguised as beggars or merchants, but wore a white pocket or a small white sash hidden under their collar as a secret sign of identification. In early 1914, Bai Lang reportedly employed seventy-six spies in four Yangzi Valley cities.[58] The third group made contact with business circles to purchase arms and dispose of stolen goods. Even officers in the government army were known to have sold weapons and ammunition to the bandits. Both sides would send emissaries to decide upon a price and designate a spot where the government troops were to bury the arms. After digging up the weapons, Bai Lang's men would bury their payment of gold in the same spot.[59]

Regular members of Bai Lang's army received a salary of ten taels in silver each month. This was in striking contrast to government soldiers, who were paid only four taels of worthless paper currency. As an additional incentive for desertion, any government soldier who surrendered to Bai Lang was given a double salary.[60] Officers who had served at the rank of battalion commander or above in the government army were offered 100 silver dollars for travel expenses and 200 silver dollars in family subsidies paid directly to their dependents. In the first two months of 1914, Bai Lang was reported already to have dispensed more than 5,000 silver dollars for this purpose.[61] In February 1914, the bandit force included some 500 former government soldiers and officers.[62]

The bandits liked to dress in colorful silks and satins that had been looted along their route of plunder. Bai Lang himself cut a dashing figure in a white fox hat and leather jacket.[63] Many of the brigands also adorned their horses with stolen jewelry.[64] Composed largely of cavalry, the force traveled rapidly; they sometimes covered more than thirty miles in a single night.[65]

Robin Hood Flavor

The discipline of Bai Lang's fighting forces, as with most bandit armies, is a matter of some controversy. Informants from Bai Lang's native area remember the troops as having been highly disciplined and discriminating in choosing their targets of plunder and ransom. Government documents and newspaper accounts, on the other hand, emphasize that Bai Lang's army was not above the rape and pillage usually associated with bandits or, for that matter, most armies. But even government reports were forced to acknowledge the close relations between Bai Lang and the populace of his native area. This can be seen in a report from the Beiyang government's command office:

> In the northern Lushan–southern Baofeng area, the village women and children . . . regard the bandits as their own family members and regard the [government] soldiers as enemies. When the bandits are behind a village and the soldiers in front of the same village, the villagers will claim to have seen no trace of bandits. . . . When there are many soldiers around, they take to the hills as farmers, but as soon as the number of soldiers decreases the entire village turns into bandits.[66]

Another government report conceded that "Bai Lang at least pretends to practice justice and to respect the weak."[67] A folk song that the bandit chief is said to have composed offers further evidence of his desire to project a Robin Hood image:

> Great Bai Lang; Bai Lang is great!
> He robs the rich, helps the poor and delivers Heaven's fate.
> Everyone agrees: Bai Lang is great![68]

There are reports of Bai Lang's army redistributing plundered grain and spreading stolen copper coins across the streets for the people to pick up.[69] Prisons were sometimes opened and prisoners released.[70] In selecting targets of attack, the bandits also evidenced some social discrimination. At Liuan, Anhui, for example, although more than 500 persons were killed in the offensive, the casualties were predominantly officials—yamen runners, wealthy merchants, landlords, and moneylenders. Bai Lang had issued specific orders to spare coolies, artisans, cripples, and anyone who had participated in anti-warlord agitation.[71] County offices were burned to the ground, but ordinary homes were to be protected. During the Liuan attack, one bandit climbed onto a roof with buckets of water to douse the flames of a house that had accidently caught fire.[72]

It is probable, however, that Bai Lang himself was more concerned with maintaining discipline than were many of his subordinates. In an early attack on a Henan landlord family, for example, subordinate chiefs Li Hongbin, Song Laonian, and "Peppery-red" Qin tried to seize the landlord's lovely concubines for their own pleasure. Bai Lang, on the other hand, admonished his men not to molest the women, but to keep them hostage for ransom money that would buy more military provisions for his army.[73]

Although discipline certainly deteriorated over time, Bai Lang continued to display restraint—and even generosity—toward friendly persons. In Nanzhao, Henan, where the county magistrate greeted Bai Lang's arrival with a lavish banquet and offerings of silver, the bandits ate only one meal and departed without taking even the tendered money.[74] In Tongwei, Gansu, Bai Lang responded to the magistrate's warm reception by presenting the city with 2,000 taels to buy books for its poorly stocked school.[75]

These charitable incidents were counterbalanced by numerous reports of plunder and pillage, yet they do suggest that the bandit chief showed at least a modicum of social conscience. And, as we would expect, the discipline of his movement tightened again when the band eventually retreated to its native area in western Henan. Once home, Bai Lang ordered the execution of a subordinate (nicknamed "match head" because of his impulsiveness) who was charged with the mere crime of setting afire the gate of a local landlord's house. Another follower was ordered beaten to death for stealing.[76] Relations between the bandits and native inhabitants were, of course, much closer in this area than they had been during the brigands' distant travels. Local peasants in Henan helped to keep government suppression forces at bay by providing sanctuary and pretending that they had no knowledge concerning the whereabouts of their returned brethren.[77] From start to finish, the peasantry played a central role in Bai Lang's movement. It was peasant recruits who made up the backbone of the rank-and-file followers, and peasant parochialism that eventually took the movement back home to the hills of Henan. However, the influence of peasant participants and supporters often came into conflict with another constituent of the bandit army: members of Sun Yatsen's revolutionary camp.

Revolutionary Potential

As previous research has shown, alliance with the revolutionaries was responsible for the series of proclamations that Bai Lang issued in 1914 naming Yuan Shikai's warlord regime as principal foe. The revolutionary side supplied the brigands with weapons, ammunition, and political or military advice.[78] Now, with the aid of new documentary materials, we are able to assess more precisely the impact of the revolutionaries and see how their presence generated tensions within the ranks of Bai Lang's army.

The earliest contacts between the brigands and revolutionaries aligned with the Sun Yatsen camp were apparently forged in March 1912. At that time the governor of Henan, who was contemplating a military assault on Bai Lang's home area of Lushan, sent ahead an emissary named Xiong Siyu to explore the possibility of persuading the bandits to surrender. Xiong, an educated young intellectual, was secretly a member of Sun's party. After contacting the outlaws in the mountains of Lushan, he posted notices in the county seat proclaiming that the bandits were basically good and should be encouraged to overthrow their corrupt rulers.

The following year Xiong Siyu met with another member of Sun's group, Jia Yi, in the city of Hankou. On Bai Lang's instructions, the two men returned to Henan intending to blow up the railroad bridge over the Yellow River and thus prevent Yuan Shikai's army from proceeding south. While on this mission, however, they were seized and executed by forces loyal to Yuan.[79]

The warlord regime's knowledge of the bandit–revolutionary connection was based in part on a letter written to Bai Lang by Sun Yatsen's close associate, Huang Xing. Intercepted by the authorities, the letter expressed admiration for Bai Lang's accomplishments and encouraged the bandit chief to destroy the railroads so as to obstruct the southward advance of Yuan Shikai. Huang Xing acknowledged that Bai Lang would have to requisition some provisions from the local populace, but admonished him to maintain discipline to avoid arousing popular hostilities.[80]

The problem of obtaining supplies was in fact a major impetus for the bandits' willingness to cooperate with the revolutionary camp. Sun Yatsen's forces did attempt to provide the bandits with military equipment. An old peasant informant from Bai Lang's home village of Daliuzhuang recalled that in 1914 as he was fleeing from famine he was accosted by a man in a military uniform who asked if he knew the whereabouts of Bai Lang. The soldier explained he had come from Wuchang on orders of Sun Yatsen to deliver a cache of ammunition to the bandit chieftain.[81] More important than direct aid itself may have been the contacts that the revolutionaries could offer. Government reports indicated that introductions from the revolutionaries enabled Bai Lang to arrange for the purchase of 3,000 automatic rifles and considerable ammunition from Japanese suppliers.[82] While the brigands stood to gain materially from such contacts, the revolutionaries also saw a military advantage in the relationship. As evidence of the value he placed on Bai Lang's cooperation, Huang Xing reportedly promised him the governorship of Henan Province in exchange for aid in toppling the Yuan Shikai regime.[83]

For all the evidence of strategic collaboration between the two groups, it does not seem that the revolutionaries exerted much influence on the beliefs of Bai Lang's followers. To be sure, proclamations posted by Bai Lang's forces as they moved across the North China plain in 1914 did express certain political aims that paralleled the goals of the revolutionaries: antagonism to Yuan Shikai's dictatorial regime and commitment to a more just form of governance.[84] Informants recall that the posters were in fact written by advisors sent to Bai Lang by Sun Yatsen, but it is doubtful that the views contained in these proclamations reflected the persuasions of the bandit rank and file. Interviews with Bai Lang's closest surviving associates established that, although they had heard the terms "revolution" (*geming*) and "oppose Yuan Shikai" (*fan Yuan*), they were unable to explain their meaning. One informant recalled that "Yuan Shikai was an official of the Great Qing Dynasty who usurped the Qing throne; he was thus a villain who certainly could not be supported."[85]

Bai Lang's closest relations with the revolutionaries seem to have been with a splinter group known as the Reform Corps (*gaijintuan*) that was active among Hubei military circles in early March 1913. The Reform Corps had been founded by a good friend of Bai Lang's, a man named Ji Yulin who held high rank in the Hubei army. Dissatisfied with the rule of Yuan Shikai and, more immediately, the rule of Governor Li Yuanhong in Hubei, Ji Yulin had created through his Reform Corps a kind of shadow government that intended to engineer an uprising and assume command of the province. The conspiracy was detected and summarily quelled by the forces of Governor Li. Many of the leaders of the Reform Corps, however, escaped northward with a contingent of Hubei soldiers to join up with Bai Lang.[86]

Government reports claimed that the influx of the Reform Corps contributed to a greater sense of purpose and determination on the part of Bai Lang himself.[87] In any event, the fact that Bai Lang's army grew by incorporating disparate elements—southern revolutionaries superimposed on a core of impoverished hill peasants from western Henan—

created certain strains within the movement. These tensions surfaced at times when the bandit army was facing critical decisions of strategy. Whereas the brigands from western Henan tended to advocate that the group confine its sphere of activities to their native area, the southerners argued for a more ambitious plan.

The first of these tests came in mid-1913 when a military offensive initiated by the governor of Henan threatened Bai Lang's home base. The brigand chief convened a council of advisors to decide on the proper course of action. Although some of the cooperating bandit chieftains from western Henan advocated digging in to defend their home territory, a southern revolutionary—Liu Tie[88]—prevailed in arguing that the band should proceed south to Anhui. Liu's plan was for the bandits to link up with forces in Nanjing and prepare a joint northern expedition to rid the country of the Yuan Shikai menace. He argued that the band must transcend its parochial ethic of robbing the rich and helping the poor to become a force of national political significance. At first Bai Lang was reluctant to accept the advice, but when another councillor performed a divination pronouncing that to remain home would invite disaster, Bai Lang was convinced; the group proceeded toward Anhui. At this time Bai Lang may have intended to march southward through Anhui to join Huang Xing in Nanjing, but when the bandit chief learned—in the aftermath of the Second Revolution—that the Guomindang was in disarray, he traveled eastward to Hubei instead.[89] A more severe test of the internal cohesion of Bai Lang's army developed in May 1914 when the brigands, fighting in the inhospitable setting of Gansu Province, had clearly lost the upper hand. An outbreak of plague took the lives of a number of Bai Lang's followers.[90] Even more problematic was the overt hostility of the local Tibetan and Muslim populations. The enmity of the latter group was aroused when Bai Lang's troops killed a Muslim governor in battle.[91] Revenge exacted a severe toll on the bandit forces; in the fighting, Bai Lang himself lost two teeth to Muslim women armed with clubs. Although his army managed to take the city of Taozhou, they continued to face serious local resistance.[92]

In this demoralized (and demolarized) state, Bai Lang called together his subordinates to decide on a plan of action. His councillors again offered a diverse array of suggestions. One advisor advocated that the bandits make contact with royal Manchu remnants in an effort to restore the fallen Qing dynasty.[93] Another proposed instead that Bai Lang declare himself emperor. If he proved less successful than Zhu Yuanzhang (founder of the Ming dynasty), he might at least do as well as Hong Xiuquan (leader of the Taiping Rebellion). Both suggestions were quickly dismissed by the bandit chieftain. He noted that when the Manchus had occupied the dragon throne they had done nothing for him. But Bai Lang laughingly pointed out that his own family was not known for small heads or large veins—both said to be the marks of royalty! He asked for more practical proposals.[94] At this point an envoy from the southern revolutionaries offered his suggestion: The band should retreat to Sichuan Province to rest and build a secure base area. Bai Lang himself expressed agreement with the proposal, but was shouted down by his rank-and-file followers from western Henan who desperately wanted to return to their families. Weary of defeat and unmoved by the arguments for the need to establish a revolutionary base area, the peasant bandits longed instead for the security of home.[95] By this time the brigands had amassed a substantial store of plundered loot. Now their overriding desire was to return with their riches.[96]

Reluctantly, then, Bai Lang led his band across the bleak Gansu and Shaanxi plain toward the comfort of the western Henan hills. Although he had been impressed by the arguments of some of his more ambitious advisors, the bandit chief was ultimately dependent upon the support of his rank-and-file followers. Admittedly, his band had by this time grown to include a motley assortment of diverse groups; nevertheless, its hardcore membership was still drawn from the *tangjiang* of western Henan. Bai Lang's favoritism toward those from his native place was demonstrated on the return journey. When his band approached a particularly treacherous river, the bandit chief would order the soldiers from Hubei to cross first, thereby sparing his Henan brethren if the river proved impassable. The Reform Corps contingent was decimated in this fashion, and most of the surviving Hubei soldiers deserted in protest.[97]

Finally, in the summer of 1914, after months of roving banditry, the force (by then somewhat bedraggled) made its way back to the Baofeng area. Although Bai Lang attempted to set up camp at an inaccessible mountain stronghold on the Baofeng–Linru border, the majority of his followers elected to return directly to their own homes. Bai Lang himself made a quick visit to relatives in Lushan to collect about thirty rifles that were buried in his kinsmen's backyard.[98] But with only a few stalwart supporters, the chieftain was unable to hold out against the government troops and militia that were soon mobilized in opposition.

In mid-August, mortally wounded by government fire, Bai Lang went home to Daliuzhuang to die. Later, his corpse was dug up by government soldiers and its head was severed and sent to Lushan County seat for identification. When Bai Lang's eldest daughter recognized the head as that of her father, the bandit's case was officially closed and the now decomposed head was sent on to the provincial capital of Kaifeng to hang in ignominy on the southern wall.[99]

The effects of Bai Lang's activities continued to be felt for some time after the demise of the bandit chief. His kidnapping of foreign missionaries in the fall of 1913 and subsequent attacks on churches and Western business enterprises created friction with foreign powers that lingered beyond the life of the bandit movement itself. The Chinese government was required to pay compensation for the substantial losses that the British American Tobacco Company and other foreign concerns suffered from the assaults.[100] Despite proclamations claiming to protect commerce, Bai Lang's attacks had been directed against Chinese merchants as well.[101] It often took years to restore areas subjected to brigand assaults to earlier levels of marketing activity.

Conclusion

Scholars have debated the ways in which brigandage resonates with local social relations, the extent to which bandits display social justice, and the degree to which banditry can be transformed into a revolutionary movement. A single case study can, of course, add only limited evidence to one or another position in this ongoing debate. Nevertheless, the case of Bai Lang seems particularly well suited to such an exercise inasmuch as it has inspired many of the existing interpretations of Chinese brigandage.

Links between bandits and peasant families were a central feature in Bai Lang's movement. The bandit chief himself took to brigandage only after receiving his mother's approval; his son and uncle served as trusted subordinates in his army; and he returned to visit relatives shortly before his death. Bai Lang's basic strength was drawn from the support of poor peasant followers rather than from the protection of local powerholders. In this respect, our findings depart somewhat from Edward Friedman's view that Bai Lang's army is not correctly portrayed as a peasant movement. To quote Friedman, "It is . . . ex-tillers and ex-villagers and not the tillers remaining in the village who form the backbone of so-called peasant rebel movements. . . . They were marginal men, not tillers. Men with land to till do not make sustained rural revolutions."[102] It is not obvious, however, that Bai Lang's army qualifies as a "sustained rural revolution." And the limitations of the bandit movement, as Hobsbawm would predict, have much to do with the peasant quality of its participants. In the end, most of Bai Lang's followers were drawn back to the rural hills from whence they had issued.

Friedman is certainly correct to emphasize the mobility of Bai Lang's recruits. But to suggest that such mobility disqualified a person from peasant status seems to contradict rural realities. For many Chinese peasants—especially those living in ecologically insecure places such as the western Henan hills—mobility was a regular part of the peasant life cycle (see Chapter 1). As Eric Wolf has argued, a "tactically mobile" peasantry is particularly prone to rebellion (1969). Its mobility does not, however, deny its peasant character.

In part, we are faced here with a semantic riddle: When are peasants not peasants? When are they bandits? Robert Somers notes that "whatever the background of the individual gang member, in T'ang China, Republican China or twentieth-century Mexico, it is essential to recognize a simple but critical fact: by joining a bandit gang . . . he becomes a bandit."[103] To this we can all agree—bandits are indeed bandits—but must we also accept the stronger contention that those who become brigands necessarily "gave up their lot in life"[104] and assumed "a new identity"?[105] For most Chinese peasants the choice of banditry may have not been so dramatic and irrevocable a decision. In many parts of China—the western Henan hills included—banditry was an ever-present feature of rural life. Just as some peasants migrated out as beggars on a seasonal or short-term basis, some turned to brigandage to supplement their meager livelihood. Most would return home to take up plow and hoe again when circumstances allowed. For many of its rank-and-file participants, banditry was a temporary survival strategy rather than the embodiment of some new religious or political commitment.

To be sure, not all Chinese bandits replicated the Bai Lang pattern. For example, Bai Lang's contemporary, Du Qibin, was less close to Hobsbawm's "social bandit" than to Anton Blok's depiction of the bandit as dependent upon the favor of local powerholders. Still, Du Qibin's misplaced trust in the authorities resulted in his early execution, whereas Bai Lang's peasant base facilitated his survival.

Without attempting to determine how "typical" Bai Lang was of Chinese bandits, his case underlines the usefulness of Hobsbawm's conceptual schema. In his peasant base, his Robin Hood flavor, and his limited revolutionary potential, Bai Lang well exemplifies the model Hobsbawmian social bandit. While it is true that the bandit chief came to accept the advice of revolutionaries who joined his force, there is no evidence in the primary sources that ordinary members of his army saw themselves as engaged in a cause that superseded parochial peasant loyalties. On the contrary, when the choice between serving the revolution and returning to the security of home presented itself, most bandits stubbornly insisted on the latter course. A politically ambitious leader proved unable to convince his subordinates to abandon homely concerns in favor of higher revolutionary goals.

In the case of Bai Lang, some of the difficulties in converting this bandit outfit into a revolutionary force must be attributed to the revolutionaries themselves. Sun Yatsen, Huang Xing, and members of the Reform Corps were attempting to overthrow the warlord regime of Yuan Shikai and replace it with a republican form of government. They were thus advocating a political revolution in which Bai Lang's bandit army could serve as a useful ally. Opposition to Yuan Shikai did not take the form of a social revolution predicated on mass mobilization. Hence while revolutionary advisors offered strategic council to Bai Lang, they did not endeavor to mobilize his ranks. This was in striking contrast to the Communist revolutionaries who ventured into bandit zones of the North China plain only a decade later. And yet, as these latter-day social revolutionaries would also discover, the preexistence of bandit forces by no means ensured an easy transition to revolutionary victory.[106] Accustomed to fighting for limited goals of peasant survival, bandits were not easily attracted to the rigorous demands of revolutionary struggle and sacrifice.

Notes

Grateful acknowledgment is made to the Committee on Scholarly Communication with the People's Republic of China for the year in China during which research for this article was completed, and to the Graduate School Research Fund of the University of Washington for write-up support. Thanks are also due to Professors Cai Shaoqing and Mao Jiaqi of Nanjing University for their generous help in obtaining materials, and to Stephen Averill, Lenore Barkan, Philip Billingsley, and Edward Friedman for comments on an earlier draft. This chapter was originally published as an article in *Modern China* (July 1983).

    1. Hobshawm, 1972: 504–505.

    2. Chesneaux, 1972: 16; 1973: 35, 63; Mancall and Jidkoff, 1972: 125–134; Nagano, 1933: 270.

    3. Dai Xuanzhi, 1973: 61–78; He Xiya, 1925; Metzger, 1974: 455–458.

    4. Price, 1937: 829.

    5. The point that bandits must elicit protection from local powerholders is also made in Linda Lewin's article (1979).

    6. Blok, 1972:496; 1974: 99–102.

    7. Friedman, 1974b: 2–3.

    8. Friedman, 1974a: 131.

    9. Ibid., 147.

    10. Davis, 1977: 176–177.

    11. There has been considerable speculation about the origins of Bai Lang's name. According to the authoritative testimony of his daughters, the "Lang" of

his given name was written with the Chinese character meaning "clear and bright." Later, when Bai Lang had become a notorious bandit, government sources substituted the homophonic character meaning "wolf." Thus English accounts that refer to Bai Lang as "White Wolf" are reproducing a slanderous epithet that was not used by Bai Lang or his followers themselves. See *Kaifeng Shifan Xueyuan Xuebao* (hereafter KSXX), 1960: 81 for a discussion of this issue.

12. Banno, 1970; Billingsley, 1974, 1981; Chesneaux, 1973: 63; Friedman, 1974a: 117–164; Hegel, 1969.

13. These include the report of an investigation of Bai Lang's descendants conducted by Chinese researchers in 1959 (KSXX), an eight-volume chronicle of the Republican period published in China for internal circulation in 1973 (Cai and Xu, 1973), a 1981 compilation of archival materials and eyewitness narratives (*Bai Lang qiyi*, 1981), and a 1981 internal circulation collection drawn from more than twenty unpublished accounts of the Bai Lang movement (*Henan wenshi ziliao*, 1981). Despite the richness of the newly available materials— upon which this chapter is based—it must be admitted that many aspects of Bai Lang's movement remain obscure and open to diverse interpretations.

14. Friedman, 1974a: 123–125.

15. Ibid., 125.

16. Ibid., 146.

17. Ibid., 135.

18. Ibid., 136.

19. Actually, Friedman is a bit confusing on the "peasant" character of the movement. He insists at the outset that the bandit army was composed of a core of "ex-tillers" who "could move on, move anywhere because it had no place to move back to" (1974a: 125), who had enter[ed] a new life, tak[ing] on a new identity" (1974a: 146). Yet at the end he concludes that Bai Lang could not forge a national movement "out of rural dwellers with a narrow focus" (1974a: 162) and notes that government suppression efforts included an order to "exterminate the robbers' relatives, confiscate their farms and burn down their homes to prevent uncaught brigands from returning to their homes" (1974a: 164).

20. Ibid., 158.

21. Ibid., 122.

22. Ibid., 154.

23. Ibid., 154.

24. Billingsley, 1974: 57.

25. Banno presents considerable evidence (corroborated by the newly available materials) that Bai Lang consciously attacked both merchants and foreigners. This contrasts with Friedman's contention that Bai Lang provided "succor for the merchants" (1974a: 123) or Charlotte Hegel's claim that Bai Lang's movement showed "no evidence of any anti-imperialist sentiment" (1969: 50). It may be, as Philip Billingsley has suggested, that Bai Lang continued to attack merchants until he was affected by Guomindang pressure, after which he gradually desisted.

26. Banno, 1970: 11–12.

27. Much of the following account is based on field work carried out in Bai Lang's native area in November 1959 by a team of eleven researchers from Kaifeng Teachers' College. In three and a half weeks of intensive investigations, the researchers conducted interviews with 85 informants in 97 individual ses-

sions. They also convened 23 group discussion meetings to elicit information on Bai Lang and his movement. Since the respondents included two of Bai Lang's own daughters, as well as many of his close associates, the interviews yielded a remarkable fund of reliable data. The results were published in the May 1960 issue of the *Kaifeng Teachers' College Journal* (KSXX); a preview summary had appeared in *Shixue yuekan* (Historiography Monthly) in January 1960.

28. KSXX, 1960: 75.

29. Ibid., 77.

30. The character *tang* means to trudge through muddy waters; thus *tang-jiang* were people who performed their work in the midst of muddy water.

31. KSXX, 1960: 73, 77.

32. Ibid., 78–79.

33. Establishment of the Baofeng Tax Bureau was part of a national trend of tax increases to pay for the Boxer indemnities and the Qing government's "New Policies" (*xinzheng*). The exaction elicited a wave of rural tax resistance that swept China in the first decade of the twentieth century.

34. KSXX, 1960: 79.

35. Cai and Xu, 1973: 269–270.

36. KSXX, 1960: 80.

37. Ibid., 80.

38. Ibid., 82; *Bai Lang qiyi*, 1981: 20.

39. *Bai Lang qiyi*, 1981: 339; *Henan wenshi ziliao*, 1981: 52.

40. KSXX, 1960: 83.

41. *Henan wenshi ziliao*, 1981:12.

42. KSXX, 1960: 83; Qiao Xuwu, 1956: 133; *Henan wenshi ziliao*, 1981: 14–15.

43. KSXX, 1960: 84; *Bai Lang qiyi*, 1981: 5–7; *Henan wenshi ziliao*, 1981: 17–18.

44. *Bai Lang qiyi*, 1981: 282.

45. KSXX, 1960: 87–88.

46. "Bai Lang zhi zhenxiang," 1914: 6.

47. *Bai Lang qiyi*, 1981: 364.

48. *Henan wenshi ziliao*, 1981: 43.

49. *Bai Lang qiyi*, 1981: 222.

50. Ibid., 202.

51. *Henan wenshi ziliao*, 1981: 49; *Bai Lang qiyi*, 1981: 364.

52. *Henan wenshi ziliao*, 1981: 53.

53. *Bai Lang qiyi*, 1981: 190.

54. KSXX, 1960: 87.

55. *Bai Lang qiyi,* 1981:153.

56. Ibid., 181.

57. Ibid., 323.

58. Ibid., 52,111.

59. Ibid., 382.

60. Ibid., 382; "Bai Lang zhi zhenxiang," 1914: 8.

61. *Bai Lang qiyi*, 1981: 232.

62. Ibid., 242.

63. Ibid., 316; *North China Herald*, February 7, 1914: 391.

64. *Henan wenshi ziliao*, 1981: 37.

65. *Bai Lang qiyi*, 1981: 285.
66. Ibid., 205.
67. Ibid., 56.
68. Tao Juyin, 1957: 39.
69. *Henan wenshi ziliao*, 1981: 14, 20.
70. *Bai Lang qiyi*, 1981: 335.
71. *Henan wenshi ziliao*, 1981: 26; *Bai Lang qiyi*, 1981: 312.
72. *Bai Lang qiyi*, 1981: 312.
73. Cai and Xu, 1973: 207–209.
74. *Henan wenshi ziliao*, 1981: 21.
75. *Bai Lang qiyi*, 1981: 343.
76. *Henan wenshi ziliao*, 1981: 47.
77. *Bai Lang qiyi*, 1981: 405.
78. Friedman, 1974a: 144–152; Hegel, 1969: 35–44; Banno, 1970: 18–19.
79. Friedman, 1974a: 144–152; Hegel, 1969: 35–44; Banno, 1970: 18–19.
80. Zhou Yanfa, 1963: 54.
81. KSXX, 1960: 90–91. Perhaps the emissary was Ling Yue, a Guomindang member from Henan sent by Sun Yatsen in 1914 to make contact with Bai Lang, but who was unable to complete the mission (Qiao Xuwu, 1956:140). Further information on Sun Yatsen's willingness to supply the brigands with military aid can be found in *Bai Lang qiyi* (1981: 134, 364).
82. *Bai Lang qiyi*, 1981: 228, 233.
83. Cai and Xu, 1973: 269; *North China Herald*, February 14, 1914: 457.
84. Xian Yun, 1956: 144–152; *Bai Lang qiyi*, 1981: 223–223; *North China Herald*, April 25, 1914: 268; Qiao Xuwu, 1956: 139.
85. KSXX, 1960:91.
86. Cai and Xu, 1973: 207–208. Joseph Esherick (1976: 253) records that the Reform Corps leaders fled to Shanghai. The *Minguo tongsu yanyi* (Cai and Xu, 1973: 207–208), however, asserts that although Ji Yulin himself fled the area (possibly to Shanghai), other Reform Corps leaders—Xiong Bingkun, Zeng Shangwu, Liu Yaoqing, and Huang Jun—all linked up with Bai Lang.
87. *Bai Lang qiyi*, 1981: 339.
88. The *Central China Post*, of October 9, 1913, reported that Liu Tie, "the revolutionist who declared the independence of Shayang on the Han River two months ago," was serving as Bai Lang's chief advisor. See *Records of the Department of State*, 893.00/2000.
89. Cai and Xu, 1973: 270–271.
90. *Henan wenshi ziliao*, 1981: 46.
91. *North China Herald*, June 13, 1914: 180.
92. KSXX, 1960: 92; Qiao Xuwu, 1956: 137.
93. Research by Philip Billingsley shows that Bai Lang's band had in earlier days enjoyed close links with the pro-Manchu restorationist party. (See Phil Billingsley, *Bandits in Republican China* [Stanford: Stanford University Press, 1988].)
94. Cai and Xu, 1973: 332–333.
95. KSXX 1960: 92; Cai and Xu, 1973: 333.
96. *Bai Lang qiyi*, 1981: 349.
97. KSXX 1960: 93.

98. Xian Yun, 1956: 154.
99. KSXX, 1960: 94–95; Cai and Xu, 1973: 335; Qiao Xuwu, 1956: 138. A photograph of Bai Lang's (unrecognizable) head on the Kaifeng city wall can be found in White (1942: 30).
100. *Bai Lang qiyi*, 1981: 61.
101. Ibid., 3, 135; Xian Yun, 1956: 147.
102. Friedman, 1974a: 124–125.
103. Somers, 1979: 16.
104. Ibid.
105. Friedman, 1974a: 146.
106. Perry, 1980.

References

Bai Lang qiyi (The Bai Lang uprising). 1981. Nanjing: Chinese Academy of Social Sciences, Institute of Modern History.
"Bai Lang zhi zhenxiang" (The real facts about Bai Lang). 1914. *Yongyan* 2,4:1–9.
Banno Ryokichi. 1970. "Hakuru kigi no rekishiteki igi o megutte" (A look at the historical significance of the Bai Lang uprising). *Rekishi hyoron* 243:4–24.
Billingsley, Philip. 1981. "Bandits, Bosses and Bare Sticks: Beneath the Surface of Local Control in Early Republican China." *Modern China* 7,3:235–288.
———. 1974. Banditry in China: 1911–1928. PhD. Dissertation, University of Leeds, England.
Blok, Anton. 1974. *The Mafia of a Sicilian Village*. New York: Harper and Row.
———. 1972. "The Peasant and the Brigand: Social Banditry Reconsidered." *Comparative Studies in Society and History* 14:495–504.
Cai Dongfan and Xu Jinfa, eds. 1973. *Minguo tongsu yanyi* (Popular chronicles of the Republic). Beijing: Zhonghua.
Chesneaux, Jean. 1973. *Peasant Revolts in China, 1840–1949*. New York: Norton.
———. 1972. *Popular Movements and Secret Societies in China, 1840–1949*. Stanford: Stanford University Press.
Dai Xuanzhi. 1973. *Hongqianghui* (The Red Spear society). Taibei: Shihuo.
Davis, Fei-Ling. 1977. *Primitive Revolutionaries of China*. Honolulu: University of Hawaii Press.
Dong Kechang. 1960. "Guanyu Bai Lang qiyi de xingzhi" (Concerning the nature of the Bai Lang uprising). *Shixue yuekan* 5:22–27.
———. 1958. "Bai Lang qiyi xingzhi ji zuoyong de yanjiu" (Study of the nature and function of the Bai Lang uprising). *Xueshu luntan* 3:34–48.
Du Chunhe. 1981. "Guanyu Bai Lang qiyi de jige wenti" (Several questions concerning the Bai Lang uprising). *Jindaishi yanjiu* 1:292–304.
Esherick, Joseph. 1976. *Reform and Revolution in China: The 1911 Revolution in Hunan and Hubei*. Berkeley: University of California Press.
Friedman, Edward. 1974a. *Backward Toward Revolution: The Chinese Revolutionary Party*. Berkeley: University of California Press.
———. 1974b. "Primitive Rebel Versus Modern Revolutionary: A Case of Mis-

taken Identity?" Presented to the annual meeting of the Association for Asian Studies.

He Xiya. 1925. *Zhongguo daofei wenti zhi yanjiu* (A study of the Chinese bandit problem). Shanghai: Taidong.

Hegel, Charlotte. 1969. "The White Wolf: The Career of a Chinese Bandit." M.A. thesis, Columbia University.

Henan wenshi ziliao (Materials on Henan literature and history). 1981. 1:10–55.

Hobsbawm, Eric J. 1981. *Bandits*. New York: Pantheon.

———. 1972. "Reply." *Comparative Studies in Society and History* 14:504–507.

———. 1959. *Primitive Rebels*. New York: Norton.

Huang Guangguo. 1960a. "You guan Bai Lang qiyi de yixie ziliao" (Some materials concerning the Bai Lang uprising). *Shixue yuekan* 2:24–27.

———. 1960b. "You guan diguozhuyi dui Bai Lang qiyi ganshe de ziliao" (Materials concerning the imperialist interference in the Bai Lang uprising). *Shixue yuekan* 4:33–34. *Kaifeng shifan xueyuan xuebao* (KSXX) (Journal of Kaifeng Teachers' College). 1960. "Bai Lang qiyi diaocha baogao" (Report of the investigation of the Bai Lang uprising). KSXX 5:68–104.

Kaifeng shiyuan lishixi (History Department of Kaifeng Teachers' College), ed. 1960. "Bai Lang qiyi diaocha jianji" (A summary report of the investigation of the Bai Lang uprising). *Shixue yuekan* 1:18–23.

Lai Xinxia. 1957. "Tan Minguo chunian Bai Lang lingdao de nongmin qiyi" (A discussion of the peasant uprising led by Bai Lang in the early Republic). *Shixue yuekan* 6:11–16.

Lewin, Linda. 1979. "The Oligarchical Limitations of Social Banditry in Brazil: The Case of the 'Good' Thief Antonio Silvino." *Past and Present* 82:116–146.

Mancall, Mark, and Georges Jidkoff. 1972. "The Hung Hu-tzu of Northeast China." In Jean Chesneaux, ed., *Popular Movements and Secret Societies in China, 1840–1950*, pp. 125–134. Stanford: Stanford University Press.

Metzger, Thomas A. 1974. "Chinese Bandits: The Traditional Perception Reevaluated." *Journal of Asian Studies* 33:455–458.

Nagano, Akira. 1938. *Shina hei dohi kosokai* (Chinese soldiers, bandits, Red Spears). Tokyo.

———. 1933. *Shina nomin undokan* (A view of the Chinese peasant movement). Tokyo: Kensetsu.

———. 1931. *Dohi guntai kosokai* (Bandits, soldiers, Red Spears). Tokyo: Shina mondai kenkyujo.

North China Herald. Various issues. Shanghai.

Perry, Elizabeth J. 1980. *Rebels and Revolutionaries in North China, 1845–1945*. Stanford: Stanford University Press.

Price, Willard. 1937. "Bandits of the Grand Canal." *Blackwood's Magazine* 241:829–843.

Qiao Xuwu. 1956. "Ji Bai Lang shi" (A record of the Bai Lang incident). *Jindaishi ziliao* 3:132–140.

Records of the Department of State Relating to Internal Affairs of China, 1910–1920. Microfilm collection.

Somers, Robert M. 1979. "Banditry, Militarization and State Formation in the Late T'ang: The Origins of Sung China." Presented to the China Colloquium of the University of Washington. Quoted with author's permission.

Tao Juyin. 1957. *Beiyang junfa tongzhi shiqi shihua* (Historical stories of the period of Beiyang warlord rule). Beijing: Sanlian.

Wang Zhongyu. 1964. "Shi lun Bai Lang qiyi de xingzhi" (A preliminary discussion of the nature of the Bai Lang uprising). *Shixue yuekan* 12:20–24.

White, William Charles. 1942. *Chinese Jews.* Toronto: University of Toronto Press.

Wolf, Eric R. 1969. *Peasant Wars in the Twentieth Century.* New York: Harper & Row.

Xian Yun. 1956. "Bai Lang shimo ji" (A complete record of Bai Lang). *Jindaishi ziliao* 3:141–157.

Young, Ernest P. 1977. *The Presidency of Yuan Shih-k'ai: Liberalism and Dictatorship in Early Republican China.* Ann Arbor: University of Michigan Press.

Zhou Yanfa. 1963. "Guanyu Huang Xing zhi Bai Lang zhi mihan" (On the secret letter from Huang Xing to Bai Lang). *Beijing shifan daxue xuebao* 1:54.

5

Skilled Workers and the Chinese Revolution: Strikes Among Shanghai Silk Weavers, 1927–1937

Studies of the Chinese labor movement generally end their story in the spring of 1927, when Chiang Kaishek's bloody Shanghai massacre drove a shattered Communist Party out of the cities and into the countryside. From that point on, we are led to believe, the urban proletariat was politically insignificant. The Chinese revolution became a peasant war, fought and won in the rural hinterland.

The focus of Communist activities did indeed shift away from the urban workers after April 1927. But the history of the Chinese labor movement is not identical with Party history. Just as Chinese workers had been active well before the founding of the Communist Party, so they continued their struggles well after the mass executions and forced exodus of Communist labor organizers in 1927. Indeed, certain sectors of the work force grew much more feisty during the Nanjing decade (1927–37) than they had ever been under Communist inspiration. One such group was the Shanghai silk weavers.

The silk weavers of Shanghai were known in the 1920s as China's "labor aristocrats" (*guizu gongren*). Occupying skilled jobs that paid well, these laborers were notably absent from the massive strikes that swept through most of the city's factories in that period. While workers in other Shanghai industries responded actively to the spirit of the May Fourth (1919) and May Thirtieth (1925) movements, silk weavers remained quietly at their jobs. By the turn of the decade, however, the situation had changed. As producers of a luxury commodity tailored toward an international market, silk weavers were especially vulnerable to fluctuations in the world economy. That economy brought them prosperity in the 1920s, but a few years later—in the wake of the Great Depression, the Japanese invasion of Manchuria, the disastrous Yellow River flood, and the Sino-Japanese conflict in Shanghai—the picture was notably less bright. Scores of small silk-weaving enterprises suspended operations, putting thousands of Shanghai's skilled weavers out of work.

Strike Waves

The difficulties of the silk-weaving industry were reflected in the strikes of its workers. The years 1930, 1934, and 1937 all saw massive strike waves among Shanghai silk weavers. The pattern is very different from that which obtained in the city as a whole. For most of the city's workers, 1925–27 was the period of greatest labor unrest. The years 1930 and 1934, in most Shanghai factories, actually saw a decrease in the level of strike activity; and although 1937 was a year of increased strikes, the magnitude of that increase was far greater among silk weavers than was found in the city as a whole.[1]

The silk weavers' increased protest activity was obviously related to the fact that by the early 1930s their industry had fallen on hard times. Exports of finished silk products fell steadily during the Nanjing decade. But the relationship between economic hardship and labor unrest was not as straightforward as may at first appear, for the depression years saw not only a general *decline* in the silk-weaving industry, but also a fundamental *restructuring* of the industry. While the smaller silk-weaving factories found themselves forced to lay off substantial numbers of workers or suspend operations altogether, a few of the larger concerns continued to expand, thereby coming to dominate the industry. Strike activity, as we will see, was heavily concentrated in these more prosperous enterprises.

The most successful survivor of the depression years was the Meiya Company, founded in 1920 with comprador capital as a small factory of only twelve looms and thirty to forty weavers. Business improved rapidly the following year when the comprador's son-in-law, Cai Shengbai, was hired as general manager. Recently returned to Shanghai from an educational stint at Lehigh University, Cai quickly put his American know-how to use by importing the latest model U.S.-made looms and recruiting educated workers to operate them. Cai's two personnel managers, natives of eastern Zhejiang Province, made frequent trips home to Shengxian and Dongyang counties to enlist bright young women apprentice weavers. Only those who passed a difficult technical test were admitted as apprentices. Thanks to the skill of its enthusiastic young workers, Meiya had by 1927 developed into the largest silk-weaving concern in all of China, with 408 looms and more than thirteen hundred employees, over half of whom were serving a four- to five-year term as apprentices. To encourage high output among the young weavers, the company sponsored production contests, paid generous wages, and provided a variety of services: dormitories, cafeterias, clinic, library, night school, recreation club, sports teams, and the like. Aided by such forward-looking management, Meiya in the space of a decade grew into a ten-factory conglomerate with more than a thousand looms. Most silk-weaving establishments in the city had fewer than ten looms in operation.[2]

With both its source of materials and its market outlets more diversified than other silk-weaving operations, Meiya was better positioned to withstand the upheavals of the depression. As many of its less fortunate competitors fell by the wayside, the Meiya Company continued to enjoy hefty profit margins. By 1934, Meiya's one thousand looms accounted for half of all the silk-weaving looms in operation in Shanghai.[3]

Success itself bred problems for Meiya's managers, however. The highly skilled and productive young employees, aware of the company's prosperity, began to press for additional perquisites. In early 1927 a portion of the Meiya work force—inspired by the urgings of He Datong, a Marxist student who hailed from eastern Zhejiang—engaged in a brief work stoppage to demand a wage increase, greater job security, and recognition of a labor union. Although General Manager Cai initially balked at these requests, he reversed his position when He Datong paid a visit to Meiya headquarters with revolver in hand. The company agreed to a 40 percent wage hike, strike pay, no dismissals without just cause, and subsidy for a labor union. On March 21, 1927, the Meiya union was inaugurated. Shortly after Chiang Kaishek's April coup, however, He Datong was put under surveillance by the Guomindang authorities. When police raided a clandestine meeting of Communist labor organizers, He Datong fled to the street below—only to slip on a watermelon rind.

Immediately apprehended, he was executed shortly thereafter at the age of twenty-four.[4]

With the demise of He Datong and the attendant dissolution of the Meiya labor union, the company, in an attempt to improve discipline among its newly hired employees, reneged on its earlier collective agreement. In 1930 a worker was fired on grounds of incompetence, and the remaining employees were required to sign an employment contract that substantially reduced their earlier rights. In protest, weavers at eight Meiya factories (1,229 men and women) struck for two weeks. The outcome was a partial victory for each side: in theory, the 1927 collective agreement would be honored, but at the same time workers would have to submit to an employment contract. Dissatisfied with the result, the weavers struck again two months later, in the summer of 1930. This time the protest lasted thirty-five days and ended with a settlement more favorable to the workers, negotiated by the Shanghai Bureau of Social Affairs: the 1927 agreement was completely upheld, workers' bonuses were to be distributed, and recently hired temporary workers would be given permanent-worker status.[5]

The unrest of 1930 spelled not the end, but the beginning, of serious labor troubles for Meiya. A few years later, the sharp decline in the price of silk fabric (which dropped by some 50 percent from 1933 to 1934) precipitated another, more dramatic conflict. With a large supply of unemployed silk weavers milling about the city, Meiya's profit-hungry managers decided this was a convenient time to cut labor costs. In 1933, Meiya reduced workers' wages by 10 percent. The following year, the company announced a second round of wage cuts (averaging 15 percent). This time, however, the employees were not so compliant. In the spring of 1934, workers at all ten of Meiya's factories—4,500 men, women, and children—went on strike. Pointing out that the company had enjoyed record sales in 1933, the strikers demanded restoration of their pre-1933 wages. For more than fifty frenzied and often violent days, they pressed their case—with management, city and Party officials, police, and the public. In the process the strikers forged links with outside allies, most notably the Communist Youth League. These connections would cost them dearly, for the strike ended with the abrupt dismissal of some 143 workers accused of radical sympathies. But government suspicions notwithstanding, the strike was not simply the brainchild of outside Communist agitators. Its impressive organization and articulate demands were features commonly found in the protest of factory artisans: the classic artisan strike is one in which skilled workers resist capitalist initiatives by recourse to pre-existing organizations and moralistic claims. Meiya weavers practiced a style of politics befitting their reputation as "labor aristocrats."

The unsuccessful strike of 1934 marked the end of this particular type of silk-weaver protest, however. In subsequent years, as weavers became more "proletarianized," outside parties played a greater role in their political activities. With the recovery of Shanghai's textile industry in 1936–37, dozens of small silk-weaving enterprises reopened. Officially sponsored unions found ready recruits among the recently rehired employees. The 1937 strike wave, which touched more than two hundred of the city's silk-weaving factories, was testimony to the broad reach of the newly established unions. Thanks to government (and gangster) connections, the union-sponsored strikes proved somewhat more successful in attaining their demands, but not without a substantial decline in worker independence.

Had the story of the Shanghai silk weavers ended with the close of the Nanjing decade, it would be a sad tale indeed. By the time of the Japanese invasion in the summer of 1937, the weavers seemed to have lost many of the distinguishing features of a labor aristocracy: pride, control, autonomy. More exploitative forms of management and increased political interference had left these once fortunate workers in a much less enviable position. But of course the Shanghai labor movement did *not* disappear in the wake of the Japanese occupation. During the Sino-Japanese War (1937–45) and subsequent Civil War (1945–49) periods, worker activism—inspired increasingly by Communist revolutionaries returned from their sojourn in the countryside—grew in both frequency and political impact. At the forefront of this resurgence in labor unrest stood the silk weavers; proletarianized and politicized by their experiences under the Nanjing regime, these workers were to play a key role in the development of the radical labor movement that eventually helped unravel Guomindang control and usher in a new socialist regime (see Chapter 6).

"Modern" and "Traditional" Weavers

Who were these silk weavers and how did they manage to become such a significant political force? The numerical strength of Shanghai silk weavers fluctuated dramatically in these years: at the height of the depression, employed silk weavers numbered fewer than ten thousand, but with the recovery of the industry in 1936–37 more than forty thousand silk weavers were working in the city.[6] Within this sizable and shifting work force, we can distinguish two rather different types of weavers. The most secure and most prestigiously employed group hailed from the eastern Zhejiang counties of Shengxian and Dongyang. These workers were educated young men and women who began their weaving careers with employment in the new, modernized factories of Meiya and other large companies. The move to Shanghai was for them a form of upward mobility. From the more than twenty-five hundred job application forms that remain in the Meiya archives, we can see that the great majority of new recruits came from peasant families. Yet these young weavers, most of whom were still in their twenties when they entered the factory, were unusual peasant sons and daughters inasmuch as nearly all had received at least an elementary education.[7]

A different sort of worker came from the traditional rural handicraft areas of Hangzhou, Huzhou, and Suzhou. Raised in families that had practiced small-scale silk weaving for generations, these workers tended to be older and less well educated, driven out of their homes in the countryside by the decline of the rural handicraft industry. For them, the move to Shanghai represented an unwelcome process of "proletarianization" in which they lost much of the freedom and control characteristic of traditional artisan production. Such weavers usually worked in small factories for lower wages and less job security than that enjoyed by their counterparts in the more "modern" sector of the industry.[8]

The contrast between the two types of weavers is suggested by a look at their literacy rates. A 1938 investigation among Shanghai silk weavers found that male weavers from eastern Zhejiang had an amazingly high literacy rate of 95 percent, with 30 percent having a middle school education, 40 percent a primary school education, and an additional 25 percent at least some minimal degree of literacy. Among women weavers from eastern Zhejiang, the literacy rate was found to be 35 percent. In large part, this impressive literacy level was the result of Meiya's early hiring practices. By contrast, silk weavers from Hangzhou, Suzhou, and Huzhou—who comprised the overwhelming majority of workers at smaller factories—had far lower rates: 20–30 percent literacy among males and even lower levels for females.[9]

About half of those employed in the Shanghai silk-weaving industry were women. In the smaller factories, women tended to be confined to the Preparation Department (*zhunbei bu*), whereas men worked in the Weaving Department (*jizhi bu*), performing the skilled work of operating the looms. This division of labor by gender perpetuated long-standing practice in the Zhejiang countryside; silk weaving had usually been a male occupation in which weavers were responsible for the operation, maintenance, and repair of their looms. Women, it was widely believed, should not be engaged in the unseemly behavior of climbing about fixing complicated machinery. At the Meiya Company, Cai Shengbai's new management procedures led to a break with this traditional division of labor. Finding that women weavers were often as productive as (or even more productive than) men, Meiya hired large numbers of female weavers at wages only 80–90 percent of the pay for males. The intention was to reduce costs as well as to create a more docile labor force, since popular wisdom held that women workers were less demanding than men. Weavers at Meiya—whether male or female—were relieved of the burden of machine repair by specialized mechanics trained at the Hangzhou Technical Institute.[10]

Differences in native place, educational level, and employment conditions were also reflected in the popular culture of these two groups of Shanghai silk weavers. The young, securely employed literates from eastern Zhejiang prided themselves on being sophisticated urbanites, fully attuned to the ways of the big city. When they had saved up some money, they spent it on the accoutrements of a "modern" life-style: Western clothing, leather shoes, trolley rides, movie tickets, foreign food. These weavers were seldom religious, and their friendship and mutual aid clubs were not of the traditional secret-society or sworn-brotherhood sort. Marriages among them were rarely arranged by family heads back in the countryside; instead they were often love matches with a simple wedding ceremony—or no ceremony at all for those who preferred the cohabitation popular among the Shanghai students whose ways they so admired.

The young weavers had not abandoned all their native eastern Zhejiang customs in the move to the big city, however. Many of them were talented singers of Shaoxing opera, a skill they parlayed as guest performers in local teahouses. At the Meiya Company, weavers formed a Shaoxing opera troupe that served as the organizational nucleus of the 1927 strike.[11] It was said that their stage experience and penchant for the dramatic made these weavers effective public speakers; certainly the Meiya strike of 1934 offered ample evidence of their ability to inspire a crowd. Identification with native place was thus still salient among these "modern" labor aristocrats. The early Communist network at Meiya was in fact organized along native-place lines.[12]

The largely illiterate workers from Hangzhou, Huzhou, and Suzhou adhered to a rather different set of norms. Peasant-artisans by upbringing and instinct, these older weavers brought along much more of their rural heritage to soften the trauma of adjustment to life in Shanghai. Wearing the familiar clothing of the countryside (blue cotton jacket and trousers), they lived together in crowded, squalid conditions. For the most part, they were deeply religious: many were Buddhists, a few were Christian converts, and virtually all believed in the unalterable power of fate. Marriages and funerals were an opportunity to rehearse rural rituals, complete with raucous drinking and feasting, which reinforced native solidarities. Kinship ties remained strong among these weavers, who often entered the silk factory in entire families. When these immigrants sought a Shanghai role model for emulation, it was not the student but the gangster to whom they turned. Sworn brotherhoods, sisterhoods, and secret societies such as the Green Gang helped provide some social identity for these uprooted rustics.[13] As one woman weaver recalled,

> Ten of us in the Preparation Department of the Dacheng silk-weaving factory formed a sisterhood. Elder sisters one and two were from Hangzhou, as were sisters five and six. On our day off we met at a pavilion in a park and the one of us who could write scribbled all our names on a red piece of paper. She also wrote our group motto: "Share good fortune and troubles alike." The paper was kept by the eldest sister. After the ceremony we all went to an amusement center to enjoy ourselves.[14]

Such groups could constitute an important informal support structure within a factory. The informant above remembered that she once avoided paying a hefty fine imposed by her supervisor only because her nine sisters threatened to engage in a slowdown unless she was pardoned.[15]

This basic division between "modern" and "traditional" silk weavers in Shanghai was reflected in their political activities. To oversimplify somewhat, the literate, urbane workers from eastern Zhejiang (active in the strikes of 1930 and 1934) tended to undertake well-organized protests for clearly articulated demands—demands that might even lay claim to new rights and resources. Workers from rural weaving backgrounds (active in the 1936–37 strikes) tended, by contrast, to engage in briefer protests that seldom went beyond an effort to reclaim lost ground. Yet despite this (often blurred) distinction, the gulf separating Shanghai's silk weavers was not so vast as to preclude cooperation. Unlike the situation in many other Shanghai industries, among silk weavers fights between rival native-place associations were rare—at least until union organizers purposely stimulated such tensions. Sharing a sense of pride in their work as artisans, silk weavers were capable of uniting in pursuit of common goals. While Meiya's educated employees stood in 1934 at the forefront of agitation among Shanghai silk weavers, workers in smaller enterprises were quick to lend support. Just as Meiya's general manager functioned as an industry leader (having formed the Shanghai Silk Weaving Employers' Association in February 1934), so his workers played a vanguard role for other silk weavers in the city.

The Meiya Strike of 1934

The wage cut that precipitated the famous 1934 Meiya strike was prompted by anxiety over recent market trends. In 1928–31, buyers in India and Southeast Asia had accounted for more than half the company's total sales. Over the next few years, however, Japanese competitors made significant gains in both markets; by 1934, Meiya's exports had dropped to 28 percent of total sales. While 1933 had certainly been a boom year for the company (with sales reaching a record high of more than 6 million yuan), Cai Shengbai feared that the shift to reliance on the domestic market spelled hard times ahead.[16] He therefore hoped to reduce operating expenses in anticipation of a business decline. According to company figures, wages at Meiya comprised an unusually high proportion of operating expenses, equivalent to 18 percent of sales. Thus it was from the payroll that Cai hoped to make the reductions to ward off a feared drop in profits.[17]

Management announced the decision to cut wages on March 2, the day after workers had returned from their New Year's holiday. The following morning, weavers at the company's Number Six factory—the branch that housed Meiya's experimental laboratory and therefore employed many of its most skilled craftsmen—refused to show up for work.[18]

Protest was no stranger to the artisans at Number Six. Several months earlier, ten of the most skilled craftsmen at the factory (operators of the complicated "five-tiered looms") had started a slowdown to demand higher wages. They were soon supported by others at Number Six: a small progressive reading group that had predated the strike expanded into a larger friendly society (*youyi hui*) of forty to fifty people, which also joined the work stoppage. After a month's agitation, the weavers succeeded in winning the wage hike for which they had struggled. Energized by this victory, the workers at Number Six inaugurated an all-company friendly society, with branches at each of the ten Meiya factories.[19]

Behind the scenes, a clandestine network of politicized workers buttressed the openly established friendly society. At Meiya Number Four, for example, some ten to fifteen weavers had joined the underground Communist Party during the initial years of Guomindang rule.[20] At Number Six, ten weavers had entered the Communist Youth League. Several of these league members elected to remain at their factory over the New Year's holiday in 1934, preparing for an anticipated additional round of wage cuts by Meiya management.[21]

Thus there was already an organizational network in place when on March 3 the strikers at Number Six dispatched deputies to the other branch factories in search of support.[22] They went first to nearby Number Nine, which had an all-female work force of relatively unskilled laborers. The superintendent of Number Nine, who happened to be at Meiya headquarters when the strike first began, boasted confidently to the general manager that the docile workers at his factory fully accepted the wage cut and would definitely not join the protest. Much to his chagrin, however, the women weavers at Number Nine were the first to follow the lead of their neighboring strikers. Within a few days the rest of Meiya's workers, except for the apprentices (numbering five hundred youths), had also joined the protest.[23]

Workers at each of the ten branch factories rapidly organized into small groups of about five to ten people. Each small group chose its own group leader, who thereby became a member of that branch factory's strike committee. The ten branch committees, in turn, selected three delegates to form the central strike committee, headquartered at Number Six and chaired by a Communist Youth League member from that factory. Under this central governing committee were established five functional units: general affairs, organization, propaganda, liaison, and security. The general affairs unit handled documents and accounts; the organization division was in charge of registration, investigation, and marshaling of strikers; the propaganda office, directed by another Communist Youth League member from Number Six, solicited monetary contributions and published a weekly newsletter about the strike; the liaison department was responsible for initiating negotiations and keeping in contact with outside parties; the security personnel were charged with maintaining order, protecting delegates at meetings, gathering intelligence, guarding factory machinery, provisioning food, and the like.[24]

These rapid organizational developments reflected pre-existing informal networks among the workers. At Number Six, for example, the picket group in charge of security comprised a twelve-man sworn brotherhood association that had predated the strike by five years.[25] Native-place bonds were also used in organizing workers. Zhang Qi, a skilled weaver at Number Six who hailed from the Zhejiang county of Pujiang, quickly succeeded in mobilizing the many women weavers at Number Seven who shared his native-place affiliation.[26] Probably because of such long-standing bonds, strikers were notably responsive to the directions of the strike leadership. As one participant recalled,

> During the strike the workers were very disciplined. Every day we went to the factory to receive instructions. When we got to the factory, first we bowed three times in front of a portrait of Sun Yatsen. Then we followed the instructions of the strike leaders. Some of us were assigned to guard duty, while others were sent out to collect contributions.[27]

Fortified by their remarkable organizational apparatus, the Meiya strikers proceeded to articulate their grievances. On March 9, they issued a statement of their position, notable for its defensive, moralistic tone: "So long as we can survive [*shengcun*], so long as management sustains our survival, we will gladly suffer tribulation and oppression. . . . All we demand is survival. . . . Now wages have been cut again and survival cannot be sustained, so why must we continue to suffer day after day? Under such pressures, we have no choice but to resort to our ultimate weapon: strike!"[28]

Judged by comparison with workers in other industries, the silk weavers' plight was in fact not nearly so dismal as the Meiya manifesto suggested. In 1934, silk weavers remained one of the most highly paid groups of workers in Shanghai, below only shipbuilders, printers, and mechanics. Their hourly wage rate (Ch$0.087) was a full three times the amount that workers in the unskilled silk-reeling industry received, for example. Moreover, even among silk weavers the Meiya workers were especially fortunate, with wages averaging double those paid to weavers in smaller, more traditional enterprises in the city.[29] Cai Shengbai's wage cuts were designed to bring the Meiya pay scale in line with prevailing wages in the industry, thereby increasing the competitiveness of his products.[30] It was not *absolute* deprivation, but rather the sharp *relative* decline in income, that drove the weavers to protest.

Meiya's silk weavers hoped to halt their recent reversals by appealing to the sympathy of their employer. They argued that the key issue was the "moral" question of whether wages were sufficient to maintain a decent livelihood for a worker's family, rather than the "rational" question of whether wages occupied too high a percentage of company expenses.[31] Having learned from past experience that the Bureau of Social Affairs—the city's official agency for labor dispute mediation—was often ineffective, the strikers decided initially to negotiate directly with Meiya management. Accordingly, the central strike committee notified

General Manger Cai Shengbai of its intention to open discussions on the afternoon of March 11 at the Number One factory on rue Bremier de Montmorand in the French Concession.

On the agreed-upon day, some forty workers' representatives—accompanied by more than two hundred of their security personnel—arrived on schedule at the appointed location. The general manager did not show up, however; instead he sent word that the negotiation site should be changed to the company's head office, in the International Settlement. Suspicious of the sudden alteration in arrangements, the workers' representatives refused to budge from factory Number One. A party of French police soon arrived on the scene to try to disperse the crowd, which had now grown to some three thousand people. To separate the negotiators from their thousands of supporters amassing outside Number One, an electric fence at the front gate of the factory was activated on orders from General Manager Cai. A battle then ensued between the police, equipped with tanks and machine guns, and the workers, armed just with stones. One woman worker was killed and many others seriously injured in the two-hour fray. The fighting abated only when the workers retreated to a public recreation ground at the city's West Gate. After an emotional mass meeting in which indignant spokesmen rebuked Meiya management for having betrayed their trust, the strikers decided to change strategy and petition the Bureau of Social Affairs for redress.[32]

Following a series of brainstorming sessions to agree on specific demands, in a couple of days the strikers were ready to submit a formal petition to the Bureau of Social Affairs. On March 13 more than a thousand workers marched on Civic Center to present their appeal, requesting that (1) the Meiya management be held responsible for the medical expenses incurred by the injured and for compensation to the family of the deceased worker, and also be instructed to issue pay for the strike period and restore the previous wage scale; and (2) the French authorities be ordered to bring the police officers responsible for the assault to justice, to compensate the strikers, and to print an apology in the newspapers providing assurance that such incidents would not be repeated. The Bureau of Social Affairs promised only to give the requests due consideration.[33]

While awaiting some official government action, the strikers turned to the public for support. The heavy-handed tactics of the French police had provided a powerful weapon in the fight for public sympathy. Shortly after the March 11 incident, a strike support committee was established among workers in the eastern district. Weavers in other parts of the city—the French Concession and Nandao in particular—were also quick to lend assistance in the form of both money and moral support. Even Shanghai's rickshaw pullers displayed sympathy for the strike by allowing Meiya propaganda teams to ride free of charge.[34]

To spread their message as widely as possible, members of the Meiya central strike committee—making good use of their literary skills—issued an open letter to the citizens of Shanghai. This manifesto, which was quickly reprinted in the major newspapers, blamed Meiya's general manager Cai Shengbai for having ordered the police assault that left one worker dead and dozens more severely wounded, and indicted him for failing to share the company's growing prosperity with its workers:

> The Meiya Silk-Weaving Company is the giant of Shanghai's silk-weaving industry. Its business is flourishing, with enormous profits each year. Last year total sales were more than six million yuan, higher than in any previous year. But General Manager Cai Shengbai doesn't understand the meaning of cooperation between labor and management; he only knows how to increase company profits. He uses every possible scheme to exploit the workers. Recently he plotted to make further cuts in wages that are already at the bare minimum, leaving workers unable to maintain a livelihood and giving rise to this strike. Surprisingly, Cai Shengbai not only refused to seek an amicable solution; he has also used force to suppress the workers. On March 11 the workers had chosen representatives to meet with Cai Shengbai at the main factory on Montmorand Road for direct negotiations about conditions for resuming work. At that time Mr. Cai not only purposely avoided the meeting, but also closed the iron gates and activated the electric fence to imprison the workers' representatives who had entered the factory. Moreover, he connived with the French police to dispatch armed troops to surround the workers who were standing outside the factory patiently awaiting news. Suddenly, the police attacked with pistols and iron bars. The unarmed workers suffered many casualties. Woman worker Xu Guifen was killed by a bullet in the head. More than forty workers were seriously wounded, and countless others received lighter injuries. Weak, defenseless women workers comprised most of the wounded. This violent use of foreign police power to murder our compatriots is comparable to the May Thirtieth tragedy. The workers are determined to carry on the struggle. We will not rest until we have expelled the violent, senseless capitalist running dog Cai Shengbai, have eliminated the irrational wage standard, and have avenged the death and injuries among the workers. People of all stations in life, having a sense of justice, must feel anger about this massacre. We hope you will advocate public morality in the form of

punishment for the culprits. Moreover, we hope you will offer spiritual and material help to the starving workers.[35]

With this open letter, the strikers drew a sharp and visible line between themselves and management. No longer were China's "labor aristocrats" willing to undertake private negotiations in hopes of appealing to the moral sensibilities of their employer. Now the battle was a public one, which ordinary citizens as well as government agencies were invited to join. It was at this stage that outside Communist organizers, attracted by the apparent class consciousness of this once quiescent group of workers, became more actively involved in the silk weavers' strike.

Tea shops near the Meiya factories, where workers gathered to chat about the progress of their struggle, were a natural focus of Communist mobilization efforts. Under the pretext of looking for friends or relatives, young Communist activists sought out sympathetic types among the tea-house patrons. In this way, they managed to make a few contacts among strikers at factories Number One and Five.[36] Over the next several weeks, resolutions exhorting the workers to more radical activities were issued by a number of Communist agencies: the Shanghai Western District Committee of the Communist Party, the Jiangsu Provincial Committee of the Communist Youth League, and even the Central Committee of the Communist Party (signed by Mao Zedong in Jiangxi).[37] A series of articles in Communist Youth League publications emphasized the need for the Jiangsu Communist Youth League to assume control of the Meiya struggle.[38] Yet, despite this considerable attention, there is evidence that Communist agents were not entirely successful in their efforts to play a commanding role. An internal Party report, seized by the British police in early April, admitted that "although the attitude of the Meiya strikers is good, our own activities still remain outside the struggles." The report bemoaned a "lack of consolidated organization" and chided the workers' strike committee for being "unaware" of the division of responsibility between itself and the Communist Youth League.[39] Such "confusion" was obviously the product of a strike committee that operated independently of outside direction.

Communist agents may not have been fully effective in gaining control of strike leadership, but their efforts had important ramifications all the same. Fear of Communist direction hardened the position of Meiya's management and inclined the state authorities against the strikers. On March 15, the company issued an ultimatum: any worker who had not resumed work by March 17 would be considered to have resigned of his or her own volition, and new hands would be hired as replacements. On

March 16, representatives of the strikers were called to the Bureau of Social Affairs to meet with government and Party officials. The authorities strongly advised the strikers to resume work immediately, pending mediation by government and Party agencies.[40]

On the morning of March 17, the deadline set by management for a return to work, it was clear that government persuasion had failed to soften the militancy of the strikers. Accordingly, the authorities decided to adopt sterner measures. Plainclothesmen were sent to the various Meiya branch factories to seek out and apprehend suspected ringleaders. At Number Six, an attempted arrest was averted only because an alert member of the strikers' security force managed to sink her teeth into the hand of the policeman before he could complete his assignment! At Number Five, however, workers' pickets proved less effective. A woman weaver by the name of Liu Jinshui was apprehended on suspicion of being a Communist and was carted off to the local police station.[41]

With a martyr to their cause now behind bars, the strikers found it even easier to elicit public sympathy. On the afternoon of March 17, strikers carrying bamboo baskets and white cloth banners inscribed with the characters "Meiya Silk-Weaving Factory Propaganda Group" visited various small silk-weaving concerns in the Jessfield Park and Zhabei districts to request support. As the propagandists shared recent news of the protest movement, sympathetic listeners filled the bamboo baskets with cash contributions.[42]

The following day, the strikers were ready for a more direct show of strength. At 8:00 A.M. on March 18, more than four thousand workers and supporters gathered at the West Gate police station to demand the release of Liu Jinshui. The officer in charge replied that he had no authority over the case, explaining that Liu had been arrested under direct orders from the Guomindang Central Executive Committee in Nanjing. Dissatisfied with this answer, the crowd refused to disperse. Instead, the protesters settled in for an all-night vigil, spreading themselves across the front gate of the station and into the surrounding streets so that all traffic in the vicinity was brought to a standstill. During the evening, several hundred workers from small silk-weaving factories in the French Concession and Nandao districts joined the sit-in. Merchants in the West Gate area sent food for the strikers, whose ranks were soon swelled by university students sympathetic to the cause. The following morning, dozens of silk weavers from factories in more distant parts of the city also arrived to lend support.[43] At 10:00 A.M. the chief of Shanghai's Public Security Bureau—responding to the intense public pressure—issued orders to release the prisoner.

Overjoyed by this outcome, the victorious protesters led their freed martyr away in a boisterous and triumphant firecracker parade. Flushed with success, the strikers quickly drew up a new and more ambitious set of demands to present to Shanghai authorities. In addition to the restoration of pre-1933 wages, the workers called for full pay during the strike period, a guarantee against dismissals without just cause, elimination of fines as a form of punishment, and equal pay for men and women.[44] This last demand reflected the key role that women weavers were playing in the protest. Meiya's effort to create a more docile labor force by hiring women had evidently backfired. Women casualties in the March 11 incident, women pickets in the strike security force, a woman prisoner—all pointed to the pronounced activism of women workers.[45]

The release of Liu Jinshui gave the weavers an important psychological boost, but unfortunately for them it did not augur a more accommodating attitude on the part of the authorities. To the contrary, public security agents actually stepped up surveillance and arrests among Meiya activists. On March 27, a confidential report by a Guomindang agent sent from Nanjing to investigate the strike concluded that Communist elements had infiltrated the movement. The agent advocated harsh reprisals.[46] Over the next few weeks, more than a dozen strikers were apprehended (and several of them sentenced to imprisonment) for distributing strike literature and soliciting financial contributions.[47]

Once again, however, police intervention worked to expand the strikers' support group. To protest the police intimidation, Meiya's five hundred young apprentices (employed for the most part at Factory Number Eight) stopped work on April 5. The move came as a surprise to management, since the traditional arrangement for apprentices relieved the company of any responsibility for the wages of these youngsters. At the start of their three- to five-year training period, apprentices were required to deposit a security payment of Ch$30 to $50, nonrefundable in the event of leaving the company before completion of the apprenticeship.[48] Although apprentices were surely the poorest of Meiya's workers, the fact that they received no wages would seem to have rendered them unlikely participants in a protest against wage reductions. However, on the day after this group of workers joined the struggle, the strikers issued an updated set of demands that evidenced the concerns of their new recruits. The new list called for the company to abolish the practice of requiring security money from apprentices, to protect apprentices from assault by foremen, and to provide every apprentice with a loom at the end of his or her training period.[49]

With all the employees now on strike, Meiya served as a kind of magnet for other disgruntled workers in the area. Strikers in Shanghai's rubber factory sent delegates to Meiya's central strike committee for advice on how to organize effectively. Workers in Shanghai's pharmaceutical, tobacco, and umbrella industries launched strikes under Meiya inspiration. Even in the interior, in the traditional silk centers of Huzhou and Hangzhou, weavers followed the lead of their city cousins in striking for higher wages and improved working conditions.[50]

The Meiya strike was welcomed not only by other strike-prone workers, but by some employers as well. Other silk-weaving concerns in Shanghai naturally profited from Meiya's work stoppage. Not surprisingly, these rival factories contributed heavily to the strike fund that sustained Meiya's militants during their lengthy protest.[51]

Seeing its market captured by competitors and without even any apprentices to carry on production, Meiya management tried to retaliate. Its first step was to reduce the quality of food still being served in workers' cafeterias. Meat was withdrawn from the already meager menu, and only the cheapest of vegetables were provided. The decline in service was quickly met by heated protest. At Number Nine, two hundred women workers engaged in a brief hunger strike.[52] Weavers at Number Four (led by the secretary of the underground Communist Party branch at the factory) barricaded the superintendent in his room. Police who tried to climb the factory fence in a rescue mission retreated hastily when workers unleashed buckets of night soil from the roof. After two days and nights under siege, the factory superintendent signed a guarantee of improved meals and paid one hundred dollars in food subsidies.[53]

With tensions between workers and management running high, the Bureau of Social Affairs decided to attempt a more active role in settling the dispute. Green Gang leader Du Yuesheng was asked to intervene in the case, but his efforts to talk the strikers into giving up their struggle proved fruitless. With few of his own followers among the Meiya work force, Du was powerless to effect a solution. Pressed by an April 8 cable from Chiang Kaishek ordering an immediate end to the strike, the Bureau put together a formal mediation committee consisting of one representative from the Bureau of Social Affairs (as chair), one representative from the Shanghai Guomindang, one representative from the Public Security Bureau, and two representatives each from Meiya management and Meiya workers. With this committee duly constituted, an official mediation meeting was scheduled for the morning of April 10.[54]

Before 10:00 A.M. on April 10, the time when mediation was supposed to commence, hundreds of strikers converged on the Bureau of Social Affairs at Civic Center. Marching two abreast and carrying portraits and statues of Sun Yatsen, they distributed handbills proclaiming "Labor is sacred" (*laogong shensheng*). Once assembled outside the offices of the Bureau of Social Affairs, the weavers sang their strike theme song— "How sad, how sad, how terribly sad; Meiya workers' wages have been cut so bad"—and chanted in unison, "We want to work! We want to eat!" Much to their consternation, however, it soon became clear that no mediation could take place: Meiya's management had again failed to show. In place of negotiators, Meiya sent word that it had decided to shut down its factories. Since operations were being suspended, mediation was pointless. To demonstrate that the decision was more than idle talk, the company summarily closed the doors of all its workers' cafeterias, leaving the strikers without a regular source of food.[55]

Meanwhile the strikers, insisting that the Bureau of Social Affairs order a reopening of their cafeterias and enforce some acceptable settlement of the dispute, laid siege to Civic Center. At about 6:00 P.M., when the staff of the Bureaus of Social Affairs, Education, and Public Health were preparing to go home for the night, the demonstrators sealed all doors and placed a tight cordon around the building. No one was to be permitted to leave until Meiya's representatives arrived to negotiate. As a cold rain began to fall, thousands of workers settled in to enforce their blockade. One intrepid young protester even delivered her baby in the dank, open air at Civic Center that night![56]

That the Meiya strike should have assumed overtly political proportions is not surprising. As Edward Shorter and Charles Tilly have argued, strikes are by their very nature political (as much as economic) modes of activity:

> Workers, when they strike, are merely extending into the streets their normal processes of political participation . . . and the people whom these displays are intended to impress are not individual employers against whom—for reasons of political convenience—the strike is ostensibly directed, but the political authorities of the land, in the form of either the government itself or powerful members of the polity.[57]

With the Meiya strikers now occupying the heart of Shanghai's municipal government, a large force of police and public security agents was called in. By the next morning, some seven to eight hundred police and six fire engines had reached the scene. In the midst of this confusion, Shanghai's mayor, Wu Tiecheng, arrived at Civic Center and while making his way to his office was surrounded by strikers demanding his help in bringing about a settlement. Alarmed by this direct confrontation, the police decided to charge the workers. Brandishing batons and turning fire hoses on the crowd, they succeeded in dispersing the protesters—but not without inflicting a good many injuries in the process.[58]

This April 11 incident marked a turning point in the Meiya strike.[59] Although the police assault generated public support for the strikers (workers at more than a hundred small silk-weaving factories in the southern and eastern districts of Shanghai staged a brief sympathy strike soon after the April 11 affair), the state authorities had lost any empathy for the workers' cause. Having experienced firsthand the disruptive effects of the strike, Shanghai officials were now more inclined than ever to identify with the position of Meiya's management. Cooperation between capitalists and the state was also promoted by new tactics on the part of Meiya's general manager; during the course of the strike, Cai Shengbai compiled a clipping file of newspaper reports on successful suppression efforts against textile strikes around the world.[60] Perhaps taking a cue from these materials, Cai decided to adopt a more aggressive role in putting an end to the strike. Sharing native-place origin with the director of the Bureau of Social Affairs, Meiya's general manager reinforced these ties by offering handsome compensation to the director and three of his underlings for their assistance in bringing the strike to a speedy conclusion.[61] The government's hardened attitude was seen in a series of public security moves intended to weaken the strike: temporary martial law was declared, all public meetings were prohibited, and police were sent to every Meiya factory to round up activists. At Number Four, eleven strike leaders—including the Communist Party branch secretary—were arrested and sent to the Wusong-Shanghai garrison headquarters for detention.[62]

On April 13, the Executive Committee of the Guomindang in Nanjing—which had also been contacted by Cai Shengbai—cabled the Shanghai Party branch with orders to take all necessary measures to break the Meiya strike immediately. Party Central expressed alarm over the involvement of "bad elements" (*buliang fenzi*)—a euphemism for Communist agents. By the next morning, the number of arrests at Meiya factories had risen to forty.[63]

Encouraged by these stiff government measures, Meiya management adopted a similarly hard line. Factory dormitories were locked up, forcing the workers to take refuge with friends or roam the streets in search of shelter. (Many workers resorted to sleeping in the public May Thirtieth martyrs' cemetery on the outskirts of town.) Homeless and leaderless, the silk weavers began to lose their fighting spirit.

The central strike committee, weakened by the loss of so many of its key members, found it difficult to retain control over the workers. Meiya's apprentices, enticed by the company's promise to provide them with their own looms if they returned to their jobs, were the first to resume work. Weavers at Number Two and Number Five then asked the strike committee to call off the walkout, threatening to resume work on their own if necessary. In a desperate attempt to salvage the situation, the strike committee announced a mass demonstration to petition city authorities on April 21. More than a thousand bedraggled workers showed up at the local Guomindang headquarters on the appointed day to demand the release of the arrested workers and the immediate reopening of workers' dormitories and cafeterias. The limited nature of the demands (which made no mention of wages) showed the sorry state to which the movement had sunk. Guomindang authorities, confident that they now held the upper hand, were firm in their answer: Meiya would be told to reopen the dormitories, but the workers must resume work at once. Tired and defeated, the silk weavers were back on the job the next morning, bringing to an end their fifty-one-day walkout.

When they returned to work, the strikers found that things had changed in their absence. They were informed that the factories were being reorganized and that all workers must therefore re-register with the company. The process of re-registration, it soon became clear, entailed an investigation of one's involvement in the strike; as a consequence, 143 activists were dismissed.[64]

On April 27, Nanjing—responding to a direct appeal from Cai Shengbai—instructed the Shanghai authorities to deal harshly with "reactionary troublemakers" in the Meiya strike.[65] Three days later, the forty previously arrested workers were sentenced to varying degrees of punishment: most received prison terms of twenty to forty days; the Party secretary at Number Four, betrayed by two of his fellow cell members, was sentenced to five years behind bars.[66] With this legal verdict, the Meiya protest was brought to an official conclusion.

What lessons were to be drawn from this long, and ultimately unsuccessful, exercise in workers' politics? For the Meiya strikers, the lesson was a bitter realization of the limitations of their own power. Theirs had been a classic "aristocratic" protest: organization was based upon small, pre-existing networks of workshop friendship; demands were moderate, articulate, and phrased in a moral language with public appeal; outside assistance was welcomed, but leadership remained in the hands of the weavers themselves. Yet, clearly, this style of protest was ineffective against an employer whose search for profits numbed the sense of respect and moral obligation he had once felt for his skilled work force.

If workers harbored any hope that the previously cordial relationship with management might be restored, they were quickly disillusioned. Cai Shengbai, proclaiming that "this dispute has left a scar not on a single person or a single enterprise, but on our entire national industry," proceeded to take retaliatory measures. In the months following the strike, Meiya enforced a 30 percent wage cut, closed all workers' dormitories, and raised prices in factory cafeterias.[67]

Even more disheartening to the defeated weavers was the implementation of a loom rental system, whereby the company leased out its looms to members of the staff to manage on its behalf. With a guaranteed annual rental income, Meiya gained a predictable source of revenue and was relieved of the burden of dealing directly with the workers. Although the company remained responsible for raw materials and sales outlets, matters of hiring, training, and wages were entirely the personal responsibility of the staff members who leased the looms. Under this system, operation expenses were reduced (by about 15 percent) and Cai Shengbai solidified ties with his top staff at the same time that he put a comfortable distance between himself and the ordinary weavers. Among the workers, the loom rental system exacerbated divisions along native-place lines, inasmuch as staff foremen tended to exhibit favoritism toward workers with whom they shared such connections.[68]

In the aftermath of the strike, Meiya's once proud labor aristocrats lost many of the privileges that had previously distinguished them from less fortunate textile workers in the city. At the same time, other large silk-weaving factories in Shanghai, pressed by the general depression in the industry, reduced their scale of operations and adopted a loom rental system similar to Meiya's.[69] This change in the organization of the industry narrowed the gap between "modern" weavers—employed at larger factories with higher wages and better working conditions—and the "traditional" weavers who worked at smaller factories under less desirable terms.

As the structure of the industry changed, its work force attracted more interest from outside parties. The strike of 1934 had drawn attention to the political potential of Shanghai's silk weavers. Earlier labor organizers, of either Communist or Guomindang affiliation, had tended to dismiss the possibility of a major protest among this relatively skilled and well-paid group of workers. The Meiya strike, however, generated a new enthusiasm for mobilizing silk weavers.

This newfound interest on the part of outside organizers became evident during the course of the fifty-one-day strike itself. As we have seen, Communist agents attempted—albeit with limited success—to gain a deciding role in the protest. Such efforts were instrumental in igniting the interest of other outside parties as well. The Guomindang, for its part, sent agents (under the guise of newspaper reporters) to try to dilute the wording of strike petitions.[70] Official unions also showed some interest in the conflict, although at the time just one of Meiya's factories (Number Two) was endowed with such an organization. The union at Number Two became active only after the April 11 confrontation at Civic Center, when it worked to persuade weavers in that factory to withdraw support from the central strike committee.[71]

As the dust from the Meiya strike gradually settled, some two to three years after the conclusion of the conflict, a new pattern of silk weavers' politics became visible—a pattern in which officially sponsored unions played a leading role. The weavers gained powerful allies among the authorities, but at a considerable cost to their independence and integrity.

The All-City Strikes of 1936–37

The immediate aftermath of the Meiya strike saw a period of quiescence among Shanghai's silk weavers. Sobered by the defeat of their "modern" spokesmen and still suffering from severe economic depression, the city's weavers were loath to undertake further struggles. Those strikes that did occur were small in scale and limited in goals. In 1935, the average silk weavers' strike numbered only fifty-five participants, compared to an average of nearly a thousand participants per strike the year before. Occurring in a time of acute depression, the strikes of 1935 were universally unsuccessful in forestalling wage reductions or worker dismissals.[72]

By late 1936, however, recovery in the silk-weaving industry brought an increase in both the frequency and success of protest. Improvement in the industry was due in large measure to illegally imported artificial silk from Japan. Cheap and plentiful, the contraband silk made it possible for small silk-weaving establishments to commence operations with very little capital. By the end of the year, some 480 silk-weaving factories were operating in Shanghai, most of them tiny workshops with only a few looms.[73] A total of twenty-nine silk weavers' strikes occurred in 1936, by far the largest number of any year to date. The walkouts were brief in duration (averaging eight days) and modest in their goals, but increasingly effective in bringing results. Taking place for the most part among workers in smaller factories that had only recently resumed operations, these protests were a good deal less bold than the Meiya strike two years earlier. Absent now were the demands for gender equality and better treatment for apprentices that had distinguished the 1934 movement. Also missing in 1936 were many women participants. In most cases, these were all-male strikes with limited wage demands.[74] The conservatism and gender segregation that characterized these protests reflected the social composition and structure of work in smaller silk-weaving enterprises. (The one notable exception to this pattern was another Meiya strike. For two weeks in the late summer of 1936, 150 women and 100 men at factory Number Two struck to demand a reduction in the control of labor contractors, abolition of the graded wage scale, and enforcement of better treatment by job foremen.)[75]

The resurgence of widespread unrest among the silk-weaving community attracted the attention of Shanghai authorities, especially in the local Guomindang and Bureau of Social Affairs. Top-ranking officials in both agencies, embroiled in a bitter factional battle for power, saw the feisty silk weavers as a potential social base for their own ambitious designs. Accordingly, representatives of rival factions raced to found state-sponsored unions that would bring the silk weavers under their control.

On December 20, 1936, the first new silk-weavers' union was inaugurated at a meeting attended by six hundred people, including representatives of the Guomindang, the Bureau of Social Affairs, and the Guomindang-sponsored General Labor Union. Known as the District Four Silk-Weavers' Union, the new organization soon claimed three thousand members in 120 factories. The chief force behind the union was an employee of the mediation section of the Bureau of Social Affairs. Making use of his native-place connections with weavers at several of the smaller silk factories in eastern Shanghai, he convinced his friends to unionize. The new union had an elaborate organizational structure (not unlike that of the Meiya strike committee), with sections in charge of general affairs, propaganda, mediation, security, organization, and liaison. Under the district union were some thirteen branch unions, controlling the more than one hundred factory committees. Each factory was organized into small groups, numbering some six hundred in all, of about five members each.[76]

Despite this impressive structure, the new union did not function altogether smoothly. According to police reports, at least two of the branch unions were actively plotting to usurp the leadership of the district union. The Ward Road branch (which included some 800 weavers at forty factories) was closely associated with the District Four Tobacco Workers' Union—a Green Gang–controlled branch of the General Labor Union that hoped to wrest control over silk weavers from rivals in the Bureau of Social Affairs. A second branch union (which included some 350 weavers employed, for the most part, at the Meifeng factory) opposed the dictatorial manner of its parent union and identified closely with Meifeng management.[77]

District unions were formed in other parts of Shanghai as well, with politics no less complicated than those of the fourth district. In January 1937 a District Three Silk-Weavers' Union was established in the western part of the city. The instigator, Wang Hao, was a member of the Peasant-Worker Section of the Shanghai Guomindang who had been sent to settle a five-factory strike in late 1936. A follower of Green Gang labor leaders Lu Jingshi and Zhu Xuefan (who were, in turn, top lieutenants of Green Gang chieftain Du Yuesheng), Wang was also a member of the Guomindang's paramilitary corps, the Blue Shirts. Since more than a few silk weavers in western Shanghai had received training from the Blue Shirts, Wang Hao was able to draw on the connection to develop a following among the workers. With official approval from the Shanghai Guomindang, he settled the five-factory strike in a manner satisfactory to the protesters. Using the five factories as a base, Wang then proceeded to establish the District Three Union at a gala ceremony attended by Zhu Xuefan.[78]

Wang Hao's mission to organize the silk weavers was part of a concerted program by his backstage bosses, Lu Jingshi and Zhu Xuefan, to develop a base among labor in preparation for the upcoming National Assembly elections.[79] At the time, Lu Jingshi in particular was involved in an intense factional struggle with the director of the Bureau of Social Affairs (Pan Gongzhan), the head of the Shanghai Guomindang (Wu Kaixian), and the acting mayor of Shanghai (Yu Hongjun).[80] Each man had hopes of cultivating elements within the Shanghai labor movement to augment his position.

The workers welcomed unionization as a means of improving their situation. As one silk weaver recalled,

> We workers didn't realize at the time that unions were part of a Guomindang plot to drum up mass votes for its National Assembly. All we knew was that organization would give us strength. This fellow Wang, I understand, was a member of the Blue Shirts. But he had a "leftist" demeanor and was really trusted by the workers, who saw that he ate plain noodles, rode a bicycle, and lived in modest circumstances.[81]

In February, an officially sanctioned District One Silk-Weavers' Union was inaugurated in the Nandao area, where six of the Meiya factories were situated. It took considerable effort to convince the formerly independent workers at Meiya to join the unionization movement, however. Slowest to register in the new union were the craftsmen at factory Number Six, where the 1934 strike had originated.[82]

With unions now in place across the city, Wang Hao moved to assume overall command by setting up a unified Shanghai Silk-Weavers' Committee for Improved Treatment. Encouraged by this new committee, the cry for higher wages spread like wildfire throughout the silk-weaving community. On March 17, under the leadership of Wang Hao's committee, a mass meeting of more than two thousand weavers was convened at an open field near St. John's University to draw up a unified set of demands. Requests for higher wages, shorter hours, and a general improvement in treatment were agreed upon and duly submitted to an official mediation committee comprised of representatives from the Bureau of Social Affairs, the local Guomindang, workers, and employers. Arguing that their industry was recuperating from its earlier depression and could therefore afford to pay more to its workers, the weavers demanded an across-the-board raise of 30 percent. After lengthy discussions, the employers consented to a 15 percent increase for workers earning less than fifty cents a day, but refused to consider raises for those receiving more than this minimum amount. Since such poorly paid workers constituted but a small percentage of the silk-weaving community, the workers rejected the proposal and began to plan a citywide strike in support of their demands.[83]

Tensions mounted when various factories around the city received police protection, ostensibly to prevent union intimidation of workers who preferred to remain at their jobs. On March 29, 150 strikers at the Jinxin factory stormed the plant and attacked police who tried to bar them from entering the factory to meet with management.[84] That same day, a crowd of 500 union members marched to the Yuanling silk-weaving factory to try to persuade workers there to unionize. Three of the agitators got into a scuffle with British police stationed at the factory. One of the three hurled a rock at the police sergeant and then tried to outsprint him, but as the English press proudly explained, "Sergeant Lovell had represented the police in the athletic games in 1935 and had no difficulty catching up." Their heads swathed in bandages, the three activists were brought to trial a few days later.[85] Police efforts to slow the pace of unionization only intensified the resolve of union leaders. At midnight on March 30, a united strike of 220 mills and 11,944 workers—by far the largest of the year's labor disputes—was set in motion by Wang Hao's Committee for Improved Treatment. The strike reached all areas of the city.

The rapid spread of the strike was encouraged by Wang Hao's policy of "factory storming" (*chongchang*), in which Blue Shirt–trained workers' pickets rushed in and destroyed machinery in factories where workers were loath to strike.[86] Recent memoirs reveal that at the time underground Communist organizers opposed a general strike in the silk-weaving industry and advocated a more restrained strategy of separate struggles in factories with relatively "enlightened" management.[87] However, although the Communists enjoyed some strength in the District Four Union, overall leadership of the silk weavers was firmly in the hands of Wang Hao.

Wang's tactics aroused criticism not only from underground Communists, but also from his opponents within the Bureau of Social Affairs. Alarmed by this massive work stoppage in one of the city's key industries and hoping to undercut the power base of Wang and his backstage bosses, the Bureau of Social Affairs issued an emergency order declaring an end to the strike. In exchange for returning to their jobs, the strikers were promised an across-the-board wage increase of 10 percent, bonus payments, elimination of the loom rental system, and a new one-month paid maternity leave program. The offer was generous enough to erode worker enthusiasm for a continued strike; by early April most weavers had resumed work.[88]

The Bureau's order proved effective in convincing the workers to end their walkout, but it had far less impact upon the managers, most of whom refused to honor the call for a 10 percent wage hike. During the course of the strike, Meiya's Cai Shengbai—who still chaired the Silk-Weaving Employers' Association—had organized an ad hoc Committee to Counter the Strike Wave. This committee, funded by an assessment of two yuan per loom, used its resources to fight the compromise solution proposed by the Bureau of Social Affairs.[89] In mid-April Cai took his case to Guomindang headquarters in Nanjing, alleging that unionization efforts by local Shanghai officials were responsible for the rash of labor unrest in the city.[90]

Early the next month, when Chiang Kaishek happened to be hospitalized in Shanghai, the generalissimo took a personal interest in the struggles still rampant among the city's silk weavers. Perturbed by the daily newspaper accounts of strikes and slowdowns, Chiang called upon municipal authorities to bring a speedy halt to the disturbances. In response, on the evening of May 14, a large contingent of International Settlement police raided the District Four Silk-Weavers' Union on the pretext that the union had intimidated a worker at the Jinxin factory. Documents were seized, seals of office confiscated, and more than twenty workers detained at police headquarters for questioning.[91]

A few days later, representatives of the District Four Union (including the union secretary, an employee of the Shanghai Guomindang) proceeded to the Bureau of Social Affairs at Civic Center to request that the police return the stolen materials and release the union members being held in custody. It was union leaders' hope that a prompt response might forestall yet more strikes on the part of angry weavers in the eastern district.[92]

Authorities in the Bureau of Social Affairs were torn between loyalty to the union they had helped create and pressure from the central government in Nanjing. The intransigence of factory managers had undermined the Bureau's strategy of using a unionized Shanghai labor movement for its own political purposes. Nanjing, for its part, shared with the International Settlement fear of a scenario in which the now heavily unionized silk, cotton, and tobacco workers would join hands to take charge of the city's economy. As a local paper explained, "It is not the individual cases which bother the authorities seriously—it is the steady move toward union combination which undoubtedly will play a decisive part in labour relations of the future."[93] Never far from the imaginations of officials in Nanjing was the specter of Communist agents seizing control of a highly organized labor movement. As a pro-Guomindang paper described fears at the height of the all-city weavers' strike:

> The bogey of Moscow is, perhaps, all too often trotted out by labour-scared employers, but definite evidence is in the hands of official circles to show that there is a direct link between current labour agitation and both financial and ideological inspiration from the Kremlin. . . . It is not only a question of wages which is being raised, but in whose hands is to rest the dominant political power.[94]

In fact, "Kremlin inspiration" played very little part in the silk weavers' spring offensive. The most active group of Communists (denounced as "Trotskyist" by their mainstream opponents in the Party underground) were at the Jinxin factory. There, workers refused to accept the Bureau of Social Affairs compromise and continued a lengthy strike to demand a 30 percent wage increase.[95] Undoubtedly this radical connection helped to precipitate the May 14 police raid on the District Four Union, for strikers at the Jinxin factory had been using union premises as a center for free food distribution. The union's president, moreover, was a former Jinxin worker with Communist leanings.[96] But, on the whole, Communist involvement was not a major factor in the silk weavers' unrest.

Even without much Communist participation, however, the contest was most decidedly a political one in which factions within the Shanghai regime struggled for the upper hand. While state agencies jockeyed for power over the workers, previously submerged rivalries among the silk weavers themselves rose to the surface. On May 24, a gang fight involving more than five hundred unionized workers erupted at Meiya's Factory Number Ten. Workers from the same native-place association as their factory superintendent advocated work resumption, whereas other employees insisted upon a continued strike for better working conditions. From 11:00 P.M. until six the next morning, the weavers fought a bloody battle in front of the mill.[97]

With control of the situation slipping quickly from their grasp, authorities at the Bureau of Social Affairs concluded that the silk weavers' unions must be destroyed. On June 3, the Bureau ordered the closing of unions in districts one, three, and four. New unions, less likely to stir up trouble among the workers, were to be established.[98] On June 12, Wang Hao was arrested at the offices of his now defunct District Three Union. When he was released a month later, weavers in the western part of the city welcomed him back with banners and firecrackers.[99]

In the one month remaining before the Japanese invasion, ambitious Guomindang functionaries rushed forth to found new silk-weaving unions. Native-place attachments were used in the struggle to draw workers into the embrace of one or another rival union organizer. Repeated battles between these competing leaders and their fellow provincials indicated the fractionalized state into which the silk weavers had fallen by the summer of 1937.[100] When the Japanese seized control of Shanghai's silk industry in August 1937, they found a once proud "labor aristocracy" in disarray.

Conclusion

The decimation and forced retreat of Communist labor organizers in the April 1927 coup did not bring down the curtain on the drama of the Shanghai workers' movement. The activism of silk weavers is ample testimony to a continuing and dynamic pattern of workers' politics. Stimulated—in rather complicated ways—by the severe depression that wracked their industry during the early 1930s, weavers were quick to fight in defense of their own interests. Initially in 1930, and then more dramatically in 1934, the battle was led by the "modern" sector of the weaving community, concentrated in the relatively prosperous Meiya Company. Later the more "traditional" weavers, located at smaller factories throughout the city, carried on the struggle—but under the aegis of officially sponsored unions.

While the early strikes had much in common with classic artisan protests, by the end of the Nanjing decade the pattern had changed. Proletarianized by hostile employers and pressured by outside organizers whose agendas had more to do with internal Guomindang politics than with worker interests, Shanghai's silk weavers shed many of the distinctive features of a "labor aristocracy."

In other parts of the world as well, silk weavers have compiled an impressive record of protest activity. Robert Bezucha's description of the *canuts* of Lyon, France—silk weavers who launched massive strikes in 1831 and 1834—bears a strong resemblance to Shanghai strikers a century later. By Bezucha's account, these were highly educated workers (70 percent of the male weavers were literate) who enjoyed relative affluence and a distinctive popular culture. Based on mutual aid societies, the weavers' strikes were "evidence not of dislocations, but of efforts at community organization. Far from being an uprooted, 'dangerous class,' they fought only when their future appeared gravely threatened."[101]

The "threat" facing Shanghai's silk weavers in the early 1930s was the result of a drastic decline in the international market for their products. But global depression was certainly not the only precipitant. Changes in the Shanghai silk-weaving industry itself were another key ingredient. As the highly mechanized Meiya Company captured an ever greater share of a once competitive field, its search for profits (exacerbated, of course, by anxieties about the world depression) undermined earlier guarantees of worker welfare. Skilled workers then responded in what they took to be an act of self-defense. The situation resembled that described by Bernard Moss to explain the workers' struggles of mid-nineteenth-century Paris: "Industrialization had advanced far enough with respect to labor and commercial competition to threaten the security, integrity and relative value of skilled craftsmen, enough to provoke resistance and protest, but not enough in terms of complete mechanization to destroy the craft and its capacities for resistance."[102]

The early Shanghai silk weavers' strikes shared certain features in common with artisan protests that developed in other times and places, under comparable social and economic circumstances. But labor movements are not merely the product of industrial structure or market conditions. The political setting also acts as a critical force in shaping the pattern of worker protest. As Shorter and Tilly suggest, "We expect changes in the national political position of organized labor to cause strikes to increase. What is more, we expect the political dimension of the strike to expand over time, as the labor movement nationalizes."[103]

Shanghai silk weavers were no exception to this general proposition. Thanks to heightened interest on the part of outside organizers, silk-weaver strikes by the close of the Nanjing decade had become more frequent and more intertwined with political struggles—on both local and national levels. In the short run, the outcome was unfortunate; Guomindang-sponsored unions robbed the silk weavers' struggles of many of the defining characteristics of an artisan movement: craft pride, autonomy, moralism. But in the longer run, the twin pressures of proletarianization and politicization would breathe new life into the struggles of Shanghai silk weavers.

Within a year after the Japanese invasion, Communist Party branches had been reestablished at the two surviving Meiya factories. At Number Four, ten weavers joined the Party. At Number Nine, a three-member branch was set up.[104] Of the handful of Communist cadres responsible for rebuilding the Shanghai labor movement in 1938, two were former silk weavers.[105]

Following the Japanese surrender, silk weavers played a prominent role in the social unrest that plagued the Guomindang regime in Shanghai during the Civil War years. In March 1946, more than twelve thousand workers at some three hundred Shanghai silk-weaving factories initiated a strike that persisted for nearly three months. Through the personal mediation of Green Gang-cum-Guomindang labor leader Zhu Xuefan, the silk weavers were eventually granted a wage hike. This favorable outcome was due in large measure to the reduced influence of Meiya's General Manager, Cai Shengbai. During the war Cai had quietly placed his two remaining factories in the hands of Italian and German businessmen to avoid a direct Japanese takeover. While the decision proved financially beneficial, politically it opened Cai to the charge of having indirectly collaborated with the enemy. By threatening to publicize Cai's disreputable dealings, labor leaders in the silk-weaving industry after the war were able to exert a good deal of leverage over the once powerful capitalist.[106]

Further evidence of silk weavers' activism was seen in the 1946 election of Pan Yueying as National Assembly representative. A silk weaver, Ms. Pan was also an underground Communist Party member who earlier in the year had organized a demonstration by fifty thousand women workers in Shanghai to celebrate International Women's Day.[107] The following year silk weavers were again at the forefront of protest in Shanghai. On May 8, 1947, more than ten thousand weavers marched from the Bund to City Hall to demand that the cost of living index be unfrozen, to keep pace with inflation. (In a desperate attempt to stem the runaway inflation of the day, Guomindang authorities had frozen the cost of living index so that wages would no longer rise in line with price hikes.) The marching weavers distributed tens of thousands of handbills en route to City Hall, where they delivered a stirring petition that opened with the words, "We want to live! We want to breathe! We want to continue to work for the good of the nation!"[108] This much-publicized display of silk-weaver solidarity inspired similar protests among other segments of the work force and helped convince the regime to reverse its policy.

By late 1947, more than one hundred Communist Party members could be found among the silk weavers of Shanghai. Although many of them were arrested in a Guomindang offensive of March 1948, those who escaped the government roundup remained active in the labor movement. At the time of Communist victory, the Party secretary of the underground Communist Labor Committee, Zhang Qi, was a former Meiya worker (a skilled craftsman at Factory Number Six) who had been a leader in the strike of 1934.[109]

The key role that weavers eventually came to play in Shanghai's radical labor movement was very much the product of their experience during the Nanjing decade. Over the course of that difficult period, silk weavers lost many of their "aristocratic" privileges, but gained solidarity with other industrial workers. As Michael Hanagan has described the process elsewhere: "The growth of a proletariat did not by itself produce mass strikes. . . . Instead, the growth of a proletariat alongside a mass of threatened artisans, artisans who acted as catalytic agents of working-class revolt, produced mass strike protest."[110]

Developments during the Guomindang era helped to create in the silk weavers of Shanghai a "mass of threatened artisans" who would indeed come to play a "catalytic" role in the Chinese labor movement. As recent scholarship on the British labor aristocracy has made clear, factory artisans are distinguished not merely by their higher wages, but also by a distinctive popular culture that emphasizes mutual aid and inclines them quite naturally toward efforts at unionization.[111] Labor aristocrats commonly engage in collective action to maintain their privileged status. Although such activity often bespeaks a fundamental conservatism on the part of this favored segment of the working class,[112] under certain economic and political circumstances the effort to cling to customary privilege can have radical repercussions.[113] For the silk weavers of

Shanghai, the Nanjing decade created just such economic and political circumstances.

Notes

This chapter appeared originally as a chapter in Frederic E. Wakeman, Jr. and Wen-hsin Yeh, eds., *Shanghai Sojourners* (Berkeley: University of California, Institute of East Asian Studies, 1992).

1. Shanghai Bureau of Social Affairs, ed., *Strikes and Lockouts in Shanghai Since 1918* (Shanghai: Shanghai city government, Bureau of Social Affairs, 1933); "Jin sinian lai Shanghai de bagong tingye" (Strikes and lockouts in Shanghai during the past four years), *Guoji laogong tongxun* 5:5 (May 1938).

2. *Shanghai zhi jizhi gongye* (Mechanized industry in Shanghai) (Shanghai, 1933), p. 175; Zhu Bangxing, Hu Lingge, and Xu Sheng, eds., *Shanghai chanye yu Shanghai zhigong* (Shanghai's industries and workers) (Shanghai, 1939), p. 133; Luo Gengmo, "Meiya gongchao shimo" (The Meiya strike wave from beginning to end), in *Zhongguo jingji lunwenji* (Shanghai, 1936), p. 227; D.K. Lieu, *The Silk Industry of China* (Shanghai, 1940), p. 191; Zhang Shouyu, *Jindai Jiangnan sizhi gongye shi* (A history of the modern Jiangnan silk-weaving industry) (Beijing, 1988); *Meiya qikan* (Meiya journal) (Shanghai Municipal Archives, nos. 199–48–258 and 199–48–259), 1933/11/16.

3. *Meiya qikan* 1934/8/16:2.

4. *Shanghai sichou gongyunshi* (The history of the labor movement of Shanghai silk weavers) (Shanghai, 1985), pp. 13–17.

5. Shanghai Bureau, ed., *Strikes and Lockouts*, pp. 85–86; Number Two Archives (Nanjing), no. 722: 4–226.

6. "Sizhiye" (The silk-weaving industry) (unpublished manuscript in the archives of the Shanghai Number Four Silk-Weaving Factory, 1982).

7. Shanghai Municipal Archives, no. 199–48: 1–6.

8. Zhu et al., eds., *Shanghai chanye*, p. 146.

9. Ibid., p. 143.

10. Xu Xijuan, personal interview conducted at the Shanghai Number Nine Silk-Weaving Factory, 1987/6/2; "Sizhiye"; A Ying, "Chouchang de nügong" (Women workers in the silk-weaving factories), *Shenghuo zhishi*, no. 39 (1946), p. 4.

11. Li Shufa, interview transcript in the archives of the Shanghai Number Four Silk-Weaving Factory, 1969/12/24; Shen Rongqing, dossier in the archives of the Shanghai Number Four Silk-Weaving Factory, n.d.

12. Zhou Zhixin, interview transcript in the archives of the Shanghai Number Four Silk-Weaving Factory, 1982/6/5.

13. Zhu et al., eds., *Shanghai chanye*, pp. 141–143.

14. Wan Wenhua, interview transcript in the archives of the Shanghai Number Four Silk-Weaving Factory, 1982/7/21.

15. Ibid.

16. Zhang Shouyu, *Jindai Jiangnan sizhi gongye shi;* Yi Wei, "Meiya chouchang bagong de yanzhongxing" (The severity of the Meiya silk factory strike), *Nüsheng* 2:2 (1934): 2.

17. *Meiya qikan* 1934/8/16.

18. Zhu et al., eds., *Shanghai chanye*, p. 151.

19. Ibid., p. 162.

20. Zhou Zhixin, 1981/12/21.

21. Zhang Qi, personal interview at the Shanghai Federation of Trade Unions, 1987/6/16.

22. Here I take issue with the otherwise generally valuable account of the Meiya strike by Edward Hammond, who asserts that "organization of the strike proceeded relatively slowly for several reasons, the most important being the lack of any pre-existing organization." Edward Roy Hammond, "Organized Labor in Shanghai, 1927–1937" (Ph.D. dissertation, University of California, Berkeley, 1978), p. 222. The major sources for this chapter—*Shanghai chanye yu Shanghai zhigong*, the Shanghai Municipal Police File, worker interviews, and government and factory archives—offer a much fuller, and quite different, picture of worker organization. None of these informative sources was available to Hammond. Still, Hammond is correct in pointing out that unions played next to no role in the 1934 strike.

23. Zhu et al., eds., *Shanghai chanye*, p. 152.

24. Ibid., p. 152; Shanghai Municipal Police (International Settlement) Files (microfilms from the U.S. National Archives), D-5802.

25. Yu Lin, interview transcript in the archives of the Shanghai Number Four Silk-Weaving Factory, 1982/5/8.

26. Zhang Qi, 1987/6/16.

27. Ge Sulan, interview transcript in the archives of the Shanghai Number Four Silk-Weaving Factory, 1982/7/17.

28. Luo Gengmo, "Meiya gongchao shimo," pp. 229–231.

29. Number Two Archives, no. 722: 4–224.

30. Luo Gengmo, "Meiya gongchao shimo," pp. 228–229.

31. Ibid., pp. 230–231.

32. Zhu et al., eds., *Shanghai chanye*, pp. 153–154; Shanghai Police Files, D-5802.

33. Shanghai Police Files, D-5802.

34. Ibid.; Luo Gengmo, "Meiya gongchao shimo," p. 229; *Shanghai dijiu sizhichang* (The Shanghai Number Nine Silk-Weaving Factory) (Shanghai, 1983).

35. Number Two Archives, no. 722: 2–224.

36. Shanghai Police Files, D-5802; Zhu et al., eds., *Shanghai chanye*, p. 165.

37. Shanghai Police Files, D-5802; *Hongse Zhonghua* (Red China) (Jiangxi), nos. 162, 169, 171, 178, 180 (March–April 1934); *Douzheng* (Struggle) (Shanghai), April 19, 1934.

38. *Tuan de jianshe* (League construction) (Shanghai), no. 13, March 12, 1934; no. 15, April 13, 1934; no. 16, April 27, 1934; *Qunzhong de tuan* (League of the masses) (Shanghai), no. 3, April 6, 1934.

39. Shanghai Police Files, D-5802.

40. Ibid.; *Meiya qikan* August 16, 1934, pp. 3–7.

41. Luo Gengmo, "Meiya gongchao shimo," p. 234; Shanghai Police Files, D-5802; Zhu et al., eds., *Shanghai chanye*, p. 155.

42. Shanghai Police Files, D-5802.

43. Ibid.; Zhu et al., eds., *Shanghai chanye*, pp. 155–156; Luo Gengmo, "Meiya gongchao shimo," p. 234.

44. Shanghai Police Files, D-5802; Zhu et al., eds., *Shanghai chanye*, p. 153.

45. Bai Shi, "Zai Meiya bagong zhong duiyu nügong de renshi" (Getting to know women workers in the course of the Meiya strike), *Nüsheng* 4:10 (1934).

46. Number Two History Archives, no. 722: 4–224.

47. Shanghai Police Files, D-5802.

48. Lieu, *Silk Industry of China*, p. 222; Zhu et al., eds., *Shanghai chanye*, p. 140; Ma Chaojun, ed., *Zhongguo laogong yundong shi* (A history of the Chinese labor movement) (Taibei: China Cultural Service, 1955), p. 1190.

49. Shanghai Police Files, D-5802.

50. Zhu et al., eds., *Shanghai chanye*, pp. 156–157.

51. Ibid., p. 157.

52. Shanghai Police Files, D-5802.

53. Zhu et al., eds., *Shanghai chanye*, pp. 157–158; *Meiya disi zhichou-chang* (The Meiya Number Four Silk-Weaving Factory) (Shanghai, 1982), p. 33.

54. Luo Gengmo, "Meiya gongchao shimo," p. 235; *Meiya disi zhichou-chang*, pp. 33–34.

55. Ma Chaojun, *Zhongguo laogong yundong shi*, p. 1191; *Shanghai dijiu sizhichang*, p. 23; *Meiya disi zhichouchang*, p. 34.

56. Shanghai Police Files, D-1791.

57. Edward Shorter and Charles Tilly, *Strikes in France, 1830–1968* (London and New York: Cambridge University Press, 1974), p. 343.

58. Shanghai Police Files, D-5802; Zhu et al., eds., *Shanghai chanye*, p. 159.

59. Recent assessments of the Meiya strike by scholars in the People's Republic of China point to the April 11 protest as evidence of the disastrous effects of the "ultra-leftist" labor policies of the day. By this interpretation, the Meiya strike committee is blamed for having adopted a Wang Ming line of "blind adventurism" in a situation where a moderate strategy of behind-the-scenes negotiation would have been more effective. The ultimate defeat of the Meiya strike, in this view, is attributable to misguided Party policy. Shen Yixing, *Gongyunshi mingbian lu* (Ruminations on the labor movement) (Shanghai: Shanghai Academy of Social Sciences Press, 1987), pp. 140–142. While it is certainly conceivable that the April 11 demonstration escalated tensions to the point where compromise became impossible, it is less clear that the responsibility for this decision should rest with the "ultra-leftist" line in Communist Party labor strategy.

60. Shanghai Municipal Archives, no. 199–48–207.

61. *Meiya disi zhichouchang*, p. 28; Jiang Hongjiao, "Ziwo pipan" (Self-criticism), in the archives of the Shanghai Number Four Silk-Weaving Factory.

62. Shanghai Police Files, D-5802.

63. Ibid.

64. Zhu et al., eds., *Shanghai chanye*, pp. 160–161.

65. Number Two History Archives, no. 722: 4–224.

66. Shanghai Police Files, D-5802; Zhou Zhixin, 1981/12/21.

67. *Qunzhong de tuan*, no. 8, August 24, 1934; *Meiya qikan* August 16, 1934, p. 2.

68. *Meiya disi zhichouchang*, p. 19; *Shanghai dijiu sizhichang*, p. 31; Fu Yuanhua, interview transcript in the archives of the Shanghai Number Four Silk-Weaving Factory, December 1982; Shanghai Municipal Archives, no. 199–48–207.

69. *Shanghai zhi jizhi gongye*, p. 175.

70. Zhu et al., eds., *Shanghai chanye*, pp. 163–164.

71. Ibid., p. 164.

72. "Jin sinian lai."

73. *Shanghai sichou gongye jieduanshi* (A periodized history of the Shanghai silk-weaving industry) (Shanghai, n.d.), p. 3.

74. Shanghai Police Files, D-7506.

75. "Jin sinian lai"; Shanghai Police Files, D-7506.

76. Zhu et al., eds., *Shanghai chanye*, pp. 171–172; Shanghai Police Files, D-7744.

77. Shanghai Police Files, D-7744.

78. "Yijiusanqi nian sichou dabagong" (The great silk-weavers' strike of 1937) (1982), in the archives of the Shanghai Number Four Silk-Weaving Factory, pp. 1–2; Zhang Yuezhen, interview transcript in the archives of the Shanghai Number Four Silk-Weaving Factory, September 23, 1981; Zhou Yunqing, "Wo shi zenma canjia geming de" (How I joined the revolution), archives of the Shanghai Number Four Silk-Weaving Factory, October 4, 1982.

79. Zhang Pingshan, interview transcript in the archives of the Shanghai Number Four Silk-Weaving Factory, September 29, 1981; Zhang Yuezhen, September 23, 1981.

80. *Shanghai dijiu sizhichang*, p. 39; He Zhensheng, "Kang-Ri zhanzheng shiqi Shanghai fangzhi gongye yu zhigong de yixie qingkuang" (Conditions of the Shanghai textile industry and its workers during the Sino-Japanese War), *Shanghai gongyun shiliao*, no. 4 (1984), pp. 14–15.

81. Zhang Yuezhen, September 23, 1981.

82. Zhu et al., eds., *Shanghai chanye*, p. 173.

83. *China Press* (Shanghai), March 31, 1937; *Shanghai Evening Post and Mercury*, March 31, 1937; Zhu et al., eds., *Shanghai chanye*, pp. 174–175; *Shanghai dijiu sizhichang*, p. 39.

84. *China Press*, March 29, 1937.

85. Ibid., March 31, 1937.

86. "Yijiusanqi nian sichou dabagong," pp. 5–6.

87. *Meiya disi zhichouchang*, p. 46.

88. *Shanghai Evening Post and Mercury*, April 5, 1937; *Shanghai sichou gongye*, pp. 20–21.

89. Zhu et al., eds., *Shanghai chanye*, p. 176.

90. *Shanghai Times*, April 14, 1937; Number Two History Archives, no. 722: 4–19.

91. Zhu et al., eds., *Shanghai chanye*, p. 177; Shanghai Police Files, D-7744; Number Two History Archives, no. 2:2–1054.

92. Shanghai Police Files, D-7744; Zhu et al., eds., *Shanghai chanye*, pp. 177–178.

93. *Shanghai Times*, May 19, 1937.

94. Ibid., 4/3/1937.

95. Zhu et al., eds., *Shanghai chanye*, p. 181.

96. Shanghai Police Files, D-7744; *Shanghai sichou gongyun shi*, p. 50.

97. *China Press*, May 26, 1937; Zhu et al., eds., *Shanghai chanye*, p. 179.

98. *Shanghai Times*, June 3, 1937.

99. Shanghai Municipal Archives, no. 199–48–207.

100. Zhu et al., eds., *Shanghai chanye*, pp. 180–181.

101. Robert Bezucha, *The Lyon Uprising of 1834* (Cambridge: Harvard University Press, 1974), p. 158.

102. Bernard H. Moss, "Workers' Ideology and French Social History," *International Labor and Working Class History*, no. 11 (1977), p. 28.

103. Shorter and Tilly, *Strikes in France*, p. 10.

104. *Shanghai dijiu sizhichang*, p. 46.

105. He Zhensheng, interview transcript in the archives of the Shanghai Number Four Silk-Weaving Factory, July 1982.

106. Zhang Shouyu, *Jindai Jiangnan sizhi gongye shi; Shanghai sichou gongyun shi*, p. 94.

107. *Shanghai sichou gongyun shi*, pp. 101–113.

108. Shanghai Municipal Archives, no. 1–7–54.

109. *Shanghai sichou gongyun shi*, pp. 130–132.

110. Michael P. Hanagan, *The Logic of Solidarity: Artisans and Industrial Workers in Three French Towns, 1871–1914* (Urbana: University of Illinois Press, 1980), pp. 216–217.

111. G. Crossick, *An Artisan Elite in Late Victorian Society* (London: Croom Helm, 1980); Robert Gray, *The Aristocracy of Labour in Nineteenth-Century Britain* (London: Macmillan, 1981).

112. Eric J. Hobsbawm, "The Labour Aristocracy in Nineteenth-Century Britain," in his *Labouring Men* (London: Weidenfeld and Nicolson, 1964).

113. E.P. Thompson, *The Making of the English Working Class* (London: V. Gollancz, 1963).

6

Labor Divided: Sources of State Formation in Modern China

Recent generations of labor historians, disappointed by the failure of twentieth-century workers to live up to the exalted expectations of Karl Marx and Frederick Engels, have focused their explanatory energies on the limitations of proletarian politics. Central to this new wave of scholarship is attention to the fragmented character of labor. Divided along lines of gender, age, ethnicity, and skill, workers are shown rarely to have acted in the cohesive, class-conscious fashion predicted by communist visionaries. There is a pessimistic tone to much of this recent analysis, as students of labor reluctantly come to grips with the shortcomings of their object of study. There is also a note of irony, as scholars discover that what little indigenous support there was for a radical labor movement tended to be concentrated in the most privileged sectors of the working class, far removed from the heroic proletariat of the *Communist Manifesto*.[1]

In wrestling with the unfulfilled promises of Marxism, studies of labor have been obsessed with "why not" questions: Why did workers not develop a class identity? Why did workers, especially the most downtrodden of them, not flock to radical political parties? Why did working-class parties, especially in advanced capitalist societies, not engineer Marxist revolutions? When phrased in this manner, the questions prompt one to search for sources of weakness in the working class. And that search has led to sophisticated analyses of divisions within the labor force. A host of careful studies have convincingly demonstrated that contradictions between men and women, old and young, black and white, and skilled and unskilled have prevented workers from exhibiting the class-conscious party allegiances or revolutionary behaviors we might otherwise expect of them.

The disaggregation of labor that this line of analysis has entailed is indeed a salutary trend. We now have a much more realistic appreciation of the powerful centrifugal forces at play within the modern working class. But must such intraclass divisions be seen only in a negative light, as obstacles to the fulfillment of the "true" mission of the proletariat? I suggest instead that the fragmentation of labor can itself provide a basis for politically influential working-class action, not only in support of one or another political party but even in the emergence of new states. An approach linking class fractions to state formation is especially appropriate to studies of the Third World. It is commonplace to remark on the high level of social fragmentation in Third World countries. To acknowledge that a society is internally divided is not to concede that it is politically impotent, however. Different segments of society—and even different segments of one class within society—may link up with state allies in such a way as to affect decisively the fate of both parties. This is not to say that social groupings will always have their way; usually neither partner gets quite what it wanted or anticipated in these often uneasy relationships. Nonetheless, by beginning our analysis from the ground up—taking seriously the political potential of these subclasses, fragmented as they may be—we have a concrete means of exploring patterns of state–society interaction.

Outline

This essay examines the relationship of two very different "modern" Chinese states—the Nationalist regime of 1927–49 and the Communist regime of 1949–89—to the Shanghai labor arena. Although neither state was fundamentally based on the working class, both were in fact a good deal more dependent on worker support than is generally recognized. Each regime, however, drew its labor constituency from a different sector of the Shanghai working class. Whereas the Nationalists (with the assistance of organized crime) relied primarily on semiskilled operatives from

North China, the Communists attracted skilled artisans from the south. This difference in labor base helps account for fundamental distinctions in the character of the two states. The Nationalists reflected a gangster mentality, extorting money from the Shanghai capitalists yet cooperating with that same bourgeoisie if the price was right. The Communists, by contrast, operated on principles more in tune with the values of the skilled craftsman—severely curtailing capitalist prerogatives and constructing a new system of industrial relations in which the state assumed major responsibility for worker welfare.

Despite its relatively small size in a country that remains to this day overwhelmingly rural, the Chinese working class (concentrated in the industrial metropolis of Shanghai) has shown itself to be a political factor of exceptional importance This is partly for the universal economic reason that workers with access to expensive industrial equipment are capable of wreaking enormous damage—in terms of both property and production. But there is also an ideological explanation for the power of Chinese labor. Whether pledging allegiance to Sun Yatsen's Three Principles of the People or to Marxism-Leninism, political leaders in twentieth-century China (as in many other developing nations) have accorded the working class a prominent place in their vision of a new society. Since modernization was seen as virtually synonymous with industrialization, workers were esteemed as agents of development. A party claiming to represent the forces of progress thus needed a working-class constituency. This ideological consideration lent labor a far greater political voice than its small size might otherwise have suggested. Both the Nationalists and the Communists made active efforts to channel the labor movement in directions favorable to their own political agendas. In the process, parties and states—as well as labor itself—underwent fundamental change.

To be sure, the ideological formations of these rival parties were substantially different. Whereas Communist labor organizers stressed the importance of class struggle spearheaded by a militant proletariat, the Nationalists emphasized the need for class harmony, with labor and capital cooperating for the economic development of the nation. The contrasting programs help account for the bifurcated reception that their overtures elicited among the workers. Skilled artisans, who boasted a long history of struggles to maintain high wages and job control, had little difficulty in relating to the radicalism of the Communist message. Semiskilled workers, who were typically factory-trained and who lacked the independence of guild-based artisans, were more inclined to support the conservative "yellow unions" founded by Nationalist organizers.

Ideology was not the only basis of division between these two sectors of the work force. Organizational differences were also of critical importance in shaping their relationships with parties and regimes. Skilled craftsmen in China, as elsewhere in the world, lay claim to a rich tradition of corporate organization. Guilds, native-place associations, and the like imbued their members with a communal spirit that encouraged collective action on behalf of shared interests. By contrast, semiskilled workers—who lacked the occupational training and the security of skilled craftsmen—became dependent on underworld gangs to ensure their success in the competitive game of urban survival. As recent arrivals to the inhospitable world of the industrial city, these semiskilled workers were ready recruits to the powerful Green and Red Gangs that dominated the economic landscape of early-twentieth-century Shanghai.

Nationalist cadres, relying on close connections with gang bosses—more than a few of whom were also factory foremen—developed a patron–client network of labor relations. In return for delivering the support of labor, gangsters were awarded key positions in the regime. The patronage system that emerged (in which opium czars mediated between semiskilled workers and top-level politicians) set limits on the ability of the Nationalist regime to effect either economic or political reform. By contrast, Communist cadres, building on the guild traditions of skilled workers, established radical unions advocating class struggle and worker welfare. Although such organizations were, of course, effectively tamed just as soon as the Communists assumed state power, the legacy of the guilds lived on in the *danwei* (work unit) structure of urban China under the People's Republic (PRC). The state-owned enterprises of the Maoist era offered their permanent employees substantial welfare benefits in an "iron rice bowl" system that would later come to be seen as a major impediment to industrial reform.

The Battle for Shanghai Labor

In retrospect, the fact that the Chinese Communist Party (CCP) was founded in China's industrial capital of Shanghai seems only natural. At the time, however, the location struck young Marxist organizers—accustomed to the more "cultured" atmosphere of the political capital, Beijing—as anything but ideal. Chen Duxiu, cofounder of the CCP, wrote contemptuously in a series of essays on Shanghai published less than a year before the First Party Congress convened in the city in the summer of 1921:

In analyzing Shanghai society [we find] a large portion are totally ignorant laborers who suffer privation and hardship. Another portion are traitorous businessmen who make a living directly or indirectly under foreign capitalism. Another portion are swindlers who sell fake Western medicines or lottery tickets. Another portion are prostitutes. Another portion are "black curtain" writers and book sellers dealing in promiscuous romances, superstitious formulas, and profitable new magazines. Another portion are gangster politicians. Committed young students are only a small portion, and situated in this sort of environment they have barely enough strength for self-protection, let alone for overcoming the environment. . . . Because of this, I believe that *if a national congress can be convened, it should not be held in Shanghai.* . . .

What types of people are most powerful in Shanghai? A superficial look shows that major political and economic power is in the hands of the Westerners, but the internal social situation is quite different. The majority of factory laborers, all of the transport workers, and virtually all of the police . . . are under the control of the Green Gang. . . . The commands of gang leaders are more effective than those of the Municipal Council. . . . The only way of eliminating them is to publicly establish legal unions in each industry.[2]

Unionization, it was quickly discovered, was most easily accomplished among the small subset of workers who shared many of the cultural preferences of their would-be Communist organizers. The first unions to be founded under Communist sponsorship were in the trades of metalworking and printing, skilled occupations dominated by artisans from the same prosperous South China region from which many of the young CCP cadres themselves hailed. Not surprisingly, the new unions reflected long-standing concerns of skilled craftsmen. The Shanghai Mechanics' Union, whose seventy or so initial members were drawn from industries as diverse as shipbuilding and cotton, pledged in its founding manifesto to uphold customary practices of apprenticeship and mutual aid.[3]

For the Communists to move beyond the world of the literate artisan to make common cause with the less skilled rank and file of the Shanghai proletariat (many of whom were gang members from the poorer regions of the North China countryside) was a more challenging project. An early activist remembered,

Our work met with many difficulties. . . . Hardest to handle were the Green and Red gangs. Finally, we decided that several comrades should infiltrate their ranks. But at that time our comrades were all students. If we wanted them to jump up on a stage and deliver a speech or jump down and write an essay, there were always volunteers. However, to enter the Green or Red Gang one had to knuckle down and learn their customs and regulations. Then, through various guises, one could begin work. Who had the patience for that?[4]

As it turned out, conservative members of the Nationalist Party (Guomindang or GMD) were a good deal more successful at using their connections with factory foremen to generate gangster support. Thanks to gangster assistance, by 1920 more than a dozen labor unions had already been founded in Shanghai under right-wing GMD auspices.[5]

The divergent results of Communist and Nationalist efforts to mobilize Shanghai labor soon became apparent in the emergence of distinctive working-class constituencies. The general trend can be illustrated by a close look at the British American Tobacco Company (BAT) in Shanghai, the most strike-prone of any factory in the history of the Chinese labor movement. The subject of intensive scrutiny by students of Chinese labor, BAT has usually been characterized as a bastion of united proletarian support for the Communist Party.[6] In fact, however, the picture was a good deal more complicated.

BAT, like most cigarette factories, was divided into three major production departments: leaf (where tobacco leaves were removed from the stem by hand), rolling (where machines rolled the dried tobacco silk into cigarettes), and packing (where cigarettes were placed in cartons). In addition, there was a machine shop where skilled metalworkers (known popularly as "coppersmiths") built and repaired the factory equipment.[7] Before outside political parties demonstrated any interest in the workers of BAT, the factory had developed a reputation for labor unrest. Significantly, virtually all of this early protest activity (which included twelve strikes during the fifteen years before Communist cadres first arrived on the scene) was initiated by unskilled women workers in the leaf and packing departments.[8] This pronounced militancy on the part of women tobacco workers resonates with the findings of researchers focusing on very different societies.[9] However, once outside parties became embroiled in labor struggles at BAT, the situation changed markedly. Skilled male metalworkers from the machine shop (nearly all of whom were natives of South China) became active in Communist-inspired protests, while semiskilled rolling machine operators (who were also male, but hailed predominantly from the north) enlisted on the side of the GMD.

The bifurcated pattern of labor politics at BAT began to emerge only a few weeks after the establishment of the Chinese Communist Party in the summer of 1921. At that time, metalworkers at the factory had gathered to grumble about a new British manager assigned to their division. Outraged by the new overseer's attempts to curtail their customary privileges, these mechanics—inspired, most probably, by the recent establishment of the Shanghai Mechanics' Union—declared a strike. Within two days, a young Marxist labor organizer had been dispatched to the temple where the strikers had congregated. Under his tutelage, a strike fund was collected and a set of specific demands was drafted. Thanks in part to this assistance, the strike ended more than twenty days later in complete victory with management's acquiescence to all demands. To solidify their gains, a BAT union was formed with Communist guidance at another mass meeting convened at the local temple.[10]

When a walkout again erupted at BAT the following year, however, management turned to a local Green Gang mobster in an attempt to prevent another lengthy work stoppage. Promising his followers a better settlement than any that could be negotiated by the CCP–sponsored union, the gangster managed to recruit hundreds of rolling-machine operators, all of whom were prepared to cross picket lines and resume work. Although the strike ended quickly without achieving any of its initial demands, management did grant concessions to the more than three hundred rollers who had returned to work early.[11]

Gangster involvement in the BAT labor movement intensified after the Nationalists took power in the spring of 1927. Having witnessed the influence of Communist-sponsored unions, the GMD was anxious to try its own hand at labor mobilization. The BAT union was reorganized "to improve workers' living conditions, develop the tobacco industry, and further the national revolution under the Three Principles of the People."[12] A Communist with Green Gang connections remained director of the union, but was joined on the standing committee by two Green Gang leaders in the factory. With generous financial backing from the new Nationalist regime, the BAT union quickly reduced Communist influences (the director was soon arrested) and pledged its support for government policies. When the BAT Company, whose foreign owners were accustomed to favorable tax breaks under previous warlord regimes, refused to pay a new tobacco impost levied by the Nationalists, the GMD-backed union declared a strike.

Thanks to a strike fund buoyed by secret subsidies from the Ministry of Finance, the walkout lasted for nearly four months, making it the longest industrial dispute of the GMD era.[13] But a strike sustained by government funds could also be squelched by government fiat. In early

1928, the GMD—through the negotiations of Finance Minister T.V. Soong, Chiang Kaishek's brother-in-law—came to an understanding with BAT. The resulting agreement, signed during a dinner party at Soong's posh Shanghai residence and sealed by a payment of 3 million yuan, pledged the multinational tobacco giant to remit taxes (albeit at a much reduced rate) and to recognize the bargaining authority of the union.[14] Thanks to this settlement, BAT taxes became an important source of revenue to government and union alike. According to a confidential memo by BAT's general manager, the Shanghai GMD received some 1,750 yuan a month from the tobacco tax, of which it kept 550 yuan for its own purposes and divided the remainder among three Green Gang factions at the BAT union. This symbiotic relationship between local politicians and labor union leaders reminded the general manager of nothing more than Tammany Hall.[15]

Not until the Japanese invasion, when GMD forces retreated to the interior of China, did this state-sponsored form of yellow unionism weaken. By the late 1930s Communists had reestablished a foothold in the BAT machine room. After the Japanese took control of BAT following their attack on Pearl Harbor, the Communist Party branch at the factory (led by three metalworkers) instigated a number of slowdowns to interfere with production and promote worker welfare. With the Japanese surrender in the summer of 1945, CCP members were determined to reestablish a leftist union at BAT. Their first planning meeting was held at the home of a metalworker, indicating that Communist support was largely confined to the machine shop. The rolling department, by contrast, was controlled by Hong Meiquan, a Green Gang chieftain and GMD member who had been active in yellow union affairs a decade earlier. A longtime rolling-machine operator himself, Hong led a powerful sworn brotherhood society of workers from North China in the rolling department. In the spring of 1946, Hong Meiquan was appointed director of a new, government–approved BAT union.[16]

The pressing problem for the Communists was their confinement to a limited segment of the work force. As an intraparty report on the BAT situation confided, "All our foundation is in the coppersmiths' room [i.e., the machine shop]. . . . Although a few of our people work in other departments, we have been unable to develop a mass following there."[17] To be sure, the metalworkers were an active group. But their very militancy was attracting an increased level of surveillance. If the radical labor movement at BAT were to continue, it would have to shift its base of operations to a less closely monitored workshop. In the summer of 1947, as demand for a Sunday wage began to sweep the BAT work force,

Communist organizers made a bold decision to relinquish leadership of the struggle to a few trusted allies in the rolling department. A leader of the strike recalled,

> At that time the reactionary union was watching the coppersmiths closely. Since they were already very "red," we tobacco rollers were charged with this struggle. I was a sworn brother of Hong Meiquan, the head of the Yellow Union. The chief of the Rolling Department was also Hong's sworn brother. So Hong harbored no suspicions about our workshop and hadn't blacklisted any of our workers.[18]

The success of this strike led to an erosion of the gangster's power. But it was not until the GMD's flight from Shanghai in the spring of 1949 that the Communists attained unchallenged control of the BAT labor movement. A metalworker, imprisoned under the GMD was released from jail to serve as chairman of a new union at the factory. His nemesis, Hong Meiquan, although shielded for some time by friends within the Public Security Bureau, was finally arrested in the spring of 1951 as part of the campaign to suppress counterrevolutionaries.

By the time that the British American Tobacco Company fell under Communist rule, its workers had compiled an impressive history of labor protest, spanning nearly half a century. It is hardly surprising, then, that historians of the Chinese labor movement have devoted a good deal of attention to the workers of BAT, praising them as exemplary proletarian fighters. But the BAT case, important as it is, is not primarily the story of a patriotic, revolutionary working class united in the struggle to seize power on behalf of its own interests. It is instead a story shaped in important ways by the competing agendas of outside partisans: gangsters and state authorities as well as young Communist intellectuals. And, most important, it is a story that reveals the complexity of the workers themselves. Although sometimes capable of united action, the workers of BAT were divided by differences in skill, wages, gender, and native-place origins. Such divisions contributed to a complicated labor movement, some of whose participants became enthusiastic advocates of Communist revolution, some of whom threw support to the GMD and their Green Gang henchmen, and some of whom remained outside the reach of would-be organizers.

The divisions at BAT were, moreover, far from unusual. Other enterprises and industries showed a similar segmentation among the work force. In cotton mills and silk filatures, where unskilled women workers from North China constituted the vast majority of employees, a small coterie of skilled male metalworkers from the south supplied the backbone of support for the Communist movement. In silk-weaving factories, where skilled and literate men and women (from South China) worked for high wages, a substantial percentage of workers of both sexes joined the revolution—as we saw in Chapter 5. In the tramway industry, skilled southern metalworkers formed a bastion of support for the CCP, whereas among semiskilled drivers and conductors (from the north) Green Gang and GMD influence was dominant.[19]

When viewed in comparative context, the political divisions of the Shanghai labor force are not surprising. As Eric Hobsbawm has noted, during World War I metalworkers "became in most countries of the world the characteristic leaders of militant labor movments."[20] By way of explanation, Michael Hanagan observes that "nowhere was artisanal survival inside the factory more clear that in metalworking. Although shut behind factory walls, metalworking artisans continued to behave as if they were in their own small shops."[21] A Russian journalist, trying to explain the militancy of the skilled metalworkers of Petrograd at the time of the revolution, concluded:

> Workers in machine production are always in the forefront of every movement. . . . Turners, founders, blacksmiths, mechanics, and machinists—all of these are people with a well formed sense of individuality and rather good wages. . . . The worker must think a great deal, reason in the very process of work. . . . In the form of their conversation and even their language, they are almost indistinguishable from our intellectuals. In my opinion, they are more interesting because their judgments are fresher and their convictions, once taken, are very firm.[22]

In fact, the radicalism of European metalworkers preceded World War I by more than half a century. In 1851 the Toulouse police, in an effort to explain why the factory metalworkers were "almost all socialist," pointed to the ease of spreading propaganda because of their concentration in *grands ateliers.*[23]

As a consequence of close on-the-job interaction—encouraged by the apprenticeship system—skilled workers took pride in their profession. Accustomed to steady employment and decent treatment, they held their employers to high standards. A privileged segment within the work force, factory artisans nevertheless saw themselves as spokesmen for the interests of labor as a whole. In their minds there was no necessary contradiction between what we may term "craft consciousness"—awareness of the collective interests of one's particular skill group—and "class consciousness"—awareness of one's common interests with other working-class groups.[24]

Unlike unskilled laborers, whose attachment to the city was usually a temporary and insecure one, most skilled workers were committed to urban life. As permanent residents of urban society, they took an interest in public affairs that transcended the horizons of the workplace. The high levels of literacy that characterized most artisan professions further contributed to the process of politicization.[25]

Artisan trades in which these traits—of literacy, urbanization, and pride in one's product—were most pronounced, were also trades that generated a disproportionate share of working-class militants. Natalie Davis points to the printing industry as an example.[26] Robert Bezucha highlights the silk-weaving industry.[27] Eric Hobsbawm and Joan Scott identify the shoemaking trade.[28] It may be worth reflecting on the background of several of Shanghai's most active Communist labor leaders. Chen Yun—later to become architect of socialist China's industrial system—apprenticed at the Commercial Press, the city's largest printing house. (During the Great Leap Forward, when Chen Yun's economic policies were out of favor, he busied himself by writing essays on the *pingtan*, a storytelling tradition of the South China region from which he hailed.)[29] Zhang Qi—later to become director of the Shanghai Federation of Labor Unions under the PRC—was a skilled craftsman at Meiya, Shanghai's premier silk-weaving enterprise (see Chapter 5). And Liu Changsheng—later to become deputy director of the All-China Federation of Trade Unions—had been a shoemaker.

Although the European labor movement is usually held up as the standard for international comparison, in the case of Shanghai the parallels with American labor are at least as instructive. Behind this similarity lies a recruitment process that in both countries relegated workers from certain regions and backgrounds to certain lines of work. As John Cumbler has described the American pattern,

> Selective recruitment directed immigrants with various skills and experiences into particular occupations. Contacts with relatives and friends, often made before migration, steered newcomers into occupations and neighborhoods already identified with particular regions and origins. . . . Social and ethnic divisions channeled workers into worlds separated by traditions, customs and skills carried over from their past and reinforced by the experiences of their present life and work in ethnic groupings.[30]

Skill and native-place differences, in America as in China, were reflected in political orientations. In a study of the U.S. labor movement, Stanley Aronowitz has pointed out that initially the Socialists found their key base of support among skilled workers who were either native-born or of Northern European origins. By contrast, the unskilled laborers—most of whom hailed from Eastern and Southern Europe—remained largely outside the radical labor movement.[31]

But there was, in both America and Shanghai, an intermediate group of semiskilled laborers who also played an important role in labor politics. Lacking the job security or social status of the skilled worker, such individuals were often prompted to turn to gang networks in search of protection. Gangs helped rural immigrants make the difficult transition to urban life. They also served as brokers between workers and politicians. The case of Tammany Hall, the infamous Manhattan Democratic organization, illustrates the linkage clearly.

[margin note: unskilled workers need gangs for job security.]

In the United States, as in China, the 1920s witnessed a transformation of gangster operations to more sophisticated political activities. The involvement of organized crime in the Teamsters Union was symptomatic of this development. The union had been open to corruption ever since it was first formed to represent drivers of horse-drawn wagons (hence the name "Teamsters"). As a student of the mob has explained its hold over American transport workers: "Every worker was a little guy out on a limb, and therefore easy to intimidate."[32] Racketeering and conservative politics were hallmarks of the union.[33]

For rank-and-file workers, patron–client gang ties were a means of getting ahead in an otherwise forbidding environment. As Teamsters leader Jimmy Hoffa recognized,

> Personal contact is the key to service and giving the membership service is the only reason we are in the business. That political and social stuff—it's not important. I don't think the drivers expect me to be holding social gatherings for them or to go on the air and tell what's wrong in Germany or Italy. We're in the business of selling labor. We're going to get the best price we can.[34]

Much of the success of gangsters in mobilizing semiskilled workers lay in a public denial of political interests, while at the same time their unions forged close links to powerholders. As Anton Blok has analyzed the Mafia, its key distinction from common banditry lies in its symbiosis with those who hold formal political office. The mafiosi act as political middlemen or power brokers in patron–client networks that link politicians to the rank-and-file citizenry.[35] The insecure position of semiskilled workers—whose futures were tied to the city, but who enjoyed few advantages in the struggle to stake out a permanent urban niche for themselves—made them especially receptive to this variety of organized crime. As employer-trained operatives who lacked the autonomous guild traditions of the skilled workers, they were easy recruits for "yellow unions" advocating economic gain rather than political resistance.

If the political division separating skilled and semiskilled workers is a common enough feature of labor movements around the globe, the Chinese case holds a special significance in light of the fact that each of these "natural" political tendencies became associated with a major state: the Republic of China (1927–49) and the People's Republic of China (1949 to the present). By exploring the relationship that these rival polities bore to Chinese labor, we have an opportunity to analyze the impact of social movements on state formation. We begin with an examination of the Nationalists during their ill-fated tenure on the mainland, after which we turn to the contemporary Communists.

Shanghai Labor and the Nationalist State

Chiang Kaishek's momentous coup of April 12, 1927, which shattered the Communist labor movement and forced the radicals out of the cities and into their twenty-year exile in the countryside, was, of course, executed by the Shanghai gangsters. In late March, three of Chiang's closest associates—all of whom had underworld ties—had been dispatched to Shanghai to establish contact with gangster leaders. There they met secretly with the powerful opium triumvirate of Huang Jinrong, Du Yuesheng, and Zhang Xiaolin to lay plans for the anti-Communist offensive that was soon to follow.

The GMD's reliance on gangsters was a recognition of the latter's influence as local strongmen in early-twentieth-century Shanghai. Huang Jinrong, the "godfather" of the Shanghai Green Gang, had originally come to Shanghai in 1900. After leading the life of a petty gangster for several years, he was recruited into the French police force as a plainclothes criminal detective. Police work in Shanghai's French Concession certainly did not require severing ties with the underworld, and Huang kept a foot in each camp. His big break came a few years later, when he succeeded in obtaining the release of a French bishop who had been kidnapped while on a trip to North China. The bishop was a close friend of both the French consul and the French chief of police in Shanghai, so Huang was handsomely rewarded for his service with a newly created post as chief inspector for the Frenchtown police. Promotion to this powerful position greatly enhanced Huang Jinrong's standing as a gang master in the Shanghai underworld; as many as twenty thousand of the city's residents subsequently pledged their discipleship to him.[36]

Among those who took Huang as mentor was Du Yuesheng. Born into a poor family and orphaned at an early age, Du worked for several years at his uncle's fruit stand along the wharf by the old Chinese city of Shanghai. The boy's penchant for throwing rotten fruit at well-dressed rickshaw passengers did not endear Du to his uncle, however, and eventually he was fired for having stolen money for gambling. In this jobless state, Du made the acquaintance of the powerful Huang Jinrong. Huang's paramour, a former brothel madam, took an immediate liking to "Fruit Yuesheng," as he was then known, and saw that Du was given work in Huang's criminal empire. Like generations of secret society chieftains before him, Du Yuesheng rose to fame and fortune through Shanghai's lucrative opium trade. First assigned as an assistant in a Cantonese-owned opium den, Du was soon promoted to manage one of Huang's large dens in the French Concession. More entrepreneurial than his mentor, Du quickly saw the possibilities for turning Huang's Frenchtown connections to maximum advantage. With his master's sanction, Du established the "Black Stuff Company" to extract a monthly fee from every opium shop in the French Concession in return for a guarantee of freedom to sell openly without police interference. The system was maintained by substantial monthly payoffs to the French authorities.[37]

Soon Du's ambitions reached beyond the boundaries of Frenchtown. To expand the scale of opium operations, he made contact with another gangster-cum-opium magnate in the city: Zhang Xiaolin. Zhang's close relations with the Shanghai garrison command had allowed him to gain control of the opium trade at the critical juncture where the Yangzi and Huangpu rivers joined. In 1920, Zhang agreed to cooperate formally with Du Yuesheng and Huang Jinrong. The close relationship among Huang, Du, and Zhang—sealed by a sworn brotherhood ceremony—was further solidified in 1924 when Huang allocated some of his extensive land holdings in the French Concession to build adjoining residences for his two righthand men.[38]

Chiang Kaishek's Northern Expedition, by challenging the political status quo in the Yangzi valley, also threatened to undermine the opium business. Thus it was more than revolutionary spirit or personal goodwill that inspired the opium triumvirate of Shanghai to offer their services to the generalissimo in 1927. Uppermost in their considerations was the maintenance of their profitable trade. Chiang's willingness to work out a mutually agreeable modus operandi ensured the support of these powerful gangsters.

On the night of April 11, only hours before the attack began, the opium triumvirate met with Chiang's trusted lieutenants to drink wine and swear mutual loyalty.[39] At two o'clock in the morning of April 12 the offensive commenced. Hundreds of mobsters wearing armbands marked with the character for "labor" (*gong*) fanned out from the concessions into the neighboring Chinese areas to wrest control from Communist-led workers' pickets. The battles were brief, as soldiers quickly took command of picket stations and union offices. Hundreds of workers and labor organizers lost their lives in the ensuing bloodbath.[40]

Having crushed the Communist labor movement, Chiang Kaishek's men immediately undertook to impose their own organizational framework on Shanghai's workers. The objective, in classic corporatist style, was to create a network of tamed labor unions under governmental direction. [41] On April 13, only one day after Chiang's stunning coup, his lieutenants presided over the formation of the Unification Committee for Shanghai Union Organization—a gangster-staffed operation that quickly developed a reputation for extreme ruthlessness. Communists and others suspected of harboring leftist sympathies were summarily rounded up and put to death. The draconian methods of the Unification Committee proved unpalatable even to some members of the Guomindang, who soon formed their own umbrella associations to compete for allegiance of the city's labor unions.

Internecine warfare between rival GMD factions was brought to a halt only in the fall of 1928 when a newly established Bureau of Social Affairs of the Shanghai municipal government was charged with overall responsibility for the city's labor movement. In spite of the good intentions of many of the newly appointed staff members, however, the Bureau was stymied in its efforts to revamp the city's industrial system. In 1930, the director of the Bureau of Social Affairs, Pan Gongzhan, reported that only 157 unions had registered with his bureau.[42] This was a far cry from the more than five hundred unions active in Shanghai on the eve of the Guomindang takeover, although it did indicate the government's interest in the matter of labor organization. Pan complained that the Bureau faced two formidable obstacles in carrying out its responsibilities in the area of labor control. First was the continued existence of the foreign concessions, where foreign residents governed with their own councils, courts, and police. With the great majority of Shanghai's factories located in the International Settlement and French Concession, the cooperation of foreign authorities was required for Chinese officials to play their assigned role in union registration and dispute mediation. Such cooperation was seldom forthcoming. The second problem that Pan identified as an impediment to the proper functioning of his bureau was that of "people who instigate labor unrest for their own profit." No doubt Pan was here referring in part to remnant underground Communist organizers trying to resuscitate their radical labor movement. But he was surely also alluding to elements within his own Guomindang coalition. The most vexing source of intraparty dissension came from the very group to which Chiang Kaishek had turned in mounting his April coup: the Green Gang. Although the dissolution of the highhanded Unification Committee had brought to an ignominious close the Nationalists' first experiment in gangster-dominated labor control, soon to follow was another—more subtle and successful—form of gangster intervention.

Aware of the Nationalist government's inability to control labor, Green Gang chief Du Yuesheng decided to try his own hand at organizing the labor movement. Du's first move was to reach out to reformist union leaders at the Shanghai Post Office. A Chinese government agency that was nonetheless directed by a foreigner, the post office was targeted by Du as an institution with sufficient social and political clout to serve as an ideal entrée to the unions. First among the postal unionists to ally with Du Yuesheng were Lu Jingshi and Zhu Xuefan.

Under the patronage of the opium czar, Lu Jingshi quickly rose to become a member of the executive committee of the Shanghai Guomindang and director of the martial law division of the Shanghai Garrison Command. Fellow postal unionist Zhu Xuefan soon assumed the chairmanship of a newly created Shanghai General Labor Union, established to provide overall direction to the city's labor movement.[43]

But it was, of course, Du Yuesheng whose star rose most spectacularly. In 1933 an English-language "Who's Who" of China described the opium magnate as "one of the leading financiers, bankers and industrial leaders of China," with "a long and honourable record of important achievements in public and civic service, having on many occasions rendered invaluable aid to his country." Among Du's many official positions were listed those of "advisor to the Military Commission of the Nationalist government, member of the Legislative Body of the Municipality of Greater Shanghai, member of the Supervisory Committee of the Chamber of Commerce of Shanghai, and chairman of the Executive Committee of the China Merchants Steam Navigation Company, which is government controlled."[44] As a foreign contemporary remarked, Du "was a combination of Al Capone and Rockefeller."[45]

The mutually advantageous partnership between gangster Du Yue-sheng and his followers from the Post Office was built on the foundation of labor control. Through the introduction of Lu Jingshi and Zhu Xuefan, their patron was invited to intervene in virtually every major strike that broke out in the city. Du's services as labor negotiator par excellence were employed—often in a fashion quite beneficial to labor—in industries as diverse as cotton, printing, silk weaving, jewelry, journalism, and rickshaw transport. On more than one occasion Du drew on his personal bank account first to subsidize the strike committee and then to augment the financial settlement that management was willing to grant. Such displays of benevolence earned the gangster the gratitude of workers, employers, and public opinion (and often netted him a significant share of the company stock, as well).[46]

Zhu Xuefan recalls in a recent memoir how Du's intervention in strikes helped the gangster shed his unsavory reputation and become a Shanghai celebrity. Each time that Du Yuesheng negotiated a settlement, Shanghai's four major Chinese-language newspapers (whose board of directors was chaired by Du) printed glowing reports of the occasion. Coverage of these events was facilitated by the Labor News Agency, which Zhu Xuefan established specifically for the purpose of publicizing his patron's exploits.[47] As Du Yuesheng's biographer on Taiwan has argued, these activities were directly responsible for the opium czar's rapid rise to fame:

> Regardless of whether it was Du Yuesheng or Lu Jingshi who sallied forth to settle labor disputes, their actions were perfectly coordinated into the smoothest of operations. Several years later, Du Yuesheng and the Shanghai municipal party branch joined forces in leading the labor movement. Shanghai industrialists and labor leaders in both the Chinese areas and the foreign concessions, regardless of trade or occupation, rushed to enter Du's gate. The confluence of these forces gave Du Yuesheng enormous power. The ease with which he subsequently launched his monumental undertakings can be traced back to the firm foundations laid during this period.[48]

Though Du Yuesheng's ascent was certainly attributable to the support of both government and big business, the primary loyalty of the gangster chieftain and his henchmen lay with no constituency but themselves. As a result, the gangsters were quite ready to champion the cause of labor—and even to promote labor strife—when such a strategy promised greater payoff. It was actually with some justification that Zhu Xuefan could boast to a foreign visitor to his Labor News Agency that "we are the only people who defend the Shanghai workers against exploitation."[49] Zhu and several other Green Gang labor organizers even founded a small printing house surreptitiously to print up strike handbills that regular presses, subject to tight government censorship, dared not handle.[50]

The targets of gang-directed strikes were various. We have already seen how Green Gang union leaders in the British American Tobacco Company launched a strike for higher wages that quickly became linked to a Guomindang effort to extract increased taxes from the multinational giant. But governments as well as corporations could fall victim to Du's labor stratagems. In 1932, the Green Gang instigated a strike at the French Tramway Company to protest the unfriendly policies of a new French consul and police chief who threatened to curtail opium and gambling in the French Concession.[51] That same year, Du's followers in the Shanghai Post Office launched a politically motivated strike that spread rapidly to postal workers in Beiping, Tianjin, and Nanjing. Although the strikers complained that recent increases in the price of stamps had not been accompanied by commensurate wage hikes, the real target of the protest was the leadership of the Ministry of Communications. At the time, the Ministry was controlled by Wang Jingwei's "Reorganization Faction"—a rival to the "CC Clique" with which Du Yuesheng was more closely connected.[52]

These examples suggest the range of concerns that motivated Du Yuesheng's promotion of labor unrest. Sometimes, as in the BAT strike of 1927, Du's objectives coincided with those of the Nationalist government. However, at other times, as in the 1932 postal strike, the protest could be directed against an agency of the government itself. By deputing the Green Gang as its chief labor organizer, the state had created a powerful challenge to its own hegemony. The outcome was identical to the situation found in so many Third World countries whose leaders feel compelled to reach an accommodation with local strongmen. Joel Migdal writes, "The paradox . . . is: while the strongmen have become evermore dependent on state resources to shore up their social control, state leaders have become evermore dependent on strongmen, who employ their resources in a manner inimical to state rules and laws."[53]

The power of gangster strongmen in Nationalist China ultimately foiled government efforts to carry out reformist labor policies. A telling example was the case of the dockworkers. Offended by the unreasonable profits that gangster labor contractors were extracting from workers' wages and hoping to win the gratitude of ordinary dockers, Nanjing in 1928 passed a "2–8 regulation" whereby the contractors' cut of wages

would be limited to 20 percent, leaving 80 percent for the workers themselves. Such a regulation aroused the immediate ire of the contractors,
who had grown accustomed to a much larger piece of the pie. Drawing
on their gangster networks, contractors throughout the 1930s prevailed
upon gang members within the Shanghai government to subvert implementation of the regulation. Rather than giving rise to a unified and loyal
dockers' union, as lawmakers in Nanjing had imagined, the 2–8 regulation opened the door to a plethora of warring unions under the direction
of rival contractors.[54]

The fascinating interplay among state, gangsters, capitalists, workers,
and foreigners—all of whom suffered from internal divisions as well—
defined Shanghai politics under the Nationalists. When the Shanghai
branch of the Guomindang first authorized the formation of a General
Labor Union headed by Zhu Xuefan, the Bureau of Social Affairs—
which was a government, rather than a party, institution—refused to
recognize its authority. Not until three years later, when Nanjing intervened in the dispute, did the Bureau agree to accept the new umbrella
union. By that time the General Labor Union's standing committee of
five labor organizers was made up entirely of Green Gang members.
Eventually the Bureau itself was forced to open its doors to the gang.
By 1936, three of the four departments at the Bureau were headed by
disciples of Du Yuesheng. Needless to say, the Labor Dispute Department
and its subordinate Mediation Office were among the agencies that fell
under Du's command.[55]

Du Yuesheng was not content merely to reap the economic rewards
that his control over labor made possible. He was also determined to
gain social respectability. In June 1931, all of Shanghai came to a standstill for several days to celebrate the founding of Du Yuesheng's ancestral
temple. In honor of the special occasion, Lu Jingshi and Zhu Xuefan
even arranged for the local post office to dispense a special postmark.[56]
The lavish festivities (complete with colorful parade, three days of op-
eratic performances, a worship ceremony presided over by the mayor of
Shanghai, and banquets for fifty thousand guests per meal) reflected Du
Yuesheng's desire to translate his substantial economic and political capital into a commensurate cultural and social standing.[57] To complete the
genteel image, Du began to dress in long mandarin robes and to write
his name with a studied calligraphic flair that belied his lack of formal
education.[58] An institutional expression of Du Yuesheng's acquired respectability was the formation in 1932 of the Constant Club, an association of some fifteen hundred of Du's more prestigious followers.[59]

By the mid-1930s, Du Yuesheng was a cornerstone of Shanghai high society. A typical day would see him entertaining anywhere from one hundred to two hundred guests, many of them top officials and wealthy businessmen, at his posh Frenchtown residence.[60] No less a personage than Sun Fo, president of the Legislative Yuan, turned to "Mister Du Yuesheng"—as he was respectfully addressed—for a happy resolution of his complicated love affairs.[61]

The meteoric ascent of Du Yuesheng was telling testimony to the efficacy of gang connections in promoting upward mobility in Republican Shanghai. Du's obsession with social acceptance underscored the distance the parvenu had traveled on his journey from orphaned fruit seller to power broker. The thousands of followers who flocked to Du's fold in the 1930s were motivated by a similar desire for promotion and prestige. Lacking the head start of a comfortable family background, these disadvantaged yet ambitious elements of Shanghai society were attracted to Du Yuesheng's gangster network as an alternative path to fame and fortune. As one ot Du's former followers recalled, most of his fellow clients were "people with a certain ability and potential who faced formidable obstacles in fulfilling their aspirations." Affiliation with Du Yuesheng was a calculated strategy for getting ahead in an otherwise inhospitable environment.[62]

Within the working class, such recruits—although evident in virtually every industry—were especially numerous among semiskilled laborers. Lacking the remuneration and job security enjoyed by factory artisans, yet more committed to urban life than the transient unskilled worker, the semiskilled laborer was easily persuaded of the advantages of an accommodation with labor racketeers. Under the combined sponsorship of gangsters and government, the middle portion of the Shanghai labor force gained a political importance it had not previously known. This political trend reinforced developments in the structure of production that had substantially increased the size of the semiskilled sector. By the Nanjing decade (1927–37), the "second industrial revolution" that had swept European and American industries around the time of World War I was in full swing in Shanghai. Less skilled employer-trained male operatives could be found in increasing numbers in both Chinese and foreign-owned factories.

The Japanese invasion of 1937 brought to an end the Nanjing decade in which the Guomindang had enjoyed its heyday. Taking control first of the Chinese-ruled areas of Shanghai and then, after Pearl Harbor, of the foreign-ruled areas as well, the Japanese imposed their own order on the workers of China's largest city. Not until the Japanese defeat in the summer of 1945 did the GMD have an opportunity to reassert leadership over the Shanghai labor movement. Many of the same individuals who had promoted the system of yellow unions after Chiang's April coup were reassigned to positions of influence in the postwar period. Most notable among the returnees was Lu Jingshi, the former post office worker whose discipleship under Green Gang master Du Yuesheng had won him a series of prominent posts in the Nationalist regime. After the Japanese occupation of Shanghai, Lu had followed the Nationalist government westward to its wartime capital in Chongqing. There he formed a close friendship with Dai Li, head of the GMD's secret police. In 1945 when Lu was ordered back to Shanghai to wrest control over the labor movement from Communist competitors, his connection with the secret police proved immensely helpful. Thanks to a generous supply of weapons from Dai Li, Lu Jingshi was able to arm a group of faithful followers among the work force.

Influential as Lu Jingshi was in the postwar labor scene, his power did not go unchallenged. And the opposition came not only from the underground Communists. Although Lu publicly named communism as his principal foe, he actually faced more insidious adversaries within his own Guomindang Party. Prominent labor leaders with whom Lu Jingshi had cooperated in the past now cultivated their own constituencies so as to diminish his control.[63]

As a result of the debilitating factionalism of the postwar period, many individuals who had served as bulwarks of government strength in the Nanjing decade now found themselves increasingly estranged from the Guomindang regime. Lu Jingshi's patron, Du Yuesheng, had returned to Shanghai after the war hoping to be named mayor of the city. Instead, perhaps to deflect attention from his own gang connections, Chiang Kaishek named a rival of Du Yuesheng to head the municipal government. When the Shanghai Legislature was established some months later, Du again had ambitions of assuming the leading post. Again he was disappointed. But the biggest wound to Du Yuesheng's pride came in the fall of 1948 when his son was arrested by Chiang Ching-kuo, son of Chiang Kaishek, for illegal dealings on the Shanghai stock exchange. Seeing a picture of his handcuffed son on the front page of *Central Daily* was unbearable to Du Yuesheng. For more than a month the distraught father refused either to venture outdoors or to entertain guests. It was probably this incident more than any other that made Du decide to leave for Hong Kong, rather than Taiwan, at the time of Shanghai's Communist takeover.[64]

A number of other Shanghai notables chose not to leave at all, but instead to throw in their lot with the new socialist regime. Gu Zhuxuan,

Shanghai rickshaw magnate and Green Gang chieftain, agreed to cooperate with his nephew, a Communist cadre responsible for liaison with
the city's gangsters. A second-floor office in one of Uncle Gu's dance
halls became the meeting place for the Communist–gangster rendezvous
in the early postwar period. Gu Zhuxuan was rewarded for his cooperation by being made special delegate to the first Shanghai People's Congress convened after liberation.[65] By far the most significant defection to
the Communist side by a Shanghai labor leader-cum-gangster was that
of Zhu Xuefan. Contacted by Communist agents as early as 1936, Zhu
developed an increasingly close relationship with the CCP during the
war years. In the postwar period, especially after Zhu was wounded in
an assassination attempt by rival GMD agents, his allegiance shifted
irrevocably to the Communist side.[66] With the founding of the People's
Republic in 1949, the former gangster and postal unionist became first
minister of post and telecommunications in the new socialist regime. In
the post-Mao era, Zhu Xuefan served as vice-chairman of the Chinese
People's Political Consultative Conference and head of the "Revolutionary Committee of the Guomindang" in Beijing.

Built upon the foundation of gangster support, the Nationalist state
was a highly personalistic and thus highly fragile regime. Gangster networks enabled the state to make contact with workers (especially the less
skilled workers who were most tightly controlled by gangster-foremen),
but these same networks could withdraw support whenever their gangster
leaders found a more promising ally. If the Nationalists had looked like
a good bet in 1927, the Communists seemed an even better bet two
decades later.

Shanghai Labor and the Communist State

Important as turncoat gangsters were in facilitating the Communist takeover of Shanghai, the heart of CCP support in the city remained with
skilled workers. From the earliest days of Communist mobilization efforts through the 1940s, factory artisans were the most enthusiastic and
committed labor recruits to the radical cause. Thus for the Communists,
in contrast to their Nationalist predecessors, it was the guild more than
the gang that served as the prototype for state-sponsored labor
organization.

The importance of artisan support had been dramatically demonstrated
at the conclusion of World War II. The Japanese surrender precipitated,
in Shanghai as elsewhere across occupied China, a scramble between
Communists and Nationalists for control of abandoned territory. Initially

the Communists harbored the hope that with proletarian support they might claim the country's largest industrial city. A year before the war's end, in anticipation of the internecine struggle that lay ahead, CCP Central had ordered the establishment of a Shanghai workers' underground army (*gongren dixiajun*). Charged with the formidable task of recruitment for this army, labor cadres in Shanghai turned first to gangster elements. Several petty hoodlums did indeed cooperate in supplying the original manpower for the workers' army. It soon became apparent, however, that sustaining the allegiance of gangster mercenaries required substantial payoffs. Strapped for funds, the party returned to a more reliable source of recruits: South China metalworkers.[67] On August 23, 1945, more than seven thousand of these committed fighters—many of whom were party members—assembled at the Xinyi Machine Works in preparation for an armed uprising aimed at seizing weapons from nearby police stations and then marching to the city center to assist the New Fourth Army in the liberation of Shanghai. That same afternoon, however, the rebellion was canceled on orders from Party Central. After having initially approved the uprising three days earlier, Party Central had received a cable from the USSR calling for peaceful coexistence with the GMD in keeping with a new treaty of friendship between the Soviet Union and the Republic of China. The workers' army was dissolved a few days later and members whose identities had been revealed were transferred north to join the New Fourth Army.[68]

Ill-fated as the workers' army was, its development illustrated the degree to which party organizers in Shanghai were compelled in times of duress to fall back upon their staunchest ally among the Shanghai working class. Although gangster elements could be instrumental in launching militant engagements, ultimately it was the skilled workers who proved willing to sacrifice for higher political goals. Happily for the party, the size of this sector of the working class grew substantially in the postwar period. Thousands of skilled workers—copper fitters, ironsmiths, and mechanics in particular—returned to Shanghai from the interior after the Japanese surrender.[69] In addition, more than thirty thousand Chinese workers—largely educated, skilled workers from the south—were repatriated from Japan.[70]

The division of labor among members of the CCP's Shanghai Labor Committee during the civil war period reflected this heightened interest in factory artisans. Zhang Qi, secretary of the Labor Committee and a skilled silk weaver by training, was put in charge of railroads, shipping, and cotton (with special attention to mechanics). A worker at the Shanghai Power Company handled water and electricity plants as well as the machine industry. A staff worker at the French Tramway Company was in charge of that company, the silk-weaving industry, and some of the bus companies. A printer was assigned to the publishing industry—with responsibility for producing propaganda for the workers' movement as well as organizing among fellow printers. He also handled some hospitals, movie theaters, and other service enterprises.[71]

Skilled craftsmen who had long been active in the CCP labor movement became designers of the Communist industrial system after 1949. Chen Yun, widely acknowledged as China's "economic czar" in the decade following liberation,[72] had joined the CCP in the mid-1920s when he was still a worker at the Shanghai Commercial Press. The radical union at the press, of which Chen was an active member, was an outgrowth of a printers' guild that had predated the Communist movement by years.[73] It was hardly surprising, then, that the system created by people like Chen Yun put a premium on welfare and security, issues central to the guild milieu in which they had originated.

Ironically, the guild heritage was most visible in the sector of the industrial economy that most exemplified the "new" socialist system: state-owned enterprises. It was these organizations that guaranteed lifetime employment, high wages, and substantial welfare measures to their employees. As Andrew Walder points out,

> The 27 million permanent workers in state sector industrial enterprises are the only segment of the industrial labor force to participate fully in the welfare state. . . . In 1981 their average annual wage . . . was almost 40 percent higher than that of the average in urban collective industry and well over twice the average of the other groups in the labor force. Just as important, however, are the many fringe benefits, wage supplements, government subsidies, on-site services and welfare and insurance provisions that the state provides. . . . These workers enjoy virtual lifetime tenure. . . . Large and medium-sized enterprises are usually able to provide them with subsidized meals, housing, medical care, and many other services and benefits that are unavailable elsewhere.[74]

Thanks to the perquisites it brought, a job in a state factory came to be known as an "iron rice bowl," in contrast to the less durable and less desirable "earthen rice bowl" of the collective sector.[75]

The exclusivity and paternalism of the socialist enterprise were reminiscent of the artisan guild. One needed the introduction of friends or relatives to join these selective organizations, which offered lifetime benefits to their privileged members. Like its guild forerunner, the socialist factory also stipulated certain behavioral norms for its membership.[76] But whereas the traditional guild had relied on the authority of its patron deity to enforce these values, the new state enterprise claimed legitimacy from the Communist Party.

In each province and city, the special prerogatives of workers at state factories were overseen by the local federation of labor unions, an arm of the state charged with responsibility for worker welfare.[77] In the case of Shanghai, the city's federation of unions has been dominated by former activists in the Communist labor movement, most of whom rose from the ranks of South China artisans.

If the new Communist order was a dream come true for skilled craftsmen, the same was not the case for excluded sectors of the labor force. Resentment against the benefits accruing to veteran workers at state enterprises was an important precipitant of the waves of labor unrest that have rolled across Chinese cities every decade since liberation.

In 1956–57, under the inspiration of the Hundred Flowers Campaign, strikes erupted at hundreds of factories (see chapter 7). As François Gipouloux has found, these labor protests were instigated for the most part by "marginal" workers: temporary and contract laborers, workers in the service sector, apprentices, and others who failed to share in the privileges bestowed upon veteran employees at state enterprises.[78] Despite the vociferous protests of that period, the gap between permanent state workers and temporary or contract laborers grew even greater in the years ahead.[79]

In 1966–67, during the Great Proletarian Cultural Revolution, serious struggles again broke out in factories across the country (see chapter 8). Divisions within the central leadership fanned the flames of local antagonism. The strife was most severe at older factories where generational animosities were especially pronounced. When Chairman Mao called upon the proletariat to undertake revolution, many of Shanghai's veteran workers and cadres joined the "conservative" Scarlet Guards to agitate for improvements in wages and working conditions. Younger workers, including a substantial number of contract and temporary laborers excluded from the privileged state system, tended to enlist in the rival Revolutionary Rebels. Charging the Scarlet Guards with "economism" and "guild mentality," the Revolutionary Rebels advocated a direct assault upon the Party Committee and its subordinate Federation of Trade Unions.[80] As Lynn White has explained the support of disprivileged workers for the radical cause,

Unemployed and contract workers may not, at first, have been passionately excited about the errors of historians, the ideologies of novelists, or the philosophies of musicians—even though these issues concerned editorialists from the radical group that launched the Cultural Revolution in late 1965 and early 1966. Unemployed workers seem to have had some idea what political leaders they disliked, however. When men like Mayor Ts'ao Ti-ch'iu [of Shanghai], who had espoused the "worker-peasant system," were criticized for cultural policies, some enthusiasm was stirred within the lower proletariat. The famous attack on "economism" is comprehensible only in terms of the fact that extra bonuses were commonly offered only to regular workers, not to temporary workers.[81]

Subjected to repeated lectures by their elders about the revolutionary exploits of bygone days, younger workers laboring under less favorable conditions longed for an opportunity to even the score. The Cultural Revolution offered them the chance. Interestingly enough, however, the methods that young Revolutionary Rebels employed in their own struggles bore an uncanny resemblance to the protest repertoires of the previous generation.[82] It was probably no coincidence that the Shanghai No. 17 Cotton Mill, where Revolutionary Rebel commander Wang Hongwen worked, had in the mid-1920s been the scene of labor violence strikingly similar in form to that of Cultural Revolution struggle sessions. In a 1925 incident at the factory, workers had tricked a hated foreman into attending a mass meeting at which he was publicly denounced. The hapless foreman was forced to kneel in front of the crowd with hands tied behind his back, dunce cap placed on his head, and a placard reading "Down with this traitor and running dog" hung across his chest. Photographs of the occasion were posted at the factory gate to serve as warning lest the unseated overseer should ever try to resume his post.[83]

When radical workers adopted similar tactics during the Cultural Revolution, their targets were the older generation and the institutions (e.g., the Federation of Trade Unions) that symbolized that generation's privileged position in the new socialist order. In Shanghai, the year 1967 saw a string of attacks by Wang Hongwen's Revolutionary Rebels against the former party underground labor organizers who then controlled the Shanghai Federation of Trade Unions. Zhang Qi, the former silk weaver from Meiya who had served as secretary of the Shanghai party underground on the eve of liberation and was now director of the Shanghai federation, was subjected to repeated humiliation in public struggle sessions. His hands were forced behind his back in the painful "jet plane" position, a dunce cap adorned his head, and a placard across his chest announced him as a "running dog" who had committed "revisionist crimes." In December, Zhang was imprisoned in the basement of the building of the federation that he had helped to create.[84] Although Zhang Qi survived the Cultural Revolution in remarkably good health, many of his colleagues were less fortunate. A recent listing of fatalities in radical assaults on the Shanghai Federation of Trade Unions illustrates the vulnerable position of former underground party organizers—most of whom were skilled craftsmen from South China.[85]

While the communitarian rhetoric of the Cultural Revolution may have seemed consonant with long-standing artisan values, the material sacrifice demanded by the movement was anything but popular with skilled workers whose privileged status had always been reflected in higher pay. In 1974–75, a wave of strikes and slowdowns swept across China's factories to demand bonuses and wage hikes, anathema as these were to the Maoist orthodoxy of the day. The most serious work stoppage, a series of strikes in the city of Hangzhou, was resolved only when Deng Xiaoping went in person to assure the restive workers of an impending wage reform.[86]

Repeated labor protests bespoke fundamental dissatisfaction with the existing industrial pattern, but the state found it extremely difficult to reform a system around which so many embedded interests had coalesced. In many respects, the early post-Mao reforms reflected a return to the status quo ante. Walder characterized Deng Xiaoping's industrial policy as a "shift from asceticism to paternalism" in which the "state enterprise continues to play a central role in the delivery of free or highly subsidized goods and services."[87]

The arrangements reintroduced by rehabilitated economic czar Chen Yun offered certain advantages to central planners. Although Chen Yun, in contrast to Mao Zedong, envisioned an important role for the market in China's socialist economy, it was nevertheless a subsidiary role. As Nicholas Lardy and Kenneth Lieberthal point out, for Chen the market was "solely a supplement to centralized planning." Bureaucratic allocation, especially of skilled labor, remained the cornerstone of his program.[88] Under such an arrangement, the basic components of which were fashioned in the first decade of the People's Republic, reforms of a more market-oriented variety were extremely difficult to implement. The demand of the central government for a steady source of revenue, based on reliable output from veteran workers at its state-owned enterprises, impeded industrial change in a more liberal direction. Moreover, the workers privileged by such a system were an important source of its perpetuation. Permanent workers at state-owned enterprises staunchly defended basic elements of the Maoist industrial order.

Conclusion

China's Nationalist and Communist states promoted an intrusive pattern of government intervention in the labor arena. Both of these "modern" states acceded to power with substantial working-class support. Both endeavored to rechannel labor activism into government-controlled institutions: the "yellow unions" under the GMD, the Federation of Trade Unions under the PRC. Both evidenced ambivalence toward the labor strikes that persisted after their consolidation of state power.[89] And both sought, successfully, to co-opt labor leaders as state officials. (The meteoric rise of Wang Hongwen and his Revolutionary Rebels after the January power seizure of 1967 was more than a little reminiscent of the prominence that Green Gang labor organizers enjoyed in the aftermath of the coup of April 1927.)

To be sure, the gang base of the Nationalists and the guild base of the Communists imply very different social constituencies. The competing ideologies of these rival parties had elicited divergent popular responses. As we have seen, it was not coincidental that skilled artisans were attracted to the radicalism of the Communist message, whereas semiskilled workers were drawn to the moderation of the GMD. The states established by both political parties were, moreover, substantially constrained by the nature of their working-class support, dissimilar as it was.

The common restraints faced by both Chinese states, despite their contrasting ideologies, points to a problem shared by many other fledgling regimes, regardless of their espoused political values. Trying to impose their rule on highly fragmented societies, new states necessarily enter into pacts with receptive social elements. Yet such accommodations may imprison the state in preferential relationships that serve ultimately to inhibit a broader base of support. As a consequence of confining partnerships with particular class fractions, regimes are likely to prove resistant to certain kinds of economic and political reform.

In making an argument for societal constraints, I depart from a considerable body of scholarship that emphasizes the alleged immunity of the modern state from social forces. In the field of Chinese studies—thanks to China's ancient bureaucratic tradition as well as its contemporary Communist experience—the emphasis on state autonomy has been especially pronounced. This emphasis is seen even in studies of the Nationalist interregnum. Lloyd Eastman, a leading authority on the Nationalist regime, has proposed an "autonomy thesis" to argue that the GMD state "was never accountable to political groups or institutions outside the regime."[90] In presenting his thesis (intended as a challenge to earlier interpretations of the Nationalists as the hireling of China's upper classes),[91] Eastman mirrors a larger debate among general theorists about the nature of the state. Whereas a Marxist scholarly tradition had seen the modern state as the "executive committee of the bourgeoisie," a Weberian tradition pictures the state as a "rational" entity operating according to rules of its own making.[92]

Faced with these alternative views, the challenge—as Charles Bright and Susan Harding have summarized it—is to arrive at "a conception of the state that accords it neither too much, nor too little, autonomy from other social forces."[93] But what are the relevant "social forces" with which we should be concerned? In an "advanced capitalist society" perhaps a case can be made that the domestic capitalist class is indeed the critical "social force" with which the regime must interact in the state-making process. Yet can the same be said for a society like Republican China, where industry was still in its infancy? And what of Communist China, where the bourgeoisie was summarily stripped of its property base?

Like many Third Word countries, modern China has been a fragmented society over which no single class could exercise hegemony. If we are to turn to the Marxist tradition for inspiration, the appropriate *locus classicus* would not be *Das Kapital*, where advanced capitalism is analyzed, but *The Eighteenth Brumaire*—where Louis Napoleon's rise to power is interpreted against the background of a divided France in the throes of the transition from an agrarian to an industrial economy. Marx's characterization of Napoleon applies with equal force to a Chiang Kaishek, Mao Zedong, or Deng Xiaoping: "The contradictory task of the man explains the contradictions of his government, the confused groping about which seeks now to win, now to humiliate first one class and then another."[94]

The classes with which Chinese leaders were forced to deal included not only the old and new elites of landlords and capitalists, but a recently politicized working class (and its leaders) as well. Contrary to the prevalent image of Chinese workers as mere putty in the hands of outside party organizers, to be molded as the latter saw fit, the historical record reveals a remarkable level of labor activism. While GMD-sponsored yellow unions were to some extent able to define labor relations in ways amenable to state officials, workers and their spokesmen were also significant participants in the definitional enterprise. And in part precisely because of the politicization that took place during the years of GMD rule, China's socialist leaders have been compelled to reach their own accommodation with a working class accustomed to militancy. If the Nationalists exercised only "dispersed domination" when compared with the "integrated domination" of the Communists, in both cases labor has demonstrated an impressive capacity for resistance.

Although the PRC is often characterized as a "totalitarian" regime in which social forces play next to no role in shaping the political agenda, actually the reality or fear of worker protest has exerted a major influence on political events over the past half century. The waves of repression that have rolled across the Chinese polity each decade since 1949 have all followed on the heels of popular protests in which labor strife was a major concern.[95] Admittedly, the repressive response of the state demonstrates the severe restrictions on popular participation. But it also suggests the extent to which state policies are themselves shaped in reaction to this very participation. Although the outcome is certainly a far cry from the workers' paradise envisioned by Marx and Engels, it nevertheless bears witness to a more influential political role for workers than a recent generation of scholarship on labor history might lead us to expect.

Notes

This chapter appeared originally in Joel S. Migdal, Atul Kohli, and Vivienne Shue, eds., *State Power and Social Forces: Domination and Transformation in the Third World* (Cambridge: Cambridge University Press, 1994).

    1. For a sampling of this important literature, see Ira Katznelson and Aristide R. Zolberg, eds., *Working-Class Formation* (Princeton: Princeton University Press, 1986); Richard Jules Oestreicher, *Solidarity and Fragmentation* (Urbana: University of Illinois Press, 1986); Sean Wilentz, *Chants Democratic: New York City and the Rise of the American Working Class* (New York: Oxford University Press, 1984); Victoria Bonnell, *Roots of Rebellion: Workers' Politics and Organizations in St. Petersburg and Moscow, 1900–1914* (Berkeley: University of California Press, 1983); Charles F. Sabel, *Work and Politics: The Division of Labor in Industry* (New York: Cambridge University Press, 1982); Ronald Aminzade, *Class, Politics and Early Industrial Capitalism* (Albany: State University of New York Press, 1981); Dick Geary, *European Labour Protest, 1848–1939* (London: Croom Helm, 1981); Diane Koenker, *Moscow Workers and the 1917 Revolution* (Princeton: Princeton University Press, 1981); William P. Sewell, *Work and Revolution in France* (New York: Cambridge University Press, 1980); Michael P. Hanagan, *The Logic of Solidarity* (Urbana:University of Illinois Press, 1980); I. Prothero, *Artisans and Politics in Early Nineteenth-Century London* (Folkestone, UK: Dawson, 1979); Barrington Moore, Jr., *The Social Bases of Obedience and Revolt* (Armonk, NY: M.E. Sharpe, 1978); Herbert G. Gutman, *Work, Culture, and Society* (New York: Knopf, 1977); Bernard H.

Moss, *The Origins of the French Labor Movement* (Berkeley: University of California Press, 1976); Joan W. Scott, *The Glassworkers of Carmaux: French Craftsmen and Political Activism in a Nineteenth Century City* (Cambridge: Harvard University Press, 1974); Stanley Aronowitz, *False Promises* (New York: McGraw-Hill, 1973).

2. Chen Duxiu, "Shanghai shehui" (Shanghai society), *Xin qingnian* (New youth), vol. 8, nos. 1–4 (1980): 67–71 (emphasis added).

3. "Shanghai jiqi gonghui kai faqihui jilüe" (Annals of the inaugural meeting of the Shanghai Mechanics' Union), *Zhongguo gongren yundongshi cankao ziliao* (Reference materials on the history of the Chinese labor movement), vol. 1 (Beijing, 1980): 43–47.

4. *Bao Huiseng huiyilu* (The memoirs of Bao Huiseng) (Beijing, 1983), p. 67. Fortunately for the development of the Communist labor movement, it turned out that a few of their young cadres did have enough patience to work with gangsters. On the efforts of early CCP labor organizers to infiltrate the gangs, see Zhu Xuefan, "Shanghai gongren yundong yu banghui ersanshi" (Two or three things about the Shanghai labor movement and the gangs), in *Jiu Shanghai de banghui* (The gangs of old Shanghai) (Shanghai: Shanghai renmin chubanshe, 1986), pp. 1–20.

5. Jiang Peinan and Chen Weimin, "Shanghai zhaopai gonghui de xingwang" (The rise and fall of Shanghai's signboard unions), *Jindaishi yanjiu* (Studies in modern history), no. 6 (1986): 46–47.

6. *Zhandou de wushi nian* (Fifty years of battle) (Shanghai, 1960) is the most detailed of these studies.

7. *Shanghai juanyan gongye gaikuang* (Conditions in the Shanghai rolled tobacco industry) (Shanghai, 1950), pp. 35–42.

8. *Shi bao*, 6/13/1906, 2/5/1915, 3/10/1916, 8/5/1918, 8/6/1918, 8/9/1918, 10/8/1919; *Minguo ribao*, 7/21/1917, 7/24/1917, 7/25/1917, 8/2/1917, 8/10/1917, 5/2/1918, 8/4/1918, 11/10/1919, 11/4/1919, 6/23/1920, 3/7/1921, 3/18/1921, 6/25/1921, 6/25/1921, 6/28/1921, 6/29/1921.

9. Rose Glickman, *Russian Factory Women* (Berkeley: University of California Press, 1984), p. 162; Louise A. Tilly, "Paths of Proletarianization," in Eleanor Leacock and Helen I. Safa, eds., *Women's Work: Development and Division of Labor by Gender* (South Hadley, MA: Bergin and Garvey, 1986), p. 37; Patricia A. Cooper, *Once a Cigar Maker: Men, Women, and Work Culture in American Cigar Factories, 1900–1919* (Urbana: University of Illinois Press, 1987).

10. *Zhandou de wushi nian*, pp. 19–31.

11. Ibid., pp. 32–38.

12. Luo Chuanhua, *Jinri Zhongguo laogong wenti* (Labor issues in today's China) (Shanghai, 1933), pp. 97–102.

13. See Number Two History Archives, Nanjing, no. 1:2–746, for confidential memos from the director of the GMD Labor Bureau to the minister of finance, allocating generous secret subsidies for the BAT union.

14. *North China Daily News*, 1/18/1928.

15. BAT Pudong Archives: August 1933 report of I.G. Riddick.

16. Yao Haigen, October 28, 1958; and Hong Benkuan, October 24, 1958; interview transcripts in the Labor Movement Archives of the Institute of History, Shanghai Academy of Social Sciences (SASS).

17. Archives of the Bureau of Investigation, Taipei, no. 556.282/810. At the

end of 1946, the 25 CCP members at BAT included 12 metalworkers, 5 leaf department workers, 4 rolling department workers, 1 office worker, 1 printer, and 2 schoolteachers. None of these were women.

18. Huang Zhihao, September 2, 1958, interview transcript in the Labor Movement Archives of the Institute of History, SASS.

19. Elizabeth J. Perry, *Shanghai on Strike: The Politics of Chinese Labor* (Stanford: Stanford University Press, 1993), chs. 8 and 9.

20. Eric Hobsbawm, *Labouring Men* (Garden City, NY: Doubleday, 1964; Basic Books, 1964), p. 424.

21. Hanagan, *The Logic of Solidarity*, pp. 10–11.

22. Quoted in David M. Mandel, *The Petrograd Workers and the Fall of the Old Regime* (London: Macmillan, 1983), p. 13.

23. Aminzade, *Class, Politics and Early Industrial Capitalism*, p. 76.

24. On this point, see Hanagan, *The Logic of Solidarity*, p. 210. See also Bonnell, *Roots of Rebellion*, p. 444.

25. A Moscow survey of 1908 showed that skilled workers, most notably metalworkers, had a literacy rate of about 90 percent and were considerably more urbanized (measured as the percentage born in the city) than textile workers. Koenker, *Moscow Workers and the 1917 Revolution*, p. 29. Such workers—skilled, well paid, literate, urbanized—led the strike waves of the early twentieth century. Koenker, pp. 76–78.

26. Natalie Zemon Davis, "A Trade Union in Sixteenth-Century France," *Economic History Review*, no. 19 (1966): 48–69; Natalie Zemon Davis, *Society and Culture in Early Modern France* (Stanford: Stanford University Press, 1975), pp. 4–10.

27. Robert J. Bezucha, *The Lyon Uprising of 1834* (Cambridge: Harvard University Press, 1974).

28. Eric J. Hobsbawm and Joan W. Scott, "Political Shoemakers," in Eric Hobsbawm, ed., *Workers: Worlds of Labor* (New York: Pantheon, 1984), pp. 103–130.

29. David M. Bachman, *Chen Yun and the Chinese Political System* (Berkeley: Institute of East Asian Studies, University of California, 1985), pp. 72–73.

30. John Cumbler, "Migration, Class Formation, and Class Consciousness: The American Experience," in Michael Hanagan and Charles Stephenson, eds., *Confrontation, Class Consciousness, and the Labor Process* (Westport, CT: Greenwood, 1986), p. 42.

31. Aronowitz, *False Promises*, ch. 3.

32. Jonathan Kwitny, *Vicious Circles: The Mafia in the Marketplace* (New York: Norton, 1979), p. 143.

33. By the early 1950s, suspicion of Communist sympathies was grounds for expulsion. See ibid., p. 144.

34. James Clay, *Hoffa! Ten Angles Swearing* (Beaverdam, VA: Beaverdam Books, 1965), p. 163.

35. Anton Blok, *The Mafia of a Sicilian Village* (New York: Harper and Row, 1974), pp. 6–7, 177.

36. Xue Gengshen, "Jindai Shanghai de liumang" (The gangsters of modern Shanghai), *Wenshi ziliao xuanji*, no. 3 (1980): 162–163; Cheng Xiwen, "Wo dang Huang Jinrong guanjia de jianwen" (What I saw and heard as Huang Jinrong's butler), in *Jiu Shanghai de banghui,* pp. 144–148.

37. *Shanghai Municipal Police Files*, microfilm reel no. 56, D-9319; *Da*

liumang Du Yuesheng (Big gangster Du Yuesheng) (Shanghai, 1965), pp. 1–7; Huang Guodong, "Dumen huajiu" (Old tales of the Du residence), in *Jiu Shanghai de banghui*, p. 134.

38. Zhu Jianliang and Xu Weizhi, "Zhang Xiaolin de yisheng" (The life of Zhang Xiaolin), in *Jiu Shanghai de banghui*, pp. 343–344.

39. Xiang Bo, "Huang Jinrong shilüe" (An account of Huang Jinrong), in *Jiu Shanghai de banghui*, p. 134.

40. "Siyier shibian de qianqian houhou" (Before and after the April 12 incident), in *Shanghai gongren yundong lishi ziliao* (Historical materials on the Shanghai labor movement), vol. 4 (Shanghai: Laodong chubanshe, 1953), pp. 12–35; Wang Jianchu and Sun Maosheng, *Zhongguo gongren yundongshi* (A history of the Chinese labor movement) (Shenyang, 1987), p. 138.

41. On corporatism, see, for example, Phillipe C. Schmitter, *Corporatism and Public Policy in Authoritarian Portugal* (London and Beverly Hills: Sage, 1975); and Alfred Stepan, *The State and Society: Peru in Comparative Perspective* (Princeton: Princeton University Press, 1978). The characterization of the Nationalists as a corporatist regime has been made in Joseph Fewsmith, *Party, State and Local Elites in Republican China: Merchant Organizations and Politics in Shanghai, 1890–1930* (Honolulu: University of Hawaii Press, 1985).

42. Pan Gongzhan, "Shanghai tebieshi shehuiju zhi zuzhi ji gongzuo" (The organization and work of the Shanghai Bureau of Social Affairs), *Qingnian jinbu* (Youth progress), no. 133 (1930): 34–41.

43. Zhu Xuefan, "Shanghai gongren," pp. 6–9.

44. George F. Nellist, ed., *Men of Shanghai and North China* (Shanghai: Oriental Press, 1933), p. 110.

45. Ilona Ralf Sues, *Shark's Fins and Millet* (Boston: Little, Brown, 1944), p. 78.

46. This was Du's mode of operation during the French Tramway strikes of 1928 and 1930, the Nandao Tramway strike of 1932, the Nanyang Brothers Tobacco Company strike of 1933, the Shanghai Power Company strike of 1933, and the Shanghai Electric Construction Company strike of 1937. See *Shanghai Municipal Police Files*, reels no. 16–17, D-5310. The British police observed that "the old French opium gang seems to be supplementing its income from smuggling by promoting racketeering in Chinese industrial enterprises." See reel no. 14, D-4611. Although the financial rewards for Du's services were substantial, the British police offered another, equally important, explanation of the gangster's appetite for labor mediation: "His desire to settle labour disputes aims at winning the confidence of the public and especially the government authorities." See *Shanghai Municipal Police Files*, reel no. 56, D-9319.

47. Zhu Xuefan, "Shanghai gongren," pp. 6–7.

48. Zhang Jungu, *Du Yuesheng zhuan* (Biography of Du Yuesheng) (Taipei, 1968), vol. 2, p. 155.

49. Sues, *Shark's Fins*, p. 75.

50. Zhu Xuefan, "Shanghai gongren," p. 7.

51. *Shanghai chanye yu Shanghai zhigong* (Shanghai industries and Shanghai workers) (Shanghai, 1939), p. 359; Xue Gengshen, "Wo yu jiu Shanghai fazujie" (The old French Concession of Shanghai and I), *Wenshi ziliao xuanji* (June 1976): 157–158.

52. "Kangri zhanzheng yiqian Shanghai youzheng zhigong de douzheng qingkuang" (Struggle conditions among Shanghai postal workers before the

Sino-Japanese war), *Shanghai gongren yundong lishi ziliao* (Shanghai, 1954), pp. 1–30; Shen Tiansheng, "Huiyi 1927–1932 nian Shanghai youju gonghui qingkuang" (Remembering the situation in Shanghai's postal workers' union, 1927–1932), *Shanghai gongyunshi yanjiu ziliao* (1981), p. 29.

53. Joel S. Migdal, *Strong Societies and Weak States* (Princeton: Princeton University Press, 1988), p. 141.

54. Number Two History Archives, no. 720–733, no. 722:4–233, no. 722: 4–502, no. 722:4–504.

55. *Da liumang Du Yuesheng*, pp. 50–51; Zhu Xuefan, "Shanghai gongren," p. 8.

56. Zhu Xuefan, "Shanghai gongren," p. 5

57. Fan Shaozeng, "Guanyu Du Yuesheng" (Concerning Du Yuesheng), in *Jiu Shanghai de banghui*, pp. 221–229.

58. Guo Lanxin, "Du Yuesheng yu Hengshe" (Du Yuesheng and the Constant Club), in *Jiu Shanghai de banghui*, p. 304; Fan Shaozeng, "Guanyu Du Yuesheng," p. 206.

59. Guo Lanxin, "Du Yuesheng," pp. 300–320; Zhu Xuefan, "Shanghai gongren," p. 6; "Hengshe sheyuanlu" (Record of the Constant Club membership), in *Jiu Shanghai de banghui*, pp. 369–382; *Hengshe qiuji lianhuan dahui tekan* (Special issue on the spring get-together of the Constant Club) (Shanghai, 1934).

60. Huang Guodong, "Dumen huijiu," p. 253.

61. *Shanghai Municipal Police Files*, reel no. 56, D-9319.

62. Guo Lanxin, "Du Yuesheng," pp. 306–307.

63. Mao Qihua, "Luetan jiefang zhanzheng shiqi Shanghai gongren yundong de yixie qingkuang" (A summary discussion of conditions in the Shanghai labor movement during the war of liberation), *Shanghai gongyunshi yanjiu ziliao*, no. 2 (1982): 1.

64. Fan Shaozeng, "Guanyu Du Yuesheng," pp. 239–242. It may also be that Du was beginning to lean toward the Communists. According to his accountant, Du had developed a number of contacts among future leaders of both the Shanghai and the central PRC government. See Huang Guodong, "Dumen huajiu," pp. 265–267.

65. Gu Shuping, "Wo liyong Gu Zhuxuan de yanhu jinxing geming huodong" (I used the cover of Gu Zhuxuan to carry out revolutionary activities), in *Jiu Shanghai de banghui*, pp. 363–366.

66. Lu Xiangxian, *Zhongguo laodong xiehui jianshi* (Brief history of the China Labor Association) (Shanghai, 1987).

67. Of the 69 members of the workers' army on whom we have data, only 8 were from North China and the remaining 61 were from southern locations. "Shanghai gongrendui duiyuan mingdan" (Name list of members of the Shanghai workers' brigade), *Shanghai gongyun shiliao* (Historical materials on the Shanghai labor movement), nos. 2–3 (1988): 52–54.

68. "Zhongshu Shanghai gongren dixiajun" (Overview of the Shanghai workers' underground army), *Shanghai gongyun shiliao*, nos. 2–3 (1988): 1–7; Zhang Chengzong, "Zuzhi dixiajun, zhunbei wuzhuang qiyi" (Organizing the underground army, preparing for the military uprising), in ibid., pp. 13–18. *Jiefang ribao*, August 23, 1945, and *Xinhua ribao*, August 28, 1945, reported the news under headlines that read "50,000 Shanghai Workers Rebel."

69. See Shanghai Municipal Archives, no. 12–1–52, for a listing of these returnees.

70. Including a number of captives from the Eighth Route Army, most of these individuals had been working in Hokkaido for several years before being sent home. Shanghai Municipal Archives, no. 11–1, 11–9.

71. Mao Qihua, "Luetan jiefang," p. 1.

72. Nicholas R. Lardy and Kenneth Lieberthal, eds., *Chen Yun's Strategy for China's Development* (Armonk, NY: M.E. Sharpe, 1983); David M. Bachman, *Chen Yun and the Chinese Political System* (Berkeley: Institute of East Asian Studies, University of California, 1985).

73. *Shangwu yinshuguan gonghuishi* (A history of unions at the Commercial Press) (Shanghai, n.d.), pp. 1–2.

74. Andrew G. Walder, *Communist Neo-Traditionalism* (Berkeley: University of California Press, 1986), pp. 40–42.

75. Martin King Whyte and William L. Parish, *Urban Life in Contemporary China* (Chicago: University of Chicago Press, 1984), p. 33.

76. Walder, *Communist Neo-Traditionalism*, ch. 4.

77. In the early 1950s, the chair of Shanghai's municipal Trade Union Council was also the deputy secretary of the city's Communist Party Committee. See Paul F. Harper, "Trade Union Cultivation of Workers for Leadership," in John Wilson Lewis, ed., *The City in Communist China* (Stanford: Stanford University Press, 1971), p. 125.

78. François Gipouloux, *Les cent fleurs à l'usine* (Paris: Editions de l'Ecole des hautes études en sciences sociales, 1986), pp. 198–205; see also Lynn White III, "Workers' Politics in Shanghai," *Journal of Asian Studies*, vol. 36, no. 1 (1976): 105–107.

79. White, "Workers' Politics," pp. 107–115.

80. Hong Yung Lee, *The Politics of the Chinese Cultural Revolution* (Berkeley: University of California Press, 1978), p. 137; Lynn T. White III, "Shanghai's Polity in Cultural Revolution," in Lewis, ed., *The City in Communist China*, pp. 325–370; Parris Chang, "Shanghai and Chinese Politics: Before and After the Cultural Revolution," in Christopher Howe, ed., *Shanghai: Revolution and Development in an Asian Metropolis* (Cambridge: Cambridge University Press, 1981), pp. 66–90.

81. White, "Workers' Politics," pp. 114–115.

82. On the importance of learned protest repertoires, see Charles Tilly, *The Contentious French* (Cambridge, MA: Belknap Press, 1986). This theme is creatively developed for Shanghai students in Jeffrey Wasserstrom, *Student Protest in Twentieth-Century China: The View from Shanghai* (Stanford: Stanford University Press, 1991).

83. Zhang Ben et al., "Shanghai guomian shiqichang gongren douzhengshi" (The history of labor struggles at Shanghai's no. 17 cotton mill), *Shanghai gongren yundong lishi ziliao* (Shanghai, 1953), pp. 61–70.

84. Fan Wenxian, "Shanghaishi zonggonghui beiza jishi" (Annals of the assault on the Shanghai Federation of Labor), *Shanghai gongyun shiliao*, no. 5 (1986): 1–6.

85. "Zhengzheng tiegu chuiqing shi" (In appreciation of martyrdom), in ibid., pp. 13–22.

86. Lowell Dittmer, *China's Continuous Revolution* (Berkeley: University of California Press, 1987), pp. 165–167.

87. Walder, *Communist Neo-Traditionalism*, p. 227.

88. Lardy and Lieberthal, *Chen Yun's Strategy*, p. 227.

89. Mao Zedong's speech, "On the Correct Handling of Contradictions Among the People" in February 1957, called for better education and improved leadership methods as an antidote to strikes that had broken out the previous year. In the spring of 1957, Liu Shaoqi proposed more boldly that union and party officials should themselves participate in strikes to regain the confidence of the workers. See Joint Publications Research Service, 1957, no. 41889, p. 58.

90. Lloyd Eastman, "New Insights into the Nature of the Nationalist Regime," *Republican China*, vol. 9, no. 2 (1984): 11. See also Eastman, *The Abortive Revolution* (Cambridge: Harvard University Press, 1974).

91. The interpretation of the GMD as representative of the Chinese bourgeoisie or landlord classes can be found in Robert W. Barnett, *Economic Shanghai: Hostage to Politics* (New York: Institute of Pacific Relations, 1941), p. 12; Harold Isaacs, *The Tragedy of the Chinese Revolution* (Stanford: Stanford University Press, 1951), p. 182; Barrington Moore, Jr., *The Social Origins of Dictatorship and Democracy* (Boston: Beacon Press, 1961), p. 196; and Mao Zedong, *Selected Works* (Beijing: Foreign Languages Press, 1967), vol. 1, p. 55.

92. More recently, however, these "alliance" and "autonomy" perspectives have been joined by a third view that allows for the "relative autonomy" of the state. Nicos Poulantzas, *State, Power, Socialism* (London: NLB, 1978), initiated a neo-Marxist debate about "relative autonomy" by arguing that contradictions within the ruling class meant that the state could not merely reflect elite interests. Subsequently, Theda Skocpol and Kenneth Finegold have elucidated the "specific historical conditions" under which some capitalist states develop "relative autonomy" vis-à-vis industry. See their "State, Party, and Industry," in Charles Bright and Susan Harding, eds., *Statemaking and Social Movements* (Ann Arbor: University of Michigan Press, 1982), p. 184.

93. Bright and Harding, *Statemaking*, p. 4. For useful efforts to develop typologies of strong, weak, and middling states, see especially Peter J. Katzenstein, "Domestic Structures and Strategies of Foreign Economic Policy," *International Organization*, vol. 31 (1977); and Stephen D. Krazner, *Defending the National Interest* (Princeton: Princeton University Press, 1978).

94. Karl Marx, "The Eighteenth Brumaire of Louis Bonaparte," in *Selected Works* (New York: International Publishers, 1977), p. 178.

95. The Hundred Flowers Movement of 1956–57 was followed by the brutal anti-rightist campaign; the Cultural Revolution of 1966–69 was ended by the intervention of the People's Liberation Army; the Democracy Wall Movement of 1978–79 was quickly snuffed out by public security forces; and the round of democracy protests from 1986 to 1989 resulted in the tragic Tiananmen incident.

7

Contradictions under Socialism: Shanghai's Strike Wave of 1957

In the spring of 1957, a strike wave of monumental proportions rolled across the city of Shanghai. The strikes in Shanghai represented the climax of a national outpouring of labor protest that had been gaining momentum for more than a year. The magnitude of the 1957 strike wave is especially impressive when placed in historical perspective. Major labor disturbances (*naoshi*) erupted at 587 Shanghai enterprises in the spring of 1957, involving nearly 30,000 workers. More than 200 of these incidents included factory walkouts, while another 100 or so involved organized slowdowns of production. In addition, more than 700 enterprises experienced less serious forms of labor unrest (*maoyan*).[1] These figures are extraordinary even by comparison with Republican-period Shanghai when the May Fourth Movement of 1919, the May Thirtieth Movement of 1925, the Shanghai Workers' Three Armed Uprisings of 1926–27, and the protests of the Civil War years gave rise to one of the most powerful and sustained labor movements in world history.[2] In 1919, Shanghai experienced only 56 strikes, 33 of which were connected with May Fourth. In 1925, Shanghai saw 175 strikes, 100 of which were in conjunction with May Thirtieth. The year of greatest strike activity in Republican-period Shanghai, 1946, saw a total of 280 strikes.[3]

Rarely mentioned in English-language studies of the period, the labor unrest of 1956–57 suggests the need to rethink several common assumptions about the development of Chinese communism. In contrast to the conventional image of the mid-1950s as a time when basic urban problems were *resolved* in China,[4] the strike wave indicates that we might better view the era as one in which fundamental social *cleavages* became evident.[5] Scholars and ordinary Chinese alike are apt to point to the 1950s as a kind of golden age—a period of unusual harmony and goodwill marked by a special closeness between the Chinese people, particularly the working class, and their new socialist government. Weary of war and proud of their revolutionary victory, citizens and cadres—we are told—cooperated in the process of socialist transformation.[6]

Of course the *early* 1950s were racked by the campaign to suppress counterrevolutionaries, the Three Antis, and Five Antis, but these were targeted at class enemies, cadres, or capitalists. And the *end* of that decade was marred by the anti-rightist campaign of late 1957 and the launching of the Great Leap Forward the following year, but these involved mainly intellectuals and peasants. For most of the decade, we are led to believe, friction between leaders and labor was minimal. The period just prior to the anti-rightist movement is often remembered most fondly. As renowned Chinese journalist Liu Binyan summarizes popular opinion,

> Twenty years later, looking back on the turmoil of the Cultural Revolution, most people felt nostalgic for 1956 and regarded it as the best period in the history of the People's Republic, calling it "the golden year." Some thought if it had not been for the antirightist campaign of the following year, Chinese society would have developed in a far more humane way.[7]

The strikes of 1956–57, Liu Binyan's candid reportage of which resulted in his denunciation by the Communist Party, were symptomatic of the severe social strains that predated and precipitated the anti-rightist crackdown. In demanding improved welfare and decrying the bureaucratism of local officials, strikers revealed deep divisions within the Chinese working class itself. Partly a product of pre-1949 experiences and partly a result of the socialization of industry under communism, such fissures would shape labor unrest in China for decades to come.

By the same token, the strikes of the mid-1950s may also demand some revision in our understanding of subsequent outbreaks of popular protest in the People's Republic of China (PRC)—most notably the Tiananmen Uprising of 1989. The so-called Democracy Movement of 1989 is often treated as unprecedented in the history of Communist China.[8] Unlike earlier outbursts (e.g., the Hundred Flowers of 1956–57, the Cultural Revolution of the 1960s, or even the Democracy Wall Movement of 1978–79), the Tiananmen protest tends to be pictured as a *bottom-up*, rather than a top-down affair—an event that, in contrast to the earlier incidents, was neither initiated nor orchestrated by the top leadership.[9] Thus Wang Shaoguang argues that "workers' involvement in the protest movement of 1989 marked a turning point of changing class relations . . . the working class in China is no longer a pillar of continuity but a force for change."[10] Likewise, Andrew Walder and Gong Xiaoxia characterize worker involvement in 1989 as a "new species of political protest in the People's Republic" that does not fit earlier modes of worker activism "where factions of political leaders mobilized their local followers for political combat."[11] This interpretation has been picked up by general comparativists as well. Jack Goldstone asserts that "unlike other confrontations that involved mainly intellectuals, such as the Hundred Flowers Movement, or other events that were in some sense orchestrated by the regime, such as the Cultural Revolution, Tiananmen marked the first time that intellectuals and popular elements acted independently to challenge the regime."[12] Yet as early as the mid-1950s, when relations between workers and the state were purportedly at their closest, labor activism evidenced considerable independence and bottom-up initiative.

Another feature of the 1989 uprising, highlighted in both journalistic and scholarly accounts, was its rich panoply of *protest repertoires*, which drew inspiration both from China's own May Fourth heritage and from international practices. Protesters at Tiananmen put up big-character posters, presented petitions, issued handbills, threatened industrial strikes and slow-downs, organized autonomous unions, and undertook hunger strikes, marches, and even the capturing of political center stage during the visit of a foreign dignitary (Gorbachev). Joseph Esherick and Jeffrey Wasserstrom have insightfully analyzed this aspect of the movement in their treatment of 1989 as political theater.[13] But on this score, too, we find remarkable precedents in the unrest of 1956–57.

A study of these earlier incidents thus offers a corrective to some of our assumptions both about the *beginnings* of the PRC (the 1950s) and about the *post-Mao* scene (the 1980s and 1990s). Scholarship on dissent in Communist China—whether focusing on the Hundred Flowers, Democracy Wall, or the Tiananmen uprisings of 1976 and 1989—has been preoccupied with the plight of the intelligentsia.[14] Yet alongside each of these famed outbursts of protest by intellectuals have occurred little-known, but highly significant, labor movements.[15] Indeed, the draconian manner in which the state chose to terminate each of these instances of protest (with the anti-rightist campaign in 1957, the imprisonment of Wei Jingsheng and other democracy advocates in 1979, and the massacre on June 4, 1989) becomes somewhat more intelligible—though certainly no more excusable—in light of this hidden history of working-class resistance.

Moreover, when put in historical and comparative context, as I shall attempt to do in the conclusion of this chapter, the Shanghai strike wave of 1957 may also have some implications for models of labor protest in general. The distinction between a *strike wave* and a *general strike*, though rarely emphasized in the theoretical literature, underscores the importance of the relationship between workers and intellectuals and highlights the contrast between the labor movements of pre- and post-1949 China.

Sources

Although there exists, so far as I am aware, no English-language treatment of these events, we have for some time had access to fragmentary evidence about the labor unrest of the mid-1950s. First of all, hints about the magnitude of the protests appear in speeches by top leaders at the time. Mao Zedong in his famous address of February 1957, "On the Correct Handling of Contradictions Among the People," notes that "in 1956, workers and students in certain places went on strike."[16] The more candid collection of Mao's speeches published for internal circulation in 1969, *Mao Zedong sixiang wansui*, provides more references. In a January 1957 speech, for example, Mao mentions widespread strikes and notes that a recent investigation found that only 25 percent of the workers were reliable.[17] And in *The Secret Speeches of Chairman Mao*, edited by Roderick MacFarquhar et al., Mao cites a report by the All-China Federation of Trade Unions (ACFTU) in 1956 that noted, on the basis of only partial statistics, that some fifty strikes had recently taken place—the largest of which had more than 1,000 participants.[18]

Liu Shaoqi, speaking in December 1956, raised the question of how to deal with strikes and petitions—but did not answer it.[19] The following spring, when the number of labor disputes had increased exponentially, Liu boldly proposed that union and Party officials should themselves participate in strikes in order to regain the workers' sympathy.[20]

A second source for information on the strikes of the mid-1950s are central reports and directives, many of which were reprinted in the internal-circulation journal, *Zhongguo gongyun* (The Chinese labor movement).[21] In February 1957, the Party group of the ACFTU issued a report noting that it had handled 29 strikes and 56 petitions by disgruntled workers the previous year. The report pointed out that this was but a small percentage of the total number of disputes that had erupted across the country. In Shanghai, for example, 6 labor disturbances had broken out in the first 3 months of 1956; 19 in the second trimester; 20 in the third trimester; and 41 in the last trimester of that year.[22] The following month, March 1957, Party Central issued a directive on the problem of handling strikes. Acknowledging that labor strikes, student boycotts, and mass petitions and demonstrations had increased dramatically in the past half year, Party Central estimated (perhaps with some hyperbole) that more than 10,000 labor strikes had erupted across the country during this period.[23]

A third—and somewhat more accessible—source was the official press.[24] Newspapers from around the country carried stories about strikes, petitions, and other varieties of labor disputes in their locales.[25] And on May 13, 1957, the *People's Daily* ran a lengthy editorial entitled "On Labor Trouble,"[26] which attributed the problem of strikes and petitions to bureaucratism on the part of the leadership.

A pioneering study of labor unrest in this period—based upon the official Chinese media—was recently completed by a French scholar. François Gipouloux's *Les cent fleurs à l'usine* (The Hundred Flowers in the factory) is a valuable work that emphasizes the year 1957 as a point of rupture in the history of Chinese socialism.[27] But Gipouloux was dependent almost entirely upon the official press—central and provincial, trade union and Youth League. His findings are very suggestive, but also quite partial. As Gipouloux himself points out, cases were not reported in the press until they had been satisfactorily resolved. Successful resolution, more than the typicality of the incident itself, was the criterion for coverage. Thus Gipouloux provides a blow-by-blow account of the resistance of 200 returned Shanghai bathhouse workers—an incident that was treated in both the Shanghai and the central press as "a very good example of how to handle contradictions among the people."[28] Interesting as the case is, however, it turns out to have been atypical in a number of respects. As we shall see, strikes by repatriated workers comprised fewer than 1 percent of the disturbances that spring.

Fortunately we are now able to go beyond speeches, central directives, and the official press in our investigation of this subject. The Shanghai Municipal Archives hold hundreds of detailed reports compiled in the spring of 1957 by the Shanghai Federation of Trade Unions and its district branches across the city on incidents that erupted in their areas of jurisdiction. These rich data offer a new perspective on the strike wave, allowing us to pose previously unanswerable questions about the origins and objectives of the protests.[29]

Causes of the Strike Wave

As studies of the Hundred Flowers Movement have emphasized, Chairman Mao's role in encouraging the dissent of this period was of critical importance.[30] Concerned about the unrest then sweeping Eastern Europe, Mao hoped that the release of social tensions in China would avert a popular uprising at home. Whether the chairman was setting a trap for his enemies (as most Chinese assume)[31] or whether he was acting initially in good faith (as Western analysts generally believe),[32] Mao clearly was anxious to defuse domestic contradictions. He referred repeatedly in both his published and unpublished speeches to the Hungarian revolt of 1956 and expressed the hope that strikes in China might help to forestall a larger and more serious insurgency.[33]

The importance of state inspiration is undeniable. Without the chairman's explicit encouragement, it seems inconceivable that the strike wave would have assumed such massive proportions. Moreover, previous mobilization of workers in state-sponsored campaigns to monitor capitalists had prepared the ground for the outburst of labor unrest at this time.[34] Factionalism within the upper echelons of the Party leadership also fostered dissent among the populace at large.[35] Even so, one is hard pressed to characterize the events of spring 1957 as a top-down affair. The archival materials give no hint of direct instigation by higher authorities, at either municipal or central levels. Although certainly stimulated by Mao's "On Handling Contradictions" speech, the protests evidenced considerable spontaneity and presented real problems for management, Party, and trade union officials alike.

Much of the explanation for the explosion of labor unrest lies with the economic restructuring of the day. The years 1956–57 were noteworthy not only for the Hungarian revolt abroad or for Mao's Hundred Flowers initiative at home; they were also the period in which most of Chinese industry was socialized. Private firms were eliminated and replaced by so-called joint-ownership enterprises (*gongsi heying qiye*). Under this arrangement, the former owners became state employees, receiving interest on the value of their shares in the enterprise. The capitalists no longer enjoyed profits, nor did they exercise any real managerial initiative. Except for the fact that the former owners clipped coupons, the joint-owned companies were in effect wholly state-run entities.[36]

The fundamental transformation of the Shanghai economy can be illustrated with a few figures. In the fall of 1950, a year after the establishment of the new socialist regime, more than 75 percent of the city's industrial work force was still employed at privately owned factories; state enterprises claimed a mere 21 percent. In December of 1957, by contrast, 72 percent of Shanghai's laborers worked at joint-ownership firms and another 27 percent at state-owned enterprises.[37] Private industry was a thing of the past.

The great majority of strikes in the spring of 1957 were concentrated in newly formed joint-ownership enterprises to protest the deterioration in economic securities and political voice that accompanied the socialization of these firms. In most instances, the wage and welfare reforms that occurred with the formation of joint-ownership enterprises spelled a decrease in real income for workers. For example, at the Yongxing Cloth Factory, workers lost the right to glean the leftover cotton waste, forfeited a special food subsidy at festival times, and gave up bonuses for good attendance and promotions. This meant on average a loss of more than 400 yuan per person per year. Similarly, at the Zhenhua Paint Factory, eighteen forms of wage and welfare subsidies were abolished.[38] Although it seems that many of these subsidies were actually very recent in origin, having been introduced after 1949 by private entrepreneurs in response to state pressure, workers reacted to their abrogation with all the righteous indignation associated with the collapse of a "traditional" moral economy.[39] At Zhenhua, workers referred to the cuts—which resulted in an average per capita monthly loss of 45 yuan—as "18 chops of the knife" and satirized cadres at the factory as "master monks" for the enforced austerity program. When the Shanghai Water Company discontinued its practice of issuing free toilet paper to all employees, workers responded by using the company's letterhead stationery instead! At the Tianhua Gas Lamp Factory, the fifty-four laborers were accustomed to a sumptuous annual banquet—a practice that was terminated under joint ownership. In protest, the workers themselves ordered a five-table feast and sent the bill to management. When the new state managers refused to absorb the cost, a disturbance erupted.[40]

The socialization of industry also resulted in a loss of political input for ordinary workers. After the Communist takeover in 1949, most private enterprises had been forced to implement a system of mass supervision—under the auspices of the enterprise trade union—in which workers had some say in production plans, management procedures, wages, bonuses, and the like. But after joint ownership was established, this system of worker supervision was often dispensed with.[41] The workers' unhappiness was intensified by the fact that, in stark contrast to their own plight, bonuses for the managerial staff were generally unaffected by the socialization process.[42]

Of the more than 1,300 incidents that took place during the approximately 100 days from March to early June 1957 (the highpoint of labor unrest in Shanghai), nearly 90 percent were centered in newly formed joint-ownership enterprises.[43] The vast majority of the incidents were located in small-scale enterprises with fewer than 100 workers, where working conditions were especially poor and cadre–worker relations commensurately strained.[44]

The disproportionately high number of strikes at joint-ownership enterprises was not the result of wage differentials per se. In 1957 the average worker at a joint-ownership factory in Shanghai actually took home a higher paycheck than his or her counterpart at a state enterprise.[45] But growing disparities in welfare assistance, housing subsidies, bonuses, and job security strongly favored the state employee and generated understandable resentment on the part of workers at joint-ownership firms. The fact that workers at joint-ownership enterprises were somewhat better educated than state factory workers may have further contributed to the militancy of the former group.[46]

In terms of motivation, nearly half the disputes were driven by a demand for higher income or improved welfare[47]—usually in response to cuts imposed during the change to joint ownership. An additional one-third were by apprentices, protesting a recent State Council directive that extended their training period beyond the initial contract. Approximately 7 percent of the disturbances were prompted solely by poor work style on the part of the cadres. The remainder of the protests were closely connected to the newly emerging system of household registration (*hukou*), which threatened to create a neofeudal hierarchy based upon the location of one's permanent job assignment.[48] Some 4 percent of the disruptions were instigated by workers unhappy about being transferred out of Shanghai to work at industrial enterprises elsewhere in the country. Another 2 percent were by temporary workers demanding permanent worker status. Fewer than 1 percent of the strikes were by repatriated workers (*daoliu gong*) sent back to their native places—the bathhouse workers on whom Gipouloux showered such attention, for example—but the protests of these peasant/workers were especially militant and the authorities thus put particular efforts into their resolution.[49]

While the formation of joint-ownership enterprises triggered the unrest of 1956–57, some of the workers' grievances had been mounting for years prior to the explosion. At many factories, wages had been withheld—often for six months or more—during the difficult period of the Korean War. When it later came time to make restitution, the Shanghai Bureau of Labor insisted that repayment take the form of a "collective welfare fund" (*jiti fuli jin*) to be used by individual firms for the general good of their work force. The disposition of the collective welfare fund created a good deal of friction at many factories. In some cases, factory unions publicized plans to construct new dormitories or cafeterias, which never actually materialized. In other cases, dormitories were built but were open only to newly hired workers—despite the fact that money for their construction had come from the withheld wages of older workers. Incensed by such injustices, workers called for a disbursement of the welfare fund.[50]

Style of Protest

Typically, a dispute would begin by raising repeated suggestions and demands (*ti yijian, ti yaoqiu*) to the factory leadership. When these were not dealt with, formal complaints were lodged (*gaozhuang*) with the higher authorities. The workers set deadlines by which they expected a satisfactory response and often staged rowdy meetings to publicize their grievances. These initial steps were classified by union authorities under the rubric of *maoyan* or "giving off smoke." But if their demands did not meet with a timely response, the protest would evolve into a strike (*bagong*), slowdown (*daigong*), collective petition movement (*jiti qingyuan*), or forcible surrounding of cadres (*baowei ganbu*)—activities that were categorized as *naoshi*, or outright "disturbances."

Many of the protesters did demonstrate a desire to remain within the law. Pedicab drivers, before raising their demands, first sought legal counsel to ascertain that their three requests were legitimate. Other measures were also adopted in order to impress the authorities with the propriety of the protests. Thus after elections for workers' representatives were held, anyone from bad class background (capitalist, landlord) was usually eliminated from the roster. Even so, over time many of the protests grew larger and more complicated—moving beyond simple requests about welfare provisions or leadership attitudes to involve bolder initiatives.[51]

The protesters evinced a remarkably wide repertoire of behavior. Many workers put up big-character posters (*dazi bao*) and wrote blackboard newspapers explaining their grievances; some went on hunger strike, some threatened suicide, some marched in large-scale demonstrations—holding high their workplace banners as they paraded vociferously down Nanjing Road; some staged sit-ins and presented petitions to government authorities; some organized action committees, pickets, and liaison offices to coordinate strikes in different factories and districts. In many cases, workers surrounded factory, Party, and union cadres, raising demands and imposing a deadline for a satisfactory response, and refusing to disband until their requests had been met.[52]

The importance of foreign influences was obvious. Just as the example of Poland's Solidarity inspired Chinese workers in the 1980s,[53] so at this earlier juncture the Hungarian revolt was a powerful stimulus for labor unrest. A popular slogan in the Shanghai protests of 1957 was "Let's create another Hungarian Incident!" There was an awareness—as in 1989—of China's being part of an international socialist world. Another slogan in 1957 was "We'll take this all the way from district to city to Party Central to Communist International." Some workers, hearing that Khrushchev was about to visit Shanghai, planned to present their grievances directly to him.[54] Although it turned out that the Soviet leader did not actually make his visit until the following year—well after the anti-rightist crackdown had thoroughly crushed the possibility of a direct confrontation with striking workers—the parallel with 1989, when protesters presented their grievances to Gorbachev, is noteworthy.

Again as in 1989, there was evidence of a growing sophistication in protest strategies over time. In many cases strikers' game plans included assigning "good cop/bad cop" roles to different participants, or, as the workers referred to this, *ban honglian, bailian*—acting the part of the red-faced hero or white-faced villain of Peking opera. In the later stages, workers distributed handbills to publicize their demands and formed autonomous unions (often termed *pingnan hui*, or redress grievances societies). In Tilanqiao District, more than 10,000 workers joined a "Democratic Party" (*minzhu dangpai*) organized by three local laborers. Some protesters used secret passwords and devised their own seals of office. In a number of instances, "united command headquarters" were established to provide martial direction to the struggles.[55]

Divisions Among the Workers

About one-fifth of the disturbances involved all of the workers at an enterprise,[56] and in a few cases (e.g., the artisan trade of cloth-dyeing) an entire industry participated. Usually, however, fewer than half of the workers at a factory were involved, with younger workers playing a disproportionately active role.[57]

One reason for the less than universal participation in most disturbances was quite simply that divisions *among* the workers themselves were an important precipitant of many of the protests. At the Taichang Nail Factory, for example, workers from rural backgrounds demanded that their dependents still living in the countryside receive the same benefits as family members of Shanghai workers who resided in the city. Similarly, barbers stationed at construction sites demanded the same welfare provisions as the construction workers whose hair they were cutting.[58]

Apprentices distraught by the extension of their training period proved an especially unruly lot. When Shanghai's Party secretary, Ma Tianshui, explained in a radio broadcast the new State Council directive prolonging indefinitely their period of servitude, apprentices across the city wept openly at the news. Most of these laborers hailed from the countryside and had promised their families that they would send home a part of their wage just as soon as the apprenticeship was completed and they were promoted to the status of regular grade-three workers. Many owed money that had to be repaid at the end of the original apprenticeship period; others had made plans to marry at that time.[59]

The apprentices were remarkably adept at forging interfactory links. On May 10, some 800 apprentices from factories across the city staged a sit-in at the recreation club of Penglai District. On May 12, more than 300 apprentices from ten factories in Hongkou and Zhabei districts gathered at a workers' library to demand higher wages, better welfare provisions, and a guarantee of promotion to grade-three worker upon completion of the apprenticeship period. In Luwan District, apprentices printed up handbills to summon their colleagues to a mass meeting at a local park.[60] In Yulin District, apprentices from five machine factories organized a "united command headquarters" to press their demands.[61]

The shabby treatment accorded to apprentices was symptomatic of the newly emerging socialist industrial order, with its sharp division between privileged permanent workers at state enterprises and less fortunate members of the work force. The dispute at the Shanghai Fertilizer Company in May 1957 illustrates the importance of these intraworker divisions. The previous summer the company had taken on forty-one temporary workers (*linshi gongren*), planning to promote them to regular employee status (*guding gongren*) after a three-month trial period. However, due to an unexpected contraction in production, management decided to fire the new hires instead. Soon thereafter the union at the factory announced a plan to issue union membership cards to its regular employees, whereupon the discharged workers got it into their heads that access to a union card would ensure them permanent worker status. They thus marched off to the union office to apply for the cards. The union, of course, refused to issue them membership cards since the applicants had already been dismissed from the factory. Nevertheless the discharged workers set a deadline by which they demanded that the cards be made available to them. After the union failed to comply, the angered ex-workers dragged both the director and the vice-director of the union down to the banks of the Huangpu River. When the union leaders continued to deny their demand, the workers dunked the head of the union director in the polluted waters of the river. This continued, at two- to three-minute intervals, for more than an hour till the union director's face was covered with mud and blood. Afraid for his own life, the vice-director jumped into the river in an effort to swim away. A boatman who offered help was stoned by the workers. Some bystander night-soil carriers who tried to provide assistance from the river's edge were beaten off with sticks. The factory physician arrived on the scene just in time to pronounce both director and vice-director near death, at which point the discharged workers finally released them to the authorities. Two days later the small group leaders of the union and Youth League at the fertilizer factory held a meeting and declared that if the Party leadership considered this outrageous incident an example of contradictions *among* the people (which, as a nonantagonistic contradiction, did not require stern punishment), then they would take matters into their own hands and repay violence with violence. The permanent workers strongly agreed and even stockpiled weapons in preparation for killing the temporary workers who had instigated the affair. The only sympathy they evidenced for the discharged temporary workers was a pledge to take responsibility for the dependents of the workers whom they planned to kill! Fortunately, the authorities decided to handle the incident themselves by arresting the ringleaders as perpetrators of an antagonistic contradiction.[62]

Temporary workers had good reason to feel ill-served by the socialist system. In 1957, of the 4,200 "temporary" workers employed in Shanghai's underwear industry, 691 had held their jobs for more than one year. Yet these workers enjoyed no employment security. One "temporary" worker who had labored for more than four years at the Tongfu Sock Factory (where he had trained numerous apprentices) was dismissed because of illness just a few days after being transferred to another sock factory in the city.

In some instances, protests were launched by workers who had lost permanent status through job reassignments. For example, a sizable contingent of workers from the Fuxing Flour Company had recently been transferred to a local automobile factory, in the process forfeiting their permanent worker status, suffering a 50 percent pay cut, and succumbing to an inordinate number of workplace injuries because of unfamiliarity with their new jobs. In other cases, participation in public works projects fueled the workers' grievances. In the winter of 1955, a large number of former vagrants (*youmin*) who had undergone training at a vocational center in Shanghai were dispatched to help with harnessing the Huai River in northern Anhui Province. The trainees had been promised regular work at the Shanghai Number One Construction Company upon their return to the city in July 1956, but after nearly a year's delay were informed that they would not be hired because of illnesses contracted while working on the river.[63] Divisions within the work force were a significant component of the unrest of the period, but these splits did not follow the "activist" versus "nonactivist" dichotomy that we might anticipate from previous analyses of political participation in Communist China.[64] Instead of political status, we find that socioeconomic and spatial categories—permanent versus temporary workers, old versus young workers, locals versus outsiders, urbanites versus ruralites—were the more salient lines of division.

In most cases, Communist Party members, Youth Leaguers, and activists do not seem to have behaved very differently from ordinary workers.[65] At the Datong Oil Factory, six of the forty workers who signed a petition demanding back pay and restoration of previous piece-rates were Party or League members or other activists. One of the three ringleaders of this petition drive and factory walkout had been a secret society leader of the Red School Association (*Hongxue hui*) before 1949 and had also served as a yellow union cadre under the GMD, but the other two principal instigators had been guerrilla fighters on the Communist side during the revolution and one of them currently served as a member of the factory management committee. The former secret society leader is credited with the slogan, "We workers need only a working people's organization [*laodong renmin zuzhi*], not a union [*gonghui*]." One of the Communist guerrilla fighters, who also had been a secret society member, reportedly claimed that "the cadres don't empathize with our joys and sorrows. To meld us with the cadres the Americans would have to drop an atomic bomb forcing us all to die together." And the former guerrilla and current factory committee member—in other words the activist—raised the slogan "Let's all return to the factory for an 'eat-in' [*zuo chi*] and wait there for a resolution."[66] Thus a worker's political status (as Party member, Youth League member, activist, backbone element, or bad element), although duly noted in the official reports, does not appear to have played a major role in determining his or her participation in the strikes.

State–Society Relations

Economic cleavages and concerns were fundamental to the labor unrest of this period, but such matters were inextricably linked to the policies of the new socialist state. Central directives now determined everything from wage rates to apprenticeship periods. Workers were of course acutely aware of the fact that responsibility for industrial policy and factory management rested squarely with state cadres. Thus although economic demands (for higher income and improved welfare measures) dominated their requests, much of the workers' wrath was directed *against cadres*—in factory, government, Party, and union positions.

With joint ownership had come a huge increase in the size of the factory managerial staff, which burgeoned to more than one-third of all employees at most enterprises. The outcome was a greater financial burden on those employees engaged in productive labor, and a commensurate resentment against the unproductive employees. Workers decried the growth in bureaucracy (which at the Ronghua Dye Company meant a leap from two and a half full-time staff positions before 1949 to fifty-two such positions after joint ownership). And they criticized the practice of promoting Communist Party members, rather than seasoned workers, to staff positions: "If you want to sit upstairs, you first have to get yourself into the Party."[67]

Anger at the surge in bureaucratization was intensified by the state's growing interference in the labor market.[68] In late 1955, there had been an effort to transfer industrial workers to enterprises located in more remote parts of the country and to repatriate service workers (e.g., the bathhouse workers highlighted in the press) to their native places in the countryside. Cadres at the time had often exaggerated the comforts of life in these more remote areas and falsely promised that transferred and repatriated workers could return to Shanghai when the economy improved. In some cases, cadres even mobilized activists to pretend that they were going down to the countryside voluntarily so as to trick ordinary workers into following suit. The workers were, however, disappointed by the poor conditions and low pay in the rural areas, so in 1957 when the city's economy did in fact improve, these people streamed back to Shanghai to reclaim their former jobs. There they discovered they had been lied to and were not going to be reinstated. The workers pointed out that in duping them by painting such a beautiful picture of the countryside, the cadres had been like "priests reciting the sutras." And as for the cadres' current attitude, "cold porridge and cold rice are edible, but cold words are hard to swallow."[69]

The Guohua Charcoal Briquet Factory illustrates this pattern. In late 1956 the factory was to be relocated in Tianjin. Cadres in Shanghai had deceived the workers into thinking that a factory and plush dormitory accommodations had already been built there, but in fact in the spring of 1957—a year after their transfer north—the area was still a wasteland. The transferred workers had no work and only a pittance of a wage. That June, 43 of the 108 employees returned to Shanghai to petition for a permanent return to the city. Ten of them threatened to commit suicide rather than go back to Tianjin.[70]

A common sentiment was that cadres were indifferent to the plight of workers and had to be shaken up if they were to fulfill their proper socialist duties. As a popular slogan of the day put it, "Leaders are like candles; if you don't ignite them there'll be no light."[71] Union leaders were a frequent target and were put in a very difficult position by the strikes.

In many cases, protesting workers evidenced a desire to take back from unions the right to represent their own interests. They organized their own meetings from which union officials, as well as management and Party branch leaders, were excluded. They cut the wires in their workshops during union broadcasts or took over the factory broadcast systems themselves. When district Party and union officials went to the Hongfa Nuts and Bolts Factory to resolve the conflict there, workers stationed at the gate refused to give them entry since they could not produce a shoulder-badge identification issued by the striking workers. And when Party and union cadres went to the Lianyi Metalworking Plant, the protesting workers mocked them: "The emperor [i.e., the Party secretary] has come down and the emperor's grandson [i.e., the director of the union] has accompanied him."[72] At the Shanghai Pen Company, strikers called for selling off union property (electric fans, magnifying glasses, and the like) and distributing the proceeds to the workers.[73]

The protests created a real dilemma for the trade unions. On the one hand, workers often criticized union cadres for being insensitive to their interests and sometimes aimed their struggles directly at the unions. Nearly half of the disputes included a demand for disbursing the collective welfare fund—a pot of money under union control. Union directors who refused to comply were subject to curses, and in many cases beatings, from enraged workers.[74] On the other hand, trade union cadres who *were* inclined to side with workers (as the director of the union at the Shanghai Knitting Factory) might find themselves out of a job.[75] An open letter from ten members of the Shanghai Federation of Trade Unions expressed the fear that they would be accused of "syndicalism," "economism," or "tailism" if they pushed too aggressively for workers' interests.[76]

Even so, in some cases union participation—and even leadership—was a key factor in the expansion of the dispute. At the Lianyi Machine Factory, the head of the union (a Party member) became disillusioned with the Communist regime after his elder brother, a rich peasant in the countryside, had been struggled against during collectivization. His entire union organization was mobilized to help direct the protest at the machine factory.[77] In this instance, disenchantment with the Communist regime prompted a union leader's activism.[78] In most cases, however, unions were trying earnestly to live up to their obligations as defenders of working-class interests under socialism.

As in 1989, many union officials saw in the disturbances a chance to shed their image as government patsies and forge a new closeness with the workers.[79] A union report on the uprising at the Datong Oil Factory in the spring of 1957 noted approvingly that when striking workers gathered at a teahouse, pounded their fists on the tables, and loudly cursed the cadres as "scabs" (even jostling the teacups in the process), union cadres sat meekly by and listened respectfully to the criticisms. As a result, worker–cadre relations improved and the dispute was amicably resolved.[80]

The ACFTU was anxious to enhance the standing of the union apparatus by successfully mediating labor disputes. On July 1, 1957, the national union issued a notice to provincial and city unions pointing out that it had been deluged with petitioners from all over the country and complaining that it often could not resolve the problems for lack of full knowledge about the local situation. It thus requested that in the future, provincial and city unions should whenever possible give advance warning to the ACFTU if workers under their jurisdiction were planning a protest trip to Beijing. Moreover, local unions were enjoined to send their own representatives to the capital to help settle the affair.[81]

This sympathetic attitude on the part of the union leadership elicited harsh criticism during the subsequent anti-rightist campaign. A notable target of the crackdown was the director of the ACFTU—Lai Ruoyu. In June 1957, shortly before the launching of the anti-rightist campaign,

Lai had delivered a speech at a basic-level cadre conference in Shanghai in which he accorded considerable legitimacy to the widespread disturbances that had recently rocked the city. In his memorable formulation, "A so-called disturbance [*suowei naoshi*] arises only because of something disturbing [*jiushi yinwei youshi cai naoqilai*]."[82] Shanghai trade union leaders revealed a similar sympathy toward the strikes. In August of 1957, the municipal trade union issued a general work report concluding that the vast majority of disturbances were contradictions *among* the people and should thus be resolved in a peaceful manner.[83] In the ensuing suppression effort, union officials at both national and municipal levels were accused of denying class struggle and were packed off to labor reform as rightists. Not until the post-Mao period did they enjoy rehabilitation—posthumously in the case of Lai Ruoyu.

The deposed chair of the ACFTU was actually one of the most astute observers of the Chinese labor scene in 1957. That May, Lai Ruoyu delivered a very insightful speech to union cadres in which he candidly acknowledged that, after the socialization of industry, the unions had become useless in the eyes of many workers, who described unions as "breathing out of the same nostril as enterprise management" (*he xingzheng yige bikong chuqi*). Lai countered the arguments of some cadres that the huge increase in labor unrest was the result of having recently added so many new workers to the labor force who were immature, impure, and imbued with a low class consciousness. The union director acknowledged that young workers, transferred Shanghai workers, and demobilized soldiers were especially prone to protest. He contended, however, that this proved that the main cause of the strikes was not the backwardness of the workers, but the bureaucratism of the leadership. These types of workers, Lai insisted, were especially daring in struggling against injustice and bureaucratism.[84]

Lai Ruoyu further noted, in a mode of analysis congruent with that of this chapter, that there were serious divisions within the working class—between new and older workers, between locals and outsiders, and between ordinary workers and managerial staff. He pointed out that current state policies were exacerbating these differences. New workers tended to be promoted more rapidly than older workers because book learning was valued above practical ability in tests for promotion. As a result the younger, better educated workers became arrogant and disrespectful to the seasoned skilled workers, while the older workers—the backbone of production—grew resentful.[85] Furthermore, newly established factories tended to hire workers from the Northeast or from Shanghai who did not get along well with the local hires.[86] Such fissures, along lines of age, education, experience, and native place, provided fuel for many of the protests.[87]

Conclusion

As Lai Ruoyu's analysis indicates, the strike wave of 1957 grew out of deep divisions within the work force. This was not a new phenomenon, however. As Chapters 5 and 6 have shown, in *pre*-1949 Shanghai the fragmentation of labor was also a key explanation for its militancy.[88]

In China, labor fragmentation has not implied passivity. Despite, indeed in large part *because* of, important distinctions along lines of native-place origin, age, and skill level, the Chinese working class has shown itself to be remarkably feisty. This is true not only for the pre-1949 period, but for the 1950s and subsequent decades as well. Worker activism during the Hundred Flowers Movement, the Cultural Revolution, the strikes of the mid to late 1970s, the uprising of 1989, and the explosion of industrial disputes in the 1990s can all be linked to splits within the working class.

The prevailing image of urban China under the People's Republic points to the role of the enterprise "unit" (*danwei*) in co-opting the working class and thereby diluting its potential for protest.[89] As Andrew Walder puts it in his influential analysis on Chinese industry, "the network of clientelist ties. . . . provides a structural barrier to concerted worker resistance. . . . This complex web of personal loyalty, mutual support, and material interest creates a stable pattern of tacit acceptance and active cooperation for the regime. . . ."[90] But it is important to keep in mind that the large, state-owned enterprises from which Walder built his impressive model of Communist neotraditionalism have never employed more than a minority of the Chinese industrial labor force. The selective incentives available to workers at such firms, and the resultant antipathy between "activists" and "nonactivists," may indeed explain the relative quiescence of state workers—at least until recent industrial reforms threatened their privileged position. But the very benefits enjoyed by this favored minority of workers constituted a continuing source of resentment for the majority of the work force that was excluded from such paternalistic arrangements. It is no accident that workers at joint-ownership enterprises, contract and temporary workers, apprentices, and the like—subject to neither the subsidies nor the controls experienced by their counterparts at state enterprises—stood at the forefront of labor protests under the command economy. Nor is it surprising that the market

[handwritten marginalia:] Conventional belief that Chinese labor was successfully coopted in the 1950s only applies to the SOEs. Very small percentage of overall workers.

reforms of the post-Mao era should elicit a defensive reaction from the once quiescent state sector.

In each of these periods of acute labor unrest in the PRC, debates over both domestic and international developments generated serious disagreements within the ruling elite. Uncertainty over policy directions at the center, in turn, created space for popular dissent. Equally important, the protests that erupted—though often promoted by elements of the state itself and seldom viewed by the participants as a fundamental indictment of the socialist system—served nonetheless as the pretext for the application of overwhelming state repression.[91] The fragmentation of labor was thus a double-edged sword: a source not only of worker militancy, but also of vulnerability in the face of a government crackdown.

The complex ties that link Chinese laborers, even when engaged in protest, to the state apparatus make it awkward to conceptualize their labor unrest as an indication of "civil society"—defined as the autonomy of individuals and groups in relationship to the state.[92] The ambivalent position of the official trade unions ("yellow unions" under the Republic of China, the ACFTU under the PRC) in these struggles further underscores the difficulty of neatly distinguishing between "state" and "society."[93] Rather than envision labor as a *solidary* expression of social interests poised to mount an opposition to a unitary state, it may be advisable to seek the roots of worker militancy in a *segmented* labor force prepared to make common cause with responsive state agents.

The socialist state has played a major role in shaping this segmentation. Thus in 1957 the uniform imposition of regulations on a great diversity of industries created, ironically enough, conditions under which groups of workers such as apprentices now found cause to join together across enterprise and even industrial lines. Unlike previous analyses of divisions within Chinese society, however, I do not see the primary split as one of "activists" versus "nonactivists"—political categories artificially imposed by the Communist party–state.[94] Instead, the lines of fragmentation reflect a rich history of labor unrest that predates the PRC.

As Chapter 8 will show, long-standing socioeconomic cleavages were central to the factionalism of the Cultural Revolution.[95] During the early years of that movement, the ranks of Shanghai's "conservative" Scarlet Guards were filled with older state workers, predominantly from the Jiangnan region, experienced in the pre-1949 labor movement. Their leaders were largely former underground Communist Party organizers who hailed from the same region. The Revolutionary Rebels of Wang Hongwen, by contrast, were mostly younger workers led in part by cadres sent down from the much poorer Subei area of northern Jiangsu in the early 1950s. Among their constituents were more than a few "un-skilled" contract and temporary workers.[96] Enduring as some of these intraworker divisions may be, however, they are also not "primordial" cleavages, immune to all change. The fissures that rend today's working class are equally a product of history and a contemporary construction.

The importance of changing circumstances is demonstrated by the very different segments of the work force that spearheaded the protests of 1957 and 1989. As we have seen, the earlier strike wave was launched by workers who felt especially threatened by the process of *socialization*: laborers at small joint-ownership firms, temporary workers, and the like. Stripped of many of the welfare measures they had enjoyed under the private ownership system that prevailed during the early years of the PRC, yet denied the privileges that came with permanent employment at large state enterprises, such workers felt particularly disadvantaged by the industrial reforms of the mid-1950s.[97] In 1989, by contrast, the back-bone of the protest was those workers most concerned about the impli-cations of *de-socialization*: permanent employees at large state-owned enterprises. It was these beneficiaries of socialist industry who felt most threatened by the new round of economic reforms.[98]

The salient lines of division within the work force are dynamic, shift-ing in response to changes in worker composition as well as to alterations in state policy. New socialist structures have created new winners and losers, while the experiences of the Hundred Flowers, the Cultural Rev-olution, and the Tiananmen Uprising have provided new understandings of the possibilities and boundaries of labor activism. But no less than in the past, Chinese labor remains fragmented.[99] And no less than in the past, its struggles are likely to follow the lines of that fragmentation.[100]

Studies of labor in pre-Communist China have emphasized the cata-lytic role of intellectuals—whether Communist revolutionaries or mem-bers of the left-wing GMD—in stimulating the unrest of the Republican period.[101] As Nym Wales put it in her monograph on the Chinese labor movement, "The students told the workers what unions were and the workers acted."[102] While such analyses underestimate the capacity of Chi-nese workers to act on their own behalf, without outside direction, they do nevertheless highlight an important fact: the milestones of Republican-period history were laid by the concerted efforts of workers and students. The general strikes of May Fourth, May Thirtieth, the Three Armed Uprisings, and the Civil War years all exhibited close co-ordination between labor and the intelligentsia.[103]

By contrast, labor unrest in Communist China is notable for its lack of student involvement. With the exception of a brief period during the

Cultural Revolution, when Red Guards entered the factories on instructions from Beijing, workers in post-1949 China have acted without guidance from intellectuals. Thus, although intellectuals contributed greatly to the dissent of the Hundred Flowers period, there is no evidence that they attempted to join forces with the strike wave that was then sweeping the nation's factories.[104]

No central political grievance The labor protest of 1957 was, however, not a *general* strike in the tradition of May Fourth, May Thirtieth, the Three Workers' Armed Uprisings, or the Civil War years. It did not have one central political grievance—the terms of the Versailles Treaty in the case of May Fourth, the slaying of workers and students by Japanese and British police in the case of May Thirtieth, the indignities of warlord rule in the case of the Three Uprisings, the corruption of the GMD in the case of the Civil War unrest—around which public opinion could be galvanized. Workers in 1957 were protesting workplace issues—labor compensation, managerial style, and the like—matters of great importance to workers, but not ones that resonated easily with public opinion.

Theorists of labor history and industrial relations have seldom drawn a clear distinction between a *general strike* and a *strike wave*, but the record of labor unrest in Shanghai suggests that the difference may well be a significant one. To clarify the issue, we will first have to unload some of the heavy baggage that has become attached to these terms in the secondary literature. We can dispense with the romantic rapture of Georges Sorel, who saw the *general strike* as having "engendered in the proletariat the noblest, deepest, and most moving sentiments that they possess; the general strike groups them all in a co-ordinated picture . . . it colours with an intense life all the details of the composition presented to consciousness."[105] Neither need we adopt the narrowly quantitative approach of Edward Shorter and Charles Tilly, who define a *strike wave* as occurring "when both the number of strikes and the number of strikers in a given year exceed the means of the previous five years by more than 50 percent."[106] Although the scholarship on these phenomena is contradictory (Sorel as well as Shorter and Tilly use the terms "general strike" and "strike wave" interchangeably, for example), the contrast between the poetic approach of Sorel and the prosaic approach of Shorter and Tilly does hint at a central distinction between the two types of strikes. The intense and widespread fervor that characterizes the general strike is the result of a set of *political* demands that generate extensive *cross-class* enthusiasm targeted directly at the *state*. Strike waves, by contrast, tend to develop around *work-related* grievances; participation is often limited to members of the *working class* who aim their criticisms at *factory management*.

Of course the distinction is hard to maintain in practice. General strikes, even when prompted by a national political crisis and instigated by outside intellectual leadership, may serve to stimulate important workplace demands as well. And under socialism, where factory managers are also state agents, economic and political objectives are often inextricably linked. Even so, a distinction between the two types of strikes seems worth making in light of their very different impact on the course of modern Chinese political history.

The general strikes of Republican China were watershed events. The May Fourth Movement led directly to the founding of the Chinese Communist Party and heralded a new style of populist culture and politics; the May Thirtieth Movement and the Three Armed Workers' Uprisings hastened the expulsion of warlord rule and its replacement by a new GMD regime; the Civil War strikes helped to unravel GMD control over the cities and usher in a new socialist order. Under the "proletarian" People's Republic, by contrast, labor unrest has enjoyed a much less glorious fate. Rather than challenging the Mandate of Heaven, protests have elicited harsh state repression (the labor camps of 1957, the tanks of 1989). One reason for the difference lies in the success of the Communist state at isolating working-class resistance from intellectual dissent. The strike waves of 1956–57, 1974–76, and the post-Mao reform era—albeit encouraged by concomitant student protests—developed without significant support from educated outsiders. Considering the prominent role that intellectuals have historically played in Chinese protest movements, it is hardly surprising that their absence would have such profound implications. The phenomenon is not unique to China, however. A cursory survey of strikes in other countries reveals a similar pattern; whereas strike waves often arise "spontaneously" among the workers themselves, a general strike tends to develop under the guiding hand of outside organizers. Intellectual leadership may act to mute divisions within the work force and enable concerted action on behalf of unified objectives.

Take the case of St. Petersburg, which was racked by strikes in 1896–97, 1901, and of course 1905. The strike wave of 1896–97 was confined to cotton spinners demanding a shorter workday (on the order of that enjoyed by skilled metalworkers), while the wave of 1901 was launched by metalworkers enamored of new political ideas. The general strike of 1905 combined the concerns of both skilled and unskilled workers by presenting a cohesive set of demands for greater civil liberties and freedom to unionize and strike, as well as calling for an eight-hour workday. In contrast to the earlier waves, the general strike was organized by the St. Petersburg Assembly of Russian Factory and Mill Workers, a workers' club with close connections to the Social Democrats. Stunned by the humiliating loss of Port Arthur to the Japanese (not unlike the trigger of the May Fourth Movement), workers were emboldened to articulate overtly political grievances. The massacre of Bloody Sunday (not unlike the May Thirtieth tragedy) further galvanized the Russian proletariat in launching its historic general strike.[107]

Similarly, the stage for the Seattle general strike of 1919 was set by a high degree of cooperation between the Central Labor Council and the local trade unions. The concerted efforts of progressive, yet pragmatic, labor organizers had built a strong foundation for working-class mobilization in the city. Unfortunately for the fate of the protest, however, the strike erupted just when the entire top echelon of union leadership happened to be off in Chicago for a conference. The lack of central direction was reflected in the strikers' inability to enunciate a cogent list of demands—a failing that explains, in no small measure, the rapid demise of the movement.[108]

General strikes are unusual, albeit remarkably powerful, events. Because they entail the participation of very different—and under normal circumstances quite competitive—groups of workers, these incidents are typically waged for causes that transcend the divisive concerns of the workplace. Not wages and welfare but national humiliation, price inflation, and political corruption are the rallying points of the general strike. Working-class interest in these issues is often promoted by those who have a professional preoccupation with such problems: the intellectuals.

Shanghai's 1957 strike wave belongs to a more common species of labor protest, a contagious movement that stems from work-related grievances. As more than a few analysts of labor have noted, politics at the point of production are inherently divisive. Indeed, the very awareness of substantial differences among workers often encourages labor activism. Depending upon their location in the job hierarchy, workers may be militant in trying to minimize, maintain, or magnify discrepancies in wages or working conditions between themselves and other workers.[109]

Socialism, like capitalism, creates winners and losers among the work force. These are determined not only by clientelist networks, which, as Andrew Walder notes, are most pronounced in large, state-owned enterprises where only a minority of the industrial work force is employed.[110] For the majority of workers, a more salient division is the structural gap that separates the haves and have-nots of the socialist economy. In the strikes of 1957, those *excluded* from the benefits of socialist reform—the marginal temporary and contract workers—took the lead. In 1989, it was the *beneficiaries* of socialism—permanent employees at state enterprises—who emerged as vocal protesters.[111] As the segment of the work force that stood to lose the most from the reintroduction of capitalist practices, their militancy is understandable.

Differences in social composition were not the only thing that distinguished the two periods. The protesters of 1989 also undertook a more concerted effort to develop autonomous workers' organizations than did their predecessors of three decades earlier.[112] Despite such differences, however, in both periods links between labor unrest and the protests of other social elements—especially the intellectual community—remained weak. (See Chapter 10 for an expansion of this point.) In this important respect, then, the strike waves of post-1949 China are to date but a faint echo of the general strikes of the Republican era.

Notes

This chapter was originally published as an article in *China Quarterly*, no. 139 (March 1994).

1. These statistics are the calculation of the Shanghai Committee Party History Research Office. See *Zhongguo gongchandang zai Shanghai, 1921–1991* (The Chinese Communist Party in Shanghai, 1921–1991) (Shanghai: 1991), p. 472.

2. On the other hand, the figures for 1957 pale in comparison with those for late 1949—the period immediately following the establishment of the new Communist order in the city. In the six months from June through December of 1949, Shanghai experienced 3,324 strikes and major disturbances (averaging more than 500 incidents per month). This critical takeover period remains to be carefully studied.

3. Shanghai Bureau of Social Affairs, ed., *Strikes and Lockouts in Shanghai, 1918–1932* (Shanghai: City Government of Shanghai, 1933).

4. See Kenneth G. Lieberthal, *Revolution and Tradition in Tientsin, 1949–1952* (Stanford: Stanford University Press, 1980); and Ezra Vogel, *Canton Under Communism: Programs and Politics in a Provincial Capital, 1949–1968* (Cambridge: Harvard University Press, 1969), for pathbreaking analyses of the impact of socialist transformation on urban China. A. Doak Barnett, in his pioneering study of the period, *Communist China: The Early Years, 1949–1955* (New York: Praeger, 1964), p. 11, concluded that "a small but vitally important minority of the Chinese population," including organized labor, had enthusiastically accepted Communist rule.

5. Roderick MacFarquhar's *The Origins of the Cultural Revolution*, vols. 1 and 2 (New York: Columbia University Press, 1974 & 1983) and David Bachman's *Bureaucracy, Economy and Leadership in China: The Institutional Ori-*

gins of the Great Leap Forward (New York: Cambridge University Press, 1991) emphasize the conflicts of the period, but their focus is on the political elite rather than the ordinary citizenry.

6. For a discussion of socialist transformation in the countryside, see Vivienne Shue, *Peasant China in Transition* (Berkeley: University of California Press, 1980). That the process in the rural areas was also socially divisive is suggested in Elizabeth J. Perry, "Rural Violence in Socialist China," *China Quarterly* (September 1985), pp. 420 ff.

7. Liu Binyan, *A Higher Kind of Loyalty* (New York: Pantheon, 1990), p. 61.

8. Useful collections stressing the novelty of the uprising of 1989 include Tony Saich, ed., *Perspectives on the Chinese People's Movement: Spring 1989* (Armonk: M.E. Sharpe, 1990); Jonathan Unger, ed., *The Pro-Democracy Protests in China* (Armonk: M.E. Sharpe, 1991); and George Hicks, ed., *The Broken Mirror: China After Tiananmen* (Harlow, Essex, UK: St. James Press, 1990).

9. For a maverick view, stressing the close connection between student organizers and high-level members of the Chinese Communist Party in 1989, see Lee Feigon, *China Rising: The Meaning of Tiananmen* (Chicago: I.R. Dee, 1990). Feigon emphasizes the similarities between the Tiananmen Uprising and earlier student protests in Chinese history, both before and after 1949.

10. Wang Shaoguang, "Deng Xiaoping's Reform and the Chinese Workers' Participation in the Protest Movement of 1989," *Research in Political Economy*, vol. 13.

11. Andrew G. Walder and Gong Xiaoxia, "Workers in the Tiananmen Protests: The Politics of the Beijing Workers' Autonomous Federation," *Australian Journal of Chinese Affairs*, no. 29 (January 1993), pp. 3–4.

12. Jack A. Goldstone, "Analyzing Revolutions and Rebellions: A Reply to the Critics," *Contention* 3: 177–198.

13. Joseph W. Esherick and Jeffrey N. Wasserstrom, "Acting Out 'Democracy': Political Theater in Modern China," in Jeffrey N. Wasserstrom and Elizabeth J. Perry, eds., *Popular Protest and Political Culture in Modern China: Learning from 1989* (Boulder: Westview, 1992), pp. 28–66.

14. Important studies of intellectual dissent include Merle Goldman, *China's Intellectuals: Advise and Dissent* (Cambridge: Harvard University Press, 1981); Goldman, *Literary Dissent in Communist China* (Cambridge: Harvard University Press, 1967); Goldman with Timothy Cheek and Carol Hamrin, eds., *China's Intellectuals and the State* (Cambridge: Harvard University Press, 1987); and Andrew J. Nathan, *Chinese Democracy* (New York: Knopf, 1985).

15. This point is also made in Anita Chan, "Revolution or Corporatism? Workers and Trade Unions in Post-Mao China," *Australian Journal of Chinese Affairs*, no. 29 (January 1993), pp. 32–33.

16. Mao Zedong, *Selected Works of Mao Tsetung* (Beijing: Foreign Languages Press, 1977), vol. 5, p. 414.

17. Mao Zedong, *Mao Zedong sixiang wansui* (Long live the thought of Mao Zedong), vol. 1 (N.p., 1969), pp. 74–76.

18. Roderick MacFarquhar, Timothy Cheek and Eugene Wu, eds., *The Secret Speeches of Chairman Mao* (Cambridge: Harvard University Press, 1989), pp. 174–175.

19. Liu Shaoqi, *Liu Shaoqi lun gongren yundong* (Liu Shaoqi discusses the labor movement) (Beijing: 1988), p. 434.

20. Joint Publications Research Service, 1957, no. 41889, p. 58.

21. Published by the ACFTU, this journal can be found in a number of research libraries in China.

22. *Zhongguo gongyun* (The Chinese labor movement), no. 2 (1957).

23. *Zhongguo gongyun*, no. 7 (1957). Reprinted in Yan Jiadong and Zhang Liangzhi, eds., *Shehuizhuyi gonghui xuexi wenjian xuanbian* (Compilation of study documents on socialist unions) (Beijing: 1992), pp. 176–183.

24. Taiwan's mainland-watchers were the first to pick up on these press reports. See the useful discussion of labor unrest throughout the 1950s in Qiu Kongyuan, *Zhongguo dalu renmin fangong kangbao yundong* (Anti-Communist protests of the people in mainland China) (Taipei: 1958), pp. 92–101, 165–166.

25. For descriptions of labor unrest in the city of Guangzhou, see *Guangzhou ribao*, May 12, 1957, May 14, 1957, August 20, 1957; and *Nanfang ribao*, May 10, 1957. For a case in Guilin, see *Guangxi ribao*, October 16, 1957. For an example from Hangzhou, see *Hangzhou ribao*, June 26, 1957. For an incident in Chongqing, see *Chongqing ribao*, September 22, 1957. For disputes at mines in Guangdong, Hebei, and Shanxi, see the reports in *Xingdao ribao*, February 16, 1957; *Renmin ribao*, May 9, 1957; and *Zhongguo qingnian bao*, June 2, 1956. For disturbances at cooperatives in Tianjin and Jiangxi, see *Da gong bao*, May 22, 1957. And for a dispute at a Beijing paint factory, see *Da gong bao*, May 9, 1957. Charles Hoffmann, *The Chinese Worker* (Albany: State University of New York Press, 1974), pp. 145–150, offers an informative description—based upon official press reports—of a longshoremen's strike in Guangzhou between November 1956 and April 1957.

26. A translation can be found in *Survey of China Mainland Press*, no. 1536, May 23, 1957, pp. 1–3.

27. Francois Gipouloux, *Les cents fleurs à l'usine: Agitation ouvrière et crise du modèle soviétique en Chine, 1956–1957* (Paris: L'Editions de l'école des hautes études en sciènces sociales, 1986). My review of this useful volume appears in *Journal of Asian Studies* 49 (February 1989), pp. 134–135.

28. Gipouloux, *Les cents fleurs*, pp. 198–202. For Chinese press reports, see *Xinwen ribao*, April 27 and May 13, 1957; *Da gong bao*, April 27 and May 3, 1957.

29. An informative guide to the archives is *Shanghaishi dang'anguan jianming zhinan* (Concise introduction to the Shanghai Municipal Archives, hereafter SMA) (Beijing: 1991). Most of the materials for this chapter were drawn from the "C1" category of Shanghai trade union archives, described on pp. 286–287 of the guide.

30. See especially Roderick MacFarquhar, ed., *The Hundred Flowers Campaign and the Chinese Intellectuals* (New York: Praeger, 1960); and Goldman, *Literary Dissent*.

31. See, for example, Cong Jin, *Quzhe fazhan de suiyue* (The years of tortuous development) (Henan: 1989), pp. 84ff.

32. MacFarquhar, *Origins*, Part 3.

33. Mao, *Mao Zedong sixiang wansui*, pp. 74–79, 87.

34. On the role of workers in earlier "tiger-hunting" campaigns, see Lynn

T. White III, *Policies of Chaos: The Organizational Causes of Violence in China's Cultural Revolution* (Princeton: Princeton University Press, 1989), pp. 67–71.

35. See note 5.

36. Carl Riskin, *China's Political Economy: The Quest for Development Since 1949* (New York: Oxford University Press, 1987), pp. 96–97.

37. SMA, no. B31–1536–1237; no. B31–1–304.

38. Qian Min and Zhang Jinping, "Guanyu 1957 nian Shanghai bufen gongchang naoshi de yanjiu" (A study of the disturbances at some Shanghai factories in 1957), *Shanghai gongyun yanjiu* (February 1990), p. 3. This inform-ative internal-circulation report, based upon archival sources, was published in the aftermath of the 1989 uprising as a reference document for leading cadres in the Shanghai Federation of Trade Unions.

39. On the notions of customary justice that fueled labor protest among the English proletariat, see E.P. Thompson, *The Making of the English Working Class* (London: V. Gollancz, 1963), especially chapters 8 and 9.

40. SMA, no. C1–2–2234.

41. Qian and Zhang "Guanyu 1957 nian," p. 4.

42. SMA, no. C1–2–2272.

43. Ten percent occurred in previously established joint-ownership enter-prises and fewer than 2 percent occurred in state enterprises.

44. SMA, no. C1–1–187; no. C1–2–2407. More than 90 percent of the incidents occurred in these smaller firms.

45. The average annual wage in Shanghai for workers at local state enter-prises (*difang guoying*) was 796 yuan and for workers at central state enterprises (*zhongyang guoying*) was 856 yuan, whereas workers at central joint-ownership enterprises (*zhongyang gongsi heying*) earned an average annual wage of 880 yuan and at local joint-ownership enterprises (*difang gongsi heying*) a whopping 924 yuan (SMA, no. B31–1–304).

46. Among state enterprise workers, 25 percent were illiterate; among joint-ownership workers, the figure was 16 percent (SMA, no. B31–305). Although the cause of the difference in literacy rates is unclear, it may be a function of a higher proportion of (literate) workers from petty bourgeois backgrounds in the smaller firms, contrasted to a larger number of (illiterate) demobilized peasant soldiers in the state enterprises.

47. The cost of living index for workers in Shanghai had shown a steady—but gradual—increase over the preceding years. With 1952 taken as a base of "100," the index rose to 105.76 in 1953, to 106.62 in 1954, to 107.76 in 1955, to 108.15 in 1956, to 109 in 1957. Thus the *rate* of increase had actually tapered off in recent years. See *Shanghai jiefang qianhou wujia ziliao huibian* (Com-pendium of materials on Shanghai prices before and after liberation) (Shanghai: 1958), p. 463.

48. Tiejun Cheng and Mark Selden, "The Construction of Spatial Hierar-chies: China's *Hukou* and *Danwei* Systems," in Timothy Cheek and Tony Saich, eds., *New Perspectives on State Socialism in China* (Armonk, NY: M.E. Sharpe, 1997).

49. SMA, no. C1–1–189.

50. SMA, no. C1–2–2272; no. C1–1–188.

51. SMA, no. C1–1–189.

52. Ibid.

53. For a discussion of demands for a Solidarity-type independent trade union in early 1980s Shanghai, see Chen-chang Chiang, "The Role of Trade Unions in Mainland China," *Issues and Studies*, 26, no. 2 (February 1990), pp. 94–96; Jeanne L. Wilson, " 'The Polish Lesson': China and Poland, 1980–1990," *Studies in Comparative Communism*, nos. 3–4 (Autumn–Winter 1990), pp. 259–280; and Chan, "Revolution or Corporatism?".

54. SMA, no. C1–1–189.

55. Ibid.

56. SMA, no. C1–1–187.

57. Qian and Zhang, "Guanyu 1957 nian," p. 2.

58. SMA, no. C1–2–2407.

59. SMA, no. C1–2–2272.

60. SMA, no. C1–2–2234.

61. SMA, no. C1–1–189.

62. SMA, no. C1–2–2234.

63. SMA, no. C1–2–2271.

64. On the role of activists in Chinese politics, see Richard Solomon, "On Activism and Activists: Maoist Conceptions of Motivation and Political Role Linking State to Society," *China Quarterly*, no. 39 (July–September 1969), pp. 76–114. James R. Townsend, *Political Participation in Communist China* (Berkeley: University of California Press, 1968), p. 132, argues that "the primary distinction to make in analyzing . . . mass participation in any political movement in Communist China, is that between activists and ordinary citizens." Andrew G. Walder, *Communist Neo-Traditionalism: Work and Authority in Chinese Industry* (Berkeley: University of California Press, 1986), p. 166, states that "the distinction between activists and nonactivists . . . is easily the most politically salient social-structural cleavage" in the Communist factory. Wang Shaoguang, "Deng Xiaoping's Reform," takes the political divisions within the working class a step further, arguing for a tripartite schema: "The work force, whether in the state sector or in the collective sector, was largely divided into three categories: activist, middle-of-the-road, and backward element." Susan Shirk, *Competitive Comrades: Career Incentives and Student Strategies in China* (Berkeley: University of California Press, 1982), chapters 3–4, portrays a comparable cleavage among Chinese high school students.

65. A June 27, 1957, report from the Hongkou District union noted that at the fifteen affected enterprises in the district for which there were statistics, 43 percent of the protesters were union, Youth League, or Party members (SMA, no. C1–2–2407). At the Xinguang Underwear Factory, which boasted a long history of labor strife in the pre-Communist period, of the 500 or so workers who participated in the 1957 strike, nearly 100 were Communist Party or Youth League members or other activists. A strike at the Hongwen Paper Factory was instigated by 27 employees, of whom 11 had "political history problems," 5 were Youth League activists, 6 were staff members, and 5 were ex-soldiers (SMA, no. C1–2–2272).

66. SMA, no. C1–2–2272.

67. SMA, no. C1–2–2407.

68. Deborah Davis, "Elimination of Urban Labor Markets: Consequences for the Middle Class," paper presented to the Association for Asian Studies annual meeting, Los Angeles, March 26, 1993.

69. *Xinwen ribao*, April 27 and May 13, 1957; SMA no. C1–1–189.

70. SMA, no. C1–2–2407.

71. SMA, no. C1–1–189.

72. SMA, no. C1–2–2407.

73. SMA, no. C1–2–2272.

74. SMA, no. C1–2–2396.

75. *Renmin ribao*, May 9, 1957. In 1956, Mao Haigen—chair of the trade union at the Shanghai Knitting Factory—was deposed after he revealed serious problems of mismanagement to an ACFTU inspection team.

76. *Gongren ribao*, May 21, 1957.

77. SMA, no. C1–2–2407. In this case, all the Youth League members—except for the League secretary—participated in the struggle.

78. In a few instances, "enemies of the people" were charged with having incited the protests. A strike at the Yiya Electronics Factory was reportedly instigated by a staff member who had received intelligence training in Taiwan before returning to China from Hong Kong in 1953. He is said to have tried to "restore the blue sky" (i.e., raise the flag of the Guomindang) in the course of the protest movement (SMA, no. C1–2–2407). "Counterrevolutionary" slogans were also detected at a few enterprises. On the walls of the bathroom of the China Machine Tool Factory, someone had scribbled in chalk "Down with Chairman Mao!" And on a blackboard at an iron implements factory, someone had written "Down with the Chinese Communist Party!" (SMA, no. C1–2–2234). But such displays of overt hostility to the new regime were rare.

79. See Elizabeth J. Perry, "Labor's Battle for Political Space: Worker Associations in Contemporary China," in Deborah Davis, Richard Kraus, Barry Naughton, and Elizabeth J. Perry, eds., *Urban Spaces in Contemporary China: The Potential for Autonomy and Community in Post-Mao China* (Cambridge: Cambridge University Press, 1995).

80. SMA, no. C1–2–2407.

81. SMA, no. C1–2–2271.

82. Lai Ruoyu, "Dangqian gonghui gongzuo de ruogan zhongyao wenti" (Several important issues in union work at present), reprinted in *Gongyun lilun yanjiu cankao ziliao* (Reference materials on studies of labor movement theory), internal circulation document of the Shanghai Federation of Trade Unions, October 1986, p. 87.

83. Qian and Zhang, "Guanyu 1957 nian," pp. 5–6.

84. Lai Ruoyu, "Zhengdun gonghui de lingdao zuofeng, miqie yu qunzhong de lianxi, chongfen fahui gonghui zai jiejue renmin neibu maodunzhong de tiaojie zuoyong" (Overhaul the unions' leadership work style, intensify relations with the masses, thoroughly develop the mediating role of the unions in resolving contradictions among the people), May 10, 1957, reprinted in Yan and Zhang, eds., *Shehuizhuyi gonghui xuexi wenjian xuanbian*, pp. 191–192.

85. As one manager remarked of the division between young and old, "Young workers are promoted by leaps and bounds while the old ones always remain at the same place under the ironic pretext of promoting their wages. At the time of the Hungarian and Polish incidents, some young workers manifested wavering in their thinking while the old workers maintained a firm standpoint." *Guangming ribao*, May 5, 1957, translated in Roderick MacFarquhar, *The Hundred Flowers Campaign and the Chinese Intellectuals*, pp. 64–65.

86. Lai Ruoyu, "Zhengdun gonghui," p. 194.

87. A useful analysis of stratification within the Shanghai proletariat can be found in Lynn T. White III, *Careers in Shanghai* (Berkeley: University of California Press, 1978), chapter 3.

88. Elizabeth J. Perry, *Shanghai on Strike: The Politics of Chinese Labor* (Stanford: Stanford University Press, 1993).

89. Studies of the *danwei* in urban China include Gail E. Henderson and Myron S. Cohen, *The Chinese Hospital: A Socialist Work Unit* (New Haven: Yale University Press, 1984); Martin King Whyte and William L. Parish, *Urban Life in Contemporary China* (Chicago: University of Chicago Press, 1984); and Xiaobo Lu and Elizabeth J. Perry, eds., *Danwei: The Changing Chinese Workplace in Historical and Comparative Perspective* (Armonk, NY: M.E. Sharpe, 1997).

90. Walder, *Communist Neo-Traditionalism*, pp. 246, 249.

91. In 1957, intellectuals and trade unionists were not the only casualties of the anti-rightist campaign. Large numbers of workers were also imprisoned or packed off to years of labor reform for their involvement in the strike wave. Thanks to a Party directive stipulating that only intellectuals and cadres could be labeled as "rightists," these indicted workers were designated as "bad elements" instead. See Chan, "Revolution or Corporatism?" p. 33.

92. On the difficulties of applying the concept of "civil society" to modern China, see Frederic Wakeman, Jr., "The Civil Society and Public Sphere Debate: Western Reflections on Chinese Political Culture," *Modern China*, 19, no. 2 (April 1993), pp. 108–138.

93. Chan, "Revolution or Corporatism?" p. 37, adopts the appellation of "state corporatism" to characterize a trade union apparatus that could "become an advocate on behalf of the workers, *in addition* to mobilizing labor for production. . . ."

94. See the references in note 64. This is not to deny the utility of such categories for explaining certain aspects of contemporary Chinese political behavior. The peculiar blend of moral rhetoric and self-interested clientelistic manipulation—highlighted by both Shirk and Walder—is indeed a striking feature of those areas of activity most affected by the state's presence. Often, however, it appears that divisions that issued from socioeconomic differences were *rationalized* in political terms. The omnipresence in China of a Manichean political discourse—which portrays conflict at the top of the system as two-line struggle and at the bottom of the system as contradictions between activists and nonactivists—has perhaps skewed the understandings of ordinary Chinese citizens and outside observers alike.

95. Michel Oksenberg, "Occupations and Groups in Chinese Society and the Cultural Revolution," in *The Cultural Revolution: 1967 in Review* (Ann Arbor: Center for Chinese Studies, University of Michigan, 1968), pp. 1–39; Hong Yung Lee, *The Politics of the Chinese Cultural Revolution* (Berkeley: University of California Press, 1978); Stanley Rosen, *Red Guard Factionalism and the Cultural Revolution in Guangzhou (Canton)* (Boulder: Westview, 1982).

96. Interviews with former Shanghai Red Guards, May 25, 1987, July 2, 1987. See also Lynn White III, "Workers' Politics in Shanghai," *Journal of Asian Studies*, 36, no. 1(November 1976), pp. 105–107; and Andrew G. Walder, *Chang*

Ch'un-ch'iao and Shanghai's January Revolution (Ann Arbor: Center for Chinese Studies, University of Michigan, 1978), chapter 6. As Walder, p. 45, points out, "contract and temporary labor . . . formed a large reservoir of radicalized workers and constituted some of the most active and vocal of Shanghai's mass organizations, virtually all of whom were reportedly aligned with the Rebel camp."

97. In other cities, as well, those disenfranchised by socialism proved militant in 1956–57. Shanghai may have experienced an especially high level of protest, thanks to its history of labor unrest, the size and concentrated living and working conditions of its laborers, and the sympathetic attitude of its trade union. But other places (Beijing, Guangzhou, Hangzhou, Tianjin, Jingdezhen, Shanxi, Hebei, Chongqing, Guangxi) also reported a high incidence of protest led by apprentices, temporary workers, and the like. See the citations in note 25 as well as *Renmin ribao*, May 10 and July 15, 1957.

98. See Perry, "Labor's Battle for Political Space."

99. On this point, I take issue with Wang Shaoguang's stimulating analysis of the contemporary Chinese labor movement in which he argues for a newfound horizontal solidarity among the Chinese working class. See his "Deng Xiaoping's Reform."

100. See Foreign Broadcast Information Service, *Daily Report: China*, January 30, 1991, p. 67, for a description of temporary and contract workers turning to " 'regional gangs' which often create disturbances. . . . For instance, fifteen strikes took place in Longgang Town in Shenzhen, with eight of them instigated by Sichuan workers, three by Guangxi workers, two by workers from south of the Chang Jiang, and two by workers from Hunan." The phenomenon of regional gangs serving as the organizational nucleus of labor strikes is highly reminiscent of pre-1949 patterns. Whether such patterns have, however, qualitatively changed as a result of the socialist experience remains to be studied.

101. The classic English-language treatment of this subject is Jean Chesneaux, *The Chinese Labor Movement, 1919–1927* (Stanford: Stanford University Press, 1968).

102. Nym Wales, *The Chinese Labor Movement* (New York: John Day, 1945), p. 11.

103. On the activities of students in these events, see Jeffrey N. Wasserstrom, *Student Protest in Twentieth-Century China: The View from Shanghai* (Stanford: Stanford University Press, 1991).

104. The lack of cooperation was mutual; in fact, relations between workers and students were sometimes overtly hostile. See *Renmin ribao*, August 8, 1957, and *Chengdu ribao*, July 9, 1957, for descriptions of violent encounters between the two groups.

105. Georges Sorel, *Reflections on Violence* (Glencoe, IL: Free Press, 1950), p. 127.

106. Edward Shorter and Charles Tilly, *Strikes in France, 1830–1968* (Cambridge: Cambridge University Press, 1974), pp. 106–107.

107. Gerald Dennis Surh, "Petersburg Workers in 1905: Strikes, Workplace Democracy and the Revolution," Ph.D. dissertation, University of California at Berkeley, 1979.

108. Robert L. Friedheim, *The Seattle General Strike* (Seattle: University of Washington Press, 1964).

109. This point is developed in John R. Low-Beer, *Protest and Participation: The New Working Class in Italy* (Cambridge: Cambridge University Press, 1978).

110. Walder, *Communist Neo-Traditionalism*, pp. 40, 159.

111. As Walder observes, "Long the lynchpin of social and political control in urban China, in mid-May 1989 work units suddenly became centres of political organizing and protest." Andrew G. Walder, "Workers, Managers and the State: The Reform Era and the Political Crisis of 1989," *China Quarterly*, no. 127 (September 1991), p. 487.

112. See Lu Ping, ed., *A Moment of Truth: Workers' Participation in China's 1989 Democracy Movement and the Emergence of Independent Unions* (Hong Kong: Asia Monitor Resource Center, 1990); and Walder and Gong, "Workers in the Tiananmen Protests."

8

Working at Cross-Purposes: Shanghai Labor in the Cultural Revolution

The Cultural Revolution (CR) looms as one of the more important, yet less understood, milestones of the twentieth century. Having built one of the most powerful systems of state domination the world had ever seen, Chairman Mao in 1966 then called upon the masses to "bombard the headquarters"; that is, to attack the party–state apparatus itself. Charging that the party had become increasingly bureaucratized and infested with "capitalist roaders," the chairman invited ordinary people to join him in an assault upon "revisionist" enemies within the Communist Party. In responding to Mao's clarion call, Chinese citizens evidenced a capacity for political improvisation that startled even the most seasoned observers of communist systems, reliant as they had been upon a totalitarian model that downplayed the influence of social forces.[1]

Thanks in part to an explosion of new sources, especially the Red Guard press and refugee interviews, a number of sophisticated analyses of student activism during the CR appeared.[2] Worker participation was also a critical ingredient in the social unrest of this period, but the relative dearth of source materials on labor made it difficult to address this aspect of the CR with anything approaching the degree of refinement attained in studies of the student movement.[3] In this chapter, we strive to remedy the gap by utilizing a variety of heretofore unavailable sources: factory surveys, confidential reports, handbills, public security bureau confessions, and other documents held by the Shanghai Municipal Archives, as well as firsthand interviews with key participants.[4] The result, we hope, is not only to put a more human face on the workers' movement but also to facilitate a more comprehensive analysis of the bases of labor activism. The sources permit us to explore a number of questions: Why were workers motivated to join the Cultural Revolution? What divided the ranks of "rebels," "conservatives," and apolitical members of the work force? Did workers separate along lines of class background, ideological inclination, political networks, or other criteria? And what do such divisions imply about the sources of dissatisfaction and potential for change within the Chinese socialist system?

Scholarly explanations of mass activism during the Cultural Revolution have fallen into three basic camps. The dominant approach, developed by Hong Yung Lee, Stanley Rosen, and others, emphasizes the importance of socially and economically based groups—especially classes, but also age cohorts, skill levels, and the like—in inclining different categories of students and workers to enlist in rival mass organizations.[5] By this account, rebel mass organizations recruited their constituents from those groups with a grudge against the socialist system: people with "bad" class labels, contract and temporary workers, young apprentices, and so forth. Conservative outfits, by contrast, generally comprised those from "good" family backgrounds, older, skilled workers, model workers, and the like. A second interpretation, elaborated by Andrew Walder in particular, stresses the role of political networks in mobilizing workers along competing lines of patronage and allegiance. According to Walder, party-sponsored networks (which cut across other bases of group affiliation) generated much of the strife that gripped Chinese factories during the CR.[6] A third explanation highlights the centrality of psycho-cultural orientation in giving rise to CR factions. As formulated by Lucian Pye and Richard Solomon, it is the extreme psychological dependence of ordinary Chinese upon higher political authorities that produces periodic outbursts of "chaos" (or *luan*), of which the Cultural Revolution was the supreme example. Factionalism was but one expression of a larger psycho-cultural complex.[7]

Although socioeconomic, political, and psycho-cultural approaches have sometimes been posed as competing interpretations, they might better be seen as complementary. Group characteristics, party networks, and personality traits all played a role in shaping the militancy of the day.

Moreover, labor unrest during the CR era was not all of a piece; three distinctive forms can be identified: rebellion, conservatism, and economism. Each of the three types of activism, we suggest, is best explained by a different analytical tradition. While psycho-cultural orientation (albeit a substantially modified version of the Pye–Solomon argument) has much to tell us about the rebel movement, party networks are essential for understanding the conservative reaction. And in explaining the "wind of economism" that swept the Chinese work force in the winter of 1966–67, we seem best served by an emphasis on group characteristics. Let us now examine how each of these varieties of labor protest unfolded in the Shanghai context.

Rebels: The Workers' General Headquarters

The Workers' General Headquarters (WGH), commanded by Wang Hongwen (later designated one of the "Gang of Four"), was an umbrella organization of rebel worker outfits founded on November 9, 1966, whose activities were aimed at toppling party authorities from the factory level right up to the Shanghai Party Committee (SPC). Buttressed by support from Zhang Chunqiao and other members of the "Cultural Revolution Small Group" of radical intellectuals in Beijing, the WGH became a major vehicle for seizing power from the SPC in the January Revolution of 1967 and remained a factor in Shanghai politics (albeit under new names) until the close of the Cultural Revolution decade in 1976.

Chairman Mao's endorsement of the January power seizure encouraged workers to rush to join the rebel ranks, and by late 1967 the WGH was the majority force in most Shanghai factories. Prior to that point, however, rebel groups could claim but a small percentage of the industrial work force. The sudden influx of new members in January 1967 (many of whom had earlier been associated with conservative factions) propelled to top posts within the WGH those who had stood bravely by Wang Hongwen's side from the very start. Known as "old rebels" (*lao zaofan*), these stalwarts became the core leadership of the Workers' General Headquarters.

Who were the "old rebels" and how do we explain their bold challenge to the party authorities? Fortunately we are aided in this inquiry by a comprehensive registration drive conducted by the WGH of all the leaders of its subordinate liaison posts and rebel brigades.[8] The investigation revealed a demographic profile of rebel leaders that was not greatly at variance with the characteristics of the work force as a whole. For example, the overwhelming majority of rebel leaders (both "old rebels" and post-January 1967 recruits) came from "good" class backgrounds. Nearly 88 percent of the "old rebels" (and 85 percent of the rebel leaders as a whole) listed worker, cadre, poor peasant, or urban poor as their inherited class label.

The rebel leadership was fairly young, with more than 55 percent falling into the 26–35 age cohort. Since this was the largest age group in the Shanghai work force, it is not surprising that it generated a substantial proportion of rebels—yet it was represented among the "old rebel" leadership at a rate almost double what we might expect from the age structure of the work force as a whole.[9] In view of the fact that protest movements usually do recruit disproportionately from among the young, however, this statistic is not unexpected.

Most of the "old rebels" had graduated from middle school or high school, giving them a somewhat higher educational standing than the average for Shanghai workers at the time. Whereas nearly half the general work force could claim at best an elementary school education, less than one-fifth of the rebel leaders fell into this poorly educated category. In part no doubt because the CR began as a rather esoteric ideological debate fought out via the medium of big-character posters, it attracted the better educated stratum of the work force.[10]

Perhaps the most interesting finding to emerge from the registration data concerns Communist Party and Youth League affiliation. Although it is often asserted that party and league members were rare among the rebels, this was not actually the case. As Table 8.1 shows, at this time about 12 percent of the Shanghai work force belonged to the Communist Party—a figure that included units like schools and government agencies where party members were especially numerous. If we take factories alone, the percentage drops to under 10 percent.[11] Among "old rebels," however, the proportion of Communist Party and Youth League members was nearly double that of the general work force.

These relatively high levels of party and league membership (together accounting for about one-third of the rebel leaders) suggest that "old rebels" tended to be more politically inclined than the general populace. Yet since few of these rebels had attained cadre or managerial status prior to the CR,[12] we can presume a gap between their ambitions and their achievements. Unlike those who enlisted on the conservative side, rebel workers included a number of party and league activists who had been passed over for higher leadership posts. The CR, with its call to rebel against "unjust" authority, offered a golden opportunity to settle scores.

Table 8.1

Party and League Membership

Type	Members among Shanghai Workforce		Members Among Old Rebel Leaders	
	Number	Percentage	Number	Percentage
Communist Party	186,510	12.1	269	18.2
Communist Youth League	115,425	7.5	196	13.3
Masses	1,237,990	80.4	1,012	68.5
Total	1,539,925	100.0	1,477	100.0

Source: Shanghai gongren geming zaofan zongsilingbu zaofandui zuzhi qingkuang tongji biao (Statistical tables on the rebel organizations of the Shanghai worker revolutionary rebels general headquarters), Workers' General Headquarters edition (Shanghai: November 1967).

The sociopolitical profile of the rebel leaders that emerges from this investigation offers some limited support for the importance of both social groups and political networks. Although class background does not appear to have been a deciding factor, rebel leaders did tend to be younger, better educated, and more politically active than the work force at large. On the other hand, none of these attributes distinguishes them definitively from their conservative rivals.

To appreciate the key distinctions among different types of labor leaders during the Cultural Revolution (rebel, conservative, and economistic), we must move beyond summary statistics to probe individual biographies. The most influential "old rebels" in the early days of the WGH were nine individuals: Wang Hongwen, Wang Xiuzhen, Geng Jinzhang, Pan Guoping, Huang Jinhai, Chen Ada, Ye Changming, Dai Liqing, and Ma Zhenlong. Three were party members; three had been designated as "backward elements" by their work units; and three were ordinary workers prior to the CR. A review of the personal histories of these rebel leaders suggests that neither a focus on group attributes nor an emphasis on political networks can adequately capture their commonalities. (In the interest of space, we will consider here only five of the nine—two party members, two "backward elements," and one ordinary worker.)

The commander of the Workers' General Headquarters, Wang Hongwen, hailed originally from Manchuria. While serving in the military, Wang entered the Communist Party. After five years of military duty, he was demobilized and sent to the Shanghai No. 17 Cotton Mill as a machine operator.[13] Workers who knew Wang Hongwen at the No. 17 Mill remember him as an affable and loyal friend who enjoyed a certain standing among the workers. But he was also said to be afflicted with "office addiction" (*guanyin*)—a longing for political position. Wang was known to have remarked to the master craftsman who taught him his workplace skills: "I don't want to eat skilled rice; I want to eat political rice."[14] His ambition was to escape the ranks of the ordinary workers and serve as a leading cadre.

Wang Hongwen's upward trajectory was not quite as smooth as he apparently anticipated, however. According to an account written by the SPC small group to investigate the Gang of Four,

> In 1958, Wang Hongwen was chosen as party committee member of the day shift in the no. 2 spinning room, but was not made branch party secretary. He believed that he had received the most votes but that higher levels had decided the original branch secretary would continue to serve in that position whereas Wang should remain at his work post. As a consequence, Wang Hongwen frequently refused to participate in branch committee meetings.[15]

Despite this early disappointment, Wang continued to move upward. In March 1960, he was loaned to the factory security department to handle militia work. Not long after, he was formally transferred to the security department as a cadre in charge of militia work for the entire factory. From this point, Wang left behind the "blue-collar" ranks of productive laborer and gained the status of "white-collar" cadre.

Between September 1960 and October 1962, during the terrible famine that followed the Great Leap Forward, Wang Hongwen was sent to Chongming Island to participate in reclamation and flood-prevention work.[16] Despite his position as a party member and a political cadre, he is reported to have been an outspoken critic of the policies of the day:

> In 1960, during the economic retrenchment . . . Wang Hongwen exclaimed, "Damn it! What kind of socialism forces people to go to work on an empty stomach? What kind of policy makes people starve to death?"
>
> Wang Hongwen observed, "My fellow villagers in the Northeast haven't eaten and in Anhui tens of thousands of people have starved. We workers should be working in the factory. What are we doing going to Chongming to reclaim land? In my view the natural calamities were mostly a man-made disaster."[17]

Wang evidently was not an obedient apparatchik—ready to champion whatever policies the party dictated—but a feisty individual willing to think and speak for himself. He read the newspapers carefully so as to stay on top of the latest domestic developments and even listened regularly to forbidden short-wave radio broadcasts to keep abreast of international events.[18] When the CR began, Wang Hongwen was a savvy thirty-one-year-old security cadre who had been working in a factory for nearly a decade. Undoubtedly, his independent spirit contributed to Wang's rebelliousness during the Cultural Revolution.

The beginning of Wang Hongwen's "rebellion" can be dated to June 12, 1966, when he announced his open opposition to the factory authorities by posting a big-character poster at the No. 17 Mill. Wang (and several of his co-workers) accused authorities at his work unit—in particular, Deputy Director Zhang Heming—of failing to grasp class struggle, practicing revisionism, and ignoring mass opinions. The poster went up at 10 A.M. Less than an hour later, the party committee secretary of the company (*gongsi*) in charge of the No. 17 Mill arrived at the factory to convene an emergency meeting. The factory party committee then proceeded to seek out the signatories to Wang Hongwen's poster to admonish them for their insolent act.[19]

In this heated atmosphere, the Textile Bureau dispatched a Cultural Revolution work team to the No. 17 Cotton Mill to direct the ongoing struggle. Wang's "rebel" action received the instant blessing of the work team. But soon this first work team was recalled and replaced by another team sent from the SPC itself and headed by Shanghai Federation of Trade Unions' vice-chair, Shi Huizhen. Shi was an older cadre who had entered the party back in 1938 and had been active in the underground Shanghai labor movement before the founding of the PRC. Shi did not support Wang Hongwen's precipitous attack on the factory deputy director, Zhang Heming; instead, Shi selected the other deputy director, Zhang Yuanqi, as the proper target of criticism.[20]

A conflict between the two Zhangs had developed over who would assume the directorship of the No. 17 Mill. Zhang Yuanqi had relatively little formal education, but substantial work experience. Charged with overall responsibility for security matters at the mill, he had developed a close working relationship with security cadre Wang Hongwen. Like his colleague Wang Hongwen, Zhang Yuanqi was a demobilized soldier from North China. Originally from Shandong Province, he spoke with an accent unintelligible to the southern workers. By contrast, Zhang Heming had been promoted to his cadre position from among the ranks of the workers themselves, spoke with a familiar Ningbo accent, and enjoyed closer relations with the ordinary workers.[21]

Before the CR, Zhang Yuanqi's portfolio at the factory included personnel as well as security matters. Wang Hongwen's support of Zhang Yuanqi apparently stemmed not only from their previous cooperation on security issues, but also from Wang's calculation that Zhang's control of personnel appointments might facilitate his own promotion in the future.[22] In any event, Wang's refusal to denounce Zhang Yuanqi created substantial friction with Shi's work team. The differences surfaced in early August when the No. 17 Cotton Mill made plans to establish a "CR committee" to direct the struggle at the factory. Although the rebel faction among the workers nominated Wang Hongwen to serve as chair of this committee, the work team refused to consider him. At this time the rebels were still a tiny minority at the factory and Wang Hongwen was not chosen.[23] Having been the favorite of the first work team posted at his factory, Wang had come to expect a position of leadership during the Cultural Revolution. Thus when the second work team of Shi Huizhen blocked his appointment, he was bitterly disappointed. Wang admitted on more than one occasion: "In the beginning if I had been permitted to serve as CR chair I would not have rebelled."[24]

In early October, Wang Hongwen put up a second big-character poster attacking the work team at his factory. A few days later, he and his followers founded a rebel group. Unable to prevail at their own factory, the rebels decided to venture north to plead their case directly to Party Central. The next day, Wang Hongwen led fifteen followers off to Beijing.[25] Wang's trip to the capital was a bold move that won him the lasting admiration of other rebels among the Shanghai work force. Prior to his foray, the "exchange of experiences" had been the exclusive prerogative of student Red Guards. Now workers, too, were performing on a national stage. When Wang returned to Shanghai, he was lionized by rebels at nearby factories who invited him to their workplaces to discuss the situation in the capital. Later, WGH activist Huang Jinhai admitted, "I worshiped Wang Hongwen." Thus when Huang Jinhai received a telephone message on November 6 from student Red Guards inviting him to a planning meeting for the founding of an all-city rebel labor organization, he immediately informed Wang Hongwen so that he too could participate. That afternoon, Wang Hongwen led two others from his factory to the historic meeting that would seal his fate as a worker rebel.[26]

Wang Hongwen's story does indeed highlight the significance of competing party networks in structuring the factionalism of the Cultural Revolution era. The long-standing conflict in which Wang's patron, Zhang Yuanqi, was embroiled became Wang Hongwen's battle as well. These networks, moreover, developed at least to some extent out of shared social backgrounds: both Wang and Zhang Yuanqi were demobilized soldiers from North China working on security matters at the mill. However, when we survey the biographies of other rebel leaders it becomes clear that neither political networks nor social characteristics were as important as Wang Hongwen's own restless temperament and frustrated ambition—his longing to "eat political rice" as he put it so aptly—in explaining the urge to rebel.

Geng Jinzhang was a very different sort of party member from Wang Hongwen. Geng had been in the party for longer than any of the other rebel leaders, having joined in 1949. He was also one of the oldest rebels: forty-one years of age at the onset of the Cultural Revolution. But Geng had always been an ordinary worker who never held any managerial position in the factory. His educational level was also extremely low; he was functionally illiterate.

Like Wang Hongwen (as well as Wang Xiuzhen, the third party member among the top WGH leadership), Geng hailed originally from North China. The child of poor peasants in Shandong, he lost his father at the age of six and his mother a year later. At age eight he went to live with his paternal uncle, who could not afford to keep him and put his nephew up for sale. In desperation Geng fled to a nearby temple, pleading to be taken in as a novitiate. When the resident monks refused to accept him, he went off to live with his maternal aunt. At the age of ten Geng began a seven-year term working for a landlord. After his dismissal from that job, he was forced to resort to short-term stints as a hired hand interspersed with periods of begging. In January 1945, Geng enlisted in the Japanese "puppet" forces in his home county of Ningyang. The following year he again entered the military under the command of GMD general Wu Huawen. In 1948 General Wu joined the Communist forces and Geng was incorporated into the PLA. In May 1949, as his battalion was fighting its way south, Geng joined the CCP.[27]

Demobilized in 1957, Geng was assigned a job at the Shanghai Paper Pulp Factory. Ordinarily, a long-standing party member like Geng at the very least would have become a foreman at his factory. Yet he remained an ordinary worker—thanks to a reputation as a womanizer and a troublemaker. While serving in the Japanese military, Geng had been accused of rape and as a PLA soldier had received a stern intraparty warning for illicit sexual relations. Then in 1963, when one of his neighbors inadvertently burned Geng's son with boiling water, Geng delivered a sound thrashing to the neighbor and his wife, ripped their clothing to shreds and destroyed much of their furniture—a transgression for which he was dealt a second party warning.[28]

Later Geng Jinzhang's workmates at the Shanghai Paper Pulp Mill offered the following evaluations of their erstwhile colleague:

> "This person is an uncouth blockhead."
>
> "He often beat up people at the factory."
>
> "He's simpleminded, uneducated, yet ambitious. Because he was never made a foreman at the factory, he wanted to create a stir."
>
> "This guy was always barbarous. He was obsessed by a lust for office. He always wanted to be an official and the CR gave him a chance to rush forth. In the past he had beaten and cursed people."[29]

Like so many of the rebel leaders, Geng Jinzhang's turn to rebellion followed upon the heels of retribution for having posted criticisms of his factory management.[30] These rebel initiatives rendered Geng a natural candidate for inclusion in the Workers' General Headquarters. On November 9, he was resting at home—having worked the middle shift the day before—when a fellow worker from his factory stopped by to say that he had seen a poster announcing the upcoming inauguration of the WGH later that day. The two men ate an early lunch and hastened to the founding ceremonies.[31]

Different as Wang Hongwen and Geng Jinzhang most assuredly were, both (along with Wang Xiuzhen) were members of the Communist Party. This was not the case with the rest of the top rebel leadership, however. After the founding of the WGH, conservative opponents charged that the new rebel organization harbored a surfeit of ruffians, gangsters, and riff-raff. Later Zhang Chunqiao noted that those under greatest suspicion were Pan Guoping, Chen Ada, and Huang Jinhai. We turn now to the latter two individuals.

Huang Jinhai was known colloquially as a "dandy" (*afei fenzi*) because of his penchant for fancy attire. Huang's attraction to fashionable clothing rendered him a conspicuous figure in the drab atmosphere of Maoist China, where simplicity of dress was the near universal norm. At the start of the Cultural Revolution in 1966 Huang was thirty-one years old. Like so many of the rebel leaders, his childhood had been less than idyllic. Within a month after his birth, Huang's mother died of illness. His father was an opium addict who put his children up for adoption. When Huang was only seven or eight, his foster father also died of illness. His foster mother took in laundry and managed to pay for three years of schooling for him. But in 1947, with prices skyrocketing in the postwar environment, she could no longer afford to keep him. Accordingly, Huang was packed off to a shantytown in Shanghai to rejoin his natural father. Living with his still addicted and abusive father, he completed his elementary school education.

In 1952, at the age of seventeen, Huang was assigned to the Shenxin No. 5 Factory (later the No. 31 Cotton Mill) to learn to operate a lathe.[32] At first, Huang Jinhai was diligent in his work and energetic in extra-work pursuits:

> After entering the factory, I applied to join the Youth League. In my spare time, I helped write the blackboard newspaper in my workshop, led the aerobics in step to the broadcast, and later joined the company chorus, dance troupe, and basketball team. I slept at the workers' bachelor dorm. Every week on my day off I worked overtime for no pay. Additionally, I studied at night school three nights a week. My work skills also improved rapidly.[33]

In spite of Huang's success on the job, his opium-addicted father continued to present a problem. To support his drug dependence, Huang's father embezzled public funds—a crime for which he was sentenced to five years in prison. Huang Jinhai recalled, "When I heard this news I was devastated; I felt that I would never be able to cast off this terrible burden."[34] Indeed, his father's impropriety became Huang Jinhai's Achilles' heel in the years ahead, blocking the recognition he felt he deserved. In 1958, Huang and several of his fellow workers discovered a method of reusing discarded parts that resulted in a major savings in time and materials for the factory. However, when their innovation was appropriated by the workshop League secretary to make a name for himself, Huang's efforts at protest proved in vain. His father's unsavory record was an insurmountable obstacle to his own advancement. Robbed of his just due by the dishonesty of his League secretary, Huang sought solace in "dissolute" pursuits:

> I knew that my application to enter the League had been in limbo for many years and now the prospects looked even dimmer. So I became depressed and no longer participated in extra-curricular activities. . . . The more I shouldered my political burden, the more despondent I became. For a time I grew a beard and spent most of my nonworking hours playing cards in the club. On Sundays I went to the suburbs to

fish instead of engaging in proper duties. I even bought a necktie and then went to a shop that sold exotica to buy a used western suit. Sometimes I ventured to the city center in coat and tie. When I saw people wearing leather jackets, I spent more than 40 yuan to buy one. I was totally preoccupied with my playboy lifestyle. My frivolous habits gave the older workers a very bad impression. I organized dances and the like, which the older workers didn't appreciate.[35]

Although we now know that Chairman Mao himself was enjoying dance parties—and more—within the protective walls of Zhongnanhai at this very time,[36] such frivolity was not sanctioned for the populace at large. In any event, family responsibilities eventually revived Huang Jinhai's interest in political activism:

> In 1964, I felt that to continue in this way wasn't right. I already had a child and my personality was undergoing a major change. At that time I studied a copy of Chairman Mao's works and had a conversion. I was a small group leader of my union and I once again actively threw myself into social activities: family visits, political study, technical assistance. In 1965, our group was named a "5-good small group" for the entire factory. I was also named a "5-good worker." I felt that this was the only meaningful kind of existence.[37]

When the CR began, Huang Jinhai plunged into the movement. However, his bold big-character poster elicited a harsh reaction from the party authorities at his factory. Huang's opprobrious family history and his own penchant for flashy apparel made him an easy target for retribution. Fueled by resentment over this counterattack, Huang attached himself to the growing rebel movement. On November 6, he attended the preparatory meeting for the Workers' General Headquarters and was chosen as a member of its leadership group. Soon he joined the first standing committee of the WGH.

Chen Ada was another worker rebel with a somewhat unsavory reputation. Known in Shanghai dialect as *awu* (a dishonest good-for-nothing), he was widely regarded as a petty gangster—prone to profanity and coarse behavior. As a common saying put it during the CR, "wherever there's an armed battle, you'll find Chen Ada."

At the start of the CR, Chen was a twenty-four-year-old blacksmith employed at the Shanghai Valve Factory who had risen above difficult family circumstances. Born into a poor family in rural Shaoxing, Chen's mother worked as a servant and his father as a peddler in Shanghai.

When twelve years of age, Chen broke his leg and his mother—unable to care for him at home—took him to the big city to join his father. At first Chen lived with his father in the "poor people's district" (*pinmin qu*) in the western part of the city. They rented a space to sleep—father and son sharing a bed. In the same room, more than a dozen other sleeping spaces went to other vendors. During the day the peddlers ventured forth to sell their wares; at night they gathered up their stands with nothing but time on their hands. Their chief recreation was to play cards for money and tell crude jokes. Chen Ada lived in this environment for a year. The next year his father brought Ada's younger brother to Shanghai from the countryside. Unable to survive three-to-a-bed, father and sons moved to another "shantytown district" (*penghu qu*) and rented a small room in a hut made of straw and mud. Chen Ada followed the older boys to various disreputable places of recreation (dance halls, ice-skating rinks, and the like) where he learned to speak with bravado and harass girls.[38]

In 1958, as part of the Great Leap Forward, an urban commune was briefly set up in Shanghai. To rid the city of its unproductive residents, petty gangsters and others seen as local troublemakers were rounded up and packed off for labor reform. Many of Chen Ada's friends were seized in this initiative. Chen himself was assigned to the Zhonghua Shipyard that year as a temporary worker. At first he labored as a loader, then as a fitter. At that time, the factory's evaluation of him was quite favorable: "Chen Ada's work style is proper, his life style frugal, his food and clothing economical, and his family background impoverished."[39]

Three years later, Chen joined the army. Upon his discharge, he was assigned to the valve factory. Chen Ada's experiences in the military seem to have exacerbated his earlier wayward tendencies, however. At the valve factory, he did not achieve "activist" status and after work he spent much of his time gambling—an activity that was strictly prohibited at the time.[40] Considered a backward element among the workers, Chen had often been subjected to criticism by the cadres. The Cultural Revolution presented an opportunity to wreak revenge.

Chen Ada was basically uneducated and his early motivations for involvement in the CR did not imply much political sophistication: "As for the bunch of jerks in the factory, I wanted to settle accounts with all of them."[41] The "jerks" (*chilao* in Shanghai dialect) were the factory cadres. It was his participation in the preparatory meeting of the Workers' General Headquarters that propelled Chen Ada to its leadership ranks. On November 6, a rebel worker who happened to pass by the foundry of the valve factory at noontime spotted a large number of big-character posters hanging inside. He decided to go in to make contact with the authors of the posters and inform them about the meeting to be convened that afternoon. Chen Ada happened to be loitering in a corner of the workshop and, hearing about the upcoming get-together, took it upon himself to attend.

Dai Liqing was an unknown ordinary worker—neither activist nor backward element—before the CR. Like so many of the leaders of the worker rebels, Dai came originally from North China. Born into a poor urban family in Shandong, his father had served as a policeman under the GMD. As a youngster in his teens, Dai moved with his family to Shanghai; soon thereafter he began an apprenticeship at a textile mill in the western part of the city. In 1956, Dai was sent to Gansu to help in the building of Lanzhou. Six years later, his father having been hospitalized with a terminal illness, Dai returned to Shanghai. After his father's death, Dai resigned from the factory in Gansu where he had been working to help out at home. Thus began a three-year period of joblessness during which Dai operated first a cigarette stand, then a tea stand, and finally a plumbing and electronics repair stand. In late 1963, his household registration was officially transferred to Shanghai and the following year he began a brief stint at the Shanghai No. 10 Steel Mill as a temporary worker. The next year Dai was introduced by his district labor office to the Jiangnan Metallurgical Factory (later renamed the No. 1 Standard Materials Factory) as an outside contract worker (*wai baogong*). Soon thereafter his classification was changed to that of a temporary worker (*linshi gong*).[42]

Dai Liqing's personal history as well as his status as a temporary worker became grounds for suspicion once the CR began. He was criticized for having returned from the interior during the period of economic difficulties following the Great Leap Forward "because he feared hardship." His efforts at petty entrepreneurship during his years of unemployment were now portrayed as "engaging in speculation and profiteering."[43] Moreover, even the other worker rebels looked down on Dai because he was not a permanent worker. Dai Liqing's troubles were made worse by his own indiscretions. Forced to abandon his wife in Lanzhou when he returned to Shanghai, Dai took up with a young woman apprentice soon after he entered the metallurgical factory. Charges and counter-charges surrounding Dai's peccadillos fueled the unfolding of the Cultural Revolution struggle at his factory:

> An investigator dispatched by the party branch discovered Dai's improper liaison with apprentice Du at his factory. So the branch called

Dai in for a talk, asking him to make a written statement. Dai wrote a self-criticism, but he was quite enraged and felt a deep animosity toward Party Secretary Fu. Later, Dai learned from apprentice Du that although Fu was thirty-seven years old he hadn't yet married and had previously pursued Du himself. This information delighted Dai; in the name of criticizing the bourgeois reactionary line of the party branch, he goaded Du into writing a big-character poster exposing Fu.[44]

Apprentice Du's big-character poster, entitled "My Accusations," galvanized the entire factory and Dai was able to force Secretary Fu to hand over the keys to the party branch office and the archive room (which held the personnel dossiers on all factory employees). But this power seizure was soon repudiated by the district work team. Dai responded by going first to the company, then to the bureau, and finally all the way to Beijing to lodge a complaint.[45]

The capsule biographies of these five individuals offer a revealing view of the tensions brewing within the Chinese socialist system in its first seventeen years of operation. Although the official rhetoric of the Cultural Revolution would portray such contradictions as rooted in class differences, most had a more mundane basis: regional rivalries, personal ambitions, family problems, individual indiscretions, resentment against factory authorities, and the like.

Interestingly, five of the nine top rebel leaders (and four of the seven who remained active after the January Revolution) were northerners. As the situation at Wang Hongwen's No. 17 Mill indicates, regional allegiances could play a significant role in shaping loyalties that later translated into Cultural Revolution factionalism. Cooperation along lines of native-place origin was certainly not a new feature of the Shanghai labor scene (see Chapters 5 and 6). Linguistic affinities and feelings of alienation vis-à-vis the dominant Shanghai culture had long acted to forge a sense of separateness and solidarity among recent arrivals from North China.

Workplace grievances played an important role in triggering rebellion. Sometimes these problems were structural in nature;[46] sometimes (as in Dai Liqing's affair with an apprentice at his factory) they were basically personal. Virtually all of the "old rebels" harbored resentment against their factory leadership for one or another accumulated complaint. But most workers in China, or elsewhere in the world for that matter, routinely encounter a host of workplace disappointments. For these to translate into overt protest requires an additional stimulus.

Like previous campaigns of the PRC, the Cultural Revolution offered an opportunity for heretofore frustrated or obscure workers to rise on the basis of political activism. In contrast to previous campaigns, however, the CR opened the door to criticism of the party authorities themselves. Yet the boundaries of criticism were never entirely clear and the possibilities for retribution ever present. Those willing to hazard the immense risks inherent in confronting party officials were unusually bold individuals.

To understand such personalities seems to call for an excursion into the murky realm of political psychology. The Pye–Solomon approach has been roundly, and rightly, attacked for its caricature of Chinese personality formation.[47] But it would be unfortunate if such criticism were to discourage other investigations into the popular culture of the CR era. Mass violence was a distinctive feature of Mao's Cultural Revolution. Although it is now fashionable to compare the excesses of the CR to the state-sponsored terror of Stalin's USSR or Hitler's Germany,[48] there was a crucial difference: in the case of the CR, social forces were called upon to play a central role. To understand why ordinary citizens accepted Mao's invitation with such alacrity does seem to demand a foray into popular mentalities. While this chapter barely scratches the surface of a still largely unexplored terrain, we will venture a few preliminary thoughts on the psychology of the "old rebels."

The one striking point of commonality among these very diverse rebel leaders was their forceful personalities. A certain audacity was a prerequisite for the high-risk strategy of challenging party committees and work teams. The sources of this boldness were various, but they point to subcultures of opposition that were both more pervasive and more powerful than previous studies have led us to anticipate. Whereas scholarship on the political culture of Communist China has tended to portray it as an essentially static and homogeneous entity, in fact there was significant diversity.[49] The interstices of the dominant Maoist system offered some space for creative resistance. Alien native-place origins, difficult family circumstances, dissident peer groups, and even military service provided breeding grounds for rebel leaders.

For party members strictly disciplined in obedience to higher authorities, outsider status as recent immigrants to the city evidently facilitated a willingness to challenge the powers-that-be. Wang Hongwen, Wang Xiuzhen, and Geng Jinzhang—the three party members among the top nine rebel leaders—all hailed from North China. For party and non–party members alike, arduous family circumstances seem to have helped mold venturesome personalities. Among those from the North, combating poverty was a constant trial. Among southerners, the shame of parental indiscretions (e.g., the opium addiction of Huang Jinhai's father) may have provided a similar challenge. Many of the rebel leaders were demobilized soldiers—individuals whose horizons had been broadened by the opportunities for travel and job mobility that came with military experience. (A number of these ex-soldiers served as militia captains at their factories.) Such personal experiences encouraged some of those who felt disadvantaged by the system to thumb their noses at party authorities. Chen Ada's youthful years in the shantytowns of Shanghai exposed him to the dissolute pursuits of itinerant peddlers as well as the rowdy ways of local toughs. His later penchant for gambling and fighting—which earned Chen the local label of *awu* (dishonest good-for-nothing)—was an outgrowth of these earlier exploits. Playboy Pan Guoping's reputation as a *xiao doulou* (hoodlum) and foppish Huang Jinhai's designation as an *afei fenzi* (dandy) were further signs of the colorful subcultures that bubbled just beneath the drab surface of Maoist China. Although we know very little about such countercultural trends, it seems clear that they helped to arm workers with weapons of resistance.

Despite differences in individual backgrounds and dispositions, we can detect a common "chutzpa" in the eagerness with which all these "old rebels" seized the initiative in denouncing party authorities. Just the opposite would be true in the case of their conservative opponents, for whom networks of party patronage had fostered a play-it-safe strategy of defending party traditions.

Conservatives: The Scarlet Guards

On November 23, 1966—exactly two weeks after the rebels had inaugurated their Workers' General Headquarters—representatives from twenty-three Shanghai factories met to establish an umbrella organization for conservative workers to counter the WGH. The group decided to adopt the historic name of "Scarlet Guards" (*chiwei dui*), the term for armed militia units in the Communist base areas during the 1927–37 period. The next day another group of Shanghai conservatives—the "Workers' Pickets to Defend Mao Zedong Thought"—held an inaugural meeting at a theater in the western part of the city. In designating themselves "Workers' Pickets" (*gongren jiuchadui*), this organization asserted a historical linkage to the Three Workers' Uprisings of 1926–27, when armed unionists had formed pickets to welcome the Northern Expeditionary forces to the city.

On the following day, the Workers' Pickets sent ten representatives to the Scarlet Guards to make inquiries about a possible merger.[50] Satisfied with their mutual interrogation, the two groups decided to unite. Soon they were joined by the "February 7 Warriors," a conservative outfit from the Shanghai Railway Bureau named in commemoration of the famous Communist-inspired strike on the Jinghan Railroad of February 7, 1923. These three groups—all of which had chosen names intended to link themselves explicitly to the historic traditions of the Chinese Communist Party and all of which enjoyed tacit sponsorship by municipal party authorities—comprised the mainstay of a new organization called the "Shanghai General Command Provisional Committee of Scarlet Guards to Defend Mao Zedong Thought." Known colloquially as the Scarlet Guards, the organization was formally inaugurated on December 6.[51]

In contrast to the countless rebel organizations that sprang up across the city, representing differing points of view and rival leadership ambitions, Shanghai's conservative movement exhibited a striking feature: only one conservative organization emerged in each work unit. Virtually all of the leaders of these conservative outfits had been party activists in the years preceding the CR. Influenced by the norm of party unity, conservatives were quick to link up with other organizations that shared their basic political outlook.

If the rebels represented countercultural undercurrents in Maoist China, the conservatives embodied the mainstream reaction. Rank-and-file Scarlet Guards claimed a large representation of pre-CR activists: especially Communist Party and Youth League members, labor models, and advanced producers.[52] But they also included a number of individuals with questionable dossiers for whom enlisting on the conservative side was a calculated attempt to minimize risk. Before Chairman Mao intervened to make clear his preference for the rebel faction, the conservatives grew to rapidly outnumber their rivals in virtually every factory in Shanghai.[53]

Unlike the "old rebels," who initially enjoyed very little backing from higher-level party authorities, the conservative leaders were well plugged into local party networks and could count on substantial behind-the-scenes support for their activities. Even so, there does seem to have been a genuine element of spontaneity in their initiatives. Much of their activism was sparked by a visceral distaste for the personalities and methods of the rebels. Li Jianyu, a Scarlet Guard leader at the No. 31 Cotton Mill, recalled of the earliest rebel leaders at his factory:

> Those who put up big-character posters all belonged to a group of people whose performance (*biaoxian*) was usually pretty poor. Some

of them were not diligent workers who even after the CR didn't change their ways. They were careless and irresponsible. . . . There were also some people who suffered from problems that today we wouldn't consider problematic. For example, if one's father had been a GMD officer it was said that one's family background was bad [*chushen buhao*]. But even by today's standards, many of these people were of shoddy character: adulterers, extortionists, embezzlers—people who would be shunned in any era.

So at that time I was really dismayed. I felt that these people's basic character was bad and yet here they were, issuing commands and criticisms of the SPC. Their own ass wasn't clean but they were collecting "black materials" on others. Today they would attack this factory cadre; tomorrow they would attack that party committee member. Whenever they got off work they went wild.[54]

Or as Ma Ji, Scarlet Guard commander at the No. 17 Cotton Mill, reported:

I didn't oppose the idea of criticizing the leadership since the CR was calling on everybody to rise up and criticize. But I did oppose the idea of doubting everything and destroying everything. . . . Wang Hongwen and his followers took quotations from Chairman Mao that had been meant for criticism of landlords and used them against cadres and party members. I couldn't stand that. . . . Thus as soon as Wang established his "Forever Loyal" group, we established our "Warriors to Defend Mao Zedong Thought" to counter Wang and his followers. When Wang Hongwen seized the materials of the work team, we protected them. We believed that since the work team had been sent by the party, it wasn't right to wantonly criticize them.[55]

The conservatives formed as an indignant reaction against what they perceived as rebel excesses. Consequently they were especially numerous in those industrial sectors that had suffered the most deleterious effects of rebel initiatives and in those factories where rebel outfits were most militant.[56]

To a person, the top Scarlet Guard leaders were trusted party members—serving as political cadres at their factories—whose promotions from the ranks of ordinary workers had come as a reward for active participation in previous party-sponsored campaigns. Although they were lower staff (*ganshi*) paid according to the wage scale for regular workers, they enjoyed close relations with leading cadres and they wielded some discretionary power over the other workers.

Take the case of Ma Ji, a cadre in the security department of the No. 17 Cotton Mill who rose to the challenge of countering Wang Hongwen. Thirty-three years of age at the outset of the Cultural Revolution, Ma Ji had been born into an impoverished Shanghai family. His father worked at a beancurd shop while his mother gave birth to ten children of whom only Ma Ji and a younger brother survived. Ma began factory work at age seventeen as an apprentice. He studied at night school where after 1949 he joined the Communist Youth League and chaired the student association. During the February 6, 1950, bombing of Shanghai, Ma participated in rescue teams, gaining a reputation as an activist. Soon he was assigned to the Yufeng Spinning Mill, the precursor of the No. 17 Cotton Mill. Initially he worked as an oiler and then as an accountant. At the same time, Ma Ji continued to build his political credentials, advancing from secretary of the Youth League branch in his workshop to the factory Youth League committee. After joining the Communist Party, he was made party secretary of his workshop. In 1955 Ma's factory sent him to a cadre school for training. Upon his return, he requested a transfer to the factory security department. There he took an active part in the anti-rightist campaign and remained involved in the supervision of cadres until the start of the Cultural Revolution.[57]

Li Jianyu, Scarlet Guard opponent of rebel Huang Jinhai at the No. 31 Cotton Mill, had entered the mill in the last group of managerial trainees (*lianxisheng*). After completing the initial training period, Li became an accountant in the dye room. Like Ma Ji, he was sent away for special education at the expense of his factory. In March 1957 Li was dispatched to a cadre school of the East China Textile Bureau (later renamed the Shanghai Textile Bureau) for further training in statistics. In 1958 when Chairman Mao called on urban cadres to go down to the rural villages, Li went with other members of his factory party committee to an agricultural cooperative in the suburbs of Shanghai. After half a year in the countryside, he enlisted in the military and was sent to the No. 2 Aviation Institute in Qingdao (Shandong) to study mechanics. Half a year later, Li was retained at the Institute as a district captain (*qu duizhang*). In December 1962, he joined the Communist Party. Demobilized the following year, Li returned to his original factory as a cadre in the party committee's Organization Department. In the latter half of 1964, as the Socialist Education Movement turned into the Four-Cleans campaign, Li was assigned to a Four-Cleans work team at the Textile Bureau.[58]

The Scarlet Guard commanders were all basic-level cadres (*jiceng ganbu*) charged with serving as links between the party and the ordinary masses. As such, they wielded considerable power over the rank-and-file workers. Ma Ji, as secretary in charge of security, had the authority to detain for interrogation any suspicious worker. Li Jianyu, as secretary of the Organization Department, was in a position to investigate the personal, family, and political conditions of cadres as well as workers. Because many cadres became targets of struggle during the Cultural Revolution, basic-level Scarlet Guard organizations often explicitly excluded from recruitment cadres above the level of department chief (*kezhang*) and even lower staff (*ganshi*) who were not on the ordinary workers' pay scale.[59] This precaution was taken in order to avoid being upstaged by rebels who accused them of "loyalist" tendencies. Had such limitations not been imposed, the proportion of cadres among the Scarlet Guard ranks would have been even higher. The conservatives insisted that their organizations were independently established entities, rather than an artifact of higher-level cadre manipulation. Even so, gaining the approval of higher authorities was considered a crucial step. Li Jianyu recalled,

> The establishment of the Scarlet Guards at our factory was our own idea. The rebels had their organization. Without our own organization we had no power to constrain or challenge them. The party committee and the municipal committee were in favor of our establishing an organization. They didn't directly instruct us, but they did give us covert encouragement.[60]

The formation of the February 7 Warriors, precursor to the Scarlet Guards at the Shanghai Railway Bureau, illustrates the general pattern. The Warriors were founded during the Anting Incident as a reaction against the disruption in rail traffic. When the deputy director of the control room, Wang Yuxi (who was on duty at the time of the Anting Incident), suggested making a public appeal to the citizens of Shanghai to put a stop to the rebels' actions, the majority of workers in the control room applauded his proposal. One worker penned a supportive handbill on the spot. Thus far the process was spontaneous. But Wang Yuxi, as an obedient party man, quickly sought out the director of the political department and the party secretary of the railway bureau as well as the vice-mayor of Shanghai in charge of transportation. Only after all these officials had indicated their approval did Wang proceed to formally establish the February 7 Warriors and distribute handbills in the name of the new organization.[61]

Once the Scarlet Guards were formed, the Shanghai Party Committee provided substantial material assistance. A deputy sent to make contact with the fledgling conservative organization later remembered,

> The SPC wanted the Shanghai Federation of Trade Unions [SFTU] to contact the Scarlet Guards so the higher levels sent me as a liaison officer. When I asked how to handle the Scarlet Guards' finances, Zhang Qi [member of the SPC standing committee and chair of the SFTU] said meaningfully, "The union has so much money, now is the time to use a little." And within ten days we had provided 125,000 armbands for the Scarlet Guards.
>
> After the Scarlet Guards emerged, they were greatly praised by cadres at all levels who provided covert and overt support, helping them with tactical planning and offering all sorts of material assistance. Some factory-level unions, following the lead of the SFTU, also provided offices for the Scarlet Guards.[62]

Former Scarlet Guard Jin Ruizhang acknowledged that the SPC was a source of significant aid:

> The day after Mayor Cao Diqiu approved the formation of the Scarlet Guards, he arranged for us to have an office in the SFTU. Immediately we were allocated pens and paper, typewriters, printing presses, bicycles, and many other supplies. Later we also used the jeeps of the SFTU to procure fifty bolts of red cloth and commissioned six workers to sew Scarlet Guard armbands.[63]

Scarlet Guard commander Wang Yuxi had a similar recollection concerning the SPC's interest in his organization's activities:

> Over the space of five months they sent five liaison officers to us, to help us with strategy and tactics, to assist us with "manifestos," to revise our proclamations and some criticism materials.[64]

Just as higher-level sponsorship was helpful in launching the Scarlet Guards, so the withdrawal of such support signaled the imminent demise of the conservative movement. When Chairman Mao on January 11 instructed Party Central, the State Council, the Military Affairs Committee, and the Cultural Revolution Small Group to send a joint congratulatory telegram to Wang Hongwen's WGH—recognizing it as the sole legitimate representative of the Shanghai working class—the conservatives lost any semblance of credibility. Thanks to a decision by Wang Hongwen to welcome former conservatives to his rebel organization, most Scarlet Guards hastily jumped ship to the side of their erstwhile enemies. Wang's policy of reconciliation spelled the organizational destruction of the conservatives and spared Shanghai the sort of bloody factional fighting that wracked many other parts of the country.

The Wind of Economism

In the winter of 1966–67, a new type of labor association—neither rebel nor conservative in orientation—appeared on the Cultural Revolution scene. Dubbed "economistic" because of their relative disinterest in the political debates of the day, these organizations were not centrally concerned with the issue of attacking or defending party leaders. Their focus was directed instead on improving their own material lot. We have records of 354 such organizations in Shanghai alone.[65] The earliest type of economistic organization was comprised of temporary workers (*linshi gong*), contract workers (*hetong gong*), and outside contract laborers (*waibao gong*). Use of temporary and contract labor had functioned as a standard means of supplementing the work force since 1949. During the economic recovery of the early 1960s, state chairman Liu Shaoqi advocated expanding the temporary and contract system so that labor might be allocated more flexibly. The system had obvious advantages for the Chinese state, in terms of both efficiency and cost. Unlike permanent workers, temporary and contract laborers were employed on an ad hoc basis and received no lifetime securities, pensions, disability coverage, health insurance for their dependents, and so forth. Often they were paid not by the month, but by the day or by piecework rates.

The cries of these downtrodden members of the Chinese work force introduced a socioeconomic note to the otherwise relentlessly political discourse of the Cultural Revolution. As an eyewitness to the inaugural ceremonies of the Workers' General Headquarters remembered the distinctive contribution of the temporary workers to the convocation,

> Those up on the platform were criticizing the capitalist reactionary line of the SPC, but down below the platform were a group of women workers between thirty and forty years of age wearing tattered work clothes and hats. These women didn't look like factory workers, but like temporary workers who pulled carts. They weren't paying any attention to the speeches on the platform, but periodically shouted out "We want to become permanent workers!" "We want a pay raise!"

The exact nature of the relationship between organizations of temporary and contract workers and the WGH remains obscure. The largest and most influential such organization in Shanghai—with branches in other cities as well—was the "Revolutionary Rebel General Headquarters of Red Workers," known colloquially simply as the "Red Workers" (*hongse gongren*). It was widely rumored that Wang Hongwen's wife had joined the Red Workers and that Wang's own lack of enthusiasm for opposing economism was related to his wife's protest activities.[66]

A second type of economistic organization was composed of employees who had been mobilized to return to their native places as a result of the retrenchment campaign of the early 1960s. The largest of this type of organization was the "Revolutionary Rebel General Headquarters of Shanghai Workers Supporting Agriculture who Returned to Shanghai," known colloquially as "Support Agriculture Headquarters" (*zhinong si*). Their chief slogans were: "We want to return to work!" "We want to eat!"[67]

In 1960–62, during the severe economic crisis after the Great Leap Forward, many factories had been forced to halt or severely curtail production. In view of the surplus labor problem, the government had asked overstaffed urban factories to relocate those workers who had relatives back in the countryside or other means of resettling outside the city. This was a kind of mass layoff, with the implicit promise that as soon as the national economy improved most of the repatriated workers would have first option on returning to their old jobs.[68] After 1963, the Chinese economy began to improve. However, the demographic explosion put pressure on urban employment that made it impossible for factories to make good on their previous promise to reinstate repatriated workers. The resentment of displaced workers was heightened when they discovered that the city of Shanghai had taken liberties with central guidelines in implementing the layoffs in the first place. In an apparent attempt to save money, Shanghai had violated central policy by targeting more experienced workers (who of course garnered higher paychecks) for the relocation effort.[69]

Now these repatriated workers were converging on Shanghai from every direction, involving cadres at all levels in their demand to return to the city. According to a report of the Shanghai Labor and Wage Committee on December 15, 1966:

> The repatriated workers have established two rebel commands and have raised demands for being made permanent workers, changing the method of income allocation, and improving work benefits. We have

learned that a "revolutionary committee of repatriated employees" with more than 10,000 registered members has been established in Wuxi [Jiangsu] and has disseminated numerous handbills. They are requesting either a return to work or an official retirement settlement. At present a number of other places have also seen groups of repatriated employees demanding an immediate return to Shanghai.[70]

A third type of economistic organization was made up of workers helping out with construction in the interior. As the premier industrial city in China, Shanghai for many years had sent a large number of people to assist with development projects in other parts of the country. In some cases, whole factories had been relocated to the interior. Some of these assistance programs were carried out according to central directives, while others were direct transfers from Shanghai to the interior. Quite a few of the relocated workers were apprentices in the middle of their training periods. After the Cultural Revolution began, many of them rushed back to Shanghai to protest the disruption in their training schedule and demand immediate reassignment to their old jobs.[71]

A fourth type of economistic organization was comprised of young people who had been relocated in the "up to the mountains down to the countryside" and "support agriculture, support the frontiers" campaigns of the 1960s. To reduce the unemployment problem, Shanghai had mobilized a large number of "social youths" (*shehui qingnian*) who were unemployed or just graduated from middle school to go down to the suburbs of Shanghai or to more distant locales to work on state farms. During the Cultural Revolution these workers also took advantage of the general disruption to hurry home. As a report of February 1967 indicated:

> At present, the great majority of intellectual youths sent to neighboring state farms as well as some of those sent to the military farms in Xinjiang have already returned to Shanghai. They claim that "mobilizing city youths to go up to the mountains and down to the countryside to support agriculture and support the frontiers is a giant plot." They demand to return to Shanghai and reclaim their household registrations.[72]

Yet a fifth type of economistic organization—and one that quickly succumbed to repression by the Public Security Bureau—was formed by private entrepreneurs. The city's largest such association, the "Shanghai Private Entrepreneur Laborers' Revolutionary Rebel Headquarters," was deemed "capitalist and antirevolutionary" and its leaders apprehended by the authorities. As a rebel handbill reported unsympathetically on its operations,

> This organization was founded in December 1966. In addition to a general headquarters, it established branches in ten districts and four counties. To entice recruits, it promised that "those who join our organization in the future can enter state enterprises with labor insurance, permanent jobs, and old age welfare and disability."
>
> Its members claimed that in seventeen years of liberation the working people have "turned over" and become masters, but the private entrepreneurs are still oppressed by the powerholders. More than thirty criticism sessions were held in every district to attack the taxation policy. They charged that three big mountains rest on the heads of the peddlers: the taxation bureau, the industrial-commercial department, and the market management office.
>
> In the name of striving for a state enterprise, they engaged in economism. They demanded that "private merchants and peddlers must be state employees" and they rejected the current system of cooperatives.
>
> They even hoped to seize power from the Shanghai Industrial and Commercial Administrative Management Bureau and the industrial-commercial bureaus in each district. As a result, they were chased out by the rebel faction at these units.[73]

Although the private entrepreneurs appear to have been better organized than other "economistic" groups, their association with capitalist tendencies rendered them an easy target for repression.

The "wind of economism" first gained momentum among those who lacked secure jobs or household registrations in Shanghai.[74] Denied the privileges that came with permanent employment at state enterprises or fixed residency in a major city, the have-nots demanded access. But even those more favored by the system were not entirely free from dissatisfactions; eventually they, too, raised materialistic demands. Indeed, the wind of economism can be read as a kind of weather vane indicating the levels of deprivation among the Shanghai work force, shifting direction over time from the most disadvantaged elements toward more privileged sectors: from contract and temporary workers to repatriated workers to apprentices, and finally to permanent state employees with Shanghai residency.

Apprentices, who occupied a kind of intermediate position on the employment roster (promised permanent employment and secure benefits in the future yet still laboring under harsh treatment), were instrumental in redirecting the wind of economism from the streets into the factories. As the Shanghai Revolutionary Committee noted in its chronology published in March 1967:

> On December 27, 1966, some apprentices in the ninth district of the Port Authority, while searching for black materials, discovered documents concerning the official wage scale for apprentices. Realizing that their wages did not match what was stipulated in the documents, they went to the district bureau to demand a supplement. Li Guang, party secretary of the Maritime Transport Bureau of the northern district, agreed to issue a year's wages as recompense.[75]

News of the apprentices' success spread like wildfire and soon not a single enterprise in the city was unaffected by monetary requests from its workers. Insisting that previous wage hikes had not kept pace with official directives, employees demanded subsidies to compensate for years of substandard treatment. Even newly hired workers rushed forward to press wage claims; for example, a group known as the "58 Regiment"—the membership of which was primarily young workers who had entered the factories in 1958—insisted that new hires had been subjected to wage discrimination for which restitution was due.[76]

Another strategy for raising wages was to change the ownership form of an enterprise, thereby altering the employees' status. In a number of instances insistent workers convinced SPC secretary and vice-secretary Chen Pixian and Cao Diqiu to sign agreements that converted formerly private and collective enterprises into new state-owned units. A group known as the "Elementary Teachers' Headquarters," claiming at its height some 30,000 members, was established to demand that private schools be redesignated as publicly owned institutions.[77] In the case of one privately run elementary school, the conversion to state ownership resulted in a 70 percent wage increase for teachers.[78]

Wages constituted only a fraction of an urban employee's total income—much of which was in the form of subsidies. Workers at state enterprises received cash allowances for transportation, baths, meals, nutritional supplements, uniforms, towels, soap, shoes, gloves, and the like. The "wind of economism" stirred up a concern over subsidies that was almost as feverish as that over wages. In some cases, workers at collective enterprises demanded treatment equivalent to that enjoyed by workers at state enterprises; in other cases, workers at state enterprises asked for the restoration of benefits that had been lost during the economic troubles of 1960–62.

Along with wage and subsidy increases, workers raised a demand for various Cultural Revolution "living expenses." Fees to exchange revolutionary experiences, spread propaganda, produce armbands, purchase broadcasting equipment, procure vehicles for transportation, and so forth were demanded.[79] A particularly costly manifestation of the economistic wind was a call to divide up various pots of money—such as union operating expenses, year-end production accumulation funds, shares of coops, and so forth. In Yimiao District, one cooperative disbursed the entire 50,000 yuan it had accumulated since 1963; similarly, the Huaihai Weaving Factory completely divided up its union's 16,000-yuan cash surplus account.[80]

In addition to claims for monetary compensation—whether in the form of higher wages, subsidies, Cultural Revolution expenses, or shares of accumulated funds—workers demanded the right to unionize. Behind the quest for unionization lay a desire for medical benefits and welfare provisions (*laobao*, or labor insurance) accessible only to union members. China's trade union regulations stipulated that neither private entrepreneurs nor workers at collective enterprises were eligible to join unions. This meant that such people were denied the medical and retirement benefits obtainable only through union membership. In late August of 1966, hundreds of workers from street factories, private schools, local hospitals, and trade, government, and construction industries marched with cymbals and drums to the SFTU to demand unions.[81] But soon the federation of trade unions itself came under attack as part of the Cultural Revolution assault on bureaucratism, rendering unionization an infeasible option.

One of the more violent manifestations of the economistic wind was the seizure and occupation of housing. Population pressure had created a severe housing shortage in the city. The Cultural Revolution offered a convenient opportunity to appropriate housing in the name of "rebellion." Acts of confiscation were carried out by individuals or groups of individuals, but usually in the name of the rebel faction at their work unit. Under the pretext of expelling "capitalist roaders," "four pests," and "reactionary authorities," workers took possession of housing that they coveted for themselves and their families. In the space of five days between December 30, 1966, and January 3, 1967, "all the housing in the city that was awaiting allocation was forcibly occupied."[82]

After the "wind of economism" spread from the streets into the factories, the basic ranks of rebel and conservative workers alike became especially vociferous in pressing materialistic demands. Some of the rebels were affiliated with Wang Hongwen's Workers' General Headquarters, others with splinter groups like the Second Regiment or the Workers' Third Headquarters. As far as we can determine, however, the rebel organizations themselves did not raise economistic demands—aside from asking for subventions of expenses associated with Cultural Revolution activities. Their handbills indicate that their actions as well as their slogans were "political" attacks on powerholders, rather than "economistic" requests for increased income. Thus although rank-and-file rebels were deeply involved with economistic activities (which Wang Hongwen initially refused to condemn), organizationally the rebel forces were relatively free of such entanglements. As a consequence, when Party Central issued a directive opposing the economistic wind, the WGH was quick to place the blame entirely on the shoulders of those cadres whom its ordinary followers had forced into signing disbursement agreements—charging that these cadres had used money to corrupt the rebel ranks. The alleged criminality of the cadres in fanning the winds of economism became a pretext for the rebel seizure of power from the Shanghai Party Committee.

Conclusion

Important as social forces were in the unfolding of the Cultural Revolution, they pulled in contrary directions. Within the working class of Shanghai, we have identified three distinctive tendencies. Rebels challenged party authorities and conservatives defended them while economistic groups clamored for material improvements. Labor was working at cross-purposes: rebellion, conservatism, and economism were promoted by different sorts of leaders acting on the basis of dissimilar motivations. These distinctions, we suggest, are best captured by different analytical traditions.

The socioeconomic approach stresses the influence of favored versus disfavored backgrounds in generating a kind of "interest group" behavior that translated into rebel and conservative factionalism during the CR. Hong Yung Lee concludes that the rebel mass organizations recruited mainly among groups with grievances against the establishment: "among the workers, they were those from the smaller, poorer factories, the contract and temporary workers, the apprentices and unskilled workers in the larger factories, and the individual laborers."[83] This is an accurate characterization of workers who were active in the wind of economism. Although previous scholarship has erred in conflating economism with the rebel movement, the materialistic upsurge is indeed well explained by a socioeconomic approach. Economism was in essence a protest against the inequities of the command economy. Groups of workers criticized the administrative methods that arbitrarily divided them into different categories with differential access to benefits. Those least favored by the system—contract and temporary workers, relocated workers, apprentices, collective and private sector employees—raised the most strident complaints. The wind of economism pointed the finger of blame at the many flagrant injustices inherent in the operations of China's socialist system. In this respect, economism presented a more fundamental criticism than did the rebel movement.

Rebel leaders, like their conservative opponents, were playing a political game whose rules had been laid down by higher levels. As was true in previous campaigns, the rewards of the game remained the promise of political office—yet the rules of the game changed dramatically during the CR. Uncertainties over proper targets of struggle permitted those outside or on the edges of established party networks to seize the initiative in a manner unthinkable in earlier political campaigns.

Unlike those who participated most vocally in the wind of economism, the "old rebels" are not easily explained in terms of group analysis; some were party members, others ordinary workers, and yet others were considered "backward elements." Those who rose to challenge the mandate of party committees and work teams were audacious individuals whose feisty personalities had often been born out of difficult family circumstances and nurtured in rowdy subcultures that operated on the margins of orthodox party life. Northern origins, shantytown childhoods, and youth gangs all seem to have played a role in fostering rebel leadership. Unfortunately, we know very little about such dissonant currents in Communist China.[84] But it is certainly clear—Pye and Solomon notwithstanding—that not all Chinese exhibited a "dependent" orientation in the face of higher authority.[85] Even one of Wang Hongwen's most faithful rebel colleagues, a party member himself, criticized many of the other rebel leaders for their unrestrained temperaments:

> Wang Hongwen never forgot those who rose in rebellion with him and was always looking out for them. . . . However, I couldn't stand those other WGH leaders like Huang Jinhai, Chen Ada, or Dai Liqing. They were rascals. We were after all party members and were used to strict demands on ourselves. During the CR I never could get along with those other people.[86]

If a rebel could express such distaste for his fellow rebel leaders, we can appreciate the feelings of revulsion that gripped those on the conservative side. The disgust with which conservative leaders regarded their radical adversaries reflected the cultural gulf that distanced the persons and actions of the rebels from accepted party practice.

While rebels and conservatives were both embroiled in a high-stakes political contest, conservatives drew upon the resources of established party–state networks in mounting their offensive. As Andrew Walder has noted, "the party reaches out to the citizenry through constantly cultivated patronage relationships, in which active support and loyalty are exchanged for mobility opportunities, material advantages, and social status."[87] Although rebel condemnation forced the conservative Scarlet Guards to disavow any intimate connection to higher-level patrons, party backers did in fact play a crucial role in promoting their activities.

Such political networks are sometimes seen as having been created de novo by the Communist state during the 1950s, but they had important roots in the pre-1949 Communist labor movement—as the conservatives' preference for historical nomenclature borrowed from the revolutionary struggles of the past suggested. At the start of the Cultural Revolution, the Shanghai Party Committee and the Shanghai Federation of Trade Unions were replete with old cadres from the Jiangnan region who had been active in the pre-1949 labor movement. Both SFTU vice-chair Shi Huizhen (who led the work team that condemned the rebellion of Wang Hongwen at the no. 17 mill), and SFTU chair Zhang Qi (who authorized the provision of material aid to the Scarlet Guards) were former activists in the underground Shanghai labor movement whose initiatives during the CR offered clear encouragement to the conservative forces. Long accustomed to a modus operandi that favored reliance upon fellow party loyalists from Jiangnan, they continued this familiar tactic during the early months of the CR. Had Chairman Mao not intervened to indicate his personal support for the rebels' assault on established party networks in Shanghai, the Scarlet Guards would undoubtedly have emerged victorious.

Mao's preference for the rebel challengers unleashed many of the disruptive consequences of the Cultural Revolution decade. Eventually party networks in work units were re-established, but not without a marked deterioration in discipline. The irreverent style of the rebels was fertile soil for the growth of a general disrespect for party authority—with serious implications for the future of Chinese politics.[88]

The variety of ways in which workers responded to the Cultural Revolution cautions against too facile a portrait of working-class politics in

Maoist China. As we saw in Chapter 7, the Communist work unit (*danwei*) induced not only dependency, but also defiance. During the CR, this defiance was directed both toward individual workplace authorities (on the part of the rebels) and toward structural features of the system itself (when those most disprivileged by the *danwei* system demanded a redress of grievances during the "wind of economism").

In part because of source limitations and in part because of the prevailing image of Chinese workers as basically quiescent, studies of protest in the PRC until recently have focused almost exclusively upon students and intellectuals. This is the case not only for the Cultural Revolution, but for the Hundred Flowers Campaign, Democracy Wall, and the Tianamen incidents of 1976 and 1989 as well. Increasingly, however, we are discovering that workers played a significant role in all these movements. Indeed, one might well propose that the heavy-handed manner in which each of these upsurges was eventually suppressed was due above all to the Beijing regime's deep-seated anxieties about a restive work force. Moreover, as Poland's Solidarity dramatically demonstrated and as new theories of democratization underscore, the Chinese leadership was hardly being irrational in harboring such fears. In the industrial age, regime transitions are often closely associated with labor movements.[89]

Upcoming transformations of the Chinese polity will surely bear more than a casual relationship to worker unrest. And yet, as in the past, labor activists are likely to continue to work at cross-purposes. Only by uncovering the divergent political, psycho-cultural, and socioeconomic strains within the Chinese labor movement can we hope for a reliable guide to its future bearings.

Notes

This chapter appeared originally in Kenneth G. Lieberthal, ed., *Constructing China: The Interaction of Culture and Economics* (Ann Arbor: Center for Chinese Studies, University of Michigan, 1997). It was co-authored with Li Xun.

1. For a discussion of this interpretive change, see Franz Schurmann, *Ideology and Organization in Communist China* (Berkeley: University of California Press, 1968): vii, 504.

2. See especially Hong Yung Lee, *The Politics of the Chinese Cultural Revolution: A Case Study* (Berkeley: University of California Press, 1978); Anita Chan, Stanley Rosen, and Jonathan Unger, "Students and Class Warfare: The Social Roots of the Red Guard Conflict in Guangzhou (Canton)," *China Quarterly*, no. 83 (September 1980): 397–446; Stanley Rosen, *Red Guard Factionalism and the Cultural Revolution in Guangzhou (Canton)* (Boulder: Westview Press, 1982).

3. Pioneering studies of labor in Shanghai include Lynn T. White, III, "Workers' Politics in Shanghai," *Journal of Asian Studies* 36, no. 1 (1976): 99–116; Andrew G. Walder, *Chang Ch'un-ch'iao and Shanghai's January Revolution* (Ann Arbor: Center for Chinese Studies, University of Michigan, 1978); and Raymond F. Wylie, "Shanghai Dockers in the Cultural Revolution," in Christopher Howe, ed., *Shanghai: Revolution and Development in an Asian Metropolis* (Cambridge: Cambridge University Press, 1981): 91–124.

4. This paper is drawn from a co-authored book. The sources we rely upon for both this paper and the book have their own limitations, of course. For one thing, our study is restricted to the case of Shanghai. Although Shanghai was undoubtedly the most important center of worker activism during the Cultural Revolution, it was also atypical in a number of respects. The close links between worker rebels in Shanghai and top leaders in Beijing and the relatively nonviolent character of factional strife in Shanghai both distinguish the Shanghai experience from the situation in other Chinese cities.

5. See the sources cited in note 2. On the importance of class categories in Communist China, see especially Richard Kraus, *Class Conflict in Chinese Socialism* (New York: Columbia University Press, 1981).

6. Andrew G. Walder, *Communist Neo-Traditionalism: Work and Authority in Chinese Industry* (Berkeley: University of California Press, 1986); and "The Chinese Cultural Revolution in the Factories: Party-State Structures and Patterns of Conflict," in Elizabeth J. Perry, ed., *Putting Class in Its Place: Worker Identities in East Asia* (Berkeley: Institute of East Asian Studies, University of California, 1996).

7. Lucian W. Pye, *The Dynamics of Chinese Politics* (Cambridge, MA: Oelgeschlager, Gunn and Hain, 1981). For earlier discussions of the role of political culture in the Cultural Revolution, see Pye's *The Spirit of Chinese Politics: A Psychocultural Study of the Authority Crisis in Political Development* (Cambridge, MA: MIT Press, 1968); and Richard H. Solomon, *Mao's Revolution and the Chinese Political Culture* (Berkeley: University of California Press, 1971). See also Alan P.L. Liu, *Political Culture and Group Conflict in Communist China* (Santa Barbara: Clio Press, 1976); Anita Chan, *Children of Mao: Personality Development and Political Activism in the Red Guard Generation* (Seattle: University of Washington Press, 1985); and Lowell Dittmer, "Political Culture and Political Symbolism," *World Politics* 29, no. 4 (July 1977): 552–584; and his *China's Continuous Revolution* (Berkeley: University of California Press, 1987), esp. chapter 4.

8. Surveyed units included the 20 municipal bureaus and their subordinate companies and factories as well as the liaison posts of the 10 city districts and 10 suburban counties. Survey forms asked of each rebel leader: name, sex, age, work experience, family background, personal status, educational level, political affiliation, pre–Cultural Revolution occupation, time of joining the rebels, and current position in the rebel organization. See *Xin ganbu tongjibiao* (Statistical tables on new cadres), ed. WGH (December 1969), in Shanghai Municipal Archives (hereafter SMA).

9. Workers aged 26–35 comprised 30.8 percent of the Shanghai work force at that time.

10. Had many rebel groups not explicitly excluded anyone with university credentials from their ranks, the proportion of this most highly educated segment (5.9 percent of the old rebels) would surely have been much higher.

11. *1965 nian Shanghai zhigong jiben qingkuang tongji* (Statistics on the basic conditions of the Shanghai work force in 1965), ed. Shanghai Statistical Bureau (Shanghai: 1966), SMA.

12. More than 80 percent of the "old rebels" had been ordinary workers before the Cultural Revolution began; approximately 1 percent had been leading managers, 1 percent had served as party cadres, and less than half a percent as union cadres.

13. *Fandang fenzi Wang Hongwen zuixing nianbiao* (Chronology of criminal activities of antiparty element Wang Hongwen), Shanghai Party Committee small group to investigate the Gang of Four case, ed. (March 1977), SMA.

14. Chen, former No. 17 Cotton Mill rebel, 1987 interview with Li Xun.

15. *Fandang fenzi Wang Hongwen.*

16. Ibid. Because of a cutback in industrial production, the SPC decided to send 100,000 people to Chongming. Each factory assigned workers and cadres to participate.

17. Ibid.

18. Ibid.

19. *Shanghai 17 chang wenhua geming shiji* (Annals of the CR at Shanghai's no. 17 factory), Shanghai No. 17 Cotton Mill, ed. (Shanghai: 1975), in archives of the Shanghai No. 17 Cotton Mill.

20. Ibid.

21. Tang Wenlan, May 17, 1992, interview with Li Xun.

22. Ma Ji, July 6, 1989, interview with Li Xun.

23. Wang Hongwen's followers at the No. 17 Mill numbered at most 100–200 workers—out of a work force of some 10,000—in August–September 1966. By contrast, the conservative organization that formed in opposition to Wang's rebel initiatives enlisted between four and five thousand workers almost overnight. Ma Ji, July 6, 1989.

24. Wang Hongwen, 1967 speech to the WGH standing committee, SMA.

25. *Shanghai 17 chang.* When Zhang Chunqiao learned of the arrival of rebellious workers from Shanghai, he welcomed them to the capital and arranged for them to meet directly with Chairman Mao and Defense Minister Lin Biao. The result was a substantial increase in personal prestige for Wang Hongwen as well as a lasting connection to the CR radicals in Beijing. See Parris Chang, "Shanghai and Chinese Politics: Before and After the Cultural Revolution," in Christopher Howe, ed., *Shanghai: Revolution and Development in an Asian Metropolis* (Cambridge: Cambridge University Press, 1981): 78.

26. Huang Jinhai, October 28, 1976, testimony, SMA.

27. *Guanyu erbingtuan fuzeren Geng Jinzhang juliu shencha de qingkuang baogao* (Situation report on the detention and interrogation of Second Regiment leader Geng Jinzhang) (April 11, 1967), in Yangpu district office of the Shanghai Public Security Bureau.

28. Geng Jinzhang, November 27, 1979, testimony, SMA; *Guanyu erbingtuan fuzeren.*

29. Transcript of roundtable concerning Geng Jinzhang at the Shanghai Paper Pulp Mill (December 1, 1979), in archives of the Shanghai Middle-Level Court.

30. Geng Jinzhang, March 6, 1979, testimony, SMA.

31. Ibid.

32. Huang Jinhai, April 5, 1977, testimony, SMA.

33. Huang Jinhai, January 2, 1977, testimony, SMA.

34. Huang Jinhai, April 5, 1977.

35. Ibid.

36. Li Zhisui, *The Private Life of Chairman Mao* (New York: Random House, 1994): 93–94, 280, 345–346, 356, 479.

37. Huang Jinhai, April 5, 1977.

38. Chen Ada, August 10, 1977, testimony, SMA.

39. Ye Yonglie, *Wang Hongwen xingshuai lu* (A record of the rise and fall of Wang Hongwen) (Changchun: Shidai wenyi chubanshe, 1989).

40. Chen Ada, August 10, 1977, testimony, SMA.

41. *Jiefang ribao* (Liberation Daily), November 20, 1977.

42. *Qingkuang huibao* (Situation report), ed. Shanghai Revolutionary Committee (April 18, 1977), SMA.

43. Ibid.

44. Ibid.

45. Dai Liqing, October 18, 1979, testimony, SMA.

46. Rebel leader Pan Guoping was incensed by the unfair wage scale at the glass machinery factory where he worked. Liu Guande, 1987 interview with Li Xun. Liu was a writer who undertook a lengthy interview with Pan Guoping after the latter's release from prison in 1987.

47. See especially Richard Kagan and Norma Diamond, "Father, Son and Holy Ghost: Pye, Solomon and the 'Spirit of Chinese Politics,' " *Bulletin of Concerned Asian Scholars* 5, no. 1 (July 1973): 62–68.

48. See, for example, Andrew G. Walder, "Cultural Revolution Radicalism: Variations on a Stalinist Theme," in William A. Joseph, Christine P.W. Wong, and David Zweig, eds., *New Perspectives on the Cultural Revolution* (Cambridge: Harvard University Press, 1991): 41–61; and Daniel Chirot, *Modern Tyrants* (New York: The Free Press, 1994).

49. Further discussion of this issue can be found in Elizabeth J. Perry, "Chinese Political Culture Revisited," in Jeffrey N. Wasserstrom and Elizabeth J. Perry, eds., *Popular Protest and Political Culture in Modern China* (Boulder: Westview Press, 1994).

50. The chief of the Organization Department of the Shanghai Party Committee, Yang Shifa, noticed that the manifesto of the workers' pickets was much like that of the Scarlet Guards, which had formed the day before, and took it upon himself to introduce leaders of the two conservative organizations to each other.

51. *Zhongcheng yu dang de Shanghai gongren chiweidui* (Scarlet Guards: Loyal to the party), ed. SFTU (September 1983).

52. *Qingkuang huibian* (Situation bulletin), ed. WGH (Shanghai: April 22, 1968).

53. Only two weeks after the formal inauguration of the Scarlet Guards, they already numbered 400,000; at their height they claimed twice that following. *Zhongcheng yu dang.*

54. Li Jianyu, July 3, 1992, interview with Li Xun.

55. Ma Ji, July 6, 1989, interview with Li Xun.

56. With the railway system disrupted by the Anting Incident and the movement to "exchange experiences," many conductors, train service attendants, and workers in the control room joined the Scarlet Guards. After the Shanghai postal system was interrupted by the *Liberation Daily* incident in which the rebels insisted upon having their tabloid delivered to newspaper subscribers, numerous

postal carriers joined the ranks of the Scarlet Guards. Similarly, those factories that generated the top leaders of the WGH were the same factories that produced the commanders of the Scarlet Guards, as well: the No. 17 Cotton Mill, the No. 31 Cotton Mill, the Glass Machinery Factory, the Lianggong Valve Factory, and others.

57. Ma Ji, July 6, 1989.

58. Li Jianyu, July 3, 1992.

59. Ibid.

60. Ibid.

61. *Zhongcheng yu dang.*

62. *Chouming zhaozhu de Shanghai chiweidui* (Notorious Shanghai Scarlet Guards), WGH, ed. (Shanghai: October 1968).

63. Ibid.

64. Ibid.

65. In some cases, these groups were extremely small and engaged in rather suspect activities. For example, a "rebel headquarters" that specialized in robbery was actually comprised of a three-person family!

66. Huang Jinhai, July 16, 1980, testimony, SMA.

67. *Wuchanjieji wenhua dageming zhong Shanghai fandui jingjizhuyi da shiji* (Annals of Shanghai's opposition to economism during the Great Proletarian Cultural Revolution), ed. Shanghai Revolutionary Committee (Shanghai: March 17, 1967), SMA.

68. *Xin Shanghai 40 nian* (40 years of new Shanghai), ed. Shanghai Statistical Bureau (Beijing: China Statistics Publishing House, 1990).

69. *Jixu qingshi de jige wenti* (Several issues in urgent need of instructions), ed. Shanghai People's Commune (Shanghai: February 15, 1967).

70. *Guanyu xianzai nongcun de jingjian zhigong de anzhi yijian* (Opinions concerning the settlement of streamlined workers now in the villages), a report of the Shanghai Labor Wage Committee to the Shanghai Party Committee with copies to Party Central and the East China Bureau (December 15, 1966), SMA.

71. *Jixu qingshi.*

72. Ibid.

73. *Jianjue fencui zibenzhuyi fubi niliu, chedi jiefa pipan "gelaosi" yixiaocuo bie you yongxin de toutou de zuixing* (Resolutely smash the capitalist restoration counter-current, thoroughly expose and criticize the crimes of the ambitious heads of the "private entrepreneurs headquarters"), handbill, n.d., SMA.

74. On the importance of the household registration system in creating stratification in socialist China, see Tiejun Cheng and Mark Selden, "The Origins and Social Consequences of China's *Hukou* System," *China Quarterly*, no. 141 (September 1994).

75. *Wuchanjieji . . . fandui jingjizhuyi.*

76. *Wenge chuqi.*

77. Ibid.

78. Zhu Yongjia, *Shanghai yiyue geming dashiji* (Annals of the January Revolution in Shanghai), 1969.

79. Ibid.

80. Telegram to Party Central, Jan. 6, 1967.

81. Shen Jingbo, August 1989, interview with Li Xun.

82. Zhu Yongjia, *Shanghai yiyue.*

83. Hong Yung Lee, *The Politics of the Chinese Cultural Revolution*, p. 34.

84. Emily Honig's pioneering work on native-place divisions in Shanghai is an important contribution to our understanding of "ethnic" influences among the working class even after the establishment of the People's Republic. See her *Creating Chinese Ethnicity* (New Haven: Yale University Press, 1992), esp. chapter 7. On the culture of the shantytowns of Shanghai, see Nai Peichun's drama entitled *Dushili cunzhuang* (Village within a city).

85. In later writings, Lucian Pye acknowledged the existence of two political cultures in Communist China—a Maoist rebel culture which he identifies with the heterodoxy of Daoism, Buddhism, and folk religion in imperial days, and a Dengist restraint which he identifies with the orthodoxy of Confucianism. See *The Mandarin and the Cadre: China's Political Cultures* (Ann Arbor: Center for Chinese Studies, University of Michigan, 1988), esp. chapter 2. Unfortunately, Pye does not provide a convincing explanation for the origins and operations of these competing cultural tendencies in the contemporary context. Anita Chan's (*Children of Mao*, 1985) use of the "authoritarian personality" concept to explain student rebels during the CR also offers little help in understanding rebel leadership among workers. Her interviews with student Red Guards led Chan to highlight the centrality of the school socialization process—a factor that does not figure significantly in workers' accounts of their turn to rebellion.

86. Tang Wenlan, May 17, 1992.

87. Walder, *Neo-Traditionalism*, pp. 246–247.

88. On rebel culture, see Elizabeth J. Perry and Li Xun, "Revolutionary Rudeness: The Language of Red Guards and Rebel Workers in China's Cultural Revolution," *Indiana East Asian Working Paper Series on Language and Politics in Modern China*, no. 2 (July 1993): 1–18. For the influence of this cultural style on the uprising of 1989, see Vera Schwarcz, "Memory and Commemoration: The Chinese Search for a Livable Past," in Wasserstrom and Perry, eds., *Popular Protest and Political Culture*, pp. 170–183; and Liu Xiaobo, "That Holy Word, 'Revolution,' " ibid., pp. 309–324.

89. Dietrich Rueschemeyer, Evelyne Huber Stephens, and John D. Stephens, *Capitalist Development and Democracy* (Chicago: University of Chicago Press, 1992); Ruth Berins Collier, *The Contradictory Alliance: State–Labor Relations and Regime Change in Mexico* (Berkeley: International and Area Studies, University of California, 1992); Ruth Berins Collier and David Collier, *Shaping the Political Arena: Critical Junctures, the Labor Movement, and Regime Dynamics in Latin America* (Princeton: Princeton University Press, 1991).

9

Rural Violence in Socialist China

Collective violence is a window on the relationship between state + society.

Introduction

Have state policies under socialism radically and irrevocably transformed the Chinese countryside? Or do age-old attitudes and behaviors persist, fueled by rural social structures that remain tenaciously vigorous *despite* new socialist imperatives? These questions have shaped much of the inquiry and debate on contemporary China over the past few decades.[1] More recently, however, another promising line of argument has gained some currency. This approach does not pose the relationship between "modern" state control and "traditional" social structure as a "zero-sum conflict" in which the ascendancy of one is necessarily a loss for the other. Rather, it sees state and society as interacting in a more complex manner; a manner that is not always conflictual, and sometimes even quite complementary. In this view, certain policies of the Chinese state have contributed (albeit often unwittingly) to the survival and strengthening of long-standing patterns of activity.[2]

In any country, one type of activity that opens a particularly promising window for viewing the relationship between state and society is, of course, collective violence. The leadership, composition, symbolism, goals, and ideology of such movements can tell us a good deal about the persistence or transformation of popular beliefs and behavior. China, as heir to one of the most enduring traditions of peasant uprisings in the world, offers an abundance of material for the comparative analysis of rural collective action. But although we now have a number of illuminating studies of peasant revolt in pre-Liberation China, the subject of rural violence in the People's Republic remains relatively uncharted terrain.

This chapter examines patterns of rural unrest in China in two quite different periods: the 1950s and the 1980s.[3] By comparing the two eras (one in which the countryside was collectivized, the other in which it was de-collectivized), I hope to contribute to an understanding of changing interactions between state and peasant in contemporary China.

Social science theories of peasant violence have flourished in the years since the Vietnamese revolution, like "bamboo shoots after a spring rain."[4] A common theme of this literature is the critical role played by the twin processes of state-building and market capitalism in undermining "traditional" peasant communities and thereby generating rural unrest. China presents an instructive variant on this general model, however. Unlike many countries in both Europe and the Third World, state-building in contemporary China has been accompanied by a socialist, rather than a capitalist, mode of production. Instead of state and market acting in concert to dispossess rural families and villages, in socialist China local society has retained (and gained) control of certain key resources. The outcome is especially interesting when viewed in comparative context, for the past three decades have witnessed in China a reversal of the evolutionary pattern of collective violence observed in other parts of the world.

In Western Europe, Charles Tilly has identified a three-stage process of changing repertoires of popular violence.[5] For Tilly, protest is always rooted in an organizational base, but the nature of this base changes in response to the pressures of capitalism and state-making. Traditionally, communal organizations (e.g., families or villages) provided the networks for *competitive* violence (e.g., feuds) against other rival groups. As nation-states and international markets gained greater power vis-à-vis communal units, however, the threatened groups rose up in *reactive* violence (e.g., food riots or tax revolts) designed to defend their traditional prerogatives. Eventually, however, the forces of state and market gained the upper hand. Thenceforth, communal groups gave way to associational organizations (e.g., trade unions), and "proactive" collective action (e.g., strikes) became the norm.

In contemporary China, where state-building has taken place in the absence of capitalist revolution, we find a very different trend. The first decade of the People's Republic saw numerous instances of reactive protest against the state's strengthened presence in the countryside, but in the immediate post-Mao period rural collective violence was more likely to be of the competitive sort in which rival kinsmen or villages vied against each other for control over local resources. The explanation for this reversal of European trends, I will suggest, is to be found in the changing interaction between state policy and local social structure in rural China.

Reactive Collective Violence: The 1950s

During the first decade of the People's Republic, violent protest in opposition to rural policies erupted with varying degrees of intensity throughout the countryside. Although the resistance was directed largely against new socialist measures, in style and symbolism the protests often harked back to pre-Liberation practices. Sectarian religious beliefs and imperial pretensions were common characteristics. The Chinese press reported subversive secret-society activities in every province and provincial-level municipality during the 1950s, with the majority of rural cases recorded in the aftermath of major initiatives in agricultural policy.

Although we sometimes speak of 1949 as marking the victory of the Chinese revolution, in reality of course China continued (or in some places, began) to undergo revolutionary upheaval well after the founding of the People's Republic in 1949. Carrying out rural revolution during the 1950s involved much more than the mere promulgation of new policy directives by Party leaders. To implement these policies would mean inciting and then overcoming the resistance of unsympathetic and disenfranchised groups in the countryside.

Thus, in the initial years there were numerous cases of disgruntled persons—particularly those designated as landlords, rich peasants, or bad elements in the course of land reform—acting as leaders of protest movements to revive the status quo ante. When religious sects were involved, the leaders had often been sectarian members for years prior to Liberation. Such "feudal associations" elicited relentless hostility on the part of the new regime (just as they had from imperial and Republican regimes in earlier periods), thereby placing sectarians in an inescapably antagonistic position vis-à-vis the authorities.

By the state's definition, sects and secret societies were not religious groups, but counterrevolutionary organizations. In the first few years of the People's Republic the regime published a considerable amount of material designed to prove that sects had established close relations with Japanese and/or Guomindang forces during the war of resistance or civil war periods.[6] The authorities acknowledged that many sects enjoyed a popular reputation as religious associations. As Shanghai's deputy mayor pointed out in a major radio address concerning the outlawing of Daoist sects, a number of ordinary people believed "there is no point in prohibiting these Daoist cults, for they just burn joss sticks and live on vegetarian diets."[7] To counter this common view the deputy mayor enumerated examples of collaboration between sects such as the Yiguan Dao and Jiugong Dao and enemy Japanese and Guomindang units in pre-Liberation days.[8]

The outbreak of the Korean War gave rise to heightened government suspicions about the patriotism of the sects. Accused of trying to disrupt the war effort, these groups were now subjected to a major suppression campaign. In a manner reminiscent of imperial days, government regulations stipulated that ordinary sectarian followers would be spared punishment if they confessed their errors and pledged to sever all sectarian connections. Only the "arch leaders" were to be arrested immediately, "and dealt with separately in accordance with the seriousness of their crimes and the extent of their confessions and repentance." Minor leaders (e.g., *tanzhu* or *sancai*) would be treated with leniency so long as they registered with the local public security bureau and signed a guarantee to cease all sectarian activities in the future.[9] Hundreds of thousands of sectarians apparently complied with the regulations. In the single province of Shanxi, for example, some 734 villages carried out a suppression campaign against the Yiguan Dao in December 1950. Over 82,300 members withdrew from the sect, 1,692 minor leaders registered, and 133 "professional leaders" were put under detention.[10]

Previous Western scholarship has suggested that such suppression campaigns were successful in basically eliminating the sectarian problem, at least in cities, by 1951.[11] After all, thousands of sect leaders did in fact register as required in 1950–51. However, when socialist transformation gained momentum over the next few years, many of these individuals were arrested for having reactivated their secret society networks in opposition to government policies.

Although registered secret society elements were supposed to remain under the watchful eye of the security apparatus, it was not difficult to escape surveillance. Before the imposition of mobility restrictions toward the end of the decade, people could move about the countryside, and between countryside and cities, with relative ease. Many sectarian leaders took advantage of this opportunity to recruit new followers. By 1952

these revived sects were already reported to have instigated armed uprisings. In Shaoxing County, Zhejiang, leaders of the Jiugong Dao
launched three attacks that damaged district government offices and resulted in the deaths of more than forty cadres. Brandishing swords and
imperial banners, the rebels attempted unsuccessfully to seize the county
seat and stage a monarchical restoration.[12]

Opposition to Land Reform

A similar case to the Jiugong Dao, launched by the Doumu Tan sect,
occurred in the winter of 1952 in Guankou District, Xishui County, Hubei.[13] The county of Xishui had been regarded as a model of successful
land reform, and Zhongtai Township in Guankou was a keypoint for the
re-examination of the land reform under the personal command of the
county Party committee. However, the work team for re-investigation
unwittingly included a Doumu Tan sectarian as a principal cadre.

On the evening of February 21, several hundred Doumu Tan members
and sympathizers surrounded the government offices of Lashu Township
in Guankou, killed the Party secretary of the township, and commenced
an assault on the Guankou District government offices. Met there by
militia fire, the group returned to Lashu and seized a few rifles from the
local militia headquarters. Their numbers having dwindled to seventy or
so, the rebels proceeded to Zhongtai Township the next morning. The
keypoint for land reform re-examination, Zhongtai was a site of concentrated state power. Local militia and army units managed to kill, wound,
or capture two dozen of the rebels, although the remnants continued to
resist under the command of two Doumu Tan leaders waving white flags.
As the *Changjiang ribao* described the scene, "some of the bandits used
swords and spears in resisting us, while some of them who were unarmed
were repeating prayers and drawing charms." Of the 50 remaining diehards, 14 were eventually captured alive and the rest were drowned or
killed by government fire. Besides swords and spears, several seals and
one copy of a proclamation were confiscated. Subsequent interrogation
revealed that Doumu Tan activities had extended to sixteen townships in
five districts of Xishui. Shortly after Liberation, the group had organized
for armed struggle, calling itself the "Army of the God of War."[14] An
eight-year-old boy surnamed Zhu was designated as "emperor" in obei-
sance to the Ming imperial line. His following included "dismissed rural
cadres and backward peasants" as well as "counterrevolutionaries, landlords, scoundrels, and ex-soldiers."

A follow-up investigation by district and county Party committees showed that Xishui was indeed a major center of secret society and sectarian activity. Some 40 to 50 townships, or about one-third of the county, harbored such organizations. With peasants usually joining as entire families, secret society members constituted the majority of the township residents. The Party's investigation revealed that 2,000 people— out of a total population of 3,000—were sectarians. In addition to the Doumu Tan, the county was home to branches of the Yiguan Dao, the Big Sword Society, the Confucian Morality Society, the Red Lanterns, and the Red Spear Society.[15]

Sectarian activism was certainly a central ingredient in the Hubei uprising, but so too—it may be surmised—were national and provincial agricultural policies. Six months earlier, *Changjiang ribao* had reported on riots by Hubei peasants in protest against the state's handling of the grain purchase program.[16] In November 1951 the *People's Daily* published a self-criticism by the Hubei Provincial Committee that admitted to serious problems in the implementation of land reform and collection of agricultural taxes.[17]

Discontent over the handling of land reform incited resistance in other parts of the country as well. In September 1951 a riot of some 20,000 people in Pingliang District, Gansu, was evidently generated by dissatisfaction with land classification.[18] In the spring of the following year, Pingliang was swept by another large-scale revolt that spread across five counties and lasted for three months. Led by a prominent Muslim landlord, the uprising was a response to cadres' efforts to redistribute the land holdings of a local mosque.[19]

The large size of such movements reflected the relative freedom of mobility in these years, enabling rebel leaders and sectarians to recruit like-minded followers from widely dispersed locations. For example, members of an Yiguan Dao branch known as the "Original Principle of the Heavenly Way" (Yuanli Tiandao) spread their message across Hebei, Shanxi, and Inner Mongolia by working as mule carters or traveling herbalists. In this way, by 1954 the group had managed to attract hundreds of believers.[20] In the spring of 1955 public security organs in various counties of Hebei Province cracked down on six sects (including Yiguan Dao, Zhongyang Dao, Mingyan Jiao, Yuanli Tiandao, and Daofuo Jiao). The principal occupations of the "Daoist chieftains and their underlings" were said to include trading, transport, fortune-telling, and therapeutic practices.[21]

As had been true for centuries, and as we saw in the case of Yellow Cliff (Chapter 3) and would see again with Falun Gong (Introduction), the practice of Chinese medicine went hand-in-hand with religious proselytizing. In the 1950s, some sectarians opened herbal pharmacies.[22] In other cases, individual leaders traveled about peddling their promise of both physical and spiritual cures.[23] The hope of healing was a powerful attraction for the rural populace. And the relative ease of mobility prior to the imposition of the household registration system meant that ordinary peasants were quite free to seek out such cures.[24] When influenza broke out in Shunyi, Guangdong, in the spring of 1957 thousands of cure-seekers thronged to a temple in Dingbao Township where a magical "holy water" was rumored to be available. To add to the excitement, a group calling itself the "Fourteenth Corps of the Chinese National Revolutionary Army" (led by sectarians, landlords, and former GMD officers) proclaimed that the holy water would be most effective on the birthday of the Goddess of Mercy, Guanyin. Declaring that Guanyin would descend to earth on her birthday, the group further prophesied that three urns of silver could be uncovered in the vicinity of the temple on that day. According to the public security's account, the Fourteenth Corps was hoping to incite the multitudes of cure-seekers to stage an armed attack on local government offices.[25]

Opposition to Cooperatization

The government's push to establish new rural organizations in the 1950s met with predictable antagonism from extant sects and secret societies. When agrarian policy moved beyond land reform to advocate mutual aid teams and cooperatives, these organizations became targets of sectarian resistance and sabotage. Initially some sects found it convenient simply to declare themselves mutual aid teams. This was the case in Baoji, Shaanxi, where mutual aid teams organized by the Yiguan Dao held regular worship services under the guise of team meetings.[26] In counties of Hebei, Shandong, and Gansu, both mutual aid teams and agricultural producers' cooperatives were established by "Daoist chiefs" and their followers.[27] Of major concern to the authorities in these cases was the fact that sect-sponsored teams and cooperatives put the interests of their sect above those of the state, often pressuring their members against selling surplus grain to the government.[28]

While some sects adopted a strategy of converting their organizations into mutual aid teams or cooperatives (much as tax protesters had often assumed the appellation of officially sanctioned militias during the imperial era, as seen in Chapter 2), others actively discouraged their membership from participating in the state-sponsored associations. The Zhong Dao of Shaanxi, which boasted more than 3,000 members in nine counties, was indicted in November 1954–January 1955 for having dissuaded many of its followers from joining mutual aid teams and cooperatives.[29] In yet other cases sectarian leaders were charged with having sabotaged production by destroying farm tools and poisoning livestock in cooperatives that they had "infiltrated."[30]

The summer of 1957, in the aftermath of collectivization, saw an upsurge in rebel activities. In July, for example, a man claiming possession of a magical sword that could slaughter all human beings within a radius of 20 miles, led an armed uprising in Linhong, Guangdong. On the basis of his claim, leader Yang Daohua had managed to attract a sizable following, targeting his recruitment efforts on landlords, rich peasants, released prisoners, and young people for whom he promised to arrange work outside the rural areas. On the afternoon of July 12, Yang's followers attacked the grain station, supply and marketing cooperatives, and other departments in Linhong, killing seven cadres and inhabitants and absconding with a portion of the official funds before being subdued by the Public Security Bureau.[31]

Food grain purchases were the immediate precipitant of much of the rural resistance that developed in the summer of 1957. In August a self-declared "emperor" in Suining, Sichuan, dissuaded followers in two production teams "over which he exercised supervision" from selling grain to the state. As emperor, Zhou Licai claimed that all grain by rights belonged to him. Described in the press as a thirty-two-year-old "gangster" who had never liked to work, Zhou prophesied that the world would soon undergo a major change. Having been appointed emperor by the Heavenly God to rule "from the edge of the heavens to the end of the sea," Zhou reiterated the age-old boast of Sichuan rebels that he could "throw beans and turn them into soldiers." Villagers were encouraged to present "tribute" to Emperor Zhou by his promise that the bigger the gift, the higher the official post one could expect to receive under his regime. One evening Zhou Licai called together dozens of followers to witness his formal enthronement. Seated upon a platform to perform the rites, he predicted that a "heavenly banner" would descend from the sky that night to verify divine approval. Before the Mandate of Heaven was bestowed, however, the would-be emperor was arrested by public security officials.[32]

The consolidation of collectives and the unified purchase and marketing plan set the general milieu within which rural resistance developed during the mid-1950s. At the same time, ad hoc instances of state intervention in particular places for particular projects could also give rise to intense local opposition. For example, in the summer of 1957 public security forces in Daxian, Sichuan, arrested leaders and hardcore members of the Sword Sect (Daoer Jiao), a group charged with plotting rebellion in three townships. In January 1957 leader Gan Zairong had prophesied that warfare would break out in the eighth intercalary month of the lunar year (i.e., August–September 1957), an emperor would appear, and people should rise up to oppose the socialist state. The press publicity given to the prophecy coupled with the widespread dissatisfaction felt by local inhabitants with the government's handling of a new reservoir project enabled Gan to recruit a mass following. The inhabitants displaced by the construction project were a receptive audience for Gan's "reactionary slogans opposing the unified purchase and marketing plan." The rebels promised their followers that when the Sword Sect took power they would introduce a three-year remission of unified purchase and collection of requisitioned grains; instead, a fee purchase and sale plan would be implemented. Secret meetings were held to plot the destruction of the reservoir, after which attacks on district, township, and finally county government offices were allegedly to have been attempted. When followers gathered in the hills of Dashu Township to carry out their plans, however, they were arrested by public security officials. Incriminating evidence confiscated from the thwarted rebels included six homemade firearms, sixteen spears and swords, a ceremonial banner, a rooster for sacrifice, Buddhist scriptures, and invulnerability charms.[33]

As this case suggests, the timing of uprisings was a reflection of general government policy, specific government initiatives, and sectarian prophecy. The importance of the last factor was demonstrated in the many uprisings scheduled for the eighth lunar leap month in 1957. In addition to the above incident, a number of other resurrections were timed to occur in the intercalary month—traditionally considered an auspicious moment in which to challenge the Mandate of Heaven.[34]

In Dayi and Yangxin, Hubei, public security officers uncovered a "Daoist" sect (the Luo Daxian) that was plotting an uprising for the fifteenth day of the eighth lunar month (i.e., September 9, 1957). This particular group was led by a landlord and a Daoist priest who spread their message under "cover" of incense burning, reciting Buddhist prayers, drawing charms, and curing illnesses. The leaders claimed possession of four magical treasures that would guarantee victory in battle and eventual control of the nation. They promised that believers would be free from misfortune and disaster, and that mastery of their esoteric practices would ensure invulnerability to swords and guns. Targeting their appeal on landlords and rich peasants, the group also managed to attract others dissatisfied with the new regime. The public security suppression netted more than twenty swords, spears, and other weapons, six rolls of red and white cloth (for making protective charms), and two seals.[35]

That same month in neighboring Xiangyang District, members of a "Black Flag Peace Party" were arrested and charged with attempting armed insurrection. The group had proclaimed that severe famine and widespread chaos would occur in the eighth lunar leap month. Declaring that an eighteen-year-old emperor had appeared in Henan Province, leaders of the Hubei Black Flags predicted the imminent collapse of the Communists. In place of the socialist regime they advocated enthronement of the "real emperor" in Xi'an, elimination of the cooperatives, revival of private ownership, and termination of the unified purchase and marketing plan.[36]

Sectarian Appeals

While cosmological prophecy was clearly an important ingredient in the rash of sectarian uprisings that broke out in the summer of 1957, another consideration was the contemporary political climate. The Hundred Flowers campaign of 1956–57, in which Chairman Mao encouraged "one hundred schools of thought" to contend (see Chapter 7), apparently generated something of a renaissance of popular religious activity in the countryside. In Hubei, for example, authorities pointed out that a folk Buddhist sect (the Dacheng Men or Wuwei Jiao) had taken advantage of political relaxation during the Hundred Flowers period to "resume chanting banned scriptures."[37] When the liberalization of the Hundred Flowers wilted under the heat of the anti-rightist attack in the summer of 1957, however, sectarian groups quickly discovered the limits of religious tolerance.

Although the Chinese press provides few details on the doctrines and practices of the sects, we can probably assume that religious appeals continued to play an important role in recruiting new adherents.[38] The fact that official reports often mention having confiscated religious scriptures in the course of a suppression campaign lends further support to this assumption. A sectarian organization in Changdong, Shandong, for example, was found to have in its possession 620 copies of "Daoist books."[39]

As we have seen, the use of protective charms and "holy water" was also a feature of many of the sects. Often the ostensible purpose of such practices was to provide physical healing for members' ailments—as would be true of the Falun Gong half a century later.[40] If the sects developed rebel aspirations, however, curative practices could be redirected toward ensuring invulnerability in battle. In Wuning, Jiangxi, a sectarian leader calling himself the reincarnation of the first Song emperor urged his followers (who numbered 600 people in 13 townships of Wuning and Xinshui) to practice boxing, handle clubs and knives, and take up other types of physical training. He promised that sustained practice would do more than contribute to good health; it would eventually ensure invulnerability as well.[41] Similarly, sectarians in Xinning, Hunan, prepared paper-made robes, banners, bows and arrows, swords, and warships to equip an "army of the other world" to fight for the mandate on their behalf.[42]

Promises of religious solace, health, and invincibility were not the only attractions of the sectarian organizations. Sometimes an explicitly materialistic appeal was used. A sect in Lucheng, Guangxi, promised that anyone who joined would receive a monthly stipend of 30 yuan. If one managed to recruit enough additional members to comprise a division, one would automatically be appointed division commander, with a monthly salary of 36 yuan. Platoon leaders were promised 80 yuan per month.[43]

Political threats and pledges also made a frequent appearance in sectarian propaganda. In 1955 the leader of the Buddhist Heaven Society (Fo Tian Hui) in Yiyang, Hunan, was arrested for spreading a rumor that American and Guomindang forces were about to launch an offensive. A self-proclaimed emperor, Deng Zhongyuan had recruited some 250 followers in five villages. His wife he honored with the title of "Highest Imperial Concubine," and he bestowed titles such as "Lotus Ancestor" and "General to Guard the Emperor" upon his most trusted lieutenants.[44] An even more sinister rumor was perpetrated by an Yiguan Dao sect in Pingding, Shanxi. This group alleged that the government had dispatched 3,000 men to gouge out people's eyes and hearts for magical use on aircraft when attacking Taiwan.[45] Equally troublesome from the authorities' point of view were prophecies of a change in the Mandate of Heaven such as those spread by members of a "Daoist sect" in Qinghai; as soon as the real emperor appeared, they claimed, the People's Liberation Army would vanish.[46]

Social Composition

The social composition of sectarian groups in this period evidenced a trend that had been under way since the late Qing, and that had been greatly strengthened during the Republican period: a tendency for the old rural elite (landlords, gentry, rich peasants) to ally with less savory elements in the countryside on the basis of "heterodox" religious appeals. While gentry and landlord participation in sectarian movements had been unusual during times of dynastic vigor,[47] such behavior grew more frequent as the imperial state lost credibility in the eyes of the local elite (as we saw in Chapters 2 and 3). Once the imperial system had been overthrown altogether by the Revolution of 1911, elite leadership of sectarian groups became commonplace. Movements such as the Red Spears of the 1920s showed the explosive potential of an alliance among rural elites, local ne'er-do-wells, and ordinary peasants, mediated through the religious sect.[48]

Thus in many ways sectarian violence in the 1950s resembles patterns of earlier times. But there are important differences as well. A striking feature of sectarian and secret society movements of the imperial and Republican periods was their organizational base in natural rural units: market towns, villages, and lineages.[49] The ability of the local elite to mobilize peasant followers through these familiar units helps to explain the massive scale of sectarian and secret society movements during that period. In this respect the post-1949 situation is markedly different.

The comparatively small scale of sectarian protests in the initial decade of the People's Republic attests to the obstacles that the now discredited rural elite of the *ancien régime* faced in mobilizing popular support. In part, of course, the difficulties can be explained by the much stronger capacity of the Chinese state after the victory of the socialist revolution. But there are other explanations, too. For one thing, a majority of the rural populace almost certainly saw its interests as enhanced by the regime's agrarian policies.[50] Hence resistance to land reform, mutual aid teams, unified marketing and purchase plans, and collectivization would not strike a responsive chord among the multitudes of peasants who did in fact benefit substantially from these programs. The rebel sects drew together malcontents from disparate locations, but often with a disproportionately low involvement of ordinary peasants. Frequently led by dispossessed landlords and rich peasants, many of the sects developed—ironically enough—a much stronger interest in land reform than had been true in the past. But now, of course, the plea was for a land reform that would restore the property of the divested rural elite, rather than service the interests of the poor peasantry. As reactionary organizations, the overtly political sects were limited in their recruitment potential.

Moreover, the natural rural units that had formed the building blocks of large-scale rebellion in pre-Liberation days were thrown into disarray by the momentum of socialist transformation in the 1950s. A new rural elite of Party-designated cadres, often drawn from poor peasant backgrounds, wielded power on the basis of new rural organizations: mutual aid teams, cooperatives, collectives, and finally, people's communes. Thus, despite the relative freedom of mobility in this period, disgruntled sectarian leaders were unable to generate a mass opposition movement.

Startling as the sectarian violence of the secret societies in post-Liberation China may at first appear, the relatively small scale of the movements argues against attaching exaggerated significance to their activities. Nevertheless, an analysis of the structure and objectives of these groups does suggest some insights into the nature of rural opposition during the early years of the People's Republic. Those designated as *class enemies* usually organized their *resistance to government policies* on the basis of traditional appeals, frequently religious or imperial in flavor, that challenged the Communists' claim to the Mandate of Heaven. While this finding should not strike us as surprising, it does provide an instructive contrast with the early post-Mao scene. Under the impact of the economic reforms, as we shall see, the leadership, composition, and targets were all quite different.

The Reconstitution of Rural Society

The consolidation of collectivized agriculture was a watershed in changing styles of collective violence. As we have seen, during the initial decade of the People's Republic villagers continued to pursue their interests along lines drawn in the process of land reform. Landlords and rich peasants in particular opposed state policies of taxation, unified purchase, and cooperation. In time, however, protest tactics came to be adopted less commonly by class enemies and more by poor and lower-middle peasants and entire collective units.[51]

Ironically, the very success of state-sponsored collectivization in China gave rise to a strengthened local social organization. As John Lewis noted in 1963,

> When the Communists encouraged the pooling of land for use under the centralized management of the co-op head they had inadvertently recreated the critical ingredient of lineage and village power: the collective land holdings. Moreover, by their unrelenting stress on the proletarian collective, party leaders enforced obligations to the village and consciously reestablished many defunct village activities and functions

such as the village meeting and the collective control of family and village life.[52]

Similarly, a study by William Parish and Martin Whyte in 1978 argued that "there have been shifts in social patterns in the countryside which in some ways make villages more encysted and closed to outside contact than they were twenty years ago."[53]

By the end of the first decade of the People's Republic, state-building under socialism—rather than setting peasants adrift from the bonds of local society—worked to reinforce kinship and community allegiances. The imposition of migration restrictions in 1958 meant that villagers had little choice but to identify with the collective units to which they were assigned. More importantly, there were powerful positive incentives to do so. Under the workpoint system of remuneration, everyone's best interests were served by cooperation among team members. As teams and brigades assumed new responsibilities (e.g., income distribution, low-interest loans, limited welfare provisions), a stronger identification with one's local unit followed quite naturally.

After the reorganization of the commune structure in 1962, official units in the countryside often coincided with pre-Liberation rural divisions.[54] Communes frequently corresponded with traditional marketing areas, brigades were often natural villages, and teams were sometimes lineages. But new socialist policies worked to strengthen horizontal identification within these units: land reform equalized property relations, collectivization leveled incomes, and migration restrictions bound peasants permanently to the same residential and work unit.

Not surprisingly, the reconstruction of rural society was followed by a revival of familiar patterns of behavior. And the propensity to revert to pre-revolution practices was apparently intensified by the agricultural disaster that swept China in the early years of the people's communes. As a 1962 document from Lianjiang County, Fujian, noted,

> Since the liberation, by consistently opposing superstition and marriage by sale, we were able to correct these old patterns of thought to some extent. Last year, however, when we encountered difficulties, marriage by sale began to reappear, and the masses again began to engage in activities inspired by superstition, such as worshipping Bodhisattvas, divination, and fortune-telling.[55]

Economic difficulties did not, however, prevent substantial expenditures for religious construction in this period. As the Lianjiang document revealed,

> Superstition is very conspicuous in coastal districts. According to an investigation made by the Huang-ch'i commune, 31 temples have been built and 11 have been repaired and there are 67 temples that have idols. The total expenditure was 8,185 yuan.[56]

Of concern to the authorities was the fact that such religious activities threatened to dilute the class consciousness that had been so painstakingly imbued during land reform and collectivization. Religious worship tended to strengthen communal bonds that cut across class divisions. As the *Nanfang ribao* cautioned in April 1964 on the occasion of the annual Qingming festival, the traditional time for visiting ancestral graves,

> Visits to ancestral tombs by member of clans sharing the same surname by different ancestors is a feudal activity. Those with the same surname are regarded as a unit in which only clan relations—not class differences—are seen as important. . . . If we go with landlords and rich peasants to visit ancestral tombs, what class standpoint are we taking? This pleases landlords and rich peasants, because they are generally the clan elders.[57]

Religious worship was not the only form of pre-revolutionary behavior to witness a resurgence in this period. The style of rural violence was also familiar from much earlier days. Because the new rural units were often coterminous with old kinship and village boundaries, long-standing feuds between lineages and communities were easily rekindled. Thus in the 1960s and 1970s, especially after the onset of the Cultural Revolution, there was an increased incidence of rural collective action based upon team, brigade, and commune membership. Reports of feuds between rival units appear with some frequency.[58] Competitive violence was once again in evidence in parts of the Chinese countryside.

For rural cadres, whose incomes were also dependent upon their local unit, loyalty to kinsmen and neighbors occasionally threatened to outweigh adherence to state directives. The Lianjiang document of 1962, for example, points out that "some cadre members and their families have led the way in participating in superstition."[59] Nevertheless, there were good reasons why most local cadres were willing to enforce official policies in the countryside. It was collectivization that finally replaced an old elite of landlords and rich peasants (whose economic power had of course already been undermined by land reform) with a new elite of grassroots cadres whose power rested in the disposition of collective resources.[60]

Competitive Rural Violence: The 1980s

As the key link between state and local society in China, the grassroots cadre plays a pivotal role in forestalling or facilitating rural violence. However, following the tumultuous Cultural Revolution years, when certain forms of violent conflict were promoted by the encouragement of central officials, local authorities often found it difficult to keep the peace. Moreover, with the implementation of agricultural responsibility systems after the Third Plenum of December 1978, the position of rural cadres themselves was rendered rather ambiguous. Once peasants were permitted to make their own decisions about farming methods and the disposition of agricultural surplus, there was less need for administrative personnel to oversee these activities. When payment is determined by contract rather than by workpoints, there is little call for the complicated accounting procedures that comprised a large portion of the local leadership's work in the past.

Although the Cultural Revolution decade is frequently depicted as a period in which the authority of the Communist Party was severely undermined by the assaults of Red Guards and the Gang of Four, in fact the situation was not unmixed. While the higher ranks of Party bureaucrats and intellectuals were certainly threatened by Cultural Revolution policies, the picture in the countryside was more complicated. The Gang of Four's effort (in the Learn from Dazhai Campaign) to raise the level of ownership and accounting from the team to the brigade, for example, implied increased control for the rural Party. Since the lowest level of Party organization in the countryside is the brigade Party branch, a Dazhai scheme that empowered the brigade leadership with new authority also promised greater control for the Party. Conversely, the agricultural responsibility systems advocated by the Third Plenum threatened Party authority by giving individual peasant households much more decision-making freedom.

The problem of superfluous local cadres was recognized in the official press. *Renmin ribao* complained that many commune and brigade cadres "think they have nothing to do now."[61] *Ningxia ribao* described production team cadres in its province as "in a state of paralysis." Remaining team leaders in name alone, many had shifted their attention and energy to the cultivation of their family plots.[62] A modern Shaanxi opera, which played to packed theaters in Beijing in the spring of 1983, similarly depicted the problems arising from the agricultural responsibility systems. The characters included a commune head who considers himself freed from all official duties, and a production team leader who decides to strike it rich on his own.[63]

To deal with this situation, there were reductions in the number of rural cadres. A Xinhua press release in August 1981 noted that too large a proportion of peasants' produce was being reserved by collective units because too many administrative personnel were being provided with subsidies. To ameliorate the problem, it proposed that the number of brigade cadres be reduced to five, while team cadres be reduced to three.[64] By 1984 brigade cadres had been reduced to four and team cadres to two in many areas.[65] At the same time the press argued that local cadres should continue to play an important leadership role. One listing of team cadres' functions included the preservation of public ownership of the basic means of production, curbing and correcting encroachments on public property, and mediation in civil disputes.[66] In short, rural cadres were enjoined to protect state interests in the countryside even though their own bases of power had been substantially undercut.

Local Cadre Leadership

The wishes of the state notwithstanding, there is evidence that many rural cadres came to identify more and more with their local units. Although such identification certainly preceded the Third Plenum, subsequent policies worked to intensify parochial loyalties. This parochialism, in turn, has important implications for contemporary rural violence.

A 1979 case from northern Anhui Province gives an indication of the pre-revolutionary flavor of the post-Mao forms of collective violence. (For examples of feuds from this same region during the imperial and Republican periods, see Chapter 1.) The niece of a Party member in a brigade in Fengtai County had an altercation with a neighbor in her village. Distraught by the manner in which the Party branch in her brigade handled the dispute, she took poison and died the following day. After learning of the death of his niece, Party member Chen Shijian gathered more than a hundred members of the Chen lineage to wreak revenge on the neighbor with whom she had quarreled. The Chens marched to the village into which the niece had married and proceeded to stage an "eat-in" at the homes of the neighbor and her stepfather. They consumed the available grain, pigs, and sheep, and made off with clothing and other items of daily use. When two cadres dispatched by the commune Party committee arrived to investigate, Chen Shijian led the attack against them.[67]

The pretext for a lucrative assault could appear remarkably slight. Wuchang Lake in Wangping, Anhui, opened for fishing on January 19, 1980. That day Chang Xiaokai, secretary of the Party branch of the Dachang production brigade in Wuchang commune, got into a squabble with a policeman about a boy picking up a fish that had been dropped on the ground. One of Chang's nephews stood by him during the argument, while another of his nephews (also a member of the brigade Party branch) pulled an oar from a fishing boat in an attempt to strike the policeman. Seeing this dispute, fellow brigade members rushed to the police command post and beat up sixteen leading cadres, public security officials, and police who were trying to oversee the fishing operations. That afternoon the local peasants looted 38,900 *jin* of fresh fish. Total losses to the state incurred in the day's riot were estimated at over 23,000 yuan.[68]

Numerous cases of illegal lumbering, apple-grabbing, looting of bricks, coal, and so forth were also spearheaded by grassroots cadres.[69] Such incidents suggest that many local cadres had come to place the interests of their local communities above those of the state. In March 1983 *Renmin ribao* printed an editorial, intriguingly entitled "Why?" which reported that production in a mining area in Henan had been delayed for years because of local cadre opposition. As the paper described the problem,

> Under the pretext of "protecting the people's interests," some localities from which the state has planned to take over land have repeatedly extorted money from the state. They regard the districts within the limits of their authority as a territory which can be wantonly controlled by themselves and is free from being directed by others.... It was none other than the secretary of the brigade Party branch and the secretary of the commune Party committee in the Jiagou mining area who took the initiative in extorting money from the state. Did these Communists not have the merest thought of the oaths they took on being admitted to the Party?[70]

Despite its title, the editorial provided few clues to explain this parochial attitude on the part of rural cadres. Much of the explanation, we may surmise, lies in disaffection with the drift of post-Mao agricultural policy.[71]

As rural Party members and basic-level cadres received fewer benefits from the state, it was hardly surprising that their allegiances should shift toward the neighbors and kinsmen with whom they share much closer bonds. A striking feature of the post-Mao rural violence was its organization along communal lines. Frequently the violence occured in areas, such as southeastern China, where armed feuds among rival lineages had a long pre-Liberation history.[72] The principal departure from earlier traditions seems to be in the area of leadership; in the contemporary era it was often rural cadres, rather than lineage elders, who instigated the conflict. Take, for example, the case of a fishing commune in Hainan Island that experienced serious interbrigade friction after some fights had broken out between children of the two brigades over the New Year's holiday in 1980. Instead of trying to calm the tensions, one brigade Party secretary convened a rally to further incite the peasants in his units. With the support of the brigade militia commander he issued guns to his fellow brigade members and personally directed them in collecting stones and constructing fortifications. When peasants in the enemy brigade saw these preparations they reported the matter to the deputy secretary of their Party branch. However, "instead of taking the stand of Party principles, this man took a sectarian stand." When the two brigades had mobilized nearly 700 people, they opened fire on each other, aiming to kill. Six villagers were slain, five injured, sixty houses destroyed, and large amounts of property burned or stolen. Damages were estimated at 47,000 yuan.[73]

Religious Rituals

The procurement of weapons for these intercommunity feuds was apparently a lucrative business. In the spring of 1980 a police guard at the Danxian branch of the Chinese People's Bank in Hainan received 1,800 yuan for the sale of three guns and forty rounds of ammunition to a production team for use in armed feuds. Two months later the guard sold another two submachine guns and a rifle to a rival production team, this time gaining 2,000 yuan in the transaction. Although there is no evidence that these guns were actually used in intercommunity fighting, the police guard was sentenced to fifteen years in prison for his entrepreneurial efforts.[74] This arrest did not put a halt to the local demand for arms, however. The following September public security agents in Danxian discovered underground workshops that had been illegally manufacturing weapons.[75]

Violence between enemy lineages and communities was often accompanied by religious rituals. An illustrative case occurred in the spring of 1981 as members of a Hunan production brigade encouraged more than 2,000 members of the Zhang clan in four nearby communes to help exact revenge on a rival brigade. Under "the guise of paying respect to their ancestral tombs" the Zhangs were described in the Hunan press as:

> Waving banners, dancing the dragon dance and with hoes and clubs in their hands, they wantonly sabotaged production; destroyed public property; trod on and uprooted over four *mu* of vegetables, rape and wheat buds; cut down more than 200 large and small trees; destroyed enclosing walls and damaged commune members' houses.[76]

The feud was evidently part of a long-standing dispute over graveyards that burst into flame during the annual Qingming festival.

In the summer of 1981 armed clan fighting was reported in Changliu Prefecture, Hainan. According to press reports, the hostilities had gained momentum in 1979 "with feudal superstitious activities of tracing ancestry, building ancestral temples and shrines and public worship." A series of five armed clashes resulted in three deaths and scores of injuries.[77] Similarly, in the autumn of 1981 Party members and cadres of a brigade in Dingan, Guangdong, were charged with having planned, organized, and directed clan fights. The press reported that the feuds were associated with other "superstitious" activities: compiling genealogies, building and restoring ancestral tombs, offering sacrifices to the ancestors, setting up clan associations, and so forth.[78]

As the above examples suggest, religious activities have played an important role in many cases of competitive violence in the post-Mao period. On first glance this particular feature of the movement would seem to resemble the reactive protests of the 1950s. A closer look, however, makes it clear that religious rituals have distinctly different meanings for participants in collective violence during the two periods. In the later period, rather than provide inspiration and identity to members of discredited social groups (as was the case in the sectarian uprisings of the 1950s), rural religious activities have served to express kinship and community solidarity.

Official fears about the upsurge in communal religious activities were expressed in a series of articles in the newspaper earmarked for rural cadres, the *Zhongguo nongmin bao*.[79] The paper reported that forty-three villages in Hong'an County, Hubei, had expended nearly 200,000 yuan in 1983 for making "clan dragon-lanterns" *(xingshi longdeng)*. Anyone who refused to pay his share was "despised and expunged from the genealogy." In one commune, persons surnamed "Li" repaired an old gravesite that they claimed was the resting place of "heroic General Li." Nearly 2,000 Lis who gathered to worship their reputed ancestor beat up government personnel when they tried to interfere with the proceedings. The power of the lineages, it was charged, had provoked six fights, resulting in twenty-three injuries. Some villages had manufactured guns and other weapons and had even hired boxing teachers to enhance their martial capacities. According to the newspaper, people were spreading rumors that "the villages will restore clan rule." To demonstrate that such was not to be the case, county authorities in Hong'an leveled the 190 ancestral graves that had recently been repaired, destroyed or converted to other uses the seven newly renovated ancestral halls, and burned the 13 genealogies and more than 70 clan regulations that they confiscated.

Another instance of large-scale communal religious activity, centered in Guangdong's Yingde County in November 1982, was inspired by a supernatural vision. Claiming to have been visited in a dream by a popular deity, a local resident announced that the masses must prepare a Daoist sacrificial ceremony to forestall natural calamities the following year. Accordingly, more than 5,000 people of 15 surnames in six brigades contributed over 2,000 yuan and 2,500 *jin* of grain. A special committee of some 30 members, complete with manager and director, was established to oversee the religious festivities. "Masters" and spirit-mediums, numbering more than twenty in all, performed their rituals at the makeshift shrine that was erected to honor the apparition. An opera troupe was also hired, playing to audiences of 5,000 to 10,000 temple-goers each day. To maintain order, a volunteer security force *(baowei dui)* of more than sixty people wearing armbands inscribed with the words "Security of the Ninth Celestial Stem" *(Jiujia anquan)* was also constituted. When commune leaders tried to put a stop to the event, hundreds of peasants stoned them. Only after county and district police were called in was order finally restored.[80]

The resurgence of religious practices was surely related to the reversion to family farming that occurred under the post-Mao agricultural responsibility systems. In the summer of 1983 the Daxian, Sichuan, district people's court sentenced to death Zhang Mingle, a spirit-medium who had become active after the household responsibility system *(baogan daohu)* was introduced in his production team. For many years Zhang had apparently managed to get along by virtue of the collective's generosity, but the situation changed dramatically once the new responsibility system was in place. As *Zhongguo nongmin bao* described it, because "this loafer could not continue to muddle through," he decided to become a disciple of a master of "superstitious activity." Zhang learned the magical arts of going into a trance and controlling demons, which he used to make a living "by tricking many people." One day he offered his services to Zhang Meikun, a Party member who had quarreled with his father-in-law at the time the responsibility land had been divided. Zhang Meikun accepted Zhang Mingle as his teacher and requested that Mingle "heal" his father-in-law, who had been hospitalized with tuberculosis. The patient was brought home from the hospital so that he might benefit from the sorcerer's "cure" of wild herbs. However, when some of the herbs induced dropsy, Zhang Mingle beat the father-in-law, claiming he was possessed by demons. Soon the unfortunate patient died, after which Zhang allegedly cut off his head and genitals, asserting that this would allow the victim to revive the following day. When the prediction proved false, the brigade head finally reported the case to commune headquarters and both Zhang Mingle and Zhang Meikun were apprehended.[81]

Much of this religious activity has a familiar look to it: ancestor worship, temple building, exorcism, and the like. The motives for participation are also familiar. The promise of physical healing continues to exert a powerful attraction for many adherents.[82] As the contemporary Falun Gong case shows, the state's retreat from socialized medicine has created a strong demand for alternative sources of medical help. A *Guangming ribao* editorial noted, "places where witches and wizards are most active are usually places where there are few doctors and not enough medicine."[83] Delivery from natural disaster is another motive for religious rituals.[84] Praying for offspring is also cited as a principal purpose of "feudal superstitious" activity.[85] And one cannot assume that the birth control campaign will eliminate this trend. If the state insists upon only one or two children per family, while economic and cultural imperatives argue for male offspring, how tempting it must be to turn to one's local shaman for help; perhaps he or she will be able to ensure that the child is a male—or better yet, male twins or triplets!

The upsurge in traditional—or what the Chinese press refers to as "feudal superstitious"—collective action was closely related to state policies. The national political climate also contributed to the revival. Just as the Hundred Flowers of 1956–57 encouraged popular religion in the countryside, so the espousal of religious freedom in the post-Mao era had a similar effect. State sponsorship of temple renovation, for example, albeit largely for the purpose of providing places for leisure activity and generating tourism revenues, tended to reinforce an atmosphere of liberalization. As the *China Daily* reported with alarm,

> In Fujian and Zhejiang provinces, for instance, Buddhist idols even appear in primary schools. Some lower-level cadres, in ignorance of Party and government policies, fail to check these tendencies. They accept the argument that since the state has had many big temples repaired, small temples and ancestral halls can be built in rural areas.[86]

Local cadre leadership was a prominent factor in much of the religious resurgence. In the spring of 1981, for example, *Nanfang ribao* reported a "rather startling" news item. Several production brigades in the suburbs of Guangzhou had recently organized a festival and parade under the name of the "great king and father touring the villages and driving away the evil spirits." A female commune member, claiming to be none other than the "great king and father," sat sedately in a sedan chair holding a long sword and dressed as a temple deity. She led a team of armed People's Liberation Army soldiers who paraded in grand style for several days:

> Even the schools suspended classes. . . . Thousands of onlookers watched the proceedings but nobody dared come forth to stop the procession. . . . What was even more startling was that those who carried the sedan chair and acted as vanguards of the parade were *all members of the Communist Party.*[87]

Role of Agricultural Reforms

While the authorities tend to blame such deviations on ideological confusion created by the Cultural Revolution years, it seems clear that subsequent rural policies also played a major role in the revival of "feudal superstition." The introduction of household responsibility systems in particular led to a decline in cadre commitment (by reducing the collective's control of rural resources), a greater role for the family (by making the household responsible for production and for welfare measures), and an increased surplus labor problem (by eliminating the opportunity to "eat from one big rice pot"—or freeload from the collective). Each of these outcomes, we have seen, has had important implications for the pattern of rural collective action. Local cadres turn a blind eye to the revival of popular religion, large-scale looting, or intercommunity feuds—and may even provide the leadership for such activities. Kinship groups—lineages and clans—comprise the main participants in these movements, while the surplus labor force provides a ready source of spirit mediums and shamans.

The regime has expressed concern about all these developments. Reduced cadre allegiance is acknowledged to be at the heart of a recrudescence of traditional beliefs in the countryside:

> Many Party members and cadres . . . have become the captives and champions of these feudal superstitious activities. . . . Some people who formerly led others in trying to break superstitious activities are now scared into submission by the sorcerers and witches and, of their own accord, have repented before the gods, seeking their pardon and promising to make amends. In this way, Party basic-level organs in the countryside have lost their fighting spirit against feudal superstitious activities.[88]

The authorities have also recognized the revival of kinship identification as a threat to state control in the rural areas:

> In places where clan power is strong . . . social order declines, local headmen replace basic-level cadres, clan authority replaces government authority, clan laws replace legal statutes, Party leadership is harmed, and Party and national policies and regulations are undermined.[89]

Finally, there is fear that a restive surplus labor force may provide recruits for secret societies. A December 1982 editorial in the journal *Ban yue tan* noted:

> In the past few years, there have been indications of a revival of reactionary superstitious sects and secret societies in some places. In some areas, scoundrels and counterrevolutionaries have appeared, claiming to be "emperors" or the "Jade Emperor descended to earth."[90]

Similarly an article in the *Renmin ribao* of July 12, 1982, referred to "frequent reports" that in some areas people were taking advantage of feudal superstitious beliefs to call themselves emperor, make women their "imperial concubines," and disrupt social order.[91] In September 1983 the secretary-general of the Legislative Affairs Commission advocated the death penalty for seven types of offenders who had committed serious crimes in the past few years. Included were "those who organize reactionary sects and secret societies and use feudal superstition to carry out counterrevolutionary activities."[92] By April 1984 the vice-president of the Supreme People's Court was able to announce that stern punishment, including the death sentence, was being meted out to "those who organize secret societies and sects."[93]

Opposition to Newly Rich Peasants

On the whole, however, rebellious secret societies threatening to seize the Mandate of Heaven did not appear to pose a problem of major dimensions in the de-collectivization era. Far more widespread and numerous, it seems, were more mundane varieties of peasant violence. The household responsibility system inadvertently encouraged some of these activities, while the subsequent policy of allowing some peasants to "get rich first" further exacerbated tensions in the countryside. Feelings of envy—or what the Chinese euphemistically refer to as "red eye disease" (*hongyan bing*)—were the motivation for a good deal of hostility toward newly rich households. Often goaded by the promptings of disgruntled rural cadres, this hostility might erupt into violent attacks against the nouveaux riches.

A 1984 case in Gansu Province illustrates the explosive potential of peasant jealousy toward prosperous neighbors.[94] In a letter to *People's Daily*, a woman who had become wealthy by providing grain polishing services complained of maltreatment at the hands of local cadres. The woman's family were outsiders *(wailai hu)* to the production team in Shandan County, where she and her small children lived. With her husband employed at the county electric station, Zhou Xiuling was the only labor power available to cultivate the responsibility plot that she contracted from her team in 1981. Unable to make ends meet by agricultural labor alone, Zhou soon purchased a small polishing machine for which she was granted an operator's license by the county. Her use of electricity was also approved by the county electric station—perhaps, we may speculate, through the good offices of her husband. Popular as the grain polishing service was, after only ten days of operation the brigade Party secretary went to Zhou's house to communicate what he claimed to be a "high-level directive" prohibiting private individuals from using electricity for grain processing. He snipped the electrical wires leading to Zhou's house, and summarily departed.

Understandably distraught by the action of her brigade secretary, Zhou wrote a letter of inquiry to the provincial newspaper. When a speedy reply from the *Gansu ribao* affirmed that Zhou was completely in the right, she resumed her business. Her son was called home after middle school graduation to serve as machine repairman, and Zhou purchased additional machinery to expand her family's operations. However, the financial success of these activities only heightened the hostilities of team and brigade leaders, who repeatedly threatened to cut off Zhou's electric supply once again. The boiling point was reached when the team leader's tardiness in paying his unit's electric bill resulted in the county disconnecting the team's electric supply. Only Zhou Xiuling's house continued to receive electricity—and here again we may wonder whether her husband's intervention was not instrumental. In any event, Zhou's team leader rallied fellow peasants with an impassioned speech that he concluded by calling on team members to pull out Zhou's electrical wiring. Shortly thereafter, more than twenty peasants descended on her house, severed her high voltage line, pulled down a ten-meter electric pole, and ripped a transformer out of its concrete platform. Zhou's machines were silenced, as she recounted to *People's Daily*, "like a water buffalo that had fallen down a well"—still powerful, but of no immediate use. For several months, her family spent all its time standing guard over their broken machines. Well-intentioned friends tried to comfort Zhou by remarking, "you encountered these problems after making only a few thousand yuan. Surely it would have been much more serious had you become a 10,000 yuan household!"

A similar incident was reported in Fujian Province, again directed at outsiders who had struck it rich.[95] When an immigrant family from Zhejiang gained an income of over 8,000 yuan by cultivating abandoned lands which they had cleared in the hills of Fujian, "red eye disease" infected many of the locals. They trampled the newcomers' watermelon fields, stole their potatoes, poached hundreds of fish, and seriously injured their young son. Eventually local cadres gathered a crowd of more than thirty natives to march on the newly rich peasant's home. They stole one of his best pigs, butchered it, and divided it up among themselves. Commune authorities finally intervened, fining the pork-eaters 100 yuan apiece—to be delivered to the immigrant's house with cymbals, drums, firecrackers, and apologies. Cadres who had led the raid were removed from office and fined 30 yuan each.

As in the 1950s, so in the 1980s the limited scale of most of the reported incidents cautions against overestimating their political potential. Furthermore, the precise extent and frequency of collective violence cannot be ascertained with accuracy. Nevertheless, the basic structure, social composition, and objectives appear fairly clear. In contrast to the "reactive" anti-state rebellions of the 1950s, in the immediate post-Mao period we see movements composed largely of kinsmen or fellow villagers, led by rural cadres, and directed primarily against parochial targets. Certainly, attacks on state property and personnel also occurred, but—prior to the tax increases of the 1990s—these tended to be ad hoc assaults on lucrative targets or responses to suppression efforts, rather than a protest against state initiatives per se.

Conclusion

A number of recent theories of peasant violence assign great explanatory power to the erosion of traditional kinship and community bonds by the twin processes of state-building and capitalist development. With governments and markets exerting unbearable demands upon families and villages, these customary rural structures break apart under the weight of new pressures. As Charles Tilly has characterized the process in Western Europe, dominant repertoires of rural violence shift as communal units give way to associational bases of organization.[96]

In contemporary China, where state-building has not been accompanied by a capitalist revolution, we see a variant to the pattern suggested by the general theories. Rather than the replacement of communal groups by new, special-purpose associations, rural China under socialism witnessed a reconstitution of traditional local units. It is true that during the early 1950s a class-based revolutionary struggle (which followed upon the heels of years of foreign invasion and civil war) disrupted the pre-existing structural order in the countryside. As the state endeavored to rearrange the local areas, losers in the struggle mounted reactive protests through the organizational vehicle of the religious sect. By the second decade of the People's Republic, however, state policy meant a resurrection of communal units. Associational groups—such as poor and lower-middle peasant associations, women's federations, and youth leagues—were also established. But the more salient vehicles of contemporary rural action were the production teams and brigades, which often replicated pre-revolution communal groupings.

Clearly, long-standing beliefs and behavior have not disappeared from the Chinese countryside. Equally clearly, familiar social structures (families, lineages, villages) provide the organizational framework for much of the collective activity. It would be incorrect, however, to interpret the continuity in local society as a *circumvention* of state policy. Rather, in important ways, the communal structure of contemporary China is a direct product of government initiatives.

Specific state policies have played an important role in determining the composition and content of rural collective action. Thus, in the mid-1950s the push for collectivization and the unified purchase and marketing program, followed by the liberalization of the Hundred Flowers, helps explain the outburst of reactive protest by many who had been declared class enemies or bad elements in the course of land reform. Similarly, in the early 1980s the agricultural reforms enunciated at the Third Plenum gave rise to restive local cadres, willing to lead their local units in competitive forays against other rival units in the countryside. Encouraged by the regime's post–Cultural Revolution espousal of religious freedom, communal groups returned to familiar practices of ancestor worship, temple repair, compilation of genealogies, spirit possession, and so forth to buttress their competitive claims.

Future trends in the pattern of rural violence are of course extremely difficult to foresee. But so long as household responsibility systems remain in effect, we should probably anticipate that collective action will be organized less upon community and more upon kinship and even class. With family replacing collective as the principal guarantor of income and welfare, blood-ties have gained increased political salience. Furthermore, as income differentials within villages increase, community allegiances may well decline. Rural families may once again develop a sense of class interest, with richer families preferring different policies from those favored by their less prosperous neighbors. Finally, as mobility restrictions crumble with the demise of the household registration system, rural China could begin to approach the scenario painted by analysts of peasant protest elsewhere: pressures of state and market acting in concert to undermine communal institutions and generate participation in large-scale protest movements.[97] Under these conditions, challenges to the Mandate of Heaven might become not only more widespread, but also of far greater political consequence.

Notes

This chapter was published initially as an article in *China Quarterly* (September 1985).

1. For an early formulation of the debate, see John King Fairbank, *The United States and China* (Cambridge: Harvard University Press, 1948); and C.P. Fitzgerald, *The Birth of Communist China* (Baltimore: Penguin Books, 1964).

2. See William L. Parish and Martin K. Whyte, *Village and Family in Contemporary China* (Chicago: University of Chicago Press, 1978); Kenneth P.

Lieberthal, *Revolution and Tradition in Tientsin, 1949–1952* (Stanford: Stanford University Press, 1980); Elisabeth Croll, *The Politics of Marriage in Contemporary China* (Cambridge: Cambridge University Press, 1981); Andrew G. Walder, "Organized Dependency and the Culture of Authority in Chinese Industry," *Journal of Asian Studies* 43, no. 1 (November 1983), pp. 51–76.

3. The principal sources for this article are provincial newspapers and radio broadcasts. There is of course a serious question to be raised about the reliability of the Chinese media in reporting rural violence: How much accuracy can we expect in the description of what are often explicitly denounced as counterrevolutionary incidents? The same problem occurs in research on "heterodox" groups in traditional China, and is an almost unavoidable occupational hazard in the study of any dissident activities for which the documentation from the government side greatly outweighs that from the rebels themselves. Still, although exaggeration and embellishment is to be anticipated, I believe that the general picture presented is credible. Informal interviews conducted in China in 1979–84 further convinced me of the veracity of press reports about rural violence under socialism.

4. Eric R. Wolf, *Peasant Wars in the Twentieth Century* (New York: Harper and Row, 1969); Joel S. Migdal, *Peasants, Politics and Revolution* (Princeton: Princeton University Press, 1974); James C. Scott, *The Moral Economy of the Peasant* (New Haven: Yale University Press, 1976); and Charles Tilly, Louise Tilly, and Richard Tilly, *The Rebellious Century* (Cambridge: Harvard University Press, 1975).

5. Charles Tilly, "Rural Collective Action in Modern Europe," in Joseph Spielberg and Scott Whiteford, eds., *Forging Nations: A Comparative View of Rural Ferment and Revolt* (East Lansing: Michigan State University Press, 1976), pp. 9–40.

6. *Renmin ribao* (People's daily) (Beijing), 11 March 1951; Xinhua News Agency (Shanghai), 3 May 1951 in *Survey of China Mainland Press* (SCMP), no. 15, pp. 27–29; *Nanfang ribao* (Southern daily) (Guangzhou), 6 June 1953, in SCMP, no. 650, supplement, pp. v–vi; *Guangming ribao* (Bright and clear daily), 4 July 1955. For more information on the issue of collaboration between the sects (especially the Yiguan Dao) and Japanese or Guomindang forces, see Kubo Noritada, *Chukyo no shukyo seikaku to minshu dokyo* (The Chinese Communists' religious policy and popular Daoism), *Toyo Bunka*, no. 11 (1952), pp. 1–26; *Ikkando ni tsuite* (Concerning the Yiguan Dao), *Toyo Bunka Kenkyujo, Kiyo*, no. 4 (1953), pp. 173–249; *Ikkando hoko* (Further research on the Yiguan Dao), ibid., no. 11 (1956), pp. 179–212. The last article also contains a Japanese translation of a pamphlet entitled *Yiguan Dao shi shemma dongxi?* (What on earth is the Yiguan Dao?), published in China in August 1956.

7. *Jiefang ribao* (Liberation daily) (Shanghai), 8 June 1953, in SCMP, no. 628, supplement, p. v.

8. Ibid., pp. v–x.

9. Ibid., 5 June 1953, in SCMP, no. 628, supplement, p. ii.

10. *Da gong bao* (The worker) (Hong Kong), 8 December 1950, in SCMP, no. 26, p. 15.

11. Ezra Vogel writes of Guangzhou that "by late 1951, most former secret society members were afraid to have contact with their former associates." See

Vogel, *Canton Under Communism* (Cambridge: Harvard University Press, 1969), p. 65. And Kenneth Lieberthal writes of Tianjin that "during the Suppression of the Counterrevolutionaries Campaign in the spring of 1951, the Communists publicly executed a number of people whom they identified as former coolie association heads and secret society leaders. It seems reasonable to speculate that this campaign marked the last phase of the CCP's efforts to eradicate the secret society leadership in Tientsin, although the influence of the secret society mentality undoubtedly lingered on in the minds of many for a long time." See Lieberthal, *Revolution and Tradition*, p. 77. That sects and secret societies continued their activities in many urban centers is shown in *Changzhou gongren bao* (Changzhou worker) (Changzhou), 19 September 1956, in Union Research Institute (URI) classified files microfilm reel, no. E18; *Liaoning ribao* (Liaoning daily) (Shenyang), 22 October 1956, in URI files, no. E18; *Changjiang ribao* (Changjiang daily) (Hankou), 29 September 1957, in URI files, no. E45; *Zhejiang ribao* (Zhejiang daily) (Hangzhou), 9 October 1957, in URI files, no. E45. Subsequently, the city of Tianjin saw a revival of secret societies. Unemployed youths were reported in September 1983 to be operating in "hooligan gangs similar to the red and green gangs of old China." *Tianjin ribao* (Tianjin daily), 25 September 1983, p. 1 in Foreign Broadcast Information Service, *Daily Report: China* (FBIS), 19 October 1983, p. R5. That same month, public security officers cracked down on Yiguan Dao activities in Tianjin (ibid., 5 September 1983, in FBIS, 4 October 1983, p. R1).

12. *Jiefang ribao*, 8 June 1953, in SCMP, no. 628, supplement, p. xii.

13. *Changjiang ribao*, 15 March 1952, in URI files, no. E4, and SCMP, no. 309, pp. 16–18.

14. Allegiance to Guan Gong (the "God of War") was not uncommon among these groups. In May 1951, for example, an Yiguan Dao sect in Shanghai was reported to have changed its name to the "Guan Gong Society." See Xinhua (Shanghai), 3 May 1951, in SCMP, no. 102, p. 49.

15. *Changjiang ribao*, 15 March 1952, in URI files, no. E4.

16. Ibid., 25 August 1951.

17. *Renmin ribao*, 29 November 1951.

18. *Gansu ribao* (Gansu daily) (Lanzhou), 27 September 1951, in URI files, no. A7.

19. *Qunzhong ribao* (Masses daily) (Xi'an), 13 September 1952, in URI files, no. A7.

20. *Hebei ribao* (Hebei daily) (Baoding), 30 November 1954, in SCMP, no. 1,001, pp. 1–3.

21. Xinhua (Baoding), 16 June 1955, in SCMP, no. 1,078, pp. 27–28.

22. Xinhua (Taiyuan), 16 October 1955, in SCMP, no. 1,158, p. 24.

23. *Heilongjiang ribao* (Heilongjiang daily) (Harbin), 7 March 1959, in SCMP, no. 1,775, pp. 14–16.

24. In 1954–55 Daoist sects in Guangdong were said to have spread a rumor that holy water in Haifeng County contained magical curative properties. For months as many as 2,000 people a day thronged to the holy site from the surrounding eighty counties. *Guangming ribao*, 4 July 1955.

25. Xinhua (Guangzhou), 2 August 1957, in SCMP, no. 1,588, pp. 31–32. A Guanyin festival that did erupt in anti-state violence is described in *Guizhou ribao* (Guizhou daily) (Guiyang), 19 August 1957.

26. *Renmin ribao*, 7 July 1955.

27. Xinhua (Baoding), 16 June 1955; *Gansu ribao*, 21 January 1955 in URI files, no. A31; *Zhongguo qingnian* (Chinese youth), 1 February 1955, in URI files, no. A31; *Renmin ribao*, 18 June 1955.

28. *Renmin ribao*, 7 July 1955.

29. Ibid., 6 July 1955.

30. Xinhua (Baoding), 16 June 1955; Xinhua (Taiyuan), 16 October 1955.

31. Xinhua (Guangzhou), 2 August 1957, in SCMP, no. 1,588, pp. 31–32. For a similar incident in which followers of a sixteen-year-old "emperor" killed cadres in an armed attack, see *Xi'an ribao* (Xi'an daily), 18 August 1957, in SCMP, no. 1,641, pp. 14–15; *Shaanxi ribao* (Shaanxi daily) (Xi'an), 11 February 1958, in SCMP, no. 1,740, p. 12.

32. *Sichuan ribao* (Sichuan daily) (Chengdu), 31 August 1957, in SCMP, no. 1,647, pp. 21–24.

33. Xinhua (Chengdu), 1 August 1957, in SCMP, no. 1,588, p. 32; *Da gong bao* (Beijing), 2 August 1957, in URI files, no. A64.

34. For additional cases, see *Sichuan ribao*, 22 August 1957, in SCMP, no. 1,652, p. 27; *Guizhou ribao* (Guiyang), 14 August 1957, in URI files, no. E45; *Qunzhong ribao* (Masses daily), (Changde), 19 December 1957, in SCMP, no. 1,729, pp. 21–22; *Jilin ribao* (Jilin daily) (Changchun), 20 March 1958, in SCMP, no. 1,770, pp. 19–20; *Zhejiang ribao*, 9 October 1957, in URI files, no. E45.

35. *Changjiang ribao* (Wuhan), 18 September 1957, in SCMP, no. 1,663, pp. 35–36.

36. *Hubei ribao* (Hubei daily) (Hankou), 28 September 1957, in SCMP, no. 1,729, pp. 21–22.

37. *Changjiang ribao*, 27 September 1958, in SCMP, no. 1,915, pp. 13–14.

38. For the religious appeal of the sects in an earlier period of Chinese history, see Daniel L. Overmyer, *Folk Buddhist Religion: Dissenting Sects in Late Traditional China* (Cambridge: Harvard University Press, 1976).

39. *Dazhong ribao* (Great masses daily) (Jinan), 13 August 1957, in SCMP, no. 1,652, pp. 20–21. For titles of religious scriptures of an Yiguan Dao sect in Shanxi, see *Guangming ribao*, 29 August 1955.

40. *Changjiang ribao*, 15 March 1952; *Qunzhong ribao*, 19 December 1957.

41. *Jiangxi ribao* (Jiangxi daily) (Nanchang), 16 June 1958, in SCMP, no. 1,875, p. 17.

42. *Guangming ribao*, 9 September 1957.

43. Ibid.

44. Ibid., 4 July 1955.

45. *Shanxi ribao* (Shanxi daily) (Taiyuan), 6 January 1955, in SCMP, no. 985, pp. 2–3.

46. *Qinghai ribao* (Qinghai daily) (Xining), 17 September 1957, in SCMP, no. 1,647, p. 10.

47. For more information on the social composition of "traditional" sectarian groups, see Susan Naquin, *Millenarian Rebellion in China: The Eight Trigrams Uprising of 1813* (New Haven: Yale University Press, 1976), pp. 38–39; and *Shantung Rebellion: The Wang Lun Uprising of 1774* (New Haven: Yale University Press, 1981), pp. 43–45.

48. On the Red Spears, see Elizabeth J. Perry, *Rebels and Revolutionaries in North China, 1845–1945* (Stanford: Stanford University Press, 1980), ch. 5. An interesting account of Red Spear resistance in the early months of the

People's Republic appears in British Foreign Office records FO 371, piece no. 83271, document no. FC101020/5. The Red Spears are described as having "decided to join hands with the landlords in an attempt to upset the communist agrarian policy." My thanks to Bruce Cumings for sharing this report with me.

49. For a secret society based on marketing networks, see Winston Hsieh, "Triads, Salt Smugglers and Local Uprisings," in Jean Chesneaux, ed., *Popular Movements and Secret Societies in China* (Stanford: Stanford University Press, 1972), pp. 145–164. For village-based cases, see Roy Hofheinz, Jr., *The Broken Wave* (Cambridge: Harvard University Press, 1977), pp. 203–206; and Lucien Bianco, "Secret Societies and Peasant Self-Defense, 1921–23," in Chesneaux, ed., *Popular Movements*, pp. 213–224. For a lineage-based case, see Robert Marks, "Class Relations and the Origins of the Rural Revolution in a South China County," *Bulletin of Concerned Asian Scholars* 15, no. 1 (January–February 1983), pp. 36–49.

50. See Vivienne Shue, *Peasant China in Transition* (Berkeley: University of California Press, 1981).

51. This point is also made in John P. Burns, "Chinese Peasant Interest Articulation, 1949–1974" (Ph.D. dissertation, Columbia University, 1979), pp. 19, 304, and 350.

52. John Wilson Lewis, "The Leadership Doctrine of the Chinese Communist Party: The Lesson of the People's Commune," *Asian Survey*, no. 3 (March 1963), p. 463.

53. Parish and Whyte, *Village and Family*, p. 302.

54. G. William Skinner, "Marketing and Social Structure in Rural China," *Journal of Asian Studies*, no. 24 (1964), pp. 3–43, and no. 24 (1965), pp. 195–228.

55. C.S. Chen, ed., *Rural People's Communes in Lien-chiang* (Stanford: Hoover Institution, 1969), p. 97.

56. Ibid., p. 110.

57. *Nanfang ribao* (Guangzhou), 18 April 1964.

58. See, for example, Chung Wen, *China Tames Her Rivers* (Beijing: Foreign Languages Press, 1972), pp. 29–30.

59. Chen, ed., *Rural People's Communes*, p. 110.

60. Certainly there were exceptions to this picture of loyal cadres. A 1961 military investigation in Xiayi, Henan, revealed, for example, that virtually all the local militia leaders were descended from "ruffians, bandits, puppet troops and rightists." In Shangcheng County, 84 percent of the heads of commune armed forces, 73 percent of militia regiment commanders, and 74 percent of militia battalion commanders were found to have committed "seriously unlawful acts." See J. Chester Cheng, ed., *The Politics of the Chinese Red Army* (Stanford: Hoover Institution, 1966), p. 119. However, the majority of incidents reported in this highly classified document, the *Gongzuo tongxun* (Work bulletin) depict local cadres who duly enforced state politics in the face of restive peasants. (See Cheng, pp. 431–432.)

61. *Renmin ribao*, 29 July 1981.

62. *Ningxia ribao* (Ningxia daily) (Yinchuan), 10 May 1982, p. 3, in FBIS, 25 May 1982, pp. T3–4.

63. Xinhua (Beijing), 10 March 1983, in FBIS, 11 March 1983, p. K16.

64. Ibid., 25 August 1981, in FBIS, 26 August 1981, p. K2.

65. Field work in Anhui and Jiangsu, summer of 1984.

66. Guizhou Provincial Service (Guiyang), 24 April 1981, in FBIS, 27 April 1981, p. Q1.

67. Anhui Provincial Service (Hefei), 23 August 1979, in FBIS, 27 August 1979, p. O1. A similar case was reported in Hong'an County, Hubei, in late 1983. A newlywed woman, surnamed "He," fought with her husband and then committed suicide. Her family amassed more than 100 Hes who marched to the husband's home and caused more than 4,700 yuan in damages. See *Zhongguo nongmin bao* (Chinese peasant gazette), 20 October 1983, p. 1.

68. Anhui Provincial Service, 3 February 1980, in FBIS, 5 February 1980, p. O3.

69. Shandong Provincial Service (Jinan), 7 November 1979, in FBIS, 14 November 1979, p. O3; Guangdong Provincial Service (Guangzhou), 26 October 1980, in FBIS, 27 October 1980, p. P2; Anhui Provincial Service, 14 December 1980, in FBIS, 19 December 1980, p. O3, and 3 February 1980, in FBIS, 5 February 1980, pp. O2–3; Hunan Provincial Service (Changsha), 14 December 1981, in FBIS, 17 December 1981, pp. K16–18; Shanxi Provincial Service (Taiyuan), 12 November 1982, in Joint Publications Research Service, *China Report: Agriculture*, no. 244, pp. 152–153.

70. *Renmin ribao*, 5 March 1983, p. 2.

71. A further discussion of cadre discontent can be found in Richard Latham, "The Implications of Rural Reforms for Grassroots Cadres," in Elizabeth J. Perry and Christine Wong, eds., *The Political Economy of Reform in Post-Mao China* (Cambridge: Harvard University Press, 1985).

72. On traditional armed feuds, see Harry J. Lamley, "Hsieh-tou: The Pathology of Violence in Southeastern China," *Ch'ing-shih wen-t'i* 3, no. 7 (1977), pp. 1–39.

73. Hainan Island Service (Haikou), 21 March 1980, in FBIS, 25 March 1980, p. P7.

74. *Hainan ribao* (Haikou), 18 September 1980, p. 1, in FBIS, 15 October 1980, pp. P4–5.

75. Hainan Island Service, 11 September 1981, in FBIS, 14 September 1981, p. P4.

76. Hunan Provincial Service, 5 April 1981, in FBIS, 8 April 1981, p. P14.

77. Hainan Island Service, 19 October 1981, in FBIS, 23 October 1981, pp. P1–2.

78. *Nanfang ribao* (Guangzhou), 5 November 1981, p. 2.

79. *Zhongguo nongmin bao*, 18 October 1983, p. 3; 20 October 1983, p. 1.

80. *Nanfang ribao*, 26 January 1983, p. 2. My thanks to Graham Johnson for bringing this article to my attention.

81. *Zhongguo nongmin bao*, 18 October 1983, p. 3.

82. On 19 August 1981, an Anhui radio broadcast reported a Daoist priest on Mt. Jiuhua who claimed to be a 123-year-old immortal "sent by the Jade Emperor to heal the sick." His promises attracted a sizable crowd. Similarly, on 14 December 1980, a Zhejiang broadcast reported that a production team head in Yiwu County, claiming to be a demi-god, had set up a formal healing practice. After a patient lit three sticks of incense, the team head would have visions and draw spells on paper. Then he would burn the paper and give his patients the ashes as a cure. See *Inside China Mainland*, December 1981, p. 10.

83. *Guangming ribao*, 20 April 1981, p. 3.

84. An Inner Mongolia radio broadcast on 1 July 1980, reported that a spring

drought had stimulated a series of mass worship services in the affected areas. *Inside China Mainland*, December 1981, p. 9.

85. *Guangming ribao*, 20 April 1981, p. 3; *Ban yue tan* (Bimonthly commentary), 25 December 1982, in FBIS, 17 January 1983, p. K18.

86. *China Daily* (Beijing), 3 November 1983, p. 4.

87. *Nanfang ribao*, 5 May 1981, p. 2, in FBIS, 20 May 1981, p. P1. Emphasis added.

88. Ibid., p. P2.

89. *Zhongguo nongmin bao*, 20 October 1983, p. 1.

90. *Ban yue tan*, 25 December 1982.

91. *Renmin ribao*, 12 July 1982; also cited in *Wen hui bao* (Shanghai), 11 October 1982, p. 3.

92. Xinhua (Beijing), 2 September 1983, in FBIS, 16 September 1983, p. K12.

93. *Beijing Review*, 23 April 1984, pp. 19–21.

94. *Renmin ribao*, 24 April 1984, p. 2.

95. *Fujian ribao* (Fujian daily), 2 April 1984. My thanks to Stephen Averill for showing me this article.

96. See Charles Tilly, "Rural Collective Action." An earlier version of the analysis appears in Tilly, "Collective Violence in European Perspective," in Hugh Davis Graham and Ted Robert Gurr, eds., *The History of Violence in America* (New York: Bantam, 1969), pp. 28–38.

97. The threat of such a possibility was seen as early as the winter of 1979 when thousands of peasants demonstrated in the streets of Beijing, carrying banners and shouting slogans calling for an end to hunger and injustice. On 14 January a group of 100 or so angry peasants yelling "We're tired of being hungry" and "Down with oppression" tried to storm the residence of then Party chairman Hua Guofeng in an unsuccessful attempt to present their grievances directly to him. See the reports by Agence France-Presse correspondents Georges Biannic and Francis Deron in FBIS, 9 January 1979, p. E1; 15 January 1979, p. E1; 22 January 1979, p. E1; 23 January 1979, p. E2; 25 January 1979, p. E2.

10

Casting a Chinese "Democracy" Movement: Legacies of Social Fragmentation

Of all the momentous political upheavals in 1989, few captured wider attention and sympathy than the Chinese protests that spring. Taking full advantage of the international media (then focused on Beijing to cover first the Asian Development Bank meetings and then the Gorbachev summit), the demonstrators engaged in a style of political showmanship that seemed tailor-made for their new global television audience: festive marches complete with colorful banners and contemporary music, somber hunger strikes punctuated by the wail of ambulance sirens, even a twenty-seven-foot "goddess of democracy" guaranteed to strike a resonant chord in foreign viewers.

Undoubtedly this adept handling of symbolic politics contributed to the widespread publicity and enthusiasm that the events in China elicited around the world; the revolutions in Eastern Europe later in the year were stimulated in part by the Chinese example. And yet, whereas the Berlin Wall came tumbling down, the walls surrounding Tiananmen

Square stand more heavily fortified than ever. International opinion was obviously not sufficient to break a Chinese regime whose leadership operated according to its own political logic. Moreover, despite the apparent sophistication of the young Chinese protesters in dealing with the international media, their movement also remained for the most part within a distinctly Chinese political tradition. The shared assumptions of rulers and rebels served to reinforce pre-existing authority relations, ensuring that China's protest movement did not become its revolution of 1989.

Why No Revolution in 1989? The Standard Explanations

When compared to the head-spinning transformations in Eastern Europe, the Chinese outcome was tragically anticlimactic. To account for this difference, two sorts of explanations are commonly given. The first, ironically enough, points to China's *revolutionary heritage.* In contrast to the communism in most of Eastern Europe, Chinese communism was the outcome of a hard-fought civil war. Having been won from within, rather than imposed by alien tanks, the Chinese system was said to enjoy a considerably higher level of popular legitimacy than its East European counterparts.

In the early 1960s, Chalmers Johnson highlighted China's (and Yugoslavia's) indigenous revolutionary experience—which he termed "peasant nationalism"—as an explanation for the emergence of the Sino-Soviet rift.[1] At that time it seemed that nationalist revolutions had engendered independent and dynamic variants of socialism: Maoism in China, Titoism in Yugoslavia. Today, however, that same revolutionary heritage (lingering on in Cuba, Vietnam, and to some extent North Korea as well) reputedly acts as a brake on further political transformation.

If legitimacy was once the product of a revolutionary past, however, it is surely being eroded by a repressive present. Presumably, then, this explanation for contemporary political stagnation is a short-lived one; as the reservoir of popular support is drained by the heavy-handed tactics of obsolescent polities, the rulers' claim to revolutionary legitimacy is rendered less and less convincing.[2]

A second type of explanation would seem to have more staying power. This is the view that stresses the *peasant nature* of China. Mired in poverty and ignorance, the hundreds of millions of rural dwellers are held responsible for China's political impasse. The tendency to lay the blame for tyranny at the feet of the peasantry is a familiar theme in social science analysis on both the left and the right. Marx claimed that Louis Napoleon's rise could be attributed to those French "potatoes in a sack," a notion that parallels the explanation many a modernization theorist has proffered for Third World dictatorships. Among Chinese intellectuals, this line of reasoning has been especially pronounced. Mao's cult of personality—and the resultant tragedies of the Cultural Revolution and its aftermath—are said to have sprung from the benighted peasantry's undemocratic messianic yearnings. It was these peasants, we are told, who were so attached to the anthem of the Cultural Revolution: "The East is red; the sun is rising. China has given birth to a Mao Zedong. He works for the people's happiness; he is our great savior." The same adulation that had propped up imperial despots for thousands of years was now being transferred to Communist tyrants—first Mao and then Deng Xiaoping. Little wonder that democracy advocates like Fang Lizhi alluded to the need to limit peasant political participation; democracy demands an enlightened citizenry—something that in China only the intellectuals claim to be.[3]

The use of peasants as convenient scapegoats is an old practice. Whenever political change failed to occur in the desired manner, the fault could be said to lie with backward inhabitants of the countryside. In fact, however, most of China's twentieth-century political follies (like those of other countries) have been centered in the cities, where intellectuals themselves have played a central role. Certainly this was true for the Cultural Revolution; not ignorant peasants but educated students (and, as we saw in Chapter 8, urban workers) proved the most zealous disciples of Chairman Mao. In the post-Mao period as well, intellectuals were a bastion of support for Deng Xiaoping through much of the 1980s. History might well have taught them better. In 1957 Deng had taken charge of implementing the notorious anti-rightist campaign that ruined the careers of hundreds of thousands of the nation's finest intellectuals.[4] In 1979–80 Deng's harsh crackdown on the Democracy Wall Movement again indicated his intolerance for intellectual criticism. Yet despite this record of repression, Chinese intellectuals continued to express enthusiasm for Deng Xiaoping.

Intellectual Traditionalism

To explain the weaknesses of China's 1989 protests, one must not stop with the country's revolutionary heritage or peasant population. Rather, the very people who launched the Tiananmen protest—urban intellectuals—were perhaps the greatest fetter on its further development. The seemingly cosmopolitan and contemporary style of the demonstrations masked other features familiar to students of earlier epochs in Chinese history.

Educated Chinese have tended to identify closely with the regime in power. For much of imperial history, this identification was of course institutionalized in the examination system; the highest honor for a Confucian scholar was to win official bureaucratic position by an outstanding examination performance. Although a vigorous tradition of remonstrance did develop among Chinese literati, it remained for the most part within officially prescribed channels. In contrast to early modern Europe, an alienated academy did not emerge in China until the twentieth century under foreign tutelage. The May Fourth Movement of 1919 revealed the explosive potential of this new critical stance, but it was a short-lived enlightenment indeed. The tendency for subsequent generations of Chinese intellectuals to invoke the May Fourth model reflected nostalgia for a truncated event, rather than the completion of its critical mission.[5] Recent generations of intellectuals, while claiming to be following in the footsteps of May Fourth protesters, have often been guilty of the very "emperor-worship mentality"—characterized by submission to a familiar pattern of ceremonial politics—against which the May Fourth Movement was ostensibly directed.

A dramatic example of this recycling of tradition was seen on April 22, 1989, a day of government-scheduled memorial services for former Party general secretary Hu Yaobang. As they had on many previous occasions (e.g., the Qingming remembrance for the late Premier Zhou Enlai thirteen years earlier, which sparked the momentous Tiananmen incident of April 5, 1976), students managed to convert an official ceremony into a counterhegemonic performance.[6] The inversion of state rituals has been used to considerable effect by protesters in other parts of the world as well, of course.[7] In taking charge of the occasion (in the Chinese case by claiming control of the official site for such events: Tiananmen Square), the demonstrators are able to challenge the legitimacy of the regime and gain a forum for conveying their own political messages. Yet a striking feature of the April 22 counterceremony was its adherence to traditionally sanctioned modes of behavior. Three student representatives attempted—in the age-old manner of Chinese scholarly remonstrance— to present a petition demanding an explanation for the ouster of Hu Yaobang and a meeting with the current premier, Li Peng. Denied entrance to the Great Hall of the People, the young emissaries suddenly fell to their knees and began to kowtow. Embarrassed at being implicitly likened to the imperial court, officials eventually opened the doors, allowing the students to present their petition to a low-ranking functionary who summarily rejected the demands.[8] The obsequious demeanor of the petitioners was an ironic reminder of the degree to which contemporary intellectuals—even in the act of protest—remain drawn to ancient modes of behavior.

Perry Link, a specialist in Chinese literature who was an eyewitness to the memorial demonstration, offers an insightful account:

> The students knelt on the steps of the People's Hall and asked the Premier, "Will you just come out and see us, just give us your acknowledgment of our trying to be patriotic and trying to help?" From our point of view the demand for dialogue with somebody might not really have punch. But for them it was really important, and in fact I can view that whole square through those thrilling days of April and May as a Beijing Opera stage . . . in that morally charged Beijing Opera sense . . . when one after another unit would come out, and say, "Here we are with our banner." This to me meant two things. It meant literally, "We have shown up," but it also meant, "We have presented ourselves in this drama."[9]

The presentation of banners representing one's unit was both a theatrical convention and part of the standard protest repertoire.[10] It was, moreover, a tradition not to be confined to Beijing. When a delegation of graduate students from the Shanghai Academy of Social Sciences attempted on May 25 to present their banner to the Shanghai Garrison Command,[11] the scene was reminiscent of the Shanghai worker militia's presentation of its banner to Chiang Kaishek following a major labor uprising in spring 1927.[12] In all these instances, the protesters were in effect seeking recognition from the ruling authorities of their unit's place on the political stage.

The Limits of Tradition

To be sure, the protesting units had changed somewhat since the Republican period. Though schools remained central, gone now were the native-place associations, guilds, and professional societies that had served as the building blocks of urban unrest during the first half of the twentieth century. Thanks to the reordering that took place under communism, in 1989 many of the participating groups were the *danwei* (or units) created by the state itself. In fact, at one point members of more than ten organs directly under the Central Committee of the Chinese

Communist Party—including the Propaganda Department—could be counted among the marchers.[13]

The incestuous relationship between state and society that had developed as a consequence of communism rendered familiar forms of protest ineffective. Although the *danwei* could serve as a vehicle to mobilize millions of people for a Tiananmen demonstration, because these units (whether schools, factories, or Party organs) were ultimately dependent on the state for their very survival, they could easily be *de*mobilized once the state leadership was united in its determination to take action. The frailty of "civil society" in contemporary Chinese cities, even when compared to the late imperial and Republican scene,[14] has made much of the old protest repertoire anachronistic. Lacking autonomy from state domination, urbanites restage the pageant of May Fourth without the *social* power that invigorated the initial performance.

The actors in the most recent rendition of this continuing drama were certainly capable of putting on an exciting show. Joseph Esherick and Jeffery Wasserstrom characterize the 1989 protest as "street theater: untitled, improvisational," but following "a historically established 'repertoire' of collective action." They rate Wuer Kaixi's performance in the May 18 dialogue with Li Peng as "one of the best acts" in this "instance of political theater"; costuming, timing, and props were all exquisitely handled.[15]

But if the theatrics were first-rate, the politics were less impressive. A notable feature of this self-styled "democracy" movement was its fickle search for patrons. Hu Yaobang, posthumous hero to the students of 1989, had been vilified in the huge demonstrations that broke out during his tenure as general secretary just a few years earlier. In winter 1986–87, a popular protest slogan had called for the overthrow of Hu Yaobang, comparing him unfavorably to the Gang of Four of Cultural Revolution notoriety.[16] Yet once Hu was ousted in January 1987, and particularly after his death from a heart attack on April 15, 1989, he became a martyr to the movement. Hu's successor as general secretary, Zhao Ziyang, now suffered the wrath of the students. Whereas Hu had been criticized for his buffoonery, Zhao was attacked for the corruption of his children.[17] Even so, when Zhao Ziyang deigned to visit the hunger strikers in Tiananmen Square on May 19, he became an instant hero, with students clamoring for his autograph. And just as soon as Zhao was deposed, he too attained instant martyrdom.

Although it would be grossly unfair to accuse the 1989 activists of anything close to the degree of adulation that surrounded Mao's cult of personality during the Cultural Revolution, nevertheless the longing for heroes remained disturbingly evident. Among many young intellectuals, this tendency found expression in support for the doctrine of "New Authoritarianism" (*xin quanweizhuyi*), which looked to a political strongman—in the tradition of Chiang Kaishek in Taiwan or Park Chung-Hee in South Korea—to push forward with economic reform. There were important differences among advocates of this doctrine,[18] but a number of its adherents played a leading role in the early stages of the 1989 demonstrations.[19] To them, state strengthening was the sine qua non of democracy—an argument that, as Andrew Nathan has shown, has been common among Chinese "democrats" since the late nineteenth century.[20] But whereas earlier generations lived under imperial and Republican regimes that were indeed too weak to effect the economic and political transformation of which young activists dreamed, the current dilemma was of an entirely different sort. Genuine reform would almost certainly require breaking, not buttressing, the state's control.

The students' deference to state authority was seen in their demand for dialogue—for a place on the political stage, as it were. Xinhua News Agency reported on April 30, "Dialogue has become a household word here as millions of Beijing residents watched last night and tonight the television program of the dialogue between Yuan Mu, the spokesman for the State Council, and the college students."[21] Dramatic as it was, the demand for dialogue was also an admission of the hold that the state continued to exert; protesters wanted a role in the official political pageant, which for them remained the only real show in town. As Geremie Barmé observes, "students and intellectuals alike have craved above all for some form of official recognition, their own place at the helm of the ship of state."[22] In sharp contrast to their counterparts in Eastern Europe, Chinese urbanites certainly had not "simply . . . [begun] to turn away from the state, by refusing to take it seriously."[23]

Perhaps the most distressing aspect of the demand for dialogue was the limited cast of characters included in the request. Perpetuating a Confucian mentality that assigned to intellectuals the role of spokesmen for the masses, students assumed that they were the only segment of society whose voice deserved to be heard. The disregard for peasants and workers was a prejudice that intellectuals shared with state leaders. Deng Xiaoping—like Chiang Kaishek and Yuan Shikai before him—was a reformer who viewed the Chinese peasantry as an obstacle to the fulfillment of his national objectives. When each of these reformers turned repressor, he pointed to the "backward" peasants as the reason why China's march toward representative government would have to be postponed. Similarly, in 1989's "democracy" movement, students were reportedly "horrified at the suggestion that truly popular elections would have to include peasants, who would certainly outvote educated people like themselves."[24] As a young intellectual in Wuhan explained, "While the people support our aims of stamping out corruption, they just don't understand the ideas of freedom and democracy."[25]

Confucian Moralism

From the perspective of the students, peasants and workers appeared motivated by crass materialism, whereas their own politics were selflessly pure. The link to Confucian morality is evident here. When hunger strikers wrote out their last testaments—vowing to sacrifice their very lives for their beliefs—they joined an ancient tradition of scholar-martyrs dating back to the third century B.C.

The intense moralism of the Tiananmen protesters has been noted by many analysts. Lee Feigon writes of the hunger strikers: "By fasting they hoped to contrast the *moral righteousness* of their behavior with that of the corrupt and despotic government against which they protested."[26] Dorothy Solinger highlights the "proclivity to *moralize* and demand high behavioral standards from rulers."[27] And Esherick and Wasserstrom point out that the manifestos of the protesters were filled with "*moral* statements of resolve."[28]

In this respect, the Chinese case would seem to fit comfortably into Daniel Chirot's interpretation of the East European revolutions of 1989; the cause was essentially moral. Chirot links "the endless corruption, the lies, the collapse of elementary social trust, the petty tyranny at every level" to a moral backlash.[29] Similarly, at the height of the Chinese protests, Fang Lizhi offered the following analysis: "The corruption is so obvious now. People see it every day in their factories and offices. Everybody understands what is going on. The blatant profiteering of state officials is now the focal point of the movement because it is this profiteering that has directly led to the failure of the economic reform."[30] An attitude survey conducted in Beijing at about the same time provided support for Fang's assertions; the overwhelming majority of respondents saw anticorruption as the most important goal of the movement and predicted that corruption was the most likely precipitant of future unrest in China.[31] A startling indication of this moralism was the nostalgia for Chairman Mao that surfaced during the spring protests.[32] One popular ditty expressed the general sentiment: "Mao Zedong's son went to the front lines [and was killed as a soldier in the Korean War]; Zhao Ziyang's son smuggles color television sets."

The 1989 demonstration was, in David Strand's words, "a morality play done in Beijing opera style."[33] As a morality play, it shared many features of the East European scenario. But its Beijing opera style limited the stars of the show to the Confucian elite: scholars and officials. Indeed, the criticisms that Mao's wife Jiang Qing had leveled against the Beijing opera during the Cultural Revolution could be applied with equal force to the Tiananmen drama: the plot followed a standard format that denied heroic roles to workers and peasants.

Rank-and-File Participation

That the ordinary populace was in fact fully capable of dramatic action is revealed not only by its revolutionary history but by its recent behavior as well. In the post-Mao era, despite major gains for agriculture under the reforms, unrest in the Chinese countryside has been remarkably prevalent.[34] As we saw in Chapter 7, this rural protest was accompanied by a strong resurgence of folk religion; many of the incidents have involved shamans, ancestral temples, "jade emperors descended to earth," and the like. Undoubtedly the popular religion of the contemporary countryside differs significantly from its pre-1949 forerunners; the socialist experience has left a visible imprint on the mentality of today's peasantry.[35] But regardless of how old or new these practices may be, they suggest the fuzzy outlines of a "civil society" in the sense of a domain of public interaction not fully controlled by the state. The drive to institutionalize this domain (as seen in the privately financed rebuilding of local earth-god temples or rewriting of lineage genealogies, for example) further attests to the efforts of the rural populace to carve out a niche of independence from state authority. We are not, of course, seeing here a Chinese Solidarity or Neues Forum. Yet we are witnessing the consolidation of organizational forms that, as we observed in Chapter 1, have for centuries provided a foundation for popular protest.[36] When they join state officials in dismissing these practices as "feudal superstition" (*fengjian mixin*), contemporary intellectuals mirror the prejudices of their Confucian forefathers as well as of the ruling regime. In failing to take seriously the peasantry's capacity for collective action, would-be democrats deny themselves a powerful and essential ally.

Equally damaging to the democratic project has been the exclusion of other key social groups: entrepreneurs and workers in particular. With the liberalization of marketing under the post-Mao reforms, an explosion in entrepreneurship occurred. Enticed by the profits to be made in commercial activity, hundreds of thousands of peasants and town dwellers

rushed to join the burgeoning ranks of the *getihu*, or independent entrepreneurs. Their transactions gave new life to the realm of nongovernment
economic activities that G.W.F. Hegel, Karl Marx, and Antonio Gramsci
all viewed as central to the emergence of civil society. The importance
of the growth of this commercial class for the advent of democratic
politics has often been posited. In Barrington Moore's memorable formulation, "No bourgeoisie, no democracy." The defense of property and
profits encourages ordinary citizens to fight for the freedoms associated
with liberal democracy.[37]

The support provided by Chinese entrepreneurs for the student protests
in 1989 was in fact substantial. In Shanghai on May 21, "hundreds of
people with 'entrepreneur' banners staged a sit-in" in sympathy with the
students.[38] Unlike most Chinese, the independent *getihu* could engage in
political action without fear of sanctions from their work units. Many of
them were, moreover, financially well off. Their largess proved crucial
in sustaining the student movement. As one private entrepreneur recalled,
"Whenever the *getihu*s passed by one of the students' donation check-
points, they would stop to give money—from ten, several tens to a thousand or even tens of thousands of dollars, to show that the *getihu*s were
sincere from the bottom of our hearts."[39] Such monetary contributions
made possible the purchase of battery-operated megaphones for the student leaders.[40] One of the largest of the new private enterprises, the Stone
Corporation, is estimated to have donated tens of thousands of dollars'
worth of sophisticated equipment—including facsimile machines—to the
protesters.[41] As military intervention grew imminent, the Flying Tiger
Brigade of *getihu* on motorbikes delivered news of troop movements to
the students. After the crackdown, the pedicabs of the *getihu* carried off
the casualties.

Despite this crucial help, the entrepreneurs received from the students
the same disparaging appellation that the regime used to discredit them.
Intellectuals and officials alike referred publicly to the *getihu* as *xiansan*
ren—idle drifters.[42] In Communist China as in Confucian China, commercial elements are scorned as rootless, amoral figures who cannot be
trusted.[43] (Significantly, the Chinese societies where merchants *have*
flourished—Taiwan, Singapore, Hong Kong, and treaty port Shanghai—
are also societies where the link between state and scholar was broken
by colonialism.)[44] The experience of Taiwan in particular establishes the
catalytic role that the commercial middle class can play in the democratization process. Chirot similarly points to the centrality of the East
European middle class in the upheavals of 1989.[45] In denigrating this

key social element, Chinese students undervalued the contributions of one of the most enthusiastic supporters of their cause.

Another group in the Tiananmen drama relegated to a role well beneath its actual performance ability was the urban working class. As noted in Chapter 8, Chinese popular movements of the past century demonstrate the extraordinary power of a worker–student alliance. The May Fourth Movement of 1919, which began as a demonstration by 3,000 students in Beijing, became a historical watershed only after it had been joined by tens of thousands of Shanghai workers in a general strike the following month. It was this participation by labor that persuaded the government to disavow the terms of the Versailles Treaty that threatened to turn China's Shandong Province into a virtual colony of Japan. And it was this same worker activism that in 1921 persuaded young student organizers to establish a Communist Party dedicated to the proletarian cause. Four years later the influence of this new party was seen in the momentous May Thirtieth Movement of 1925—again precipitated by a worker–student protest against imperialism—which marked a high point of Communist strength in the cities. Although subdued by Chiang Kaishek's "white terror" of repression against the Left in spring 1927, the urban coalition regained force after the Japanese invasion of 1937. Fueled first by anti-Japanese sentiment and then, after 1945, by anti-Americanism, worker–student nationalism was a key ingredient in the Communist victory of 1949.[46]

As we saw in Chapters 6, 8, and 9, the founding of the People's Republic certainly did not spell the end of labor unrest. In fact, every decade has brought a new round of widespread strikes. In 1956–57, the Hundred Flowers Movement saw a major outburst to protest inequalities of the First Five-Year Plan. In 1966–67, the Cultural Revolution prompted another explosion of labor protest. In 1974–76, resentment against the austere policies of the Gang of Four resulted in a further display of working-class dissatisfaction.[47] And in 1986–88, strikes erupted at factories across the country to protest the inflationary consequences of the post-Mao reforms.[48] In contrast to the pre-1949 situation, however, the contemporary upheavals elicited little enthusiasm from students. To be sure, much of the explanation for the separation of worker and student politics in the socialist era can be attributed to the effectiveness of state controls.[49] But a certain amount of the responsibility must also be assigned to the intellectuals' disdain for a working class whose aspirations are dismissed as crass "economism."

That workers are actually attracted to larger social causes than many intellectuals give them credit for is shown in their reaction to student demonstrations. When tens of thousands of students marched in Shanghai during winter 1986–87 to demand freedom of expression and an end to police brutality, an even larger group of workers gathered in support. Although a tight police cordon was formed to prevent anyone without valid student identification from entering the center of the demonstration, sympathetic workers stood just outside the police lines yelling, "Younger brothers, your elder brothers support you!" and tossing in bread and cigarettes as a gesture of solidarity. The immediate precipitant of this massive demonstration was the police beating of a college student during a concert by an American rock group in Shanghai. When fellow students erupted in fury, the mayor of Shanghai (who subsequently became general secretary of the Communist Party), Jiang Zemin, went to the campus of the injured student to offer an explanation. The police, he assured his audience, had mistaken the young concert-goer for a worker; had they only realized he was an intellectual, such heavy-handed treatment would never have been applied. Most members of the campus community reportedly found nothing improper in the mayor's line of reasoning.[50]

Many workers, increasingly disadvantaged by the post-Mao industrial reforms, had ample cause for concern about government policy. For one thing, double-digit inflation was threatening their standard of living. For another, the reforms promised to put more money into industrial reinvestment at the expense of workers' housing and bonuses. "Economistic" as such issues may be, they could form the backbone of a lively protest. Moreover, workers were no less aware or intolerant of corruption and petty tyranny than other Chinese. In short, the basis for a potent worker–student alliance seemed to exist. As in the pre-1949 era, such an urban coalition might have been constructed on the foundations of both *consumer* identity and *citizen* identity. As consumers, urbanites could unite against the debilitating effects of runaway inflation (also a central issue during the general strikes of May Fourth and the Civil War years). As citizens, they could condemn government corruption (again an issue, along with imperialism, in all the major pre-1949 urban movements). Orthodox historiography notwithstanding, it was not simply *class* identity (or protest against on-the-job exploitation) that had fueled the massive worker strikes of early twentieth-century China. Labor was accustomed to performing on a larger stage than the narrow confines of the workplace.[51]

In spring 1989, workers again sought to play a major role in the drama unfolding in Tiananmen Square. On April 20, laborers from a number of Beijing factories made speeches at the square, proclaiming that "workers and students should work together for the introduction of a more democratic and less corrupt system."[52] Fearing the dangers of growing working-class participation, especially as the May Fourth anniversary drew near, the Beijing city government issued an order forbidding any worker to take leave of absence between April 25 and May 5.[53] At this same time, Deng Xiaoping—explaining that "the movement might soon spread to workers and peasants, as in Poland, Yugoslavia, Hungary, and the Soviet Union"[54]—arranged for two divisions of the Thirty-eighth Army to be called into the city. But the leadership's fears of a worker–student coalition were in fact ungrounded. As Anita Chan and Jonathan Unger have observed, until the very end of the movement, "the students had disdainfully tried to keep the workers at arm's length."[55] This was literally the case, with students linking arms to prevent workers from joining their ranks.[56] As the member of one working-class family observed, "The workers could see that participation was being strictly restricted by the students themselves, as if the workers were not qualified to participate . . . the issues that the students raised had nothing to do with workers. For example, Wuer Kaixi in his speeches only talked about the students. If he had mentioned the workers as well, appealed to the workers, appealed to them in a sincere manner, the workers might really have come out in a major way."[57] Only during the last week of May, beleaguered by the growing threat of military suppression, were student delegations sent to the major factories to seek support.[58]

Considering the lack of student initiative, the extent of worker participation was really rather remarkable. In late April an unofficial workers' group calling itself Beijing Workers' Autonomous Association issued a statement condemning inflation and the gap between wealthy government leaders and the ordinary people. The group called for wage raises, price stabilization, and publication of the incomes and material possessions of Party and government officials and their families.[59] A month later, claiming a membership of more than 6,000 workers, the association's goal was "to set up a nationwide non-Communist union along the lines of Poland's Solidarity trade union."[60] At this time it issued a stinging attack, in cynical Marxist language, on official corruption and its deleterious consequences for the Chinese working class:

> We have carefully considered the exploitation of the workers. Marx's
> *Capital* provided us with a method for understanding the character of
> our oppression. We deducted from the total value of output the work-
> ers' wages, welfare, medical welfare, the necessary social fund, equip-
> ment depreciation and reinvestment expenses. Surprisingly, we

discovered that "civil servants" swallow all the remaining value produced by the people's blood and sweat! The total taken by them is really vast! How cruel! How typically Chinese! These bureaucrats use the people's hard earned money to build luxury villas all over the country (guarded by soldiers in so-called military areas), to buy luxury cars, to travel to foreign countries on so-called study tours (with their families, and even baby sitters)! Their immoral and shameful deeds and crimes are too numerous to mention here.[61]

To fight such "typically Chinese" bureaucratic corruption, the autonomous union pledged to support the student hunger strikers and to "promote democratization in alliance with students and citizens from all walks of life."[62]

Pressured by this competition from an unofficial labor association, the official All-China Federation of Trade Unions (ACFTU) began to assume a more active role in responding to working-class concerns. On May 1 (International Workers' Day), the president of the ACFTU conceded that government-sponsored unions "should fully support workers in their fight against corruption."[63] Thanks to this encouragement, workers became more involved in the demonstrations. On May 17, as the hunger strike entered its fifth day,

> Millions of workers, peasants, and clerks from government organs, personnel from cultural and publishing circles and from the press took to the streets to show they supported and cared for the students. . . . Particularly noticeable were the massive marching columns of workers. They came from scores of enterprises such as the Capital Steel Corporation, the main factory of the Beijing Internal Combustion Engines, Beijing Lifting Machinery Factory and the state-run Number 798 Factory. The demonstrating workers were holding banners and placards carrying slogans stating: "Students and workers are bound by a common cause" and "Workers are grieved seeing students on hunger strike."[64]

The next day the ACFTU took the bold step of donating 100,000 yuan (about $27,000) for medical aid to students in the sixth day of their hunger strike. Explained a spokesperson for the federation, "We workers are deeply concerned about the health and lives of the students."[65] The same day, the Shanghai Federation of Trade Unions added its voice in support of the movement: "Workers in the city have expressed universal concern and sympathy for the patriotism of students who are demanding democracy, rule of law, an end to corruption, checking inflation, and promoting reform. The municipal council of trade unions fully affirms this."[66]

There were limits beyond which the official unions could not go, however. On May 20, a crowd of workers gathered in front of the ACFTU offices to demand that the unions order a national strike.[67] Three days later, after the declaration of martial law, Beijing television announced: "In the last few days, there have been rumors in some localities saying that the All-China Federation of Trade Unions has called for a nation-wide general strike. A spokesman for the Federation said that this is merely a rumor with ulterior motives. The spokesman emphatically pointed out that the ACFTU has recently stressed that the vast number of staff members and workers should firmly stay at their posts and properly carry out production work."[68] By the end of the month, Ruan Chongwu, a former minister of public security, had been appointed to the post of labor minister. His brief was "to ensure that workers remain loyal to the party and government—and that they not take part in activities that challenge the regime."[69] Reported the Hong Kong press, "A top priority with Mr. Ruan and the restructured leadership of the trade unions federation will be to prevent nonofficial unions from being organized."[70]

In the drive to recapture control of labor, three leaders of the Beijing Workers' Autonomous Association were detained by the police on May 30. Also rounded up were eleven members of the Flying Tiger Brigade— the contingent of 300 motorbikers, at least 200 of whom were independent entrepreneurs—which was providing information on troop deployment to the students.[71] Once again workers and other nonstudents were being made to pay the price for a movement in which they had played only supporting roles.[72] Even so, many continued to defy the authorities. On June 9 at a huge demonstration and memorial service in Shanghai for victims of the June 4 massacre, among the marchers were about 1,000 workers holding high a banner that read "Shanghai Autonomous Federation of Labor Unions."[73]

Conclusion

The tragic ending to China's uprising of 1989 is explained neither by the salience of its revolutionary ideology nor by the silence of rural inhabitants. If the persistence of "tradition" served as a brake on political transformation, the relevant tradition was not that of the committed revolutionary or conservative peasantry. Ironically, it was the very instigators of the Tiananmen protest—the urban intellectuals—who appeared most wedded to a limiting legacy. In their *style of remonstrance* (presenting petitions and banners and demanding dialogue with the authorities), their *search for political patrons* (emphasizing the need for state strengthening and switching quickly from one "hero" to the next), and above all their *stress on moralism* (contrasting their own selfless martyrdom to the crass materialism of the masses), the students evinced a brand of political behavior and belief replete with the stigmata of the imperial past.

The neo-traditionalism of student protesters was not due to some immutable Confucian culture, forever lurking like a sea monster beneath the surface of China's political waters—waiting to seize and sink any unsuspecting would-be democrat who happened to swim by.[74] As we saw in Chapter 5, the cities of Republican China had been home to a much more inclusive mode of political protest. That the causes of student exclusionism at Tiananmen Square in the spring of 1989 were as much structural as cultural is further suggested by a demonstration that occurred a year later in Taiwan. The Taipei protest (which helped to bring about direct elections for the presidency of the Republic of China a few years later) borrowed directly from the repertoire of the Tiananmen Uprising: students occupied the central political square in Taipei where they undertook a hunger strike, donned headbands, and listened to the same rock songs that had excited their predecessors across the Taiwan Strait just the year before. However, in stark contrast to their compatriots on the mainland, the student protesters on Taiwan welcomed to their movement a wide array of other social groups, including workers. The growth of a substantial middle class as a product of Taiwan's economic "miracle," and the decline of state controls with the lifting of martial law, had blurred social distinctions on the island, encouraging intellectuals to identify more with fellow citizens than with state authorities. Clearly, then, Chinese political culture is not a permanent barrier to cross-class alliances. Rather, the intellectuals' political proclivities at Tiananmen in 1989—as in the imperial era—were shaped by the close structural links that obtained between state and scholar.[75]

Though the Confucian examination system was abolished in 1905, the Communists instituted a *fenpei* (allocation) system whereby the state assigns college graduates to jobs commensurate with their scholastic records, political loyalties, and of course personal connections. Even more than under the imperial regime, the socialist state exercised a virtual monopoly over meaningful job opportunities for intellectuals. Little wonder, then, that these intellectuals—even in the act of protest—should evince such state-centric tendencies. It was only during the Republican interregnum, when the state's hold over the scholar was effectively eased, that a different sort of student protest emerged. That "May Fourth Tradition," which held sway from 1919 until the founding of the PRC in 1949, was a brilliant but brief chapter in the history of Chinese popular protest. Occurring during an unusual period of state retrenchment (at least with respect to control over intellectuals), the protests of that generation demonstrated an unprecedented independence and enthusiasm for active alliance with workers, peasants, and merchants. It was these qualities of autonomy and mass involvement that imbued the collective action of the Republican era with such social fire. By contrast, contemporary intellectuals who attempt to resuscitate the spirit of May Fourth are hampered by the inability to liberate themselves from the hegemonic claims of the state and thereby to embrace the interests of other social elements. As a consequence, their rendition of the May Fourth drama is much less powerful—politically, if not necessarily theatrically—than pre-1949 performances.

The omnipresence of the Chinese Communist state, even more than its Confucian forerunner or its East European counterparts, has inhibited the florescence of "civil society" and rendered the formation of cross-class coalitions correspondingly difficult and dangerous. Accordingly, Andrew Walder cautions against interpreting the Tiananmen upheaval "as a direct expression of the growth of an independent society. Such independence was greatly restricted in China relative to Poland, Hungary, and the Soviet Union."[76] But if the answer lies not in a developed "civil society," how *do* we explain China's recent turmoil? For Walder, "the key to the 1989 upheaval appears to be the splintering of the central leadership and the Party–state apparatus after the initial student protests of April."[77] There is considerable merit in an emphasis on elites and political institutions. As we have seen in the case of the All-China Federation of Trade Unions, elements of the state did indeed play a significant role in facilitating the protest movement of 1989. At the same time, however, we must not underestimate the potential for self-generated political action by nonstate entities. The practices of Chinese civil society are substantially different from those of Eastern Europe. Absent in China are the Catholic church of Poland, the old democratic parties of Hungary, or the dissident intellectual circles of the Soviet Union and Czechoslovakia. Yet there is evidence that recent reforms have encouraged the resurgence of meaningful traditions of extrastate economic and associational behavior in China, just as in Eastern Europe. Today's independent entrepreneurs, practitioners of folk religion, and members of autonomous labor unions are all building on patterns of collective identity and action with proven records of resisting state domination in the Chinese context. These practices may well lack the democratic character of the institutions of civil society in Eastern Europe.[78] But as Strand has noted, "When Chinese seek to revive a democratic tradition, it is a tradition of movements, not institutions, they are drawing upon."[79] And China's merchants, peasants, and workers—as well as students—can rightfully lay claim to a vital part of that inheritance.[80]

In accounting for the timing of the 1989 protest movement, it is clear that the efforts of the Chinese state to undertake reform have played a major hand in encouraging dissent on the part of both political elites and ordinary citizens. Although the relationship between reform and revolution is poorly understood, it is obviously significant. As the history of modern China shows, reform is often the harbinger of revolution. The 1911 Revolution that toppled the imperial system followed upon the Hundred Days' reform and New Policies of the ailing Qing dynasty. Chiang Kaishek's reformist New Life Movement heralded the imminent demise of the Nationalist regime. Serious reforms exact substantial costs on at least some sectors of both state and society. Furthermore, they raise expectations to levels that can seldom be attained. Most important, reforms are admissions by the regime of its own inadequacies. As a result, they encourage widespread disbelief. This is especially unsettling in Communist systems, where claims to ideological truth have been so central. When the leadership publicly repudiates many of its past practices, it invites ordinary citizens to engage in open criticism as well.

The uprising of 1989 was a dramatic expression of Chinese students' appetite and aptitude for political criticism. Influenced by forty years of socialism as well as by international cultural currents, the demonstrators staged an innovative performance. Dunce caps from the Cultural Revolution, rock music from Taiwan, headbands from South Korea and Japan, and a hunger strike from Gandhi's India all contributed a seemingly contemporary and cosmopolitan flavor. Yet in some of its core values the student movement appeared remarkably traditional. Thanks to the special bond between state and scholar that had persisted for so long under the imperial system and was reconstituted (on different terms, to be sure) under the socialist system, Chinese students engaged in an exclusionary style of protest that served to reinforce pre-existing authority relations. At the same time, however, other social groups showed themselves ready to reclaim the spirit of the May Fourth Movement—in which a fledgling civil society had challenged a troubled Chinese state on both moral and material grounds.

Notes

An earlier version of this chapter was published in Jeffrey N. Wasserstrom and Elizabeth J. Perry, eds., *Popular Protest and Political Culture in Modern China* (Boulder: Westview Press, 1994).

1. Chalmers Johnson, *Peasant Nationalism and Communist Power: The Emergence of Revolutionary China, 1937–1945* (Stanford: Stanford University Press, 1962).

2. Of course, powerholders in Beijing see the situation differently. Jiang Zemin, general secretary of the Chinese Communist Party, offered five reasons why his country would not go the way of Eastern Europe: (1) The CCP is armed with Marxism–Leninism–Mao Zedong Thought and has grown strong through armed struggle; (2) The Chinese military is armed with Maoism and led by the CCP; (3) Chinese socialism was created by the Chinese people themselves and not forced upon them by the Soviet Red Army; (4) China is not surrounded by capitalist countries; and (5) Marxism has been sinicized by Mao Zedong and Deng Xiaoping and is thus not subject to a Soviet type of reform movement. Quoted in *World Policy Journal*, December 22, 1989, p. 20.

3. Richard C. Kraus, "The Lament of Astrophysicist Fang Lizhi: China's Intellectuals in a Global Contest," in Arif Dirlik and Maurice Meisner, eds., *Marxism and the Chinese Experience* (Armonk, NY: M.E. Sharpe, 1989), pp. 294–315.

4. On Deng's role in the anti-rightist campaign, see David Bachman, *Bureaucracy, Economy and Leadership in China: The Institutional Origins of the Great Leap Forward* (New York: Cambridge University Press, 1991), ch. 8.

5. Vera Schwarcz, *The Chinese Enlightenment: Intellectuals and the Legacy of the May Fourth Movement of 1919* (Berkeley: University of California Press, 1986), pp. 283–291. Schwarcz argues convincingly that the incompleteness of the May Fourth enlightenment is linked to the tension in twentieth-century China between commitment to cultural criticism and commitment to national salvation. Those who raised the most serious criticisms have been open to the charge of being unpatriotic.

6. Examples of this technique during the Republican period can be found in Jeffrey N. Wasserstrom, *Student Protests in Twentieth-Century China: The View from Shanghai* (Stanford: Stanford University Press, 1991).

7. See Charles Tilly, *The Contentious French* (Cambridge: Harvard University Press, 1986), for a discussion of comparable protest behavior in France.

8. Lee Feigon, *China Rising: The Meaning of Tiananmen* (Chicago: Ivan R. Dee, 1990), p. 146; Foreign Broadcast Information Service (hereafter FBIS) (April 27, 1989), pp. 11–12.

9. Perry Link, *Chinese Writers Under Fire*, pp. 21–22; quoted in David Strand, " 'Civil Society' and 'Public Sphere' in Modern China: A Perspective on Popular Movements in Beijing, 1919–1989," *Working Papers in Asian/Pacific Studies* (Durham, NC: Asian/Pacific Studies Institute, Duke University Press, 1990), pp. 30–31.

10. On the continuity with earlier student movements, see Jeffrey Wasserstrom, "Student Protests in the Chinese Tradition, 1919–1989," in Tony Saich, ed., *Perspectives on the Chinese People's Movement: Spring 1989* (Armonk, NY: M.E. Sharpe, 1990). At least since the May Fourth Movement, groups of stu-

dents had paraded with banners naming their alma mater as they marched from school to school, calling on those at other institutions to join in the task of saving the nation.

11. Wu Mouren et al., *Bajiu Zhongguo minyun jishi* (Annals of the 1989 Chinese democracy movement) (New York: privately published, 1989), p. 446.

12. Jean Chesneaux, *The Chinese Labor Movement, 1919–1927* (Stanford: Stanford University Press, 1968).

13. FBIS (May 18, 1989), pp. 49–50.

14. On the earlier situation, see William Rowe, *Hankow: Conflict and Community in a Chinese City, 1796–1895* (Stanford: Stanford University Press, 1989); Susan Mann, *Local Merchants and the Chinese Bureaucracy, 1750–1950* (Stanford: Stanford University Press, 1987); and Mary Rankin, *Elite Activism and Political Transformation in China* (Stanford: Stanford University Press, 1986).

15. Joseph W. Esherick and Jeffrey N. Wasserstrom, "Acting Out Democracy: Political Theater in Modern China," in Jeffrey N. Wasserstrom and Elizabeth J. Perry, eds., *Popular Protest and Political Culture in Modern China* (Boulder: Westview Press, 1994).

16. Personal observation, Shanghai, December 1986. The slogan was: "Dadao Hu Yaobang; Ningyuan Sirenbang!" (Down with Hu Yaobang; better the Gang of Four!).

17. A son who had allegedly used his family connections to make huge profits from an illicit trading company in Hainan was the cause of much of the public hostility.

18. The Beijing variant, formulated by Rong Jian and others close to Zhao Ziyang, argued for a coercive government to carry out radical liberalization of the economy. The southern variant, as formulated by Xiao Gongqin at Shanghai Normal University, favored a more gradual reform program. See Xiao Gongqin, "Lun guodu quanweizhuyi" (On transitional authoritarianism), *Qingnian xuezhe*, no. 2 (1989).

19. Feigon, *China Rising*, ch. 6.

20. Andrew J. Nathan, *Chinese Democracy* (Berkeley: University of California Press, 1985).

21. FBIS (May 1, 1989), p. 50.

22. Geremie Barmé, "Blood Offering," *Far Eastern Economic Review*, June 22, 1989, p. 39. As Barmé explains this phenomenon: "The traditional role of the scholar-bureaucrat dovetailed neatly with the Stalinist talk of engineers of the human soul."

23. For this argument about Eastern Europe, see Daniel Chirot, ed., *The Crisis of Leninism and the Decline of the Left: The Revolutions of 1989* (Seattle: University of Washington Press, 1991).

24. Mary S. Erbaugh and Richard C. Kraus, "The 1989 Democracy Movement in Fujian and Its Consequences," *Australian Journal of Chinese Affairs*, no. 23 (1990), p. 153.

25. Eddie Yuen, "Wuhan Takes to the Streets" (unpublished paper, 1990), p. 11. However, as Yuen notes (pp. 10, 12), hundreds of workers did in fact participate in the Wuhan protests by attending demonstrations and driving out in factory trucks after their work shifts were over.

26. Feigon, *China Rising*, p. 196 (emphasis added).

27. Dorothy Solinger, "Democracy with Chinese Characteristics," *World Policy Journal* (Fall 1989), p. 625 (emphasis added).

28. Esherick and Wasserstrom, "Acting Out Democracy," pp. 50ff.

29. Chirot, *The Crisis of Leninism*, p. 11.

30. *South China Morning Post*, May 22, 1989, p. 23.

31. *China Information*, 4, no. 1 (1989), p. 4.

32. Feigon, *China Rising*, p. 206. The carrying of Mao posters was one expression of this phenomenon.

33. Strand, "Civil Society and Public Sphere," p. 16.

34. Elizabeth J. Perry, "Rural Collective Violence: The Fruits of Recent Reform," in Elizabeth J. Perry and Christine Wong, eds., *The Political Economy of Reform in Post-Mao China* (Cambridge: Harvard University Press, 1985).

35. For this argument, see Helen Siu, *Agents and Victims* (New Haven: Yale University Press, 1989); and Elizabeth J. Perry, "Crime, Corruption and Contention in Contemporary China," in Merle Goldman and Roderick MacFarguhar, eds., *The Paradox of China's Post-Mao Reforms* (Cambridge: Harvard University Press, 1999).

36. On rural religion as a basis for anti-state rebellion, see Susan Naquin, *Millenarian Rebellion in China: The Eight Trigrams Uprising of 1813* (New Haven: Yale University Press, 1976). On kinship and village as organizational bases of rural protest, see Elizabeth J. Perry, *Rebels and Revolutionaries in North China, 1845–1945* (Stanford: Stanford University Press, 1980).

37. Barrington Moore, Jr., *Social Origins of Dictatorship and Democracy* (Boston: Beacon Press, 1966), ch. 6. For a dissenting view, see Nina P. Halpern, "Economic Reform and Democratization in Communist Systems: The Case of China," *Studies in Comparative Communism*, 22, nos. 2/3 (1989).

38. Wu, *Bajiu Zhongguo minyun jishi*, p. 355.

39. *Jiushi niandai* (The nineties) (December 1989), pp. 15–16, quoted in Anita Chan and Jonathan Unger, "Voices from the Protest Movement, Chongqing, Sichuan," *Australian Journal of Chinese Affairs*, no. 24 (July 1990), p. 264.

40. Feigon, *China Rising*, p. 183.

41. Ibid., p. 184.

42. Interviews with participants, Seattle, April–May 1990. An exception was the dissident writer Wang Ruoshui, who argued for an affinity of interests between intellectuals and entrepreneurs. See the interview with Wang in *Jiushi niandai* (The nineties) (April 1989), p. 37.

43. On public disdain for the *getihu*, see Thomas B. Gold, "Guerrilla Interviewing Among the *Getihu*," in Perry Link, Richard Madsen, and Paul Pickowicz, eds., *Unofficial China: Popular Culture and Thought in the People's Republic* (Boulder: Westview, 1989), pp. 175–192.

44. In Taiwan, the role of intellectuals was further weakened after the GMD takeover via a land reform that undermined their traditional economic base and (by compensating dispossessed landlords with stock in nascent industries) converted the intellectuals themselves into members of the bourgeoisie.

45. Chirot, *The Crisis of Leninism*.

46. Suzanne Pepper, *Civil War in China* (Berkeley: University of California Press, 1980).

47. Lowell Dittmer, *China's Continuous Revolution* (Berkeley: University of California Press, 1988).

48. Interviews at the Shanghai Federation of Trade Unions, Shanghai, May 1987 and September 1988.

49. See Andrew Walder, *Communist Neo-Traditionalism: Work and Authority in Chinese Industry* (Berkeley: University of California Press, 1986). Walder provides an insightful discussion of the operation of state controls in state-owned factories. In my view, however, he underestimates the possibility of autonomous worker protests.

50. Personal observations and interviews, Shanghai, December 1987–January 1988.

51. Elizabeth J. Perry, *Shanghai on Strike: The Politics of Chinese Labor* (Stanford: Stanford University Press, 1993); Elizabeth J. Perry, "From Paris to the 'Paris of the East'—and Back: Workers as Citizens in Modern Shanghai," in Merle Goldman and Elizabeth J. Perry, eds., *Changing Meanings of Citizenship in Modern China* (Cambridge: Harvard University Press, 2002).

52. FBIS (April 20, 1989), p. 18.

53. FBIS (April 26, 1989), p. 17.

54. Feigon, *China Rising*, p. 153.

55. Anita Chan and Jonathan Unger, "China After Tiananmen," *Nation*, January 22, 1990, pp. 79–81. See also Henry Rosemont, Jr., "China: The Mourning After," *Z Magazine* (March 1990), p. 87. Rosemont argues that for the first four of the six weeks of demonstrations, students kept their distance from workers. Workers were primarily concerned with inflation and job security, issues that did not gain student attention.

56. Feigon, *China Rising*, p. 203.

57. Chan and Unger, "Voices," p. 273. Similar sentiments were expressed in an open letter to the students from a Beijing worker. See Mok Chiu Yu and J. Frank Harrison, eds., *Voices from Tiananmen Square* (Montreal: Black Rose Books, 1990), pp. 111–112.

58. FBIS (May 26, 1989), p. 52.

59. The founding manifesto of the union can be found in Yu and Harrison, *Voices*, p. 107. See also FBIS (April 28, 1989), p. 11.

60. FBIS (May 30, 1989), p. 9; FBIS (May 31, 1989), p. 44.

61. Yu and Harrison, *Voices*, p. 109.

62. Ibid., p. 114.

63. *China Daily*, May 1, 1989, p. 1.

64. FBIS (May 18, 1989), p. 49.

65. Ibid., p. 76.

66. FBIS (May 22, 1989), p. 91.

67. Ibid., p. 45. See also Yu and Harrison, *Voices*, p. 114.

68. FBIS (May 23, 1989), p. 58. Whatever the ACFTU leadership may really have felt about a general strike, theirs was one of the last government/Party units to express support for martial law. See FBIS (May 30, 1989), p. 9.

69. FBIS (May 30, 1989), p. 9.

70. Ibid.

71. FBIS (May 31, 1989), p. 44.

72. On the detention of additional workers and entrepreneurs in early June, see FBIS (June 2, 1989), p. 11. Wuhan also saw more severe treatment for workers than for students. See Yuen, "Wuhan," p. 13. Rosemont states that at

least forty-two workers were executed after the June 4 crackdown, whereas no student executions had been reported. Rosemont, "China," p. 87.

73. Wu, *Bajiu Zhongguo minyun jishi*, p. 787. Members of the Workers' Autonomous Union and a handful of small radical workers' groups had assisted Shanghai students in erecting barricades on the morning of June 4. Official workers' militia (composed largely of Party members and cadres) dismantled these barriers on June 8, however. See Shelley Warner, "Shanghai's Response to the Deluge," *Australian Journal of Chinese Affairs*, no. 24 (July 1990), pp. 303, 312.

74. The "unchanging China" argument can be found in Lucian Pye, *The Spirit of Chinese Politics* (Cambridge: MIT Press, 1968); Richard Solomon, *Mao's Revolution and Chinese Political Culture* (Berkeley: University of California Press, 1971); and Lucian Pye, "Tiananmen and Chinese Political Culture: The Escalation of Confrontation from Morality to Revenge," *Asian Survey*, 30, no. 4 (April 1990), pp. 331–347. Pye and Solomon argue for a unitary Chinese culture (across time and social class) instilled during childhood socialization experiences.

75. In Taiwan, where the bonds between state and scholar were weakened first by Japanese colonialism and then by the GMD takeover, intellectuals have found it easier to make common cause with other social elements, especially entrepreneurs. This has been apparent in the development of the Democratic Progressive Party, the main opposition party to the ruling GMD. It is also seen in the active participation of intellectuals (along with virtually all other social groups) in Taiwan's recent stock market boom.

76. Andrew G. Walder, "Political Upheavals in the Communist Party-States," *States and Social Structures Newsletter*, 12 (Winter 1990), p. 8. See also Walder, "The Political Sociology of the Beijing Upheaval of 1989," *Problems of Communism* (September–October 1989), pp. 39–40.

77. Ibid.

78. For this interpretation, see Esherick and Wasserstrom, "Acting Out Democracy."

79. Strand, "Civil Society and Public Sphere," p. 3.

80. This is not to say that protests by peasants, workers, and entrepreneurs were invariably less exclusionist than student protests. We can, of course, point to numerous examples of labor unrest or rural uprisings that eschewed alliance with outside forces. But in contrast to the student movement, these were not self-proclaimed "democracy" protests. The argument here is simply that a successful effort at democratization must incorporate the interests of a diverse array of social elements. Another important source of potential allies left untouched by the students in 1989 were the national minorities. Disaffection in Tibet, Xinjiang, and elsewhere might well have been creatively addressed by student leaders—several of whom (including, most notably, Wuer Kaixi) were themselves of minority descent. However, any overt expression of sympathy with minority aspirations for freedom would have immediately elicited charges of lack of patriotism (not only from the government, but most likely from many ordinary Han Chinese as well).

Index

D

Dacheng Men, 284
Dai Li, 190
Dai Liqing, 242, 251–252
Daoist sects, 278, 281, 285
Davis, Fei-ling, 110
Davis, Natalie, 180
Democracy Movement of 1989. *See*
　Tiananmen Square Uprising
Democracy Wall Movement of 1979, x,
　xii, 311
Deng Xiaoping, x, 196, 198, 311, 315, 321
Deng Xin, 95
Deng Zhongyuan, 285
Diaoyutai Islands protest, xiv
District Four Silk-Weavers' Union, 156,
　159–160
Double Dagger Society, 52
Doumu Tan sect, 279
Du Qibin, 114, 116, 126
Du Yuesheng, 150, 157, 182, 183,
　185–189, 190

E

Eastman, Lloyd, 197–198
Economistic organizations, during Cultural
　Revolution, 260–267
Elementary Teachers' Headquarters, 264
Engels, Friedrich, 170
Entrepreneurs, 262–263, 317–319
Esherick, Joseph, 208, 314, 316
Ethnic feuds, 24–25

F

Falun Gong
　belief system of, xviii
　Communist Party members in, xvi
　heterodox labeling of, xvii, xx
　official recognition demands of, xvi, xxi
　repression campaign against, xiii, xv–xxi
　Tiananmen Square demonstrations of,
　　xxii–xxiii
Family size, as survival strategy, 3, 5–6
Famine, 113
Fang Lizhi, 311, 316
Feigon, Lee, 316

Female infanticide, as survival strategy,
　5–6
Feuds, peasant, 23–28, 293–294
Flooding, 10, 15, 61
Flying Tiger Brigade, 318, 323
Foreign concessions, 145, 182, 184–185
Foreigners
　kidnapping of, 17, 117, 125
　Small Sword rebellion and, 55–56
Fortified communities, peasant, 34–38
Fortune, Robert, 55
France, silk-weaver strikes in, 162
French Concession, 145, 182, 184
Friedman, Edward, 110, 111–112, 125,
　126

G

Gambling, peasant, 7
Gang of Four, 243, 290, 319
Gangsters
　-Guomintang ties, 173, 182–183, 185,
　　191
　as labor organizers, 175, 176, 181–182,
　　184, 185–189
Gansu, land reform riot in, 280
General strike *vs* strike wave, 226–228
Geng Jinzhang, 242, 246–247, 253
Gipouloux, François, 194, 210, 213
Gleaning, 29
Goldstone, Jack, 208
Gong Xiaoxia, 208
Grain
　harvest, 49, 113
　price decline, 32–33
　riot, 113
　state purchase of, 282
　tribute tax, 49, 61, 62
Gramsci, Antonio, 318
Great Leap Forward, 243
Green Gang, 141, 157, 173, 176, 177, 182,
　185, 187, 188
Guilds
　function of, 50
　in Small Sword rebellion, 51–52, 53
　state-owned enterprises based on,
　　193–194
Guomindang (GMD)
　autonomy thesis of, 198

Elizabeth J. Perry is Director of the Fairbank Center for East Asian Research and Henry Rosovsky Professor of Government at Harvard University. Born in China, she was educated at William Smith College (B.A. summa cum laude), The University of Washington (M.A.), and the University of Michigan (Ph.D.). Before moving to Harvard, she taught at the universities of Arizona, Washington, and California (Berkeley). Professor Perry has written widely on Chinese popular movements from the nineteenth century to the present. Her previous books include *Rebels and Revolutionaries in North China, 1845–1945* (1980); *Shanghai on Strike: The Politics of Chinese Labor* (1993); *Proletarian Power: Shanghai in the Cultural Revolution* (with Li Xun) (1997); and *Popular Protest and Political Culture in Modern China* (with Jeffrey Wasserstrom) (1994).